NGÔ ĐÌNH DIỆM AND I

NGÔ ĐÌNH DIỆM AND I
A Memoir by Bùi Công Văn
Edited and Introduced by Tuong Vu

Cover Design: Triet Tran
Layout: Ngoc Do Huynh Dang
US-VIETNAM RESEARCH CENTER
UNIVERSITY OF OREGON, 2025
ISBN: 979-8-3494-7040-0

NGÔ ĐÌNH DIỆM
and
I

A Memoir by Bùi Công Văn
Edited and Introduced by Tuong Vu

US-VIETNAM RESEARCH CENTER
UNIVERSITY OF OREGON
2025

Specially dedicated to:
My Beloved Wife,
NGUYỄN THỊ TRƯƠNG

(A promise made long ago,
Now kept at long last.)
B.C.V.

TABLE OF CONTENTS

Foreword by Tuong Vu i

Author's Biography xv

1. Prologue 2
2. Departure 4
3. A Fateful Meeting in New York 15
4. Work, Life & Family 27
5. The Party 51
6. Chicago 60
7. Grandpa Maryknoll 67
8. Winter 1952 77
9. Vietnamese Catholic Students' Association 93
10. The Feud 105
11. A Beautiful Chapter of My Life 120
12. Visitors 129
13. Tết 1953 137
14. The Good Time 151
15. The *Sûreté Americaine* 159
16. The Farewell 173

17. Visit to Washington, D.C. 191
18. Cornell and Buffalo 214
19. Americanisms 226
20. Grant us Freedom and Joy! 235
21. Leaving New York 253
22. Arrival in Washington, D.C. 263
23. A New Era 280
24. "Think of your kids" 305
25. Going Home 317
26. An Idealist in Hong Kong 338
27. Friendships 371
28. In Shackles rather than Free 389
29. Black Smoke 406
30. Operation "Celestine" 419
31. Who's Afraid of Winter? 436
32. A Malaria-Sufferer Stuck in Delirium 445
33. A Mad Race to Perdition 460
34. Murder in the Tank 472
35. Epilogue 492

FOREWORD

The US-Vietnam Research Center is pleased to publish the late Bùi Công Văn's memoir which he had written decades ago before his passing in 1998. We are grateful to Mr. and Mrs. Nguyễn Đức Cường for their permission and their generous support for the US-Vietnam Research Center since the beginning. Mrs. Nguyễn Đức Cường whose maiden name is Marie Bùi Mỹ Dung, is the oldest daughter of Mr. and Mrs. Bùi Công Văn. She was a witness to much of the story Mr. Văn told in this memoir. Thanks are also due to Mrs. Lucie Bùi Mỹ Châu, Bùi Công Văn's second daughter who was also a witness and who typed up his handwritten manuscript and provided the long preserved family pictures for the book.

***

Born in Cần Thơ in 1919, Mr. Văn was one of the first Vietnamese recruited to work as announcers and translators for the Vietnamese language service of the Voice of America (VOA), back in 1951 when it was still located in New York. By virtue of living in New York City, Mr. Văn and his family got in touch with Ngô Đình Diệm who was living at the time in the Maryknoll Seminary in Ossining (north of New York City) and Lakewood, New Jersey. From then on, Văn's career and life together with his family were profoundly shaped by their friendship with Ngô Đình Diệm, who in 9 months during 1952-1953 came to stay with them for weeks at a time in their apartment in New York City.

Mr. Văn was a patriot: he hated the French and wanted Vietnam to be independent. Unlike some other Vietnamese in New York or many visitors to his apartment who desired to meet and be friends with Diệm out of political curiosity or calculation, Mr. Văn was absolutely uninterested in politics. As he wrote,

> We were not rich—on the contrary, we were heavily in debt—but happiness needed no money, at least in our case. With Mr. Ngô, we found meaning in our lives and we knew that we were doing a good thing for him. Despite my dislike for politics (or probably because of it), I did not see in Ngô Đình Diệm a future leader of Vietnam. I thought he was destined to go the way of unsuccessful revolutionaries who preceded him. Men like Cường Để, Phan Bội Châu, Phan Châu Trinh, Nguyễn Thái Học, and the like. Men of principles and courage; men who would rather die than compromise with the French colonialists and secure a phony independence for Vietnam. All Ngô Đình Diệm's past spoke loudly of this, which

was why my wife and I deeply respected him. We thought he was not going to please the French and consequently he would stick to his own demands: True Independence, Genuine Freedom for Vietnam. And of course, he would never have that chance. Nothing in the U.S. policy vis-à-vis Indochina at that time induced us to think otherwise."

Ngô Đình Diệm turned out to be more than a friend to him and his family:

> As far as my family was concerned, it was fun to be with Mr. Ngô. It was a great consolation for us expatriates to have in him someone close who was not unlike a blood relation or a foster father as it were. The fact that our children called him 'Grandpa Maryknoll' without any urging on either side or *arrière pensée* [ulterior motive], was proof enough of our sincere attachment to him... [T] he sentiments underlying our behavior with him were the same [as filial duty]. And Ngô Đình Diệm appreciated us.

Thanks to their family-like relationship, Ngô Đình Diệm was comfortable living with Mr. Văn's family, and the latter had a lot to say about the future president whose private thoughts and personality have not been known much to the public. What kind of person was Ngô Đình Diệm? Was he prone to engage in hours-long monologues that many (especially Americans) dreaded when talking with him?[1] Was he a devout Catholic? Was he misogynous?

---

1 Stanley Karnow, *Vietnam: A History* (New York: Penguins, 1997 [1983]), 230.

It turns out that Diệm's monologues were even worse than what is already known. Diệm routinely talked to Mr. Văn for whole nights, night after night, while smoking. As Mr. Văn revealed,

> Ngô Đình Diệm spoke for hours and hours on end. He attacked every subject under the sun, stopping only to sip some tea, or more rarely, to listen to a question or two I put to him. [My wife] would have disappeared to the kitchen as befitted Vietnamese women—at least according to tradition—but returned once in a while to refill the teapot then discretely tiptoe out. Whenever [she] opened the door, though, she had to step back a moment, the room was so smoky she could hardly see anything inside. The two men in there were deep in conversation, oblivious to the smoke, and never stopped their chain smoking. In winter, it was worse, as we shut the windows tight against the cold and [my wife] had to open them to let some fresh air in when she came with the tea.

How did Mr. Văn and his family handle these endless monologues that took place nightly over many months?

> At first this was unbearable for us because Mr. Ngô never seemed to want to sleep and the later the night became, the more awake he looked. In the long run, we got used to it. Not only did I stay up until the last minute before I had to leave for work on my night schedule, but I also enjoyed our chats.

And it was not just Mr. Văn. Ngô Đình Diệm behaved

the same way toward guests and visitors whom he hardly knew.

> [T]he visitor, hastily bought to my apartment to have a first meeting or to renew an old acquaintance with Diệm never expected to spend so many long hours, let alone an entire night, with him talking. Most of them arrived around 6 p.m., freshly disembarked after long hours on planes or days at sea or were exhausted from a long day of shopping and sightseeing. Some had not eaten anything, no doubt intending to enjoy some American food then resume exploring New York that night. Some others came in for a few hours' visit planning to return to their hotels to rest their aching feet, and least for them, to call it a day.
>
> Not so for Ngô Đình Diệm on a full or empty stomach, at 6 p.m. or midnight, he was as fresh as ever and unless pressed to eat, would go on and on and on. Oblivious to hunger or fatigue, he talked on and completely forgot whether the men opposite him needed food or rest. Why, they had especially come so far from home, and were so eager to meet with him, he owed them a long talk.

Perhaps some visitors enjoyed Diệm's all-night monologues, but no doubt many must have felt being tortured by them. It is interesting that Diệm felt he owed his visitors a long talk, and he talked out of care and responsibility to his partners in dialogue. At the same time, it is clear that his social skills were limited and he was not able to read cues from his conversational partners.

One might even speculate that Diệm's monologues were symptoms of a mild form of autism.[2]

What made up to some extent for the long hours guests must sit to listen to Diệm was that he was knowledgeable about politics and "had a wealth of personal details and peculiar knowledge about current and past personalities of Vietnam. He was full of humor and was particularly good at mimicking people he especially disliked." Mr. Văn told us:

> As I write, I can still clearly see in my mind's eye the funny way that Ngô Đình Diệm often mimicked Lý Chánh Đức. He would stand with hands clasped and mouth twisted, then proceed to contort his back while commenting: "Đức is like an actress on stage, dancing to the music of castanets. His torso convulses and his hands jerk up and down as if pulled by puppet strings."

The idea that Ngô Đình Diệm could be funny is quite astonishing, given what has been written about him. Yet there is much more of the man revealed in the memoir. According to Mr. Văn, Ngô Đình Diệm was not "above common gossip, shop talk, or reluctant to discuss 'vulgar' details about women."

> Once, for instance, I told him about Mme. Hoàng Xuân Hãn whom I had seen that day walking *bras dessus* [arm-in-arm] with [a man] near my bank ... at 57th Street near the VOA offices.... Mr. Ngô laughed heartily and then explained to me that

2 See https://www.autism-help.org/index.htm.

Mme. Hãn was 'bisexual' and despite her seeming intimacy—in public, too!—with [that man], the latter could not and would not do such a thing.[3] It was pure shadow boxing as far as that lady was concerned, Ngô opined. There were little known details about Mme. Hãn, the wife of a renowned scholar from Hanoi and Mr. Ngô knew it and told it to us.[4] I was pleased to see him as a quite normal human being, his reputation as a 'woman-hater' and 'eternal virgin' and the like notwithstanding.

Foreign journalists have described Diệm as being "misogynous"[5] but the reality might have been more complex. Another common perception that Diệm possessed a deep religious devotion,[6] which Mr. Văn

---

3 Given the context, Ngô Đình Diệm appeared to mean "homosexual" and not "bisexual." He was likely speaking in either Vietnamese or French in 1952, and contemporary terms in sexual and gender studies or contemporary meanings of particular words may not have been used or known then.

4 Hoàng Xuân Hãn (1908-1996) was an engineer, historian, and Minister of Education in the Trần Trọng Kim government (March-August 1945). We are not able to verify the information in this memoir about Madame Hãn, whose maiden name was Nguyễn Thị Bính. For a laudatory story of her life with Hoàng Xuân Hãn published by the Police newspaper in Vietnam that we also cannot verify, see Kiều Mai Sơn, "Dược sĩ Nguyễn Thị Bính, Madame Hoàng Xuân Hãn: Một trí thức, một thiên hương" [An intellectual and a beauty], October 18, 2018. Available at https://antgct.cand.com.vn/Nhan-vat/Duoc-si-Nguyen-Thi-Binh-Madame-Hoang-Xuan-Han-Mot-tri-thuc-mot-thien-huong-i495522/

5 For example, see Karnow, *Vietnam*, 282. Karnow also mentions that as an adolescent Diệm "had a mild flirtation with a girl but she jilted him for a convent." Ibid., 231.

6 Diệm was "an ascetic Catholic," according to Karnow. Karnow,

believed to be wrong. Spending many Sunday mornings going to church with Diệm and observing his practices in public and at home, Mr. Văn told us,

> Contrary to what was said about Ngô Đình Diệm being a priest in civilian clothes or his extreme devotion to being a monk, I never once saw him receive Holy Communion or otherwise conducting himself any differently from us ordinary and not-so-devoted Catholics. In fact, Ngô did not carry a missal or rosary, and he never stayed any longer in church than my family and I did. For that matter, we never saw him pray or devote himself to any religious observances at home. If he was an especially fervent Catholic, he was unobtrusive about it, and I was at a loss from what sources came those observations about Ngô's 'monkish' epithets attached to him. I would not be surprised to find out that those were insults invented by political foes aimed at turning Ngô into some *moine manqué* [failed monk] and thus unfit for statesmanship.

While we do not have to believe entirely in Mr. Văn's account of Ngô Đình Diệm, we have no reason not to believe either, including the following remarks about Diệm in late 1952 not appearing to have a grand plan of action for the future:

> On the future, however, Ngô Đình Diệm was unsure. He did not know—and would not venture to predict—what was to happen to our country.

Vietnam, 229.

> As for his personal activities, he was quite sincere and stated that he did not, nor did he plan to, have anything important to accomplish nor did he really intend to act. Mr. Ngô's favorite word was "study." He was in the United States mainly to serve and to "study," he said.

Yet it is possible that Diệm was still waiting for the course of history to change in his favor and did not want to speculate about the future, especially with someone like Mr. Văn who was not his close collaborator. We will perhaps never know.

***

Although Mr. Văn did not expect much from Diệm, after he became president, Diệm did return Mr. Văn's favor when he appointed the latter in 1956 to represent the Republic of Vietnam in Hong Kong. As the Consul of Hong Kong and an official who served under Diệm, Mr. Văn believed in the mission and integrity of the president, but he encountered many problems that have been reported about Ngô Đình Diệm's government, including corrupt officials, disloyal and arrogant family members who had too much power, and the president being surrounded by sycophants and inaccessible to those who could have told him the truth about his government. Again, we do not know to what extent Mr. Văn was fully informed of Saigon politics while living and working in Hong Kong. Yet he did not mince words when mentioning President Diệm's family, from his brothers Ngô Đình Nhu, Ngô Đình Thục, Ngô Đình Cẩn, and Ngô Đình Luyện, to Madame Nhu, her parents Trần Văn Chương and Thân Thị Nam Trân, and many other officials.

By 1960, Mr. Văn became deeply disillusioned when he came back to participate in a week-long conference for the Heads of Diplomatic Missions abroad. The purpose of this conference was to showcase what the government touted as "accomplishments" of Khu Trù Mật (Prosperity Zones), with trips to local sites having been hastily and incompletely developed. As he described in detail his feelings and observations,

> The conference that began with a bang ended with a whimper. President Diệm thought that showing his ambassadors these 'accomplishments' would strengthen their dwindling optimism about his government's efforts, but the contrary must have been produced. Not one mission head was fooled by what he saw, and they all returned to their posts, perhaps hoping never to be called back again.

After his wife was asked to give money by a man allegedly sent by Ngô Đình Nhu on a secret political mission in Hong Kong, Mr. Văn returned to Saigon to present this case of "extortion" to Diệm. He had a tense moment with the president who later sent him to see Nhu. This whole affair made Mr. Văn want to resign from his position although he retained his belief in Diệm:

> A rush of being sick and tired of this whole business overcame me: of Vietnam under the U.S. umbrella, of Saigon-style government and politics, of Võ Văn Hải and Political Advisor Ngô Đình

> Nhu. The only redeeming shadow, although faint and tired, was Ngô Đình Diệm but he was kept inaccessible behind the ramparts of Independence Palace. I did not realize how close my thoughts were to the truth.

He eventually decided to stay. As he explained, "Looking at him a last time [before leaving the Palace] I felt: Here is the same Ngô Đình Diệm I knew. He may have changed but deep down, he remains my friend. I will stay on in my post because of him." Watching from afar the events in the last years of the First Republic before Ngô Đình Diệm was overthrown, Mr. Văn suspected that the president was being sidelined by his brother Nhu. He and his wife wished that Diệm would resign and come to live in exile with them in the US as in the old days. Diệm would be a grandfather to his children again. But history did not unfold that way as we already know.

***

Although the biography focuses mostly on Ngô Đình Diệm, it contains fascinating details about Mr. Văn's work for the VOA and his and his colleagues and friends' lives and activities in the U.S. in the 1950s. They included vignettes about well-known politicians and scholars such as Đỗ Vạn Lý, Phan Huy Đán, and Huỳnh Sanh Thông, as well as many now forgotten figures. As all the individuals involved, including Mr. Văn, have long deceased, we are not able to verify any details and the personal stories must be taken with a grain of salt.

Mr. Văn did not simply tell a story but immersed it

in deep thoughts and occasionally sprinkled it with poetic verses. This paragraph below gives a sense of his philosophy in presenting the story:

> I took the liberty ... to merge or amalgamate the present and the future, not through any impatience or lack of recognized methodological storytelling, but by a compelling sense of continuity and never ending even long after death. So present-past-future is nothing but eternity in a capsule, ready and colorful for whoever has a knowing eye to contemplate it.

Readers will appreciate Mr. Văn's honesty and modest sense of himself and those around him:

> We were certainly not revolutionaries. We were a starry-eyed bunch of kids inadequately and ineffectively trying to oppose the French colonials and their sycophants in Vietnam. Some of us were more ambitious but we were basically just a bunch of kids—inexperienced, ludicrous, and immature despite all of us approaching middle age.

Above all, readers will appreciate Mr. Văn's great memory and his skills as an entertaining writer and storyteller. His memoir is rich in lively detail of things and people with a subtle sense of humor. An example is his description below of the apartment of a female graduate student at Cornell University:

> I have yet to see a filthier apartment, especially the sink and pile of unwashed dishes filling it and stinking like carrion. The floor seemed to be

> a three-inch-thick pile of dirt caked into a slimy, malodorous carpet. And the beds hovering just above the unsavory damp rug, were jungles of pillows and sheets and blankets. A battlefield right after a skirmish when remnants of bloody encounters were not removed could not look any more distasteful.

And the resident of the apartment, Marjorie Weiner, who was[7]

> a not unpretty girl, but untidy from head to toe. Her light blue eyes were unwashed, and it was a real pity to see them cloudy, as if veiled by a thin mist, and the corners crusted with tiny lumps of dirt. Just a few years later, we were to meet her in Saigon, transformed into a totally different ripe fruit, so tantalizing a girl that the fairy tale image of Cinderella metamorphosed flashed into my head. Rosy-cheeked and gracious in every gesture, her curly locks fell in undulating golden waves over her shoulder, Marjorie was the picture of Madame Récamier in her salon, especially when she received visitors every Wednesday and Thursday afternoon in her tastefully furnished apartment on Bà Huyện Thanh Quan Street.

***

Although the story in this book is told by a single

7 Marjorie Weiner's MA thesis is still a valuable study of the first two years of the Ngô Đình Diệm government. See "Government and Politics in South Vietnam, 1954-1956," MA thesis (Ithaca: Cornell University, 1960).

individual decades after the events, it will be of great interest to historians of Vietnam and students of Vietnamese history. Ngô Đình Diệm was indisputably among the most important figures in Vietnam's modern history, yet not much has been known about him as a person, and what is known has been told mostly by foreigners. It is our hope that this memoir by a Vietnamese who lived for nearly nine months under the same roof with Diệm at an important moment in his life will contribute to our knowledge about him. As editor, I let the author speak for himself while adding (most of) the titles of the chapters to make the story easier to follow. I also made sure the Vietnamese words are spelled correctly with their tonal marks, and provided a few footnotes where necessary. Those footnotes by the author are specifically marked by "(Au.)."

Tuong Vu
Professor, Department of Political Science
Director, US-Vietnam Research Center
University of Oregon

AUTHOR'S BIOGRAPHY

Bùi Công Văn was born in Cần Thơ, South Vietnam, in 1919 and passed away in Dallas, Texas in 1998. With all his travels around the world and the many years that he lived outside Vietnam, Van remained a man who deeply loved his country yet no longer fit there.

Early in his youth Văn traveled with his grandfather to nearby villages, which piqued his wanderlust so that he became a steward for Air France to allow him to visit Cambodia, Laos, and Thailand. He found he had an affinity for languages, learning French at the lycée during Vietnam's colonial period, teaching himself English, Cantonese, and some Japanese. Văn's English was good enough that, after a short stint at the British Council in Saigon he applied to the Voice of America (VOA) for a Vietnamese broadcaster position in the U.S. When the VOA accepted his application, Văn's family became the first in the clan and in the village of Cần Thơ to move overseas, a dream far out of reach for many Vietnamese at the time.

Shortly after arriving in New York in April 1951, Văn met Ngô Đình Diệm for the first time. Eventually Ngô Đình Diệm became Văn's mentor and the family's honorary grandfather as Diệm spent much of his time in Văn's small apartment, chain smoking and talking far into the night with Văn and visitors about Vietnam's state of affairs. Văn became an important link in the U.S. for Diệm and his supporters before he returned to become president of Vietnam.

Văn served as Vietnam's Head of Mission in Hong Kong for President Diệm in 1956 through years of significant political upheaval in Vietnam that abruptly ended with Diệm's assassination in November 1963. When all diplomats were ordered to come home, Văn felt it was wiser to avoid being jailed or killed, given his connections to Diệm, and focused instead on resettling his family abroad. The family lived in France for a year and then sailed to the U.S. on the SS Rotterdam, docking in New York Harbor on 54th Street in late 1964. The circle closed with Văn's return to the city where his entire family's life was changed by coming to know Ngô Đình Diệm.

Văn always told his family that he was a writer but found it difficult to write his stories until many years had passed. Deep down, he had never recovered from the assassination of President Diệm. Eventually, Văn did keep his promise to his wife to write about his life and completed three memoirs, two of them about his relationship with Ngô Đình Diệm.

This book is the story of how he met Ngô Đình Diệm and how that encounter shaped his life.

Bùi Công Văn and wife Nguyễn Thị Trương (1996)

1. PROLOGUE

The bells of St. Paul's Catholic Church chimed the hour in long peals that resounded in the quiet night. It is an old, dilapidated 12th century church dominating the Old City of Hyères, France.

I came here in the spring, and like a pilgrim, I was trying to retrace the steps of the past. Not the past of the old cathedral, now disused and a standing relic of centuries gone by on the Côte d'Azur.

Nor was I looking for the memorabilia of a Captain of Artillery, Napoleon Bonaparte, who during the siege of Toulon, lived in the same house our good friend Bùi Kiến Thành now lives and I happened to share with him and walk in its historic rooms.

My "Remembrance of Things Past" rather concerned a more modest man, son of a more modest country. Both Man and Country, however, fought valiantly for independence and liberty, and in this regard were second to none.

The man was NGÔ ĐÌNH DIỆM. His country, Vietnam. His friends and youthful early comrades in arms, Bùi Kiến Thành and I, among others. I came here, then, and with

Thành's help, was piecing together the early days of that part of NGÔ ĐÌNH DIỆM's life that I had the good fortune to share that led to a short, if tumultuous and finally dramatic episode of pre-1975 Vietnam.

The story began when my family and I left a French-occupied Vietnam for the United States in the spring of 1951....

2. DEPARTURE

ON APRIL 19, 1951, WE LEFT VIETNAM FOR THE UNITED STATES. I was recruited, together with Miss Bài, Lâm Chấn Quan, and Trịnh Văn Chẩn, to work as translator-announcer for the Voice of America whose offices and studios were in New York City.

Vietnamese families, as Oriental families have always been, were large and sticking together and ours was no exception. At that time, my family in Gia Định, a suburb of Saigon, was composed of my grandparents; my wife and myself; our three children Marie (10), Dominic (3), Mỹ-Châu (8 months); my three brothers Minh, Hiến, Lập; a cousin of mine, Xuân; and my sister-in-law, Eighth Auntie, or Dì Tám. Twelve people.

Now part of this, namely my wife, me, and our three children were about to leave the family for a long voyage to an unknown country, and for an indefinite length of time. We might come back after two years as stated in our work contracts, or we could choose to stay in America. The latter seemed more likely, as conditions in Vietnam were very unstable. The first Indochina War which started in

Saigon and throughout South Vietnam in September 1945 was going on fiercely. The French Expeditionary Corps reoccupied the cities and towns throughout Indochina, but the countryside remained in the hands of the Việt Minh. There was no end to war in sight.

Ours, then, was the "largest" family to go to the U.S. at that time and in that contingent of radio announcers, the first of its kind ever recruited in Vietnam by the U.S. Government. The only other "family" on the contingent was Miss Bài and her mother as Quan and Chẩn were bachelors.

At 5 a.m. that morning, we left our little house at Gia Định. The night curfew had just ended, and we made our leave-taking in great trepidation. We were very much afraid lest the French, who did not like the Americans at all, might have their henchmen waylay us, or arrest us even before we departed. Such arrests in the dark of night were almost routine.

Bùi Công Văn on a bicycle in Saigon (2/14/1951)

Bùi Công Văn at a busy Saigon street (1951)

Bùi family in Gia Định before leaving for the U.S. (1951)

Bùi family arrives in New York on 4/25/51
(courtesy Air France)

AT TÂN SƠN NHỨT AIRPORT, everyone in our family was there to see us off with the exception of grandpa. In addition, my father, my father-in-law, and my wife's elder sister, Third Auntie or Dì Ba, had come up from Cần Thơ for the occasion. We entered the waiting room like a little army, and Margaret, the tall American girl who worked at the Embassy whom we nicknamed 'Half-Track' because of her size, greeted us with hearty laughs. Once again, we said goodbye to our loved ones, tears welling in our eyes, and departure time struck.

The Air France super-constellation lifted off at dawn and we had a last glance at Saigon below. Houses, tamarind trees, large boulevards and winding lanes, then over the suburbs with myriad clusters of shacks and shrubs and small churches among the coconut trees, and the open countryside with meandering rivers. We were flying to Paris via Pakistan, India, Lebanon, and Turkey on the first leg of our trip to New York City. I had never been west of Indochina and the West, especially Paris and France, the capital of every French-educated Vietnamese of my generation, presented an unspeakably strong appeal.

We were all excited with anticipated joy and fulfillment of the dream of our youth: to see Paris, and in our case, even to see New York, which was another world not only for us, but for colonial Frenchmen in Saigon as well. My father related how, on asking his French boss and the Cần Thơ branch of the Banque de l'Indochine for a leave of absence in order to see us off, the latter expressed both his surprise and envious admiration: "Your son is going to New York?!!"

In flight, we had the company of such personalities as Princess Yukanthor of Cambodia and Messrs. Trần Thiện Vàng and Trương Quốc Định, all three members of the French Union Council on their way to one of its regular meetings in Paris. The princess and Mr. Vàng sat next to Dominic and they were quite chummy with him. My son sang loudly the patriotic songs of the day—"Lên Đàng" and "Quyết Tiến"—to the merriment of both the Cambodian and Vietnamese councilors.

Marie had a window seat and watched the scenery and clouds flying down below. Mỹ-Châu was sleeping on a little hammock hanging over our heads. One night, she fell out of the hammock, tumbling down onto her father and elder sister and we quietly and quickly picked her up. She didn't even wake up and as we pressed a bottle to her mouth, she smilingly continued her sleep. My wife alone, sitting next to Miss Bài's mother, did not seem to enjoy the flight. She had her usual airsickness (even automobile rides made her sick) and kept her eyes closed. I glanced at Miss Bài's mother and saw her nylon stockings, and I regretted that through ignorance and perhaps also our tight finances, I had not given my wife a proper outfit.

We traveled to Paris in early spring in tropical clothes. My wife and children had flimsy silk and cotton dresses. I wore a blue gabardine suit, the only suit I had from my flying days with Air France as a steward. As for Dominic, his Third Auntie had confectioned for him a white safari jacket which he now sported with a white cotton skullcap. We were country bumpkins going to town! Even our luggage was old leather suitcases, half worm-eaten and so outmoded that we might as well be a family of peasants going to Saigon for the first time, let alone flying to Paris in a super constellation and having such fellow travelers as a Royal Highness and a couple of Excellencies! But we were not ashamed, nor were we inhibited in any way. Especially the kids. They had their field days for many weeks to come.

In Paris, the U.S. Embassy had reserved rooms at the plush Hotel de Castiglione at the Faubourg de St. Honoré just around the corner from the Place de la Concorde which was near the embassy. We had three days shopping and sightseeing. Paris, here I come! The Paris of my boyhood, ever since the first day when I was taught that "Our ancestors were the Gauls," Paris was nothing less than Paradise. Then during my adolescence, I used to dream of Paris as sung by Josephine Baker in such alluring, unforgettable lyrics: *Et sous les grands arbres noirs, chaque soir vers elle s'en va tout mon espoir* (And under the great black trees, every evening all my hope goes to her).

Even before we reached the heart of Paris where the Castiglione Hotel was at, we had our first encounter with a compatriot. Long, the son of Mr. Hunt, a friend of my father's. He had word of our coming to Paris and as a student there, he made it his obligation to meet us and show us the marvels of the city of light. But when Long accompanied us to the hotel it was his turn to be astonished. Never in his student days had he been inside such a splendid hotel. And he never stopped praising our good luck. We were given a large suite with two bedrooms and a luxuriously furnished living and dining room complete with bill buttons for the maid, the valet, and the cook in each room long jumped around, enjoying the luxury much more than we who had to pay for meals and fare.

The first night in Paris, we sailed down the grand boulevards, and spotting a modest looking restaurant we trooped in rather hesitantly. We ordered a simple French omelet, bread and wine. The kids enjoyed their meal with gusto as they were drunk with novelty and the fresh weather made them quite hungry. At a nearby table, an elderly gentleman watched us with a grandfatherly smile on his lips and I told him: "Comme vous voyez, Monsieur, nous venons de loin" (As you see, sir, we have come a long way). I particularly apologized for our rather outlandish outfits, paper thin cotton cloth and white homemade cap and all. "Je m'en suis douté" (I suspected it), replied the old man. And we were at ease.

Back at the hotel, we ordered a big dinner to be served in our room by way of celebration and compensation for the parsimony we had been observing so far. I had gone into debt for this trip, as my salary hardly covered the $400.00 or so I had to obtain before we left Vietnam. Hứa Xiêu, a half Chinese friend of mine, introduced me to black marketers who consented to pay double the amount in piastres which I used to buy dollars for my trip at the Exchange Office. Only with the proceeds of the transaction could I afford to buy the necessary dollars. Besides, as the French then permitted, each traveler was entitled to transfer a sum of francs at the official rate of one piastre for 17 francs. This was the kind of transfer which enriched many a Frenchman and not a few Vietnamese. Despite all these operations however, I still owed half the amount in dollars I bought and the balance of $200 would be paid to a Chinese man when I arrived in New York. We ignored the debt for the moment and enjoyed our Paris stopover to the hilt. I was 32 years old, in the prime of youth, and all whipped up and enchanted with our first trip abroad. Ever since my school days, I always wanted to go abroad. At 17 years of age, with a classmate, I scurried up and down all the French liners moored at the Saigon docks, innocently hoping to find a way either to hide myself, stow away, or somehow to bribe a cabin boy to smuggle me to France. I was injected with a sense of adventure, a thirst for faraway places, and the desire to live in or at least see the West. I wanted Marie, our eldest child on this trip, at least to thoroughly enjoy our dream come true life in America.

My English, which I began to learn late, much later than the French which was taught from the first day of elementary school, was very much self-taught and learned by ear. Even after some years of experience, having worked for both English and American Information Services in Saigon, I had to guess at many English words spoken to me by strangers. Thus, it was with hilarious bewilderment that the U.S. Embassy in Paris left me nonplussed after some exchanges on the telephone. The word "Embassy" for instance, was pronounced "M.C." and I lost a minute or two before realizing that they wanted me to get to the Embassy instead of some mysterious M.C. I kept saying M.C. anytime I referred to the Embassy, both to make sure that I made myself understood, and to not let them suspect that I didn't get it in the first place.

3. A FATEFUL MEETING IN NEW YORK

ON APRIL 25, 1951, my family took the early morning Air France flight to New York. Some type of super constellation plane, same routine of service on board, almost the same crew we had on the trip from Saigon. But it was an entirely different flight insofar as we were crossing the Atlantic for the first time. There were no Vietnamese passengers on board except for us, and when the aircraft approached New York in the late morning (there is a time difference with New York 6 hours behind Paris), the stewardesses offered Miss Bài, her mother, my wife, and Marie a small bouquet of fresh orchids. That was special to our group: no other women passengers were offered any flowers.

We landed at Idlewild Airport. Voice of America sent photographers to take our pictures. We still have a photograph of our family going down the steps of the aircraft ladder: Dad, Mom carrying Mỹ-Châu wrapped in a woolen shawl we'd bought at the Marché aux Puces in Paris, Marie with a colorful muffler around her neck, and Dominic smiling happily as he sported, as always, his

Auntie's homemade white cotton cap.

A representative of the Voice met us and took care of our entrance procedures then we boarded a bus to go into New York City. We were brought to the Henry Hudson Hotel on West 57th Street, quite near the studios and officers of the Voice of America, which were just down the block across the street. Our room was on the 12th floor, and it was a new experience for us: we had never lived that high above ground! The kids and I spent hours watching tiny people and cars on the streets far below. Then, we had our first experience with pay radio feeding quarters into the machine and listening for the very first time to authentic American music. We spent an eventful night at the hotel as we did not realize that babies were fed with fresh milk in America. We had ordered condensed milk and hot water and while we struggled with bottles and pots, the bell boy stood watching us in open mouth bewilderment.

Next morning together with Miss Bài, Chẩn and Quan, myself at the Vietnamese unit of the Voice of America. It was located in the Argonaut Building on 57th Street. The chief of the unit was Alfred W. Pruett, a former Protestant missionary in Vietnam. There were only three full-time Vietnamese on the staff of the unit before our group of four newcomers joined them. They were Nguyễn Đức Thanh, Lý Đức Lâm, and Nguyễn Đình Hoà.[8] Thanh and Lâm were sailors on the French liners of Messageries Maritimes, and Hoà was a student at New York University. Later in the

---

8 Nguyễn Đình Hoà (1924-2000), a noted linguist, university professor and author of many books on the Vietnamese language besides his memoir, *From the City Inside the Red River: A Cultural Memoir of Mid-Century Vietnam* (Jefferson, NC: McFarland & Co, 1999).

day, Miss Bài's mother and my wife came up to say hello to Mr. Pruett and I remember how my wife had a hard time taking off her new gloves to shake hands with him.

That second night in New York was commemorated by the visit en masse of the very few Vietnamese residents of New York. They were about 5 or 6, former sailors mostly and even one or two stowaways or "jump ships" as well. They were all excited by the news that, for the first time, Vietnamese women were in New York. And they had been away from home since before the war period in some cases for decades, as a Mr. Cụ Tư who had been living in Europe and America for more than 20 years who was then in his late sixties.

Very soon we moved to new hotels for a lower rate and our family settled down at the Whitehall Hotel on 100th Street and Broadway. (The hotel is still standing today as an apartment building called The Whitehall). I rented a TV set there for $1 a day and we had our very first look at television. President Truman appeared with his well-known gesture of "chopping" both hands down on either side of the microphone in front of which he stood. We stayed in this hotel for the rest of April then well into May. Each day, on my way back from work, I stopped at the delicatessen stores along Broadway to bring back to my family some cooked ham, fish, or salami for our evening meals. One day, a Jewish shopkeeper took me for a Korean as the Korean War was going on at the time, and he insulted me: "So, you Koreans are famished over there, and you flock here and eat our food!" I was angered but didn't try to explain anything to the ignoramus because no one we met in the streets of New York had ever heard of Vietnam. Whenever we explained that we were from Vietnam, they often exclaimed, "Oh, I see, you are from Vienna!"

While I was away at work, my family must have been terribly lonely and a little worried, as they were confined in a room high on the 14th floor, spoke no English, and were too new to New York to venture down its streets. Most nights were a family gathering when dad tried to introduce some elementary English words and notions of geography of the city to mom and Marie. Then, after mom and the kids went to bed, dad used to stay up late and sometimes took Marie down to have tea with him in some nearby cafes. Oh, how this reminded me of the early 40s, when Marie was a tiny baby and mom and I lived in Cần Thơ in grandpa's house.

Then, during many nights too, dad used to carry Marie in his arms and walk to Chinese tea shops in town to give her hot milk for in the paternal house there was none, and Marie would not stop crying unless she was fed.

Mỹ-Châu get with her bed many times and mom had to wash the linens lest the hotel maids discover it and blame us. We were so afraid of many things.

One night in early May while still at this hotel, dad and mom left Dominic and Michael in their beds for Marie to look after them and set out to a rendezvous with Ngô Đình Diệm.

Before we left Saigon, Mr. Dư Phước Long, a translator

at USIS[9] gave me a letter and asked me to deliver it to a Mr. Ngô Đình Diệm. In the U.S., Mr. Ngô was a national personality well known for his integrity as a former Minister of the Interior at the court of Emperor Bảo Đại who resigned because the French disapproved of the reforms he wanted to carry out. At a time when the French came back to Vietnam with an Expeditionary Corps and tried to reimpose their colonial administration against the wishes of the Vietnamese people, Ngô Đình Diệm stood out as the most respected potential leader on this side of the resistance. The other side, of course, was led by Hồ Chí Minh.

Because of his staunchly nationalist aspirations, which of necessity must be anti-French, Ngô Đình Diệm had been carefully watched by the *Deuxième Bureau* in Vietnam.[10] He found an opportunity to escape their surveillance, however, by obtaining an exit visa to go to Rome on the occasion of the Holy Year of 1950 and from there, to go and stay in the US. But in Saigon, any letters addressed to him were confiscated and to circumvent this, Mr. Long asked me to serve as mail carrier. I pocketed the letter without much thought of having anything further to do with Ngô Đình Diệm, except just hand deliver his mail to him.

After a few weeks at the Whitehall Hotel, I telephoned Đức Thanh and ask him whether he knew Mr. Ngô's

9 The United States Information Service (USIS) was the overseas arm of the United States Information Agency (USIA) that operated public diplomacy and exchange programs worldwide.

10 "The Second Department," which refers to the intelligence section of the French armed forces.

address somewhere in New Jersey, Thanh proposed that a meeting could take place when Mr. Ngô would come to New York City. According to Thanh, Mr. Ngô always let him know in advance if and when he came to New York City. And he even did not say so in his own words, but let me understand that he served as some kind of representative for Mr. Ngô in this city, if not in the U.S. As I would rather hand deliver the letter to Mr. Ngô and mail it, I didn't insist on getting his address but just waited for the next opportunity to see him in person.

ON THE APPOINTED DAY, Đức Thanh called me and told me to go to the Tudor Hotel where Mr. Ngô would be, and he had been informed of my coming to see him. It was about 7:00 p.m. when my wife and I left our hotel. We took the subway downtown to Times Square, then shuttled east to come up at 42nd street where the hotel was. As soon as we entered the revolving door, Đức Thanh was there to meet us.

Đức Thanh was one of the three translator-announcers already on the Vietnamese staff of the Voice of America when our group of four came from Saigon to join them. He was the eldest of the whole staff except for Mr. Pruett, the chief of the unit. He, Lý Đức Lâm, and another colleague, Bùi Văn Thinh were sailors on the French liner of the Messageries Maritimes and got caught in the middle of the Pacific War when the allies attacked Japan in 1945. Stranded in the Philippines, the U.S. fleet had given them the option to either stay on board with the French or to join the staff of an American ship. They all opted for the American ship and sailed to the U.S. Soon after that, the

Voice of America started its broadcasts in Vietnamese, and they were employed as the very first announcers ever to broadcast in the Vietnamese language from the United States. Later, when the Second World War was over and a few Vietnamese students arrived in the United States in the late 40s or early 50s, some of the initial staff were dismissed. Thanh and Lâm remained and were later joined by Nguyễn Đình Hoà shortly before my group arrived from Vietnam.

Now Đức Thanh, despite his lack of higher education, was a smart aleck. He had been sub-manager of some French hotel back in Vietnam and had a 'flair' for business, being an out-and-out opportunist. At that time, he played two games at the same time. On one hand, he speculated on Ngô Đình Diệm as a potential Prime Minister at some future date to succeed the Prime Minister of the French-sponsored government of Vietnam then, Trần Văn Hữu.[11] On the other hand, Đức Thanh would display his self-styled 'knowledge' of Indochina and, in his usual showy manner, try to impress businessmen who had an interest in Southeast Asia. In this way he succeeded to open a so-called Indochina Department in an American firm—an import and export establishment owned by an American of German descent. Thanh would sit at his desk smoking a pipe, and although the firm had no business whatsoever in Indochina nor any salary ever paid him, a visitor entering his door bearing the imposing brass plaque marked 'Indochina Department' would have been deeply impressed. Like an angler setting out his magnificent gear

11 Trần Văn Hữu (1895-1984) was Prime Minister of the State of Vietnam under Bảo Đại from May 1950 to June 1952.

and using the best bait, Đức Thanh sat there day in and day out, waiting for the opportunity to catch a big fish. He worked only a few hours at night for the Voice of America, so his full-time pay was secure, and his days were free.

In his other role of "Angler in Politics," Đức Thanh set his net around Ngô Đình Diệm, a prospective big fish in his eyes. Unasked, he acted as an agent for Mr. Ngô and made it—if at all possible—that anyone who wanted to get in touch with Ngô Đình Diệm had to do it through him. An experienced wheeler and dealer on a small scale, Đức Thanh offered his services free of charge, but made himself indispensable. He kept a list of important and not so important visitors from Saigon, met them at their hotels, took them on New York tours and shopping outings, and located the parties they needed to contact.

As Mr. Ngô was secluded at the Seminary of the Maryknoll Fathers in Lakewood, New Jersey, his only contacts with the outside world were made by Đức Thanh. So it was that Đức Thanh greeted me and my wife at the Tudor Hotel's revolving doors. He led us to a corner of the lobby where Ngô Đình Diệm sat by himself, away from the noisy crowd, and introduced us in his theatrical manner.

Ngô Đình Diệm was a name we had heard much about but had never seen before. Before us was a youngish-looking man in his early fifties, jet- black hair, rather short of stature, and a beaming sunburnt face. He wore a dark-brown suit with a nondescript necktie. His appearance in this first encounter was of a rather modest and poorly dressed man. Although he didn't rise to meet us, his gentle fatherly gesture in welcoming us with slightly raised hands and a large smile on his face immediately took us in. He gestured that we sit down opposite him, while Đức Thanh stood beside him in a posture of a busy and zealous lieutenant.

I opened the conversation by explaining to Mr. Ngô the circumstances of our departure from Saigon and how Mr. Dư Phước Long gave us a message to personally deliver to him. Mr. Ngô did not ask me much about either the letter or its sender but rather, he asked about the situation at home when we left Saigon. He listened attentively to my words, lighting one cigarette that he snuffed out after a short draw. He did this by rubbing its burning head against the ashtray bowl. It was a gesture so typical of him that for many years to come we would watch him do it again and again, mesmerized by the act, all while conducting a monologue for hours on end: lighting the cigarette, drawing on it, slowly rubbing it out against the glass, then lighting another. It was his way of occupying his hands and fixing his eyes on the cigarettes while talking rather than looking at his interlocutor. If Mr. Ngô looked at you at all, he seemed to look through you and his eyes would fix at some point behind you.

After a while, he invited my wife and me to follow him upstairs to his room, but he did not extend that invitation to Đức Thanh and the latter quickly excused himself and disappeared.

Mr. Ngô's single room was furnished with two hard chairs and a bedside table covered with a red cloth. He sat on the bed while we took the chairs. Only then did he ask for the letter I had brought, and I passed it to him. After reading it in silence and putting it in his jacket pocket, he began an intimate conversation—quite different from the rather aloof attitude he adopted when Đức Thanh was present.

Ngô Đình Diệm inquired about our parents, where we were from, what part of Vietnam we were born in. He even asked if my present radio announcer position paid well enough to keep a family with three children in New York City. Before the talk took a more mundane turn, I had to ask him something: "Sir, please allow us to address you as 'Ông' (Sir or Mister in Vietnamese) rather than the term I hear people use to refer to you by—namely, 'Cụ' which is a term used only in Central and North Vietnam. Southerners put a lot of respect in addressing older people, why we even call our grandfather 'Ông.'" Diệm replied: "I quite agree as I have lived a long time in the South, and I know its customs quite well." This was how, right from the beginning, Mr. Ngô and my family settled the matter of proper appellation. We never again had to discuss it: everyone else addressed him as 'Cụ' while my family stuck to the southern 'Ông.'

Then came my closing salvo concerning my attitude towards politics in general and his political expectations in particular. I told him point-blank that I had no interest in politics and that my bringing the letter to him was but a favor for a friend, Dư Phước Long. I bluntly said that I did not expect to engage in anything political no matter how slight the matter seemed to be. In fact, I was very much afraid of any difficulty my family and I could get into if we were somehow involved in politics. It has never been a tradition in my greater family nor in my upbringing to concern ourselves with things political, and the French *Sûreté*[12] had long been a menace even in our innocent daily activities that we did not want troubles here in a foreign land any more than we needed them back home. One experience of being jailed as a suspected Việt Minh was enough for me.

"I too," Mr. Ngô replied, "I have had enough troubles with the French, and I am not now pursuing any political goals." Smiling, he concluded, "Why, even if I wanted to be active, I have no means to do so. Perhaps Đức Thanh thought that I came to the U.S. to seek some political support. He is wrong. As far as I'm concerned, I only want to get in touch with the Vietnamese residents and students in America. My brother, Bishop Ngô Đình Thục, could help me financially by remitting *piastres*[13] to the families of the Vietnamese living abroad and the latter would pay me here in dollars. Without money, how could I move around, let alone do any political work? And when I brought up the idea with Đức Thanh, he took me all wrong and even asked me for money before he could help me!"

On this note, my wife and I took our leave of Ngô Đình Diệm. It was late and we hurried back to our hotel where we had left our young children unattended. We were relieved to find them all sound asleep. Days passed without us thinking even once of this first encounter with Mr. Ngô. It was a fateful meeting, however as developments in the future would prove, and we could not but appreciate the

12 The *Sûreté* was the French secret police in Indochina.

13 *Piastre* was the local currency in French Indochina.

profound truth contained in the Buddhist-Taoist teaching: "Even one mouthful of food or a drink of water has been preordained and destined to happen ever since the unknown beginning."

4. WORK, LIFE & FAMILY

OUR FAMILY MOVED to an apartment on Eighth Avenue and 15th Street sometime toward the end of May 1951. One month's stay in a hotel was quite enough and we were looking forward to living in a place of our own. I recall the early spring evenings when the weather was still quite fresh, and we took our children on walks from Broadway to Riverside Park. Mỹ-Châu was wrapped in her white wool shawl, a tiny little thing, and she looked around with big round eyes while mom carried her propped up against her shoulder. Marie and Dominic enjoyed these walks too as they were the only outings they had during their first month in the U.S. We were too new to America to venture out much. My 9-to-6 workday kept me separated from my family and they had to wait for my return for practically everything. Once in a while, Marie was sent out on an errand, but she could not go too far as she neither spoke English nor knew her way around yet. In any case, we were eager to move out of the Whitehall Hotel.

Our apartment on 8th Avenue and 15th Street was on the second floor, next door to the apartment of Miss Bài and her mother. In point of fact, I didn't choose the apartment of my own volition. It was Bài who got her apartment first then, without consulting us if we wanted to live next door, in that neighborhood, or if that type of apartment would suit us. She had signed the lease, moved into it first, and then made me take the apartment next to hers. I was very reluctant to pay an exorbitant rent of $120 a month for a miserable one-bedroom apartment for a family of five. For the sake of my wife, as well as Bài's mother, I did sign the lease in order to let the two expatriated women live side by side while I was away at work whole days on end.

Nonetheless, we were happy in our new home. Little by little, Marie picked up more English and went out with her mother more and more often. I took Marie to Chinatown and put her in the care of Father Smith at the Catholic parish there. Marie did not attend any school yet but played with American and Chinese kids and learned English by ear. Every morning, dad and Marie would ride the subway together to Chinatown at Canal Street stop. I left Marie there for the day and picked her up after 6:00 PM. It was her only preparation for elementary school in September.

After our first month in the new apartment, Bài and her mother moved out of theirs! With the help of American acquaintances, Bài succeeded in breaking her lease, but she left us stranded there not even trying to help us. So, we parted company and had to endure the bad landlord, a Mr. King, until our lease finally expired.

DURING THAT SUMMER, we were busy with visitors from Vietnam, former colleagues of U.S.I.S., such as Bích and Ngoan who were given a paid tour of the United

States. They became our uninvited house guests, as was the behavior of Vietnamese abroad then and still today. My poor wife and Marie had to shop, cook meals, and run errands for them, which doubled and tripled their usual household workload. We were young, inexperienced, and still too attached to Vietnam to imagine turning visitors out.

We began to explore New York City and adapt ourselves to our new American way of life. I remember well one night shopping at Times Square. My wife wanted to buy a girdle, but I didn't know the word in English, so I asked the salesgirl if she had what the French call a "gaine." Of course she didn't. We resorted to lots of gestures before she finally understood what we needed.

Also, we went by subway to Coney Island, enjoyed once in a while a Chinese dinner, and learned a little more of both the English language and the American way of life. One night, baby Mỹ-Châu got sick with a high fever. I telephoned a Puerto Rican doctor I knew, Dr. Mazzia. He was the younger brother of an employee of Caltex who used to work with me in Saigon. The good doctor came and took good care of my baby with no charge. That Christmas, we sent him a gift as a way of thanks. As for Dominic, he stayed home with mom all day long except when we went out together for walks or to the park. He ate well and grew taller, but he stayed skinny.

AMONG OUR VIETNAMESE friends at that time there was Bùi Văn Thinh, who had been a sailor and used to work for the Voice of America but was dismissed before we arrived. Thinh was a very kind man and as he was a bachelor with some money and nothing to do, he called on us often and took the children out for treats. He bought them toys like a cowboy shoot for Dominic complete with guns and hat. All day long Dominic played around the apartment, sometimes climbing out on the fire escape just outside our windows. Next door lived the Mahoneys whose son, Mike, was about Dominic's age and taught him his first few English words. The two would climb out on the fire escape that connected the windows of both apartments, playing cowboys or cops and robbers. We had for a long time a snapshot of Dominic sporting his cowboy suit and drawing his guns. It was taken on the sidewalk just below our fire escape on 15th Street.

Mounted police patrolled the streets at night. There was also a Nabisco factory in the neighborhood, so the smell of biscuits and caramel invaded our noses day and night. Especially during that first summer, when the temperatures reach the 80s or more, The sweet smell would sweep full strength into our apartment. It was a noisy, dusty, dirty neighborhood right at the intersection of 14th Street and 8th Avenue, but we were too happy to be away from Gia Định and Vietnam to care. Fresh in our memories were scenes of night kidnappings, bloody assassinations, attacks and machine gun bursts, not to mention floods of water inundating our little house during the monsoon season when river water reached its highest level. America in comparison was paradise. And we did not mind our modest salary of $400 a month, out of which already $120 went to the landlord first. Our children, especially Marie and Dominic, who were old enough to remember the horrors of wartime in Vietnam, thrived in this unhealthy American climate. Still, Marie did have her little disappointment. One day, she told me: "Dad, before we came to America, I imagined it was a golden country where gold would be literally glittering in the streets. Now that we are here, I'm disappointed to see dust and dirt and sad people mixed in the noise and tall buildings." Marie's dream-image of America was not an exception; many Vietnamese had the same idea of the United States as she did.

Quickly the summer passed, and autumn came with busy preparations for Marie's entrance to school. Her knowledge of English learned with the help of Father Smith and her playmates in Chinatown, plus the French she was taught by the nuns at the École Ste. Thérèse in Tân Định, Saigon, was enough to gain her entrance to Saint Patrick's Parochial School on 14th Street. Marie had stopped school in April last year, so she was happy to start again. In the new school, she learned English in no time and made some good friends like Catherine and our Mahoney neighbors' daughter, also named Mary. Would Marie remember her school days back in Saigon when her dad brought her to and from school twice a day on his velosolex from Gia Định to Tân Định?[14] For the day when dad had just bought his fellow selects and put her and Dominic on the back seat and drove them around? Dominic got his foot into the turning spokes of the wheel and got hurt and Marie was blamed for not watching her little brother who didn't know any better. The ride was cut short and great grandma had to nurse Dominic's foot for

14 Velosolex was a moped or motorized bike made in France.

many days.

WITH AUTUMN CAME the first chill of the season and new wool clothing was bought for the kids. Then November came and the approaching Christmas meant our first Noel away from home. One night around 7 pm, Marie's little friends burst into our apartment with great excitement. They begged Marie to put on her national dress and join them for a Halloween "Take-a-Treat," which neither she nor I understood what this was about. Marie was quick to comply but couldn't help wondering why her classmates had on such outlandish outfits or smeared their faces with soot. They all left in a hurry, and her parents were a little at a loss, worrying they might get into trouble. The girls safely returned sometime later, giggling, sharing their candies, and declaring that Marie was a great success with her pale green Vietnamese dress *áo dài*.

This time we learned with trepidation and a little joy when it was confirmed that my wife was again with child. We worried quite a bit because my salary was hardly enough for our family, and we knew nothing of maternity care or hospital expenses in this country. After inquiries, we started to go to the Women's Hospital in uptown New York twice weekly for mom to be examined and taken care of. We had a plan where we paid monthly that covered mom for both prenatal care and through delivery. So, we took it easy and prepared ourselves for our first Christmas in America.

We were particularly happy around this time because Christmas has always been the greatest holiday for us except for Tết, which we knew would not be celebrated in this country. For many weeks, we prepared in advance and bought our very first Christmas tree—never in Vietnam did we have a tree before. Christmas as celebrated in Vietnam was almost a Pagan affair, resplendent with multi-colored lanterns and throngs of strollers out to see the lights on Christmas Eve. Nor could we forget the procession of the infant Jesus which, in many far away corners of Vietnam, are very similar to Buddhist or Taoist processions where villagers sometimes brought out all the paraphernalia of pagan rituals, such as large high-stemmed Chinese style parasols and pennants and wore Mandarin clothing.

ON CHRISTMAS EVE, Emily had a party and many Vietnamese came. Among them were not only New York residents, but also students from other states such as Miss Nguyễn Minh Đẩu from Ohio, Lý Chánh Đức from somewhere west of north of New York, and so on. Bùi Văn Thinh was the unofficial M.C., since he had spent time and money to prepare and decorate everything—and my children were overjoyed! We enjoyed a turkey dinner and before the party broke up, someone took a color picture of us all that I still have: Thinh reclined at the foot of the Christmas tree like a lazy beaming Buddha; Miss Đẩu and Nguyễn Thanh Vân, a student from Seton Hall University in New Jersey was squeezed in the middle of the group crowded around them, the two appearing to be in a deep embrace which caused lots of merriment.

On this occasion, I had sent an invitation card to Mr. Ngô Đình Diệm, but he declined and did not get in touch with us again for a long time. However, he did send a Vietnamese priest to us, Father Trần Văn Kiệm, who was studying physics at Fordham University.[15] Father Kiệm was from the diocese of Phát Diệm about 100 kilometers south of Hanoi and sent to study in the U.S. by the Council of Vietnamese Bishops along with several other priests from the Bùi Chu or Saigon dioceses. Representing the Vietnamese Bishops was Father Jacques Houssa, a missionary of the Order of Auxiliaries to Priests in Brussels, Belgium (*L'Ordre Auxiliaire des Prêtres*). Father Jacques had taught at the Collège de la Providence in Huế and had the confidence of the Council of Bishops for he was entirely devoted to both Vietnam and its Christendom. Father Kiệm became a frequent visitor to our home and in later years, became a most devoted friend and benefactor to my family. He took turns with Bùi Văn Thinh to pay us almost daily visits and took our children on outings. The kids became attached to these two Vietnamese friends of ours and it was no little help because they brought to the kids and to us not only material assistance sometimes, but also the closeness and sense of relationship that we missed having back in Vietnam.

15 Father Trần Văn Kiệm (1920-2012), from Phát Diệm, Ninh Bình, was ordained in 1946 and later studied Physics in the US. He was the author of *Từ Điển Văn Học Việt Nam* [A Dictionary of Vietnamese Literature] (N.p.: self-published, 2007). He left a memoir which was published posthumously as *Sự Thực Có Sức Giải Phóng* [Truth Can Liberate People] by Trịnh Kim Dung (N.p.: self-published, 2013).

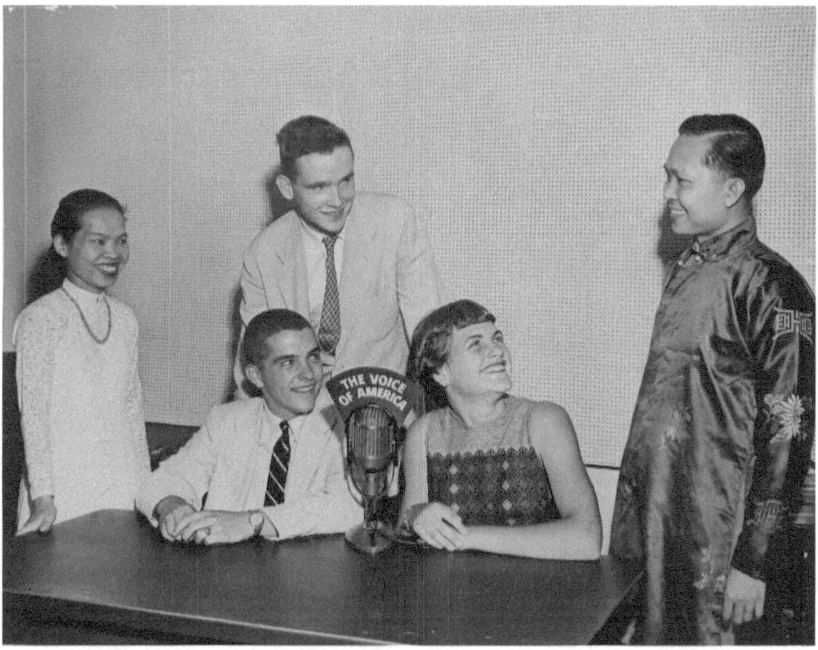

Bùi Công Văn and Lê Thị Bài with their Voice of America colleagues (Voice of America publicity photo, New York 1952)

Father Trần Đình Kiệm with the Bùi family at 306 15th St., New York (1951)

Visitor Đinh Lê Ngoạn at the Bui apartment at 306 15th St, New York (1951)

Finally, the year 1951 came to an end—our first year in America! Our new year would come later with Tết, so on America's New Year's Eve, we didn't celebrate or do anything special. My family was still too poor to afford a TV set and besides, we had no idea how New Year's were celebrated in the U.S. After mom and the children went to bed, I set out with some friends to join the crowds at Times Square. We went first to the Bronx apartment of Bùi Văn Thinh and Lý Đức Lâm, the two sailors working on a French liner who got stranded in the Philippines during a 1945 allied attack and brought to the U.S. on an American ship. We had dinner there and drove down to Times Square. On the way there, I remember how I foolishly put my scarf out the window to celebrate and let it fly in the wind like a banner. Of course, the strong wind blew it away and I was too shy and ashamed to have the car stopped to pick it up. I often thought it would be hilarious to anyone who retrieved my scarf that New Year's Eve in 1952: to see the scarf flying out of nowhere in the midst of dense traffic in the Bronx. Another feat of daring savoir-faire was demonstrated to newcomers like me by Nguyễn Tư Bân, a young student from somewhere I don't remember who spent his holidays in New York as a guest of Santa Claus Thinh. In the huge crowds at Times Square with horns blaring and all kinds of merry-making going on around us, Bân solemnly declared that at the stroke of midnight, you can kiss any girl you want and no one would remonstrate or even push you away. Sure enough, when old Lang Syne was playing and the big-time piece on Times Building struck midnight, Bân looked around and seized the girl next to him who was in the company of a sailor. Before she could utter a word, Bân planted a lengthy kiss smack on her mouth and only when he released her could she cry out, "Hey! Where's this guy from anyway?" For a while there, I was scared that the girl's sailor friend would beat Bân up while he administered the prolonged kiss.

Looking back at these eight months, from April till December 1951, which marked an abrupt and complete change in our lives, I was often wondering whether we would have remained in Vietnam and led a better life for our children and ourselves, at least the life we as Vietnamese had always known and cherished for better or for worse. In the thick of tumultuous events, however, we were often subject to whatever change circumstances would have brought us. True enough, we could have chosen to stay home in Vietnam, but the new life we embarked upon for us and for our young children did promise a better future and we had no reason to regret it. Years later, one of the many Vietnamese visitors from Saigon asked me this question which at the time sounded rather farfetched: "Don't you fear for the day when your children will grow up to be complete strangers to you and your country?" Well, I felt that day was yet in the far, far future and its consequences I would leave to tomorrow to worry about. Each day had its sufficient load of labor and anxiety to deal with.

I was glad to be in America. I had left behind my grandparents, my father and stepmother, and all my brothers and sisters, and so did my wife. Insert behind insecurity, poverty, and untold dangers that could happen every day, including sudden death. And above all, I felt for the first time like a man. Back in Vietnam, French colonial power treated Vietnamese like third-rate citizens. We could not and did not feel proud to be Vietnamese. In New York at least, I was not stopped and searched by any cop like a criminal in the streets—which happened to me back home. My children at least had a fair chance to grow up free from any colonial domination and a better chance to get an education that only rich and powerful Vietnamese at home could afford to give to theirs.

That's why I look back with delight at these first few months we lived in New York City. We were not rich, but you don't need to be rich to be happy. Contentment is all a matter of the heart and the soul. Even slavery could have moments of happiness. It is only when we refuse it and start to revolt that our "condition humaine" or complexity of our fate becomes intolerable.[16]

Had I ignored my former status as a colonial subject and been content with the standing in life that my average fellow Vietnamese got, I would still have been there at the end of 1951. As it was, my family and I were instead in New York and the subway rides every morning at 3:00 AM from 15th Street to 57th Street for my early morning broadcasts were not as disagreeable as they could be if I were to dream of delicious hours of sleeping late. Neither were the long hours in the office where Mr. Pruett, nicknamed 'Slave driver' for his missionary mien and zeal at work, made us over produce our translations as if they were so many pieces of wood to be chopped in so many

16 The phrase refers to Andre Malraux's 1933 book *La Condition Humaine* (Man's Fate) and the existential dilemmas we all face. [Au.]

hours. Nope, the Romans came later on.

LIFE AT 15TH STREET in downtown Manhattan these first few months until halfway through 1952 was routine, except that my wife got heavier everyday with her pregnancy. By now, we were used to our new way of life and even mom began to chat with neighbors or go out shopping more often by herself. The next block, 14th St. was an attraction for mom with its many department stores and she walked up and down the large avenues window shopping mostly and for exercise.

One day in late spring 1952, Dr. Trần Đình Đệ came to our apartment from his school somewhere far away and brought his five-year old daughter to stay with us for a few days as his wife, also attending a nursing course in New York, had to go out of the city.[17] At that time, my home was the only Vietnamese ménage (household) complete with children, and it was the best and only choice for the doctor to entrust his small child to, as she was also a newcomer and stranger in America. We took in the little girl whose name was Dung. She played with Dominic and Mỹ-Châu, ate with them, and spent the night without much fuss. When her father came to pick up his little girl, I remember he needed to rest a little, but our place was too small to invite him anywhere to have a rest and the poor doctor had to slumber right at the dinner table after lunch.

We had been looking for another place to stay and found an apartment on 111th Street between Broadway and

17 Trần Đình Đệ (1917-2003), graduate of Medical School in Hanoi, would later become Minister of Health in the Republic of Vietnam's First Republic and a professor in the Saigon Medical School.

Amsterdam avenues. We were to move there by the end of May, and I would let the landlord use the security deposit equaling one month's rent that the landlord already held to cover that last month. Well, the landlord sued me for not paying that last month and I had to appear in court. The judge, an old man in a black robe fringed with white fur, very kindly leaned over and asked me, "Why won't you pay the rent, son?" I explained my reasoning to the judge, who nodded and ruled: "Case dismissed." I resented that greedy King, that money-hungry landlord who was not content to such $120 a month out of my meager salary for the wretched little box he called an apartment but wanted to steal an extra $120 or at least a part of it too. I also could not but blame Miss Bài for having gotten me into that dire rental spot and then got out of it herself, leaving me and my family behind high and dry without as much as one word of goodbye. Mother and daughter just disappeared from the scene as if we were strangers to each other in a new city.

ON MAY 31, 1952, we move to our new abode. We were so happy to have a new home four times larger than the previous one and beautifully furnished for exactly the same rent. We had to pay one month's rent to the agent as commission for securing this apartment for us, but the charge was all right. After all, "Who believes that beautiful things in life are free of charge?" went the lyrics of a popular song at the time. But we had been hardly in the new "deluxe" apartment, the kids running about trying this bed and that sofa and exploring the places many rooms, when mom began feeling her first birth pangs. Ah, the time has come! The children and I brought mom to the woman's hospital and returned to our new apartment, our first night would be without mother. It was a long and anxious night for me, and I expected to be called and told that my wife had given birth to a new child. But no calls came during that night.

We had been married 13 years almost to the day when this fifth child of ours was given to us. Marie Mỹ-Dung was born in February 1941 at Cần Thơ; Tuyên, our second child and first son, was born in March 1943 also at Cần Thơ but he died in 1946 at Gò Cát, Mỹ Tho, where no medical care was available in a village infested with Việt Minh to which we returned after being evacuated to the wilderness; Dominic Nghiệp was born in January 1948; and Lucie Mỹ-Châu in August, 1950. This coming fifth child, an American citizen by birth, would it be a boy or a girl? That night at the new apartment, a father and his children waited for news with a mixture of joy and anxiety. Marie, already conscious of her new status as the eldest sister of two small youngsters and an infant soon to come, behaved as the circumstances expected of an adult although she was but an 11-year-old girl and had so far acted like a little mother in every way. It is the way of Vietnamese families where girls, especially the first born, became responsible much sooner than boys, and women in general shoulder all tasks, menial or not, leaving the men of the house to deal with outside society and see to it that the financial needs of the household be met. By instinct, if not necessarily by education, our children were more of a help to their parents than a burden. This was a habit I would see in later years but not likely to survive long in America, or anywhere else in the West for that matter.

Marie Mỹ Dung, Dominic Nghiệp, and Lucie Mỹ Châu in New York living room (Winter 1952)

EARLY MORNING OF June 1, 1952, Muriel Josephine Mỹ-Nga Bùi was born. The Women's Hospital informed dad that mom and baby were fine, and that the child had been delivered sometime in the early hours of the first day of June. However, we all had to wait until evening to see mom and the newborn as I had to go to work, and Marie had to care for the kids at home. On my way to the office, I stopped to buy some candy and even cigars, as I had heard that this was the custom in America: offer sweets and pass around cigars when you have a new addition in the family. I triumphantly announce my happy news to everyone in the Vietnamese unit and every neighboring Southeast Asian unit of the Voice of America.

I loved my wife, my children, and my family and each new child given to me was an opportunity for great rejoicing. Marie, our first-born, I carried high above my shoulders and walked exuberantly in the streets as if to show her off for the whole world to see and admire. I was young, and it happened that I was jobless then, so I could devote all my time and effort to love my child who was in every way my very own unique and unequaled creation. Mentions had been made earlier about the nights in my father's house at Cần Thơ as I was mindful of not interrupting my father's sleep in the middle of the night. In 1945, when Marie was four years old and American bombing raids occurred almost daily in Saigon, sometimes the alarm got sounded in Cần Thơ too. One morning, such an air raid alarm sounded, and father and first daughter hurried to seek shelter to the great laughter of neighbors and onlookers who called us poltroons ("cowards"). People around me had never been under an air raid before but I had the year before in Saigon when the Americans bombed the Municipal Theater or Saigon Opera House, I can't remember which, and I crouched fearfully in a flimsy shelter not more than 300 meters away.

Except for little Tuyên who died in the village where we went to hide after forced evacuation from Saigon, Marie was the lone child who with her parents fled from bombs and evacuations in the dismal and dangerous months 1945. Dominic and Mỹ-Châu had been born in the relative security of the vicinity of Saigon. This new princess of ours, whose birth was announced to me this very day—whom I hadn't even seen yet—Ah! How joyfully and proudly I would look upon her tonight!

That evening, I went to the woman's hospital alone and Marie stayed home with her brother and sister. When I walked to my wife's bedside and stood close to her what did I see? My wife was still half unconscious from the aspect of anesthesia and only vaguely recognized me. She convulsively grabbed my hand and silently cried, tears rolling down her pale cheeks. Oh, my love. What did I do to you? I brought you to this country, a faraway place, and separated you from everyone in our extended family! Your mother who always stood nearby when you were in labor, who held your hands and stayed by your side until after each child was born, or my grandmother, or any other member of our extended family, for that matter. For we in Vietnam are very sensitive to the labor pains of the women in her hours of childbirth. We have a saying that describes the loneliness of the mother at this moment that recounts how, no matter how many people stand with the woman to help her, the laboring mother still goes alone through the pain and danger. It goes like this: "*Man goes to sea in the company of other men/But woman gives birth, like an orphan, all by herself.*"[18]

But she didn't know she was crying. I bent down and murmured some comforting words in her ear, but she apparently neither heard nor understood me. Just kept rolling down her cheeks and while I wiped them off with my handkerchief, she was trying to say something inaudible and unintelligible. Months later, mom told me that she felt like she was in a dream. She knew she was in the hospital, that the child had been born, but somehow had no idea that she was in America. Everything was a blur and even I didn't appear real to her either. She was surprised the next day when she was herself and I told her she had cried. She had no idea, but we think it was her first childbirth with anesthesia despite having previously birthed four children before. Another reason could have been because when she emerged from anesthesia she was at a complete loss: she saw no familiar face, she was in entirely strange surroundings, she might as well have woken up on another planet. And the child, where was it? She had given birth four times before and each time she saw her child lying next to her when the pain stopped and she was fully conscious and eager to look at the result of so many months, so much pain, so much love. To look at her trophy as it were. Here in America though, her child was kept apart from her and when my wife was half awake, she must have felt something was missing,

18 In Vietnamese, "Đàn ông đi biển có đôi/Đàn bà đi biển (or vượt cạn in some version) mồ côi một mình."

and all her instincts cried out that something important, some part of herself, some precious for being here in the hospital—was amiss! Her tears were tears of panic almost, but also of loneliness, archer loneliness as described in that Vietnamese saying. After a few moments in which I failed in calming her down, with my wife's tears and maybe her even blurred vision, I pulled over a chair and shaft there holding her hand. We did not talk, or rather, I talked, and she seemed to be in a trance too far removed to follow what I had to say. She didn't cry anymore and little by little her color returned so her face looked more normal, and she even gave me a half-conscious smile, too. Visiting hours were over and I took leave of my wife, confiding her to the good care of the duty nurse. My beloved wife was healthy in every way after giving birth, and I had no reason to worry about her. In my view, the anesthesia was a new experience that had a strong effect on her, but the duty nurse matter-of-factly shrugged off my wife's odd behavior as it did little lasting harm.

I made my way to the viewing room where I could admire my newborn daughter. She was a lovely little creature, dark of hair and round of face, wrapped up in white linen. The nurse held her up for me to see her tiny arms, a small bead chain around her wrist bearing the letters V-A-N good morning. Ahh! She was the latest scion of the Văn family, according to the incorrect way Americans read my name—first name first, last name last! I had to go to the Birth registry office and declare my little one's name as BUI, MY-NGA, the same way I did for my other children on entering the US. The lady there corrected me on how to write my name. "No! Add your 'last' name first and your first name last!" What she did was reverse the name my wife and I had chosen for our beautiful daughter. It was ugly and nonsensical for they made me put my given name of "Van" last so that the birth certificate looked like this: Child's name: BUI MY-NGA VAN, Father's name: BUI CONG VAN.

AFTER FIVE DAYS, mother and child came home to a new place that they would live in for the first time, as if both had come back from a trip during which dad, Marie, Dominic and Mỹ- Châu prepare the nest for them to come home and roost. For Mỹ-Nga, it was her first home in this world, and we were quite proud to have a better more decent home to receive our "Chinese Princess." I had already started to nickname her this after her rather accentuated oriental traits, especially her long arched and well refined eyebrows similar to those described by Nguyễn Du in Kiều:[19]

Vân xem trang trọng khác vời,
Khuôn trăng đầy đặn, nét ngài nở nang.
Hoa cười, ngọc thốt đoan trang
Mây thua nước tóc, tuyết nhường màu da.

Vân's dainty appearance is above the common,
Her radiant face the moon, her eyebrows the silkworms.
Her hair more lissome than feathery clouds,

19 "Kim Vân Kiều Tân Truyện," a long narrative poem written by Nguyễn Du (1765-1820) in early 19th century in the Nôm script, is one of the masterpieces of classical Vietnamese literature. For an English translation paired with vernacular Vietnamese verses, see Nguyễn Du, Huỳnh Sanh Thông, and Alexander Woodside, *The Tale of Kiều: A Bilingual Edition of Truyện Kiều* (New Haven: Yale University Press, 1983), 2.

And snow-white would be a poor description of her complexion.

I am glad Nguyễn Du made such a portrait of my Chinese Princess, especially as Thúy Vân, Kiều's younger sister, had an uneventful if less interesting and therefore tempestuous destiny than did Kiều's. My wife and I did not plan it so, but the events of Mỹ-Nga entering the Bùi Clan proved to be a good omen, auguring great and splendid things to come.

Mỹ-Nga was baptized when she was ten days old. To be her godparents, we chose the Mahoneys, our former neighbors at 15th Street (and she got her American godmother's name). Unlike the American custom to have different godfather and godmother for a child, we stuck to the Vietnamese tradition to choose a couple to whom we would entrust our child for lifelong spiritual guidance, and to act in every way as a new set of parents to care for their godchild not only spiritually but materially too, if necessary. Her baptism certificate registered at the Ascension Church at 108th Street West reads: MURIEL JOSEPHINE BUI MY-NGA.

5. THE PARTY

OUR NEW APARTMENT on 111th Street West was No. 4, on the 4th floor. It had a spacious front part looking down on the street below, divided into living and dining rooms. We turned the dining room into a den where a divan served as a bed for me when I worked late at night, and I had a desk with a glass top and a built-in bookcase. One night I brought home a desk lamp, ceremoniously placed it on the desk, plugged it into the wall socket, and switched it on. Boom! The lamp burned up in a small explosion and a trail of black smoke—I didn't realize that it ran on direct current!

The living room would serve as combination living-dining room, with an early colonial style mahogany table, a couch mom covered with a red and white flower cloth she bought at a bargain basement store on 14th Street, an old-fashion dark brown radio set that didn't work put there by the landlord as a decorative piece, add a set of four straight-backed wooden chairs that we arranged against the partition wall between the den and the living room. The communicating door was shut tight except when we threw a party and needed the whole space in the front part of the apartment. The wallpaper was a light pink shade with elongated crimson flowers and light green leaves. The kitchen with its gas range and Frigidaire was an extension of my den but separated by a wooden door and a window that mom used to put out crumbs for the pigeons. Our entry door opened onto a long corridor off our living-dining room that was lit by a naked bulb in an iron sconce on the wall. Bedrooms lined the corridor for mom and infant Mỹ-Nga; Marie, Dominic, and Mỹ-Châu; and an unfurnished guest room.

We were so happy for our good fortune. We had all these nicely painted and furnished rooms for the same $120.00 monthly rent we had to pay for an entire year to that avaricious Mr. King down on 15th St. for the small one-bedroom box he called an apartment. We had reason to celebrate our home. And more than that, we could throw a party in our space to mark Muriel's first month of life!

For many days in advance, Bùi Văn Thinh and Nguyễn Tư Bân came and helped us prepare for Muriel's Day. Thinh was jobless "deluxe" for he had nothing to do and plenty of dollars in his pocket, and Bân was on vacation. Most of the expenses were paid by Thinh, our Santa Claus. Bân helped in every way possible, and never minded being sent down 20 times a day for something at the newspaper and candy store at the corner of 111th and Broadway where he liked to flirt with the shop owner's daughter. We concocted an "Atomic Punch," which consisted of five parts vodka and three parts orange juice diluted with plain tap water and mom bought a huge punch bowl to serve our powerful drink. We later gave it to Yến, Huỳnh Sanh Thông's wife, and she still had it decades later, complete with ladle and all its small cups.

On July 1, 1952, when Mỹ-Nga was exactly 1 month old, we had an open house to celebrate our child's first month of life as was and still remains the custom in Vietnam. I had invited Mr. Ngô Đình Diệm and all of our friends and acquaintances, as many people as I could think of.

Mr. Ngô arrived first. We opened the door and hardly recognized the man from the first night that we met him. Perhaps he had on the same dark-brown suit and green necktie as then, but he held in his right hand a bulging black briefcase and looked younger and happier than he did that night 14 months ago when we first met at the Tudor Hotel. Tonight was also the first time we noticed his very peculiar gait as we followed him down our long corridor into the living room. A rather short man, Ngô walked rapidly but his feet did not touch the ground straight and perpendicular to his legs but slightly obliquely. He gave the impression of a duck's walk advancing with his toes pointed out. In Vietnam, we call this gait the "Character Eight" walk as it resembles the Chinese character for that number.

Ngô Đình Diệm took the *fauteuil d'honneur,* the only armchair in the house, put down his briefcase, and took a pack of Phillip Morris cigarettes from his pocket. As his first lighted cigarette reached its remaining half, he snuffed it out by rubbing the burning end gently against the wall of the ashtray then relit it again a few times. My wife brought in a tray with two glasses of whiskey soda. Mr. Ngô declined the alcohol but requested strong tea instead. "I've got very good Lotus tea—Trà mạn sen—

from home," he said. "Next time I'll bring it out for you, Mrs. Văn."

Then he opened his briefcase. "By the way," Mr. Ngô went on, "here is a rosary made of lotus seeds. They tie dried lotus grains up in a pretty rosary not unlike the buddha's rosary we used to see back home. Have them for your tea—very good indeed--or you may give them to the children to play with." Our conversation went on for a good half hour before our guests began to arrive. It was 3:00 in the afternoon, a Saturday afternoon, and the hot and sticky July sunshine emitted waves of heat intermittently relieved by a light breeze from the riverside. As I turned to go answer the first doorbell's ring, I clearly recalled Mr. Ngô taking a wristwatch from his briefcase and handing it to me and saying, "Mr. Văn, will you look at this watch? It stopped working and I think, if you know something about watches you could make it work again." I pocketed the watch and went to answer the door. As the first batch of guests entered, we all exchanged polite words and congratulations. Then came another batch of guests and the party was in full swing.

There were Đức Thanh, Đức Lâm, Nguyễn Đình Hòa, Miss Bài and her mother, Quan, Trịnh Văn Chẩn, all my colleagues from VOA, Thu--a Tonkinese who stayed with Đức Thanh, Vinh Đan, Nguyễn Ngọc Linh, Miss Phạm Thị Thu (who later became Linh's wife), the septuagenarian Cụ Tư, Linh's brother Nguyễn Ngọc Nhạ who limped, and of course Bùi Văn Thinh and Nguyễn Tư Bân. There was Miss Phan, a young Vietnamese visitor whom Đức Thanh courted and stayed as close to as a Siamese twin, and a reporter named Sol Sanders, who arrived with a bouquet of gladiolas for my wife. My colleagues from the Voice of America arrived with a present for Muriel—a cot—which they proceeded to assemble and place Muriel in it. A color picture was taken, which we still have, of our infant sound asleep in her new cot.

Our "atomic punch" made most people tipsy and towards midnight, Vinh Đan put on a show. He was an optometry student, and he deemed it appropriate to show everyone his slides. Mostly they were scenic pictures taken in America but every once in a while, he'd mischievously slip in a slide of nude ladies and Vinh Đan would loudly exclaim, "Ooh, pardon my mistake!" upon which the audience roared with laughter. Fortunately, Mr. Ngô departed before the slide show, his wristwatch in his pocket. I had returned it to him saying, "I've looked at it, Sir, but I'm no watchmaker nor connoisseur of timepieces whatsoever. I am so sorry."

A FEW DAYS after Muriel's month celebration, one night in July 1952, Ngô Đình Diệm telephoned me from Lakewood, New Jersey, where he was staying at the Maryknoll Seminary. He asked me to go down to Grand Central railway station and buy a one-way ticket for him to Cleveland, Ohio. I said "yes" without the slightest inkling that this was the first in a series of debts I'd incur for Mr. Ngô. My wife and I began to worry: where would we get the money for the ticket? I should have asked for money in the 1st place. I blamed myself for having been too polite, or too rushed maybe. After all, had I not "warned" Ngô Đình Diệm at our first meeting that politics was not my cup of tea, and did he not remember my saying so? Mr. Ngô did not say what he was going to Cleveland for, nor did I ask. I just said "yes." My wife and I knew he did not go there or anywhere else for vacation. And if he did, we also knew he would not have asked us to buy a train ticket for him without mentioning any money to buy it with.

Politics, then, was involved. We thought about Đức Thanh: a phone call and he would jump to the occasion. And he—of any person we knew—would have ready cash. But we brushed the idea aside, remembering too well what Mr. Ngô told us about Đức Thanh and how he'd ask for money first before doing anything for Mr. Ngô. And we saw why the lecturer called us instead of anyone else as Mr. Ngô also was penniless. He appealed to us because we would not ask for money. He knew we knew his situation and trusted us. And we were glad to help him.

It was about 8:00 p.m. and I went right away to Trịnh Văn Chẩn, a fellow translator-announcer at the Voice, who was a bachelor but whose salary was exactly the same as mine. If anyone could lend me money, he could and he would. Chẩn was in fact a pretty close friend of mine and I would not be embarrassed to ask the favor. He and Lâm Chấn Quan shared an apartment at West 80th Street. These two bachelors had come on the same contingent of recruits from Saigon as Miss Bài and myself and they had shared an apartment ever since. Quan was rather stingy and kept very much to himself whereas Chẩn was more outgoing and I knew he would be ready to help should I run short of cash—as I often did. A train ticket, however, was no little matter of $10 or $20 which he might have on him.

I worried that we'd have to wait until morning when he could withdraw a larger sum from the bank. Sure enough, this was the case. I made Chẩn promise to withdraw the $50 I needed first thing in the morning then called Mr. Ngô to let him know that I would have his ticket for him.

The following night at 8 p.m. I met Ngô Đình Diệm at Grand Central and handed him the ticket I bought for him during my lunch break with Chẩn's money. Mr. Ngô came alone, wearing the same dark-brown suit and green tie, the same black suitcase under his arm, and a leather suitcase I helped him carry on board the train. I didn't ask him why he was going to Cleveland, nor did he say anything about it, except that some urgent business calls him there, and he thanked me for the ticket, and he would pay me back one day. I was still very much averse to politics and although I knew "business" meant 'political business,' I did not want to pursue the matter. On his side also, I thought he was reading my mind quite clearly, so no words were needed to explain our respective positions or attitudes. My wife and I only thought of helping a good man as best we could, with no mental reservation as to what Mr. Ngô was up to.

Trịnh Văn Chẩn's suspicion that something 'political' might be afoot revealed itself the next day. When I inadvertently said I'd seen Mr. Ngô off to Cleveland the night before, Chẩn asked if I'd borrowed the money for Mr. Ngô's political reasons. I managed to sidestep by chiding him for his poor opinion of the character of a respected man like Ngô Đình Diệm. Why, he wouldn't need a miserable 50 bucks from a poor man like me for politics, would he? And why was he asking, anyway?

What was to happen sooner or later did happen. A few days after the rather heated exchange between Chẩn and me, the office secretary, a Miss Loretta Napolitano, called me on the telephone saying she had Mr. Ngô on the line, calling from Grand Central station.

"Mr. Văn, could you help me? I'm at the train station. Could you come right away?"

I was a little taken aback and worried that something serious happened to urgently request my help. "I'm afraid not, Sir," I replied. "I'm going on air soon. Could you tell me what happened?"

"Oh, nothing much, but my back aches terribly. I don't think I can make it to Lakewood."

My recording session was fast approaching so I hastily said: "In that case, please go straight to my apartment. I'll call my wife and let her know you're coming over."

I WAS NAÏVE to such an extent that I did not realize that the Voice of America where I worked was a listening post for any stirrings in the politics of Vietnam and Indochina. My colleagues heard me talking to Ngô Đình Diệm and knew he was heading to my home. But unlike Chẩn who directly voiced his suspicions to me, these others kept quiet except to their superiors in Vietnam. This was what in hindsight and particle by particle what I pieced together of the situation at VOA at the time.

When I reached home that evening, I saw Mr. Ngô lying on the divan covered with the red cloth my wife had bought. He tried to sit up, but his face grimaced with pain and he fell back. I made him as comfortable as possible and he told me that on the return trip, he got a bad backache during the night. I told him to try and rest a bit while I arranged to have our neighbor, Dr. Meltzer, come see him that night despite the late hour.

I brought Mr. Ngô over to Dr. Meltzer's apartment where he was given an injection and an electric hot pad to apply to his lower back where it hurt the most. The consultation helped Mr. Ngô enough that he could walk back to my apartment much more easily and his pain somewhat relieved. My wife helped readjust the pad over many hours that night and he felt much better the next morning. In the days that followed, Dr. Meltzer contributed more to Mr. Ngô's recovery until one day, Ngô Đình Diệm was his old self again. He walked about jauntily, seemingly more jovial than ever. Before he said goodbye to us and returned to the seminary, he had this to say:

"You know, it seems destined that I came to you without any intention of burdening you. I know well how your life is here, with your family and many children to care for, and your modest salary. What can I say except 'Thank you!' from the bottom of my heart." We were touched, my wife and I, and we quickly assured Mr. Ngô that he was no burden to us. We asked him to please come again and stay as long as he wished, provided he was not troubled by our meager meals and modest lifestyle. He said a last goodbye and departed from us.

6. CHICAGO

IT WAS SUMMER IN MANHATTAN and in those hot months I badly needed my vacation. I had three weeks in August, something I chose to take all at once rather than having my vacation later in the fall or winter as did most of my colleagues. It was also my first vacation ever since I began working with the Voice of America on April 25th, 1951. My plan was simply to lie down and recapture all the sleep I had lost from late nights broadcasting and otherwise take it easy with my wife and children. But once more Ngô Đình Diệm and the hand of destiny wanted things differently for me.

The Vietnamese Catholic Students Association in North America held its first annual meeting in early August in Chicago. I hadn't the slightest idea what the Association was, nor concerned myself with what it did but one night, my telephone rang. It was Ngô Đình Diệm. He mentioned the Association and asked if I would like to go to Chicago and attend the meeting. Of course I would, I said. I was on vacation, wasn't I?

The husband and wife once more had a family meeting. Where would travel money come from? Not Chẩn again!

But I had to go to the meeting and my past reluctance to borrow had evaporated—I was almost eager to go. Money was a problem that could be solved. We decided then and there to borrow much from a bank, on a "grand scale" as it were, rather than submit ourselves to the embarrassment and the enervating curiosity of any potential Vietnamese money lender.

So, I went to the branch of a Chase Manhattan bank and borrowed $300. It was the first time I ever owed money to a bank. I was rash, but I did not care and nor did my wife. We were young yet and were influenced by Ngô Đình Diệm, only we did not know that we were. I walked out of the bank with a payment book pierced with holes for each monthly June, but not with the whole $300—the first monthly due plus interest had been deducted in advance! Yet again, I smiled to myself. I walked down to the subway and headed for 14th St., where I used to buy winter clothes and other necessities for my family. I went to Wanamaker, a big department store where I had no difficulty obtaining credit to purchase on an installment plan. One more new debt. How ironic that the popular song of the day was "Sixteen Tons" by Tennessee Ernie Ford. The lyrics partly went: "I sold my soul to the company store ..."

I left Wanamaker with a green plastic suitcase filled with a few shirts and ties and some frivolities. (Muriel still uses that suitcase—it's as old as she is). And the trip to Chicago began. To save money, I took the long, long ride there on a Greyhound bus. Once in Chicago, I took a room at the YMCA the day before the Vietnamese Catholic Students' Association officially opened. The next morning,

I was still sleeping when someone loudly banged on my door. "Who's there?" I grouchily croaked. "Friends. Open up!" a voice said in Vietnamese.

I was overjoyed! If the Vietnamese as a people have a national characteristic, it's their attachment to country and countrymen. Especially when they are abroad. There's a saying about that:

Cửu hạn phùng cam vũ
Tha hương ngộ cố tri.[20]

(There's no such delight as:)

Sweet rain in a drought
Old friends meet in foreign lands

FROM MY NARROW bed in the tiny room of the Chicago YMCA, my eyes still swollen with sleep, I reached out and turned the doorknob. The door was pushed in from the outside and a tousled head poked in. "Hey, wake up! Don't be a lazy bone—it's midday!". I sleepy narrowed my eyes and saw behind the youth a few more heads—Vietnamese heads. I stood up right away and introductions were quickly made with the youth speaking up first. "I'm Bùi Kiến Thành" then named each fellow who squeezed through the half-opened door. "This is Nguyễn Thái, current President, sorry soon to be President of the Association; this is Nguyễn Văn Mừng; and this is ..."

I was still in my pajamas so I quickly changed. Nguyễn Thái spoke up: "We heard of your arrival. Guys, aren't

20 These verses are from a poem by Wang Zhu (Song Dynasty, China) on the happy moments in life.

we showing Mr. Văn the Loop and other merveilles [wonders] of Chicago?". I quickly replied: "Thanks, but I have already been to the Loop and bars where girls drink colored water ,but charge you the price of whiskey. Yeah, last night." Laughter echoed all around!

My favorite youth was the tousled fellow, Bùi Kiến Thành, who said he was a friend of Ngô Đình Diệm, or at least his father was the friend, and he asked if I had ever met Diệm in New York. Indeed I have, and I explained that in a manner of speaking, I am attending this meeting not of my own accord but because Diệm wanted me to.

Oh, how lighthearted we all were. I was 33, their elder but not by much. I felt like one of them—I felt rejuvenated. If earlier I regretted borrowing money for this trip, I didn't anymore. I willingly joined them—and their youthful mien and activities. And I owed this happiness to Mr. Ngô.

The fellows drove me around downtown Chicago, then uphill to the college dormitory where members and guests of the association would spend the next few days. My bed was next to that of a youth named Nguyễn Văn Nghiêm who was younger brother to Nguyên Văn Thơ but at the time, I knew neither of them. Nghiêm and I spent the next week or so as roommates and we got along together quite well. Later on, when his brother Thơ became a headache for both the Association and our group of supporters of Ngô Đình Diệm, I still remembered young Nghiêm and thanked God he was not like his brother.

I was introduced to Father Jacques. I had met the real contender, the one they had already chosen as their president or chairman Âu Ngọc Hồ.[21] He was a very gentle looking youth, mild in manner and soft in speech. He was exactly the opposite of Nguyễn Thái and I liked him then and there despite Nguyễn Thái striking me as the more dynamic and intelligent of the pair. But Hồ was there for a vote, not mine, and I was a guest. Even years later, Âu Ngọc Hồ was flattered when I still referred to him as "the gentle young man."

At the luncheon immediately after the first session of the meeting when the chairman, Hồ, was nominated and installed, I was introduced to the Association members by a young girl from Huế, Miss Nguyễn Thị Quít. In my speech of thanks, I made a big mistake when I said: "Thank you, Miss Nguyễn Thị Quít, a lovely Việt girl from the village of Thừa Thiên . . ." Laughter exploded throughout the audience that naturally thought here is an ignoramus from the South! The laughter had barely subsided when I dexterously extricated myself: "I mean from Thừa Thiên Province . . ." More laughter, if a little subdued. "Particularities of each of our three parts of Vietnam," I went on rather lamely, "I am not a separatist—on the contrary. But I have yet to hear a province be changed to a village in Cochinchina, Annam (where Miss Quít is from and pardon for the colonial appellation which started the truncation, and therefore, the division of our country into three parts in the first place), or in Tonkin. The Vietnamese names for Tonkin, Annam, and Cochinchina are Bắc Kỳ, Trung Kỳ, and Nam Kỳ, my apologies." There

21 Âu Ngọc Hồ (1930-2015) would later serve as Minister of Economy from May 1968 to September 1969 in the Republic of Vietnam's government of Prime Minister Trần Văn Hương.

was general laughter now but of approval, not sneering. Later, a Vietnamese priest, a Father Trịnh, whispered in my ear: "No wonder you're a radio announcer. You're a born orator."

That day I was made an honorary member of the Association. It was at this first plenum of the Association, indeed its founding day, that I met most of the Vietnamese students in America. Many came to study here under the sponsorship of Vietnamese bishops, whether the students were Catholic or not. Âu Ngọc Hồ was not and the fact that he was elected the first chairman of the Association spoke highly of its liberal and non-sectarian character. Some of the students, such as Trương Đình Phú, an agricultural student, were very friendly and interested in talking to me despite knowing we might not see each other again after they dispersed for far away campuses and I was not to attend any other plenum of the Association.

Father Jacques was made chaplain and advisor to the Association, a function he had always held (unofficially, as the Association had not been formed yet). As representative of the Vietnamese bishops, he was responsible for every scholarship given and he devoted himself to each student in the U.S., Catholic or not, and whether they came under his sponsorship or not. He was indefatigable, and if possible, he looked after the welfare of any student who asked him for help. He wore a black silk cassock that was almost gray from wear—he seldom cared about his appearance—he would drive thousands of miles, knock on all doors, and leave no stone unturned for the sake of his Vietnamese student flock.

Father Jacques of course knew Ngô Đình Diệm well. He had been a teacher at the Collège de la Providence in Huế and spoke Vietnamese fluently. Besides, Bishop Ngô Đình Thục, Mr. Ngô's brother, was the most influential of the Vietnamese bishops. There were not too many of them, not more than a dozen total, as the creation of Vietnamese bishops was an event of recent date.

At the luncheon that day, the name of Ngô Đình Diệm was mentioned, and Father Jacques proposed that I help him by receiving students coming to the U.S. by way of New York. The newcomers would stay with my family for a few days before traveling to their campuses. I accepted his request with some worries as doing this would certainly take up a lot of my time and a lot of my budget. That same night, the Association received a congratulatory telegram from Ngô Đình Diệm on behalf of the students and the priests residing in New York City. I never suspected that Mr. Ngô would have come to my home and sent the telegram from there.

Notes on this first plenum: Nguyễn Thái was to become more and more active in the affairs of the Association, and although he did not know it himself, it was his stepping stone onto future political ambitions and successes. Thái was assiduously courting Miss Tuyết Mai. Students then were unambitious and pretty much in the mold of old traditions: devoted to filial duties, mindful of their parents' wishes, and as a rule, studied hard. A few exceptions could not help but confirm the rule.

7. GRANDPA MARYKNOLL

I LEFT THE CONVENTION and came home to find Ngô Đình Diệm waiting there for my return. Mom had turned our living room into a private room for Mr. Ngô with the couch as his bed and the door connecting it to my den had been nailed shut for good. This room would be Mr. Ngô's for the next nine months, except when he infrequently returned to the Maryknoll Seminary and stayed for only a few days. He told me and my wife, by way of apology: "I know I may be an extra burden for you, but I'm so lonely at the seminary and too secluded to be able to follow outside events. I would beg for your generosity and understanding to allow me to stay with you here several days at a time. And besides, events at home seem to be astir..."

He did not have to plead. We were more than ready to take him in. In fact, we were eager to have him as member of our family. By now, we were used to him and considered him almost like our father. For a Vietnamese abroad, what could be more precious and comforting than to have your own parent living under the same roof? My wife and I made ourselves clear in a few simple words and Mr. Ngô was pleased.

From then on started a series of long nights—in fact, entire nights—of talking and smoking. At first this was unbearable for us because Mr. Ngô never seemed to want to sleep and the later the night became, the more awake he looked. In the long run, we got used to it. Not only did I stay up until the last minute before I had to leave for work on my night schedule, but I also enjoyed our chats.

When my regular working hours were days from 9 to 6, Mr. Ngô would spend the day with our children. He brought them to Riverside Park on long walks, chatted with them, and also took beautiful photographs of them on his battered Leica. He composed a particularly nice photo of Mỹ-Chậu standing on a park bench: it was an artistic tableau of stone, trees, and a little girl holding a large red autumn leaf in her hand that she studied as if admiring its color, her little green handbag lying at her feet. Mr. Ngô brought the children back in time for lunch with mom and rested or read until I got home.

Ngô Đình Diệm in his favorite armchair
in Mr. Bùi Công Văn's apartment (New York 1952)

Ngô Đình Diệm with Bùi family and supporters (New York 1952)

Standing left to right: Nguyễn Hữu Hanh, Dư Phước Long, Marie Mỹ Dung, Mrs. Văn, Mr. Văn

Seated left to right: Dominic Đỗ Văn Quý, Ngô Đình Diệm, Dominic Nghiệp, Lucie Mỹ Châu

Bùi family with the newest member, Muriel Mỹ-Nga (New York 1952)

When the weather was fine, especially during the lingering summer evenings when the sky was still bright with the sun's last rays and fresh breezes blew in from the Hudson River, we all walked together to Riverside Park. Muriel was in a baby carriage we borrowed from a colleague at the Voice of America who lived nearby, Mr. Jim Lanigan, as we were still too much in debt to afford our own carriage for the infant. I pushed the carriage, Dominic and Mỹ-Châu walked behind me, and mom and Mr. Ngô made up the end of the procession. Sometimes, visitors to our home joined us in our evening walks in the park.

On one such evening, our procession was joined by Father Kiệm, Bùi Văn Thinh and Nguyễn Thanh Vân from Seton Hall University in New Jersey who had come to New York to spend the day with us. We were chatting and exchanging pleasantries in Vietnamese when we heard an American voice calling loudly: "Hey, Vietnam!" It was Jim Lanigan. He was one of the few Americans at that time who even knew where Vietnam was, let alone know what Vietnamese language sounded like. We introduced him to Mr. Ngô and Lanigan later told us he had heard of him and was delighted to meet him.

Dominic, meanwhile, was rolling on the grass, a thick carpet of green clover, playing with a small boy his age. My son wanted to show his friend a somersault he just learned to do but got his English mixed with Vietnamese in a cute manner. In Vietnamese, "lộn mèo" is putting your head on the ground and pushing off with both legs to flip over on your back. "Do you know how to lộn mèo?" Dominic asked. His pal shook his head, perplexed.

"Then," Dominic said, "Let me lộn mèo you coi'" (let me somersault, watch).

His friend didn't even shake his head, this time; he was completely at a loss as to what my son was saying or about to do. We adults all laughed our heads off. Dominic proceeded to demonstrate his lộn mèo skills over and over again on the soft green clover carpet.

One other evening walk, Lý Chánh Đức, another visiting student was with us. But as far as I can recall, at the time there was no other Vietnamese in New York or elsewhere, resident or student. Mr. Ngô knew all his visitors for he was quite circumspect—and rightly so, I thought. Quite a few Vietnamese in the U.S., especially in Washington, D.C. and New York, were favored by the French and their puppet government in Saigon headed at the time by Trần Văn Hữu. More than that, some Vietnamese were in the pay of the French or at least tried to gain favor with the Vietnamese Embassy then headed by Ambassador Trần Văn Khá. Mr. Ngô, on the other hand, preferred to have his whereabouts unknown and keep the French and their henchmen in the dark.

We would thus linger in the park until dark. When we returned to our apartment, street lights were on and on the other side of the Hudson River, the multicolored lights of the Palisades Amusement Park twinkled and glistened, reflecting in the water like so many long, coiling snakes.

Back home, a simple dinner (as we could hardly afford sumptuous meals) and then the long nightly "vigil" began. Mom by now was quite used to the routine. She brought in a steaming teapot filled to the brim. On the table was a carton of Philip Morris cigarettes. Sometimes, when available, a glass of whisky for me. The ritual of Mr. Ngô lighting his cigarettes, slowly snuffing them out, then relighting them began, and the seeming interminable conversations started.

Ngô Đình Diệm spoke for hours and hours on end. He attacked every subject under the sun, stopping only to sip some tea, or more rarely, to listen to a question or two I put to him. Mom would have disappeared to the kitchen as befitted Vietnamese women—at least according to tradition—but returned once in a while to refill the teapot then discretely tiptoe out. Whenever mom opened the door, though, she had to step back a moment, the room was so smoky she could hardly see anything inside. The two men in there were deep in conversation, oblivious to the smoke, and never stopped their chain smoking. In winter, it was worse, as we shut the windows tight against the cold and mom had to open them to let some fresh air in when she came with the tea.

I availed of the opportunity to ask Mr. Ngô about his past and Vietnamese politics in general. He would launch on long discussions of colonialism and colonial policies, on this and that Vietnamese personality past and present, with many particular details about them—at least for me, who was admittedly ignorant of those.

On the future, however, Ngô Đình Diệm was unsure. He did not know—and would not venture to predict—what was to happen to our country. As for his personal activities, he was quite sincere and stated that he did not, nor did he plan to, have anything important to accomplish nor did he really intend to act. Mr. Ngô's favorite word was "study." He was in the United States mainly to serve and to "study," he said. He explained: When the time comes, or when the opportunity presents itself, and if he judges it worthy and useful, he will see what the proper action to take would be.

Mr. Ngô observed and studied America but I also learned from him. One night Mr. Ngô asked me if I knew what "filibuster" meant. I was totally ignorant at the time and responded with the first idea that came to mind: "a buccaneer, a pirate on the high seas." He laughed and explained what it meant in the U.S. Congress. That was one of many occasions when Ngô Đình Diệm acted as teacher to me, and he seemed to enjoy the role. He was more fitting in the role of teacher than conversationalist. He taught me a lot about politics and needless to say, he influenced me profoundly and as the months passed, I came to adopt every one of his viewpoints on almost any subject.

I had for Mr. Ngô the respect and filial attachment not unlike the love I had for my own father. As a matter of fact, our children began to address him as Ông Nội, or paternal grandfather. And because Marie and Dominic certainly remembered their own Ông Nội back in Vietnam, even if Mỹ-Châu did it, to make the distinction, we referred to Mr. Ngô as Ông Nội Maryknoll, or Grandpa Maryknoll. The appellation, used by the parents when speaking to their children of Mr. Ngô, served to confirm the sentiment we developed and retained for him through many years to come. Indeed, even to the present, despite the children's growing up and forgetting most of their early experiences with their Grandpa Maryknoll. For Dad and Mom, we continued to call him Ông as was agreed on first meeting him at the Tudor Hotel.

8. WINTER 1952

VERY QUICKLY TIME flew by. Summer left, then autumn came and went and the year 1952 was about to end. Mr. Ngô's routine had not changed. He would go back to the Maryknoll Seminary in Lakewood, New Jersey or to the one in Ossining, New York (he had a room in both places and shuttled between them and our apartment in New York). But he would always return to be with us after just a few days' absence, staying with us for ten days or so at a stretch. By this time, he had entered into contact with his younger brother in Saigon, Ngô Đình Nhu, who sent to my home his weekly newsletter called *Xã Hội*, or Socialism, to distribute to Vietnamese students in the U.S. Also, students and visitors started coming to New York and as I had agreed with Father Jacques, I often went to the airport or the docks to meet them and bring them home for a few days' stay before sending them off to their final destinations.

How well I remember those early winter days when Ngô Đình Diệm walked in through our front door, his black briefcase bulging as usual with his pajamas and other little necessities, his shoes snow-covered and battered hat all wet. Sometimes, he brought home fruit or a package of crackers he liked which he called "rackets" in his poor French-accented English. At other times, he would simply walk in the house and say to Marie: "Daughter, go to the grocery store and get this or that item I saw on the shelves." And Marie would run out quickly and bring back whatever he wanted.

On several occasions Mr. Ngô brought home toys for the children. He bought one black plastic toy phone for Dominic and a green plastic handbag for Mỹ-Châu—the one at her feet in the photo he took of her inspecting an autumn leaf. At other times, he just played with the children and became quite chummy with Dominic. Often, he would lift the boy high up in the air and swing him back down several times; or he pretended to wrestle with him, teaching him one or two judo moves, laughing and enjoying himself as much as Dominic. Mr. Ngô would say, "Here, son, what would you do if a thief entered the house and was about to attack you?" Dominic clenched his tiny fists like a boxer and threw punches and kicked out. Grandpa Maryknoll would tussle with Dominic, and both would tumble to the floor laughing their heads off.

That winter I was scheduled to work night shifts and on returning home after dinner, Mr. Ngô and I sat and talked as usual. I was mindful of my working hours from 3 a.m. to 10 a.m. the next morning. Of course, Mr. Ngô knew my hours and toward midnight would remind me to go to bed for a few hours' sleep. I was no sooner halfway through the door than he would call me back to ask me something or other, or continue what he was saying before, thus forcing me to unwittingly resume the talks. These routines would be repeated many times before I was able to successfully leave Mr. Ngô and go to my den next to his room. More often than not, I stayed up all night then left for my morning broadcast at the Voice of America.

I was young yet and did not mind, really. I preferred the night shift as it allowed me to work fewer hours and spend more time at home. Translation of the news did not take longer than an hour or so and the broadcast was no more than 15 minutes. I had plenty of time to read or do whatever I liked after we went on-air at 5 a.m. and sometimes I recovered my lost sleep until 9 a.m. when the day shift began, and we worked on translations until 10 a.m. Back home, I could sleep until noon and then the routine with Ngô Đình Diệm began anew.

Mr. Pruett, our Unit Chief, did not like us to have too many free hours at night, especially after he 'caught' me and some other nightshift colleagues sleeping when he arrived at the office at 9 a.m. Thus, he started leaving texts, features, or commentary for nightshift staff to translate. We proceeded to slow down our work and instead of finishing the translations, we left half or more of it undone. Several times we didn't translate anything at all, causing heated words to be exchanged between me and our "slave driver," Mr. Pruett. I particularly took exception to his way of timing our translations. We had to knock out a certain number of lines in so many minutes—as if we were woodchoppers at the log pile!

THIS SITUATION OF course created a feud, if not between Mr. Pruett (who was a nice man, really) and me, then between me and some of my colleagues who didn't like the idea of Ngô Đình Diệm living with me and my family. The leaders of this group were Đức Thanh and Hoà, the latter being more influenced by the former rather than starting the feud himself. Đức Thanh thought Mr. Ngô's living with my family as my "monopolizing" him, and especially disliked this as he was his client first. Nguyễn Đình Hoà and Đức Thanh shared an apartment and most, if not all, of their living expenses were paid by Đức Thanh. Their apartment downtown on 23rd Street was at first a gathering place where students on vacation flocked to for free lodging and free meals during their stay in New York City. Đức Thanh was not a stingy man and was generous with penniless students—and this largess was highly appreciated. However, the underlying motive was his relentless drive for profit, and even more than profit was nurturing a reputation of being Big Brother to the Vietnamese community. Still, no one was fooled by his suave and grandiose mannerisms or his pompous and showy way in which he went about his daily business.

Nguyễn Đình Hoà was a young student from Hanoi. When I first met him and Đức Thanh on a nightshift at the Voice of America in April 1951, they were already sharing an apartment. Hoà was a handsome, brilliant young Vietnamese fellow who did well in his studies. However, he was also extremely conceited and never hesitated to criticize in a rude and insulting manner any Vietnamese person he disliked. Perhaps this was because he had only poorly educated, half-ignorant, and weak-kneed and self-effacing Vietnamese to deal with in those early days in America. I'll never forget, for example, the summer evening in 1951 when we had just finished our dayshift work and ran into Bùi Văn Thinh on 57th Street as we left our offices on the 14h floor of the Fisk building.

Thinh had come to the office for no reason whatsoever as he was a "De Luxe Unemployed" with plenty of time to fool around and quite a few dollars in his pocket to spend, not recklessly or foolishly, but on kids of poor families such as mine. I believe it was the first time Thinh was introduced to Mr. Pruett, our Unit Chief. Thinh had done work for the Voice before under a different supervisor and had been hired because there was not enough Vietnamese talent to draw upon. This was the reason that Miss Bài, Chẩn, Quan and I were recruited from Saigon in the first place.

FOR SOME REASON, Hoà did not like the way Thinh talked to Mr. Pruett. Thinh was not a university student and in fact didn't have higher education, but he was not the ignoramus that Hòa called him. True, he had never held any higher position than that of sailor on a French liner—but so did Đức Thanh! Đức Thanh footed most of the bills for Hoà whereas Thinh used his money on other wiser things. An ugly scene erupted on the sidewalk: Hoà, red with anger, gesticulated and yelled furious gutter insults at Thinh, declaring he was the shame of all Vietnamese vis-à-vis his manner of speaking to Mr. Pruett and other Americans. Poor Thinh had an embarrassed smile on his face as he tried to defend himself, but Hoà shouted over him. All the Vietnamese staff and even some others stood watching, aghast, before they scattered to dive into nearby subway entrances. Never once, during the many years in New York did I hear Thinh refer to this incident or remonstrate in any way. For all I knew, Thinh was no coward and he also spoke fluent English. And in one instance, he resolutely disagreed with Phan Quang Đán,[22] a politician of much higher standing than Hoà, right at Đức Thanh's apartment while Hoà, Đức Thanh, and company remained silent, awed by the "esteemed" politician in their midst.

Hoà had become arrogant and insufferable with his ego flattered and inflated by the ilk of Đức Thanh, his expenses paid for by 'Big Brother,' and his valuable work fully appreciated by Boss Pruett and finding no peers in or out of his office—at least, until I came along. He found fault with almost every Vietnamese translation except mine which he conceded, behind my back, to be "tolerable." Hoà and I had a few heated exchanges nonetheless, apropos of some terminology I used in the translations we churned out every day. He used some Sino-Vietnamese words instead of common well-known terms found in any Vietnamese newspaper. And he claimed to be an undisputed authority on Chinese characters, which was true, since none of us could read or write Chinese. But who needs Chinese to do a piece of Vietnamese writing anyway? Hoà's results sometimes sounded not just incorrect, but outlandish and ridiculous, too. For example, he persisted in writing and voicing in his broadcasts the term 'Phun Xa' for jet

22 Phan Quang Đán (1918-2004), also known as Phan Huy Đán, was once a member of the Vietnam Nationalist Party; an opposition politician in the Republic of Vietnam during the First Republic (1955-1963); and a member of the Lower House in the National Assembly and Deputy Prime Minister under the Second Republic (1967-1975).

planes while ignoring the commonly used word, "Phản Lực" because he never read any Vietnamese newspapers! He read Chinese newspapers, though, and if the Chinese called a jet plane 'Phun Xa,' then Phun Xa it must be. Pedantic, muddleheaded, and narrow-minded Hoà may have been during these youthful years of his but who cared about propaganda broadcasts such as broadcast by the Voice of America or The Voice of the Soviet Union? So, we just let his silliness go, not even laughing under our hats.

Mr. Pruett came round, little by little, to appreciate my work more than Hoà's, which became an added reason for his personal antagonism long before our political feud even started. It was election year 1952 and Eisenhower was elected president. Mr. Pruett had been for Adlai Stevenson and so were Hoà and his friends. It didn't matter to me one way or another, except that my wife liked Ike, for some reason, and so I did too. Pure sentimental reason. My politics were, if anything, elementary: I didn't care who became President of the United States.

Ngô Đình Diệm, however, pointed out to me that Vietnam could have some advantages with Eisenhower, a Republican. Since 1945, if not earlier, Democrats had been strong supporters of the French and the State Department played the French game in Indochina. With a new administration, U.S. policy could turn in another direction vis-à-vis Vietnam, and we could try to put a dent in the operations of French colonialists and their henchmen. As far as I can remember, nothing of any importance was done during the rest of 1952, nor did I really care. I was more interested in Mr. Ngô as a sort of foster father to me and as Ông Nội Maryknoll to my children. Of course, I listened to all his explanations and kept them in mind, but I was far from active politically.

Politics never interested me much. Patriotism to me was a quite different thing that attracted me strongly, especially in a foreign land where your national identity is the only value you can claim as your own. It is a truism to state that Vietnamese living abroad are bound to return because they miss their country more than their fellow countrymen back home. I did not doubt their patriotism, or at least the homesickness of even my political enemies because for them, all that counted was any method to achieve success in politics, not the true service to their fatherland. I could not stomach them; they were despicable to me, frankly. And I let them know that they did not carry much weight in my eyes. Consequently, the feud augmented with each passing day, but I was not aware of this until the noisy fracas burst in my face. This, though, was yet to come and for the time being, I was quietly and without care just going along, oblivious of enemies plotting and making all sorts of comments behind my back.

NGÔ ĐÌNH DIỆM did try, once, to look for support, admittedly in a small way. One day, he asked me to speak to Mr. Pruett about securing the support of the American Protestant churches, at least that of Mr. Pruett's Baptist church. I brought up the subject, but Mr. Pruett gave me a rather cold shoulder. When I reported this to Mr. Ngô, he suggested that I get Pruett's consent for a personal visit at the latter's home in New Jersey, which I did.

On the appointed day, a Sunday in fall 1952, Father Trần Văn Kiệm drove Ngô Đình Diệm and me to the Pruett's residence. We were received correctly, if coldly. I felt that Pruett disliked Ngô, which I attributed to the fact that Protestants and Catholics, at least in Vietnam, did not exactly see eye to eye in religion and perhaps not in politics either. And Mr. Pruett had been a missionary in Vietnam for over twenty years and loved the Vietnamese and loathed the French and almost anything French. It transpired that Ngô was not Pruett's idea of a national leader. He stayed aloof and kept a reserve throughout our visit, without venturing as much as a simple question on Ngô's political viewpoint or on Vietnam in general. A homemade cake was served with tea. The conversation was mostly on banalities and the host's noncommittal attitude discouraged Ngô's hopes—if he had had any. After some exchanges of platitudes and pleasantries, we took leave of the Pruett's and drove back home. Father Kiệm drove, I was in the front passenger seat, and Mr. Ngô sat alone in the back. Incidentally, this was the only time I ever rode in a car with Mr. Ngô. He may have gone somewhere with Father Kiệm in his second-hand Plymouth, but never again with me in tow.

During Mr. Ngô's stay with my family at 111th Street, except for walks in the park, Ngô sat practically all day long in his armchair. On Sundays, he walked with us to church. Many times, we heard mass in his company at our neighborhood Ascension Church on 108th Street. He knelt next to me, usually in the first or second row and next to him were Marie, Dominic, and sometimes Mỹ-Châu. My wife did not go to church at the time for she had to look after baby Mỹ-Nga.

Contrary to what was said about Ngô Đình Diệm being a priest in civilian clothes or his extreme devotion to being a monk, I never once saw him receive Holy Communion or otherwise conducting himself any differently from us ordinary and not-so-devoted Catholics. In fact, Ngô did not carry a missal or rosary, and he never stayed any longer in church than my family and I did. For that matter, we never saw him pray or devote himself to any religious observances at home. If he was an especially fervent Catholic, he was unobtrusive about it, and I was at a loss from what sources came those observations about Ngô's 'monkish' epithets attached to him. I would not be surprised to find out that those were insults invented by political foes aimed at turning Ngô into some *moine manqué* [failed monk] and thus unfit for statesmanship.

When mass was over and we trudged out of church amid the throng of worshipper, we did not stop to chat with the parish priest nor linger. We slowly walked back to our apartment, stopping *en route* to buy the Sunday *New York Times* or *Herald Tribune* from a little newspaper and candy store along Broadway. And we did not go to any other church than Ascension, either. Back home, Sunday or not, Ngô's routine followed its course: interminable monologue, sometimes including anecdotes, other times lecturing me about things political or historical. He had a wealth of personal details and peculiar knowledge about current and past personalities of Vietnam. He was full of humor and was particularly good at mimicking people he especially disliked.

Neither was Ngô Đình Diệm above common gossip, shop talk, or reluctant to discuss 'vulgar' details about women. Once for, instance, I told him about Mme. Hoàng Xuân Hãn[23] whom I had seen that day walking *bras dessus* [arm-in-arm] with Đức Thanh near my bank, the Excelsior Savings Bank, at 57th Street near the VOA offices. I commented that Mme. Hãn was not a bad-looking lady being young and quite pretty. Was she trying to lure Đức Thanh into withdrawing some money for her to enjoy a shopping spree?

Mr. Ngô laughed heartily and then explained to me that Mme. Hãn was 'bisexual'[24] and despite her seeming intimacy—in public, too!—with *Monsieur* [Mister] Đức Thanh, the latter could not and would not do such a thing. It was pure shadow boxing as far as that lady was concerned, Ngô opined. There were little known details about Mme. Hãn, the wife of a renowned scholar from Hanoi and Mr. Ngô knew it and told it to us. I was pleased to see him as

23 Hoàng Xuân Hãn (1908-1996) was an engineer, historian, and Minister of Education in the Trần Trọng Kim government (March-August 1945). We are not able to verify the information in this memoir about Madame Hãn, whose maiden name was Nguyễn Thị Bính. For a story of her life with Hoàng Xuân Hãn published by the Police newspaper in Vietnam that we also cannot verify, see Kiều Mai Sơn, "Dược sĩ Nguyễn Thị Bính, Madame Hoàng Xuân Hãn: Một trí thức, một thiên hương [An intellectual and a beauty]," October 18, 2018. Available at https://antgct.cand.com.vn/Nhan-vat/Duoc-si-Nguyen-Thi-Binh-Madame-Hoang-Xuan-Han-Mot-tri-thuc-mot-thien-huong-i495522/

24 Given the context, Ngô Đình Diệm appeared to mean "homosexual" and not "bisexual." He was likely speaking in either Vietnamese or French in 1952, and contemporary terms in sexual and gender studies or contemporary meanings of particular words may not have been used or known then.

a quite normal human being, his reputation as a 'woman-hater' and 'eternal virgin' and the like notwithstanding.

Among the books Ngô advised me to read for my enlightenment on things political and otherwise to get a judicious appraisal of men and politics were 'dirty' books like *Vice in Washington* or the like. Indeed, I found those books among his own possessions. He used to offhandedly comment: "Politicians are no saints." Noticing my revulsion toward opportunists and easily bought-off politicians in the service of French colonialism, Mr. Ngô wryly admonished: "Yet, sometimes we have to use those men and women in order to get things done." A means to an end—politics!

Again, by way of political education, one day Mr. Ngô told me about Nguyễn Hữu Trí, then the Governor or North Vietnam. His comments were derogatory, his judgments were harsh, and his adjectives were unflattering, so much so that I completely despised the man. In my inexperience and lack of both *savoir vivre* and *savoir faire* [knowledge of life and work], I soon repeated the whole description to Trịnh Văn Chẩn who admired the governor and saw him as no less than the rightful leader for Vietnam. Poor Chẩn! I never saw him angrier: he, who had always been calm, composed, and soft-spoken. And poor Mr. Ngô! He could not have a worse apprentice than me. When I told him about describing Trí to Chẩn, he remained silent for a long time and never again did he so freely comment about any political person to me. This, I strongly believed, was why Ngô later put me in the Vietnamese diplomatic service to get me away from Saigon where I might unwittingly create unnecessary enemies for him. Finally, Mr. Ngô said to me: "You cannot get along well with politicians at home."

The fact was that in any Vietnamese group there is a Mandarin, as the French used to say. With most Vietnamese I knew there was a potential officeholder, but I hardly suspected it until Chẩn himself told me he was aiming for a post as Consul General—in New York, no less. When Prime Minister Trần Văn Hữu came to the U.S. and the VOA dispatched us to get an interview with him. I knew that after the session, Chẩn asked for and got a private meeting with Hữu who was staying in a state suite at the Waldorf Astoria hotel and he and Chẩn had a personal half-hour tête-à-tête. I did not know the substance of the conversation or the purpose of Chẩn's meeting until he said: "You know, Đức Thanh or Hoà and the other guys for that matter, had been doing. The same with Trần Văn Khá so I took a more daring step for a better chance to get what I wanted!

Imagine if Trịnh Văn Chẩn of all people, a guy I thought was an unambitious, unpretentious, Francophobic anti-colonialist in every way, would stoop to begging for a post as any third-rate collaborator with the French colonial master, what could I expect of the likes of Đức Thanh and company? No wonder they were so secretive and then so angry when their potential sponsor (Ngô) seemed to take interest in someone other than them. It was a competitive market and even for—or should I say, especially for—a sycophant, the *démarche* [approach] was arduous, the path long, and the ladder was particularly slippery. Ngô Đình Diệm could be such a potential sponsor and although his chances to become President were nil at that time since his anticolonial demands displeased the French, who knew if the near future might be different?

In the eyes of Đức Thanh and company, I was a potential wrench in their achieving their desired posts in a new government. I came to despise them all, those ring-kissers, including my heretofore close friend and benefactor, Trịnh Văn Chẩn. Fortunately, I did not know anything of my enemies' schemes and went about my daily chores in tranquility until they inadvertently revealed all or a simpleton like Chẩn committed the fatal error in politics—revealing your ambitions too soon and to the wrong party. What extra work and expenses I incurred to my own and my family's detriment, I did it willingly for a patriot I had come to know and respect and love as much as my own father.

Ngô Đình Diệm was a kind, sensitive man. He was shy and did not easily express his feelings, but he always appreciated sincerity and honesty. Therefore, he chose my family as his home away from home and, if at all possible, he would not have brought up any political topic during our endless talks, knowing well my aversion to politics. Even after my unconscious conversion to political acceptance of certain methods to gain independence for Vietnam, Mr. Ngô never overplayed the game. He would rather—and only if necessary—gingerly tackle certain 'solutions' he referred to in his roundabout way as suggestions which, more often than not, I would think were my own ideas as well as his. And even after so many blunders on my part, he continued to trust me and while not saying so, he surely preferred honesty and outspokenness to the smooth ways of smart alecks. He respected my family as he loved us. And this respect proved durable, lasting long after Mr. Ngô became President of the Republic, and indeed to the end of his days.

One of his favorite stories concerned a simple private first class, a civil guard attached to his household when he was governor of a province. The man was a peasant, blunt in manners and words, uncouth in every way so he was deemed suitable only for medial tasks, in fact, to be a servant. Over the years, the man never distinguished himself or otherwise made the governor change his mind about him. He stayed at his lowly station, neither complaining nor showing any desire for advancement and he might as well have been a non-entity until the day when trouble arrived. The governor and his family were in danger and feared for their lives. Faced with the threat of death, all the governor's 'faithful' assistants fled and only the uncouth private remained with the family. The soldier managed to hide them, feed them, and at the appropriate moment, sent them away to safety using his own meager savings—a small bundle of piasters he always carried on his person, stacked up in a tiny pocket sewed into his leather uniform belt.

Ngô Đình Diệm told us this story many times, and each time on reaching the end, his eyes grew misty there was a hint of tears. He was decidedly sentimental and no matter what changes would come over him later when he held power in his hands, we believe they were not fundamental changes from the heart. Later events proved our thinking to be correct.

9. VIETNAMESE CATHOLIC STUDENTS' ASSOCIATION

WE DID NOT know it then, but in hindsight we now realize that the second half of the year 1952 was the most active part of Ngô Đình Diệm's stay in America despite nothing important really transpiring from his or our activities. At least, it is so from my viewpoint insofar as I was, and still am, an unenthusiastic political activist and have always looked at things political with a dubious eye. I enjoyed Mr. Ngô's friendship and constant company but little else. Indeed, many times he urged me to do certain things of a political nature and without so much as an excuse, I invariably postponed doing them or didn't do them at all.

For instance, soon after the founding of the Vietnamese Catholic Student's Association in America, Mr. Ngô asked me to write to Đỗ Vạn Lý,[25] a Vietnamese translator for the language school of the Department of Defense in

25 Đỗ Vạn Lý (1910-2008) was a revolutionary, politician, diplomat and later high-ranking Cao Đài leader in the diaspora. For a study of him, see Janet Hoskin, "Diaspora as Religious Doctrine: An 'Apostle of Vietnamese Nationalism' Comes to California," *Journal of Vietnamese Studies* 6:1 (2001), 63-86.

Washington DC and invite his cooperation with out group: Mr. Ngô himself, me, Nguyễn Thái, Huỳnh Sanh Thông at Cornell University in Ithaca, N.Y.,[26] and whoever joined us later, in or out of the Association. After a few days seeing that I did not budge, he reminded me to write Lý. He said nothing when I didn't write anything and only after some time had elapsed did Ngô finally say with a sigh: "I see that you haven't written to Đỗ Vạn Lý, after all."

According to what Mr. Ngô told me, Đỗ Vạn Lý had been in Japan as a would-be revolutionary in a group formed by Vietnamese Prince Cường Để.[27] However, in one unhappy incident, Lý incurred the wrath of the prince who in feudal princely fashion, ordered his batman to 'get rid' of Lý and 'waste him' in modern parlance, without in the least meaning what he said. Lý had to go into hiding, and never forgave the Prince for that. Soon after, Lý left the company of the Prince, the Group, the Cause, and Japan. With the help of a Hawaiian-American girl whom he married, Lý came to America. In 1945, when the Việt Minh took power in Vietnam and established the Democratic Republic of Vietnam in Hanoi, Đỗ Vạn Lý was one of the staunchest supporters of Hồ Chí Minh in the U.S. Together with André Pham and others, he founded the Vietnam-American Friendship Association in New York and was

26 Huỳnh Sanh Thông (1926-2008) was a renowned scholar and translator, best known for his translation of *Kim Vân Kiều Tân Truyện* (Tale of Kiều). Nguyễn Du, Huỳnh Sanh Thông, and Alexander Woodside, *The Tale of Kiều: A Bilingual Edition of Truyện Kiều* (New Haven: Yale University Press, 1983).

27 Cường Để (1882-1951), a Nguyễn prince and a revolutionary in exile in Japan.

actively propagandizing for Hồ when in 1946 in the wake of the French Expeditionary Corps landing in Saigon and the return of French colonial administration, American policy vis-à-vis Vietnam and Indochina, heretofore undecided, followed suit and the F.B.I. cracked down on Lý's association. Perhaps to enlist my sympathy, Mr. Ngô took the time to describe in moving terms the ordeal poor Lý went through at that time.

Đỗ Vạn Lý lost whatever job he had, hid himself during a manhunt Herbert Hoover may have ordered against him, and suffered hunger and misery. When things calmed down a bit, Lý cautiously left his hiding place but would not dare search for a decent job. Instead, he did menial or manual work such as being a delivery boy or pushing heavy carts in the dusty streets of New York. Mr. Ngô's told me himself that it was thanks to his intercession with the Department of State and the F.B.I. that Lý finally could feel safe and out of danger, even if still on a 'surveillance' list.

This explained Lý's furtive character, the secrecy, suspicious nature, and of course, his grudge against everyone. He had a respectable job with the Department of Defense and lived comfortably but he was absolutely a lone wolf. He trusted no one and in return, no one trusted him. Moreover, Lý had abandoned his Hawaiian wife despite her devotion to him. Had it not been for her, he would still have been in Japan, admittance to the U.S. being particularly difficult for Vietnamese at that time. All these details about Đỗ Vạn Lý I learned piecemeal from Bùi Văn Thinh and others who had been here before me and knew Lý well—not from Mr. Ngô who only told me about Lý's best side.

Nonetheless, the determining reason why I didn't hurry to get in touch with Lý was Huỳnh Sanh Thông's comment upon hearing that Mr. Ngô desired Lý's cooperation with his group. Thông said: "Lý has no love for Ngô Đình Diệm whom he calls a 'staunch Catholic.' Lý doesn't like Catholics at all." In my usual tempestuous matter when angered by such a highhanded attitude as I myself was a Catholic, I hastened to report to Mr. Ngô what I had learned on Lý's account. He tried to appease me but didn't change his mind, attributing Lý's bitterness and suspicions to his previous ordeals. Ngô appealed to my Christian charity and insisted that Lý was wrong about Prince Cường Để's real intentions to 'get rid of him,' no doubt wishing me to transmit his own words to Lý when I wrote him to dispel what lingering hatred Lý apparently still nourished toward the Prince.

IT WAS THE period when the Vietnamese Catholic Students Association started its first activities which were practically thrust into the hands of two men: Nguyễn Thái and Huỳnh Sanh Thông at Cornell in Ithaca, N.Y. The Association President, Âu Ngọc Hồ was all but unheard of. Thái sent me letter after letter asking me to help in such things as making a seal for the Association (I composed the name that is still retained today and gave it to the seal maker), getting Mr. Ngô's approval for certain projects, and so on. Thái used as return address a combination of his and Thông's names and later added Nguyễn Chí Hiền's to it: THÔNG-THÁI-HIỀN, Cornell University, Ithaca, N.Y.

A year or so later, Hiền left Ithaca for New York where he took up residence on Riverside Drive. But in late 1952 and early 1953, the trio in Ithaca handled practically everything for the Association whose official headquarters were at Chicago where Father Jacques lived and worked.

IT WAS ALSO the period when the first students and visitors from Vietnam came, either under the Association's sponsorship or on their own but using the facilities of the Association as set up recently with Mr. Trần Hữu Phương in Paris and me in New York. In San Franciso, Dr. Nguyễn Thành Nguyên whom Bishop Thục and Mr. Ngô contacted on their way to America in 1950, was supposed to be in charge but there were many more Vietnamese coming by way of New York and Dr. Nguyên was not very active. All in all, like the sunflower, the Association and its activists turned to where the sun was--New York, where Ngô Đình Diệm was. Vietnamese visitors flocked to New York via Paris because of the presence of Mr. Ngô Đình Diệm in the Empire State.

Among the first arrivals were the Nguyễn Đức Hiệp family from Phát Diệm, North Vietnam that consisted of Mr. Hiệp and numerous children. They stayed with my family for a few days and as it was the tail end of the U.S. presidential campaign, they posed for pictures at streetcorners with Ike supporters and wore IKE buttons on their coats. Then came Father Chu Công and several seminarians like Nguyễn Hữu Toản and Nguyễn Ngọc Lan. Father Kiệm's battered Plymouth was overworked on trips to the docks or Idlewild Airport and bringing newcomers back to our apartment at 111th Street. I went with him but more often I went by myself since Father Kiệm had classes to attend at Fordham University.

I was on the nightshift at VOA at the time and had the whole day free. It goes without saying that my wife and Marie were busy day and night when batches of students arrived. Of course, the Association did not have the means or personnel to help me, nor did it aid me financially, leading to my having to contract more debts. However, I was young yet and determined to help Mr. Ngô and his Association, for it had been his creation from the beginning. I cannot but think back on those days and marvel at the patience, largesse, and untiring efforts of my wife and Marie (the other children being too small to help) who gave themselves unsparingly in service of Mr. Ngô and the Association.

Precisely because the Association was the de facto handiwork of Ngô Đình Diệm, those Vietnamese who either played ball with the French and consequently opposed him or wished to cooperate with him but were not agreeable to him were kept at a distance, gradually formed their own group and joined forces to sabotage Ngô. One such group was the self-styled Association General of Vietnamese Students in America, organized by (who else?!) Nguyễn Đức Thanh and his acolytes Hòa, Nguyễn Ngọc Linh and Linh's brother, Nguyễn Ngọc Nhạ.[28] Their

28 Nguyễn Ngọc Linh (1930-2017) was a prominent journalist, director of the Vietnam News Agency of the Republic of Vietnam, and a founder of college-level professional programs of journalism and mass media in the RVN. His obituary is available at https://thanhthuy.me/2017/04/11/nha-bao-nguyen-ngoc-linh-cuu-tong-giam-doc-viet-tan-xa-qua-doi/

headquarters were at Đức Thanh's place (where else?). They found a fifth member in the person of Nguyễn Văn Thơ, a malcontent dental student.

Thơ came to the US on a scholarship obtained by Father Jacques who not only helped him as he did every other Vietnamese student but had a paternal love for him dating back to the days Thơ was a student of his. Special favors not available to others were heaped on Thơ. Father Jacques, however, opposed Thơ's desires in certain things, the most important being his proposed marriage to Miss Pauline Nguyễn Thị Nguyệt Minh, a girl from Bến Tre and a protégée of Father Jacques. The General Association of Vietnamese Students in America made Thơ its President and issued a bulletin. Its first copy included a manifesto that expressed the subtle desire to see Vietnamese students in the U.S. united in one association and the not-so-subtle suggestion that the Vietnamese Catholic Students Association in America represented but a restricted portion of its students. The implication was clear: the General Association, as its name announced, was the only group qualified to represent all Vietnamese students in America. Whatever 'smaller' organizations there were, such as the Vietnamese Catholic Students Association, would be and must be assimilated into the larger group and submit to its control and direction as well.

It was pretentious, arrogant, and stupid for five young men to impose their will on the entire Vietnamese student community. The question arose as to why they did that, with what means supplied by whom, and who was behind all this? It was transparent that the five were launching an operation of great importance—at least to them—and that they had ample means at their disposal. They issued a bulletin whose printing cost far surpassed anything the Catholic Students' Association could afford and mailed it to all Vietnamese students and residents in the U.S. together with pamphlets, circulars, and invitations to attend the first convention to be held at Đức Thanh's place in New York.

It was not difficult to see why these young men did this. It had been clear for some time that Đức Thanh was smarting under the impression that Ngô Đình Diệm had given him the boot. He, the first Vietnamese ever to pretend to lead other Vietnamese in the U.S. He, the first person ever to 'guide' Ngô Đình Diệm through the labyrinth of New York City during his debut with people and things American. He, whose presence was indispensable for anyone, Vietnamese or American, who wanted to get in touch with Ngô Đình Diệm could do so only through him and with him. He, of all men, had been summarily dismissed by Ngô! Not bluntly, not openly, not even with a visible cold shoulder. Mr. Ngô simply avoided contact with Đức Thanh, thanked him very politely but firmly for offers of service, and altogether disappeared from his horizon of clever calculations.

AS A MATTER of fact, Ngô Đình Diệm did not see Đức Thanh again after the letter introducing me and my wife to him at the Tudor Hotel that spring night in 1951. Đức Thanh did not see us again until July 1952 when our party to celebrate Mỹ-Nga's first month started the series of events leading to the start of a feud. Mr. Ngô set up his command post at my apartment at 111st Street and I served, willingly or not, as his second-in-charge.

In point of fact, I only commanded my children. I was a poor choice in every way for Mr. Ngô and he and I both knew it. By nature, if not by trade, I was a whiskey drinker, albeit not an alcoholic. I was far from even-tempered and easily worked myself into a frenzy at the smallest provocation. In short, I was totally unsuitable for politics, and I couldn't have cared less. On the other hand, Nguyễn Đức Thanh presented like a born politician: suave of speech and smooth of manner, he dressed smartly and conducted himself with pompous dignity, spoke Vietnamese and English in a *recherché* [research] style of his own with a terrible accent, and dexterously combined savoir-faire with savoir-vivre to go out and conquer.

Đức Thanh had also been a card-carrying member of the hapless Vietnam-America Friendship Association and a strong supporter of Hồ Chí Minh. He could have disputed a leadership role with no less than Đỗ Vạn Lý had the Association existed longer. He got out of it in time, however, before J. Edgar Hoover's thunder struck his organization. What a smart aleck! Immediately, Đức Thanh launched holier-than-thou tirades against his former associates, professed a sincere sacred hatred for Đỗ Vạn Lý, and otherwise behaved so wisely and circumspectly that even the FBI could not find a trace of previous suspicious activities.

This 180-degree turnaround may have shed an unfavorable light on him as a reliable comrade, let alone a would-be leader, but saved his neck. He did not fail to learn his lesson for future enterprises. Đức Thanh quickly learned that patriotism does not pay and with the new turn in American overseas policies, his best chance for advancement would be to tag along with the French. He was not much impressed by Ngô Đình Diệm with his shabby clothes, lack of funds, and still less with his principles and his anti-French opinions. But Đức Thanh did not mind betting a bit on this dark horse. Who knew if he might yet win: if not tomorrow, then the day after. It flattered his ego to have a man of Ngô's character under his protection. Win or lose.

At Mỹ-Nga's one-month-old party, Đức Thanh saw Ngô Đình Diệm among us, no doubt with surprise. When the Catholic Students' Association was founded and he learned of Mr. Ngô's staying with my family, he became angry. All his planning had been for naught, so he started scheming. Đức Thanh's *bête noire* was me. I not only failed to bring him into the game with Mr. Ngô, I kept my mouth shut about his comings and goings with the result that Đức Thanh and his protégées imagined many 'important' plans Mr. Ngô and I were hatching. The more they imagined, the more their anger grew, and when students were making initial stops at my home and I ignored him, his antagonism reached its paroxysm. Đức Thanh, the 'doyen' and his group of Hoà, Thu, and Linh considered themselves the elite of the New York Vietnamese community in New York and decided to strike back. They found temporary satisfaction with a puppet leader in the 'intellectual' Dr. Nguyễn Văn Thơ.

Thơ eagerly accepted the role Đức Thanh's group

assigned him. He had ambitions of his own and on top of them, he hated Father Jacques. This was killing two birds with a single stone and Thơ didn't have much to do either: take one step and lo! He was made 'President of the General Association of Vietnamese Students in America' —not bad at all! What could be more impressive than such a title, such an honor (at least in the eyes of his paramour)? Thơ then applied his signature in big, flowery letters to letters, circulars, and 'Declarations of the President' printed in his Association's bulletins. I can never forget the tall looping "N" that started his signature which he finished off with a great flourish. They say how you sign your name reflects your view of yourself: I could see all the puerile vanity in Thơ that dotted his signature.

The feud between me and Đức Thanh rapidly came to a head at the General Association's first convention. Everyone received an invitation to attend the opening night, and I brought mine home to show to Mr. Ngô. We talked a little about our friction and how Đức Thanh and his acolyte's forming a competing group to Ngô's association was a ridiculous enterprise done out of pique. I understood that none of us would attend the Convention but said nothing about it to Mr. Ngô before he left us for the Maryknoll Seminary.

On Convention opening night, while I rested for my 3 a.m. newscast, my telephone rang with Mr. Ngô on the line:

"Aren't you going to the Convention?" he asked.

"Of course not," I replied. "I thought you didn't mean

for us to go."

"Oh, no" he disagreed. "Please go now and bring your wife and Marie, too. Every vote counts and they are but a few people. We must suppress their association," Ngô urged.

It happened that we had a new houseguest in our apartment that night. He was no other than Dư Phước Long, the very man who had given me the letter to deliver to Ngô Đình Diệm back in April 1951. Long had arrived in the city a few days earlier and was staying in our spare guestroom. Ever since Long started working for the cause of bringing Mr. Ngô back to Vietnam, this was his first chance to see him again after Ngô departed the country on his 1950 Holy Year trip, a simple tactical maneuver to avoid the French *Sûreté* in Vietnam. Poor Long was so homesick that when I entered the guestroom to ask him to come with me, I saw him standing in front of the photos of his wife and children, his eyes brimming with tears.

I quickly brought Dư Phước Long out of his room, poured him a glass of wine to cheer him up. I told him about the convention I had to attend and asked would he like to go to the meeting with me? Indeed, Long would, not just because Ngô Đình Diệm's "request-order" was sacred to him, but also because he had taken a strong dislike to the Đức Thanh group whose anti-Ngô and pro-French activities aroused his political sense that had been dormant with Ngô's absence from the scene.

10. THE FEUD

WE SET OUT to go to the Convention at Đức Thanh's new apartment near Greenwich Village. I had been there once before when he had thrown a party just after moving in. Here I must record my first impressions of Vietnamese living away from home: they are exceedingly competitive among as to who has the nicest-looking apartment, whose standard of living was more comfortable, and the like. If Americans try to "Keep up with the Joneses", Vietnamese in America aim to "Keep up with other Vietnamese." Đức Thanh didn't lack in this. When he heard I'd moved into a new apartment, he was the first to come and have a look, speak derogatorily about a few things, and immediately began hunting for a better home. He left his old apartment on 23rd Street and moved to the new place not long after my family and I moved to 111st Street.

Long and I trudged into Đức Thanh's apartment which also served as headquarters of the General Association. My wife, Marie, Dư Phước Long and I confronted Đức Thanh, President Nguyễn Văn Thơ, Hoà, Nguyễn Ngọc Linh, and his brother, Nhạ. To the side of these men stood Lý Đức Lâm and Bùi Văn Thinh because they didn't belong to the hardcore of the group. These were the two sailors on the same ship as Đức Thanh but who he later looked down on as inferior to him given his new station in life in America. Lâm continued to work at the Voice of America and wanted to stay neutral in the feud. If anything, he leaned a bit to Đức Thanh's side should there be a showdown. For old time's sake, I guess. Thinh, on the other hand, didn't like either Thanh or Hoà but he was timorous and not a little awed by Hoà. Toward Đức Thanh, Thinh maintained a not too distant or too cordial a modus vivendi. He came to Đức Thanh's place as he would visit anyone's place when invited. With his usual generosity, Thinh contributed substantially to the expenses of the occasion without being asked to do so. He also helped prepare for parties or if the occasion was dinner, he simply washed dishes. He was so useful and uncomplaining that Đức Thanh and company didn't hesitate to use Thinh as a factotum without pay and good only for manual labor.

The meeting—a more accurate name than 'Convention' which implies a crowd of people—opened immediately in unveiled anger. Without so much as a preliminary, we began to attack the creation of a 'ghost' Association.

"Look around you," I said, "and show us those students that you claim to represent in your self-styled General Association."

"They couldn't come," Đức Thanh lamely answered, "because of their school schedules. But I assure you that they had sent in their acceptance as members. And we *are* the General Association."

"'General,' my eye," a voice said. It was Bùi Văn Thinh. "There are no other members besides you, Linh, Hoà and Nhạ." Thinh astonished his host just as much as he did me, my family and Long.

"We do not need to have members", Nguyễn Ngọc Linh interjected. "We can create an Association without even one member. And serve as President, Vice-President, and member, all rolled into one!"

So that was how they conceived of their Association—a mere charade! When I calmly invoked Ngô Đình Diệm as the authority behind whom all Vietnamese should stand and that he had expressed his disapproval of Dr. Thơ's so-called Association, Đức Thanh replied: "Ngô Đình Diệm's voice is but one voice. We are at least five here." He had also counted Lâm.

The meeting turned into a noisy quarrel. On Đức Thanh's condescending observation regarding Ngô Đình Diệm's single voice we almost left but Dư Phước Long could not let that pass. He launched into a long, tiresome speech that we had to listen to although we could sit back. The farce had gone too far: it had to end, or we would just be wasting our time. Whereupon Thơ presented a compromise: he would put aside the question of the General Association which he called "our own business." And he went on:

"We will continue with our Association, be it a one-member or two-member thing. And since you aren't in it, we don't need to discuss it tonight. Would 'your side' consent to make peace with ours so right here we can form a 'Mutual Help' society of our own?" Thơ demanded the compromise be put to a vote and even before we could speak up, his 'side,' that is, the five of them raised their hands. Hòa, who did not speak much throughout all this felt it was time to pipe up. He smiled sweetly at us and after a few words of explanation as to his sincerity and goodwill which we suspected was to motivate us, he wept. Tears rolled down his face and he became choked up by his own emotions. It was quite an unexpected scene and I for one, was deeply touched, I wanted so badly to believe him. It was my turn to be conciliatory, I felt. I explained the importance of disbanding their General Association as it would encourage more dissension among the Vietnamese. But I was quite willing to sidestep the question now, for the sake of peace.

The rest of the evening was reluctantly devoted to voting for members of the innocuous-sounding 'Mutual Help Society' that Dr. Thơ proposed. It was done in a matter of minutes and all I can remember now is that I voted in Lý Đức Lâm as Treasurer of something that never came off the rug of Đức Thanh's sumptuous flat. Like the other "General" thing, the Mutual Help Society soon disappeared into oblivion.

This was a memorable incident in my early years in New York despite its tedious nonsense. I would not have come to Đức Thanh's place at all were it not for Mr. Ngô's insistence that all my group attend. It was memorable to me because Mr. Ngô seemed to take the whole laughable affair rather seriously and personally. Long afterwards, he would still recount from memory what Đức Thanh said on his account that night. He would repeat in mocking seriousness a part of Đức Thanh's phrase: "Just one voice!" And sarcastically, Mr. Ngô would comment with feeling, "Eh! Whoever heard of a person with two voices unless he is a Siamese twin?! He was angry in his subdued way. And he always remained slow to forgive or forget.

As for Nguyễn Văn Thơ, it was also Mr. Ngô who, like a fount of information, gave me all the details I needed about him. I never ceased to marvel at the man's seemingly inexhaustible knowledge about mice, men, and events. Name a name, refer to an event and happenings in Vietnam and he would launch into an interminable lecture remarkably rich in unexpected and detailed descriptions and saucy comments. This explains the night-long monologues he subjected me to, which, unless interesting and humorous, would have had me yawing or falling asleep on the spot. It so happened, however, that I enjoyed listening to Mr. Ngô as much as he relished talking. He was an irresistible mimic and illustrated his talks with descriptive gestures and facial expressions that exactly copied and exaggerated whoever he was ridiculing.

For him, Đức Thanh and Dr. Thơ were villains, although the latter was a lesser degree of villain than the former. In any case, the event of the so-called General Association hurt him deeply. It was not so much a rejection of his Vietnamese Catholic Students' Association that the General Association wanted to rival: it was the rebuke of Ngô Đình Diệm himself, an affront to his very person. We should keep this in mind in order to understand why Ngô held a grudge for so long against Đức Thanh, Hòa, Dr.

Thơ, Nguyễn Ngọc Linh—in fact, the whole 'politburo' of the General Association. Two years later, when Ngô returned to Vietnam to take power, these early offenders belatedly tried to mend fences, but it was too late. When Ngô was elected President of the Republic, Đức Thanh sent Ngô a letter from America, awkwardly addressing him as 'Mister President.' Needless to say, this letter went into the waste basket and if Ngô Đình Diệm didn't tell me about Đức Thanh's letter, it might as well have never been written. As for Hòa, he succeeded in making himself Dean of the Faculty of Letters at Saigon University in 1956 but was promptly dismissed as soon as Ngô Đình Diệm got wind of it. Dr. Nguyễn Văn Thơ had to wait many years before his protector, Dr. Trần Đình Đệ was made Minister of Public Health by President Ngô, rightly judged that so much water had flowed under the bridge that he dared to take Thơ in as Chief of his Ministerial cabinet. Linh had to wait until after the Ngô family's demise in November 1964 to join the new Junta and serve as Press Officer under Nguyễn Cao Kỳ.[29]

IN THE WAKE of the ill-fated General Association of Đức Thanh's group, the relationship between the two 'camps' was anything but easy. A line had been drawn between pro-Ngô and anti-Ngô groups. I was alone in New York to face them all. My comrades-in-arms, so to speak, all lived outside Manhattan. Ngô Đình Diệm and I alone were what Nguyễn Đình Hòa referred to as the "Party of Ngô Đình Diệm." There was also a 'Third Force"

29 Nguyễn Cao Kỳ (1920-2011), an Air Force major general and Chairman of the Central Executive Council in the military government of South Vietnam during 1965-1967.

composed of 'neutrals,' those who belonged neither to Đức Thanh's nucleus nor to the Ngô clan. They were, in New York again, Miss Bài and her mother, Trịnh Văn Chẩn, Lâm Chấn Quan (my fellow-travelers on that first trip from Saigon), Bùi Văn Thinh, Lý Đức Lâm, and a few straggler students from out of state who spent a few days in New York staying either with Đức Thanh or with me and my family as they couldn't afford to stay in hotels.

Among this group there was Lý Chánh Đức, a young student from Saigon who stayed with us. He was on a scholarship that Father Jacques obtained for him. Now, it happened that when Đức was in our apartment, two girls from Hanoi came to America, Miss Phạm Thị Lý and Miss Đinh. We picked them up at the airport to spend a couple of days with us before moving on to their respective campuses. That night, Đức undertook to show them New York City and I told him not to come back too late as they were leaving early the next morning for their colleges. After several hours and the hour got late, I got a phone call from Đức telling me they were at Hòa's apartment. I was furious: these girls were under Father Jacques' sponsorship, and they were not supposed to visit with the very enemies of the Catholic Students' Association. I ordered Đức to come home forthwith.

He obeyed but after the girls had left the next day, Đức and I had an ugly scene. He had lost face because I ordered him to bring the girls back. We both lost our tempers and I almost hit him because as far as I could see, here was another foe of Father Jacques. Đức stormed out of my apartment never to be seen again. Afterwards, I learned he became somewhat active in opposing the Vietnamese Catholic Students' Association—fighting against Father Jacques and Mr. Ngô, but neither Đức nor 'the other camp' ever amounted to much and all Đức earned was a long-lasting hatred on the part of Mr. Ngô.

As I write, I can still clearly see in my mind's eye the funny way that Ngô Đình Diệm often mimicked Lý Chánh Đức. He would stand with hands clasped and mouth twisted, then proceed to contort his back while commenting: "Đức is like an actress on stage, dancing to the music of castanets. His torso convulses and his hands jerk up and down as if pulled by puppet strings."

Was this Mr. Ngô's way of telling me that Đức was a puppet controlled by others? He never explained further but repeated the mocking performance many times whenever Đức's name was mentioned. Ngô had a word, a collective he used to designate the group of Vietnamese in New York who opposed him that meant "pertaining to" or "the likes of" Đức Thanh and his cohorts: "Đức Thanh đức đồ!" It described a metonym rather than the group itself or its members. As Grandfather Maryknoll was not above cavorting with Dominic for his pleasure, he never hesitated to poke fun at his foes or ridicule people he disliked. When I reported to him how Ho wept *chaudes larmes* [hot tears] in front of everyone that General Association night at Đức Thanh's, Mr. Ngô immediately reacted with an admonition: "Beware! Hòa is an actor—he acted. There was not an ounce of sincerity in what he did." Then Ngô mimicked Hoà, wiping dry eyes with the back of his hand and thumping his chest in mock *mea culpa*.

Later on, when he faced more serious foes and had to more cautiously weigh the consequences of a break or reconciliation, Mr. Ngô nevertheless maintained first convictions once he made them, and I never saw him change his mind. It is safe to deduce that Ngô Đình Diệm was a man of *idées fixes* [fixed ideas]. Rightly or wrongly, he reached a conclusion and stuck to that decision. Of the Đức Thanh group, and later on, their newfound Phan Huy Đán episode that I'll relate presently, Ngô Đình Diệm was not going to have a different opinion. When for the sake of peace among Vietnamese and also to recruit more hands to his cause, Father Jacques and I wanted to forgive and forget and as far as possible write off the past in order to start with a clean page, but Ngô Đình Diệm remain adamant. I don't remember who proffered the phrase "Christian charity" as an argument for reconciliation, but when I reported that to Mr. Ngô, he angrily rejoined: "They speak of Christian charity—but they forget Christian justice!"

PHAN HUY ĐÁN came to New York in late 1952 or early 1953.[30] He had been a Minister in one of the cabinets of Emperor Bảo Đại and was practically unknown to us when he showed up. One day, I received a phone call from Miss Bài inviting me to attend a meeting at her home. I was rather surprised as she would not tell me what the meeting was about but cryptically said that I would know soon enough. Curious, I came and saw the entire Đức Thanh group, some neutrals, a few new faces among the Vietnamese residents of greater New York, and two 'political' figures. One, the *clou de la soirée* (highlight of the

30 Phan Huy Đán: see footnote 13 on page 66 on Phan Quang Đán.

evening), was Dr. Phan Huy Đán whom we met for the first time and saw he was seated in the place of honor. The other figure, hidden in the kitchen, and whom I met for the first time only much later that day, was no other than the famous Đỗ Vạn Lý.

To this day, I have no idea who called the meeting and at whose initiative it was held at Miss Bài's apartment. Was it Dr. Huy Đán? Was it Đức Thanh's scheme to start something new in 'neutral' territory? Suffice it to say that the whole event had been cooked up in advance and I knew nothing of it until the hour it happened. There was connivance not only between Miss Bài and the Đức Thanh and Huy Đán group, but was it also between Bài and Đỗ Vạn Lý? Or was it a combination of all three disparate elements? Most mystifying, though, was Ly, who chose that door to enter the town (in this case, New York) instead of knocking at Ngô Đình Diệm's gate.

Phan Huy Đán opened the meeting. He shook hands all around and distributed copies of a book with a blue cover, written in French and entitled *Le Parti Republicain du Vietnam,* with him as the author.

Then, he spoke up. His subject was abolition of royalty, or Bảo Đại, in favor of Republicanism. Đán did not elaborate much, contenting himself with generalities and poking fun at, not Bảo Đại in particular, but King Farouk of Egypt. He paraphrased the latter's remark that, "The whole world is in revolt. Soon there will be but five kings left—the four kings on playing cards and the King of England," without acknowledging its authorship. Đán stopped as abruptly as he started speaking. Not a sound came in response to his "Any questions?" that he threw at the audience. We were bored, and he knew it as he claimed the meeting was just a simple gathering of the Vietnamese community, that he wasn't there to advocate anything but to make the acquaintance of "our countrymen and women" in the U.S.

The eating and drinking part of the meeting was more interesting. Bùi Văn Thinh as usual, cracked jokes right and left and quickly got busy in the kitchen where Đỗ Vạn Lý gingerly introduced himself. Ly was a new face only to the newcomers like me. When I entered the room, I was the only one who had not met Lý yet. Nor had my wife and Marie, who came with me to the meeting.

At this first meeting with Lý, I told him how Mr. Ngô asked me to write him to ask if he would be one of his supporters. Lý was all smiles and niceties but noncommittal. He preached unity but glanced with unmistakable fierce hatred at Đức Thanh, his former rival. Lý pleaded lack of time but vaguely said he would get back to me with an answer. Then, the meeting was over. When I reported to Mr. Ngô that night, he looked concerned and asked me for Phan Huy Đán's book. To this day, I have not read that book. Mr. Ngô kept it and never gave it back to me. About Đỗ Vạn Lý, he told me to be patient, for he knew Lý well and the trauma he still suffered from Emperor Bảo Đại was the cause of all this seeming aloofness.

There the matter rested until a few days later, when Mr. Ngô had gone to the Maryknoll Seminary for a visit, that Đức Thanh invited me over to his 23rd Street apartment for a chat with Dr. Đán. When I arrived, Đức Thanh, Hoà,

Linh, Nhạ (the General Association of Students didn't exist so there was no Dr. Thơ yet), Thu, Lâm and Thinh were present. And again, Phan Huy Đán was sitting in the chair of honor. Đức Thanh undoubtedly had brought Đán to his apartment so he could freely speak his mind in privacy—and he did. After a long tirade of denigrating remarks against Bảo Đại, thereby disassociating himself from his former boss the Emperor of Vietnam, Đán presented his *pièce de résistance*, the reason he was in the U.S.

Ostensibly, Đán had a scholarship for medical training at Harvard, but he didn't even mention it. With a studied seriousness, his forehead wrinkled up, his eyes tensed in concentration, and he looked around at all of us and dipped his head confidingly: "I have a secret I'm going to impart to you." He stopped and blew his nose. A pause for effect. "Did you know that ***WE*** have at this moment a volunteer army fighting the Communist Việt Minh?" Another pause. "I represent that army," he continued "and I am here to recruit volunteers. If you are interested, I can send you to Thailand where you will go through training before actually joining the ranks of fighting guerillas in action against the Communists."

Đán stopped and looked around. No one was interested. No one asked him anything about the ***WE***, the army, or where the money for this came from. The chief of the imaginary Republican Party was disappointed, but he was clever. Not two minutes elapsed before he rose from his chair, shook hands all round, told us to forget the Republican Party, but please he asked, "Would any of you, or anyone you could recommend, would you go to

Thailand?"

In the embarrassed silence that ensued, Hoà fixed Thinh in his truculent regard and shouted: "You!" All eyes swiveled to poor Thinh who, like a deer under the searchlight of a night hunter, twisted and turned in his chair and tried to resume his composure but to no avail. Đức Thanh immediately followed suit. "If anyone could and should go," he said to no one in particular, "it looks to me like our friend Thinh here…"

He didn't finish his sentence as a furious Thinh defiantly looked Đức Thanh in the face and demanded, his voice trembling with anger: "Why me? Why not you? Or Hoà over there?" The circle was stunned back into silence. Hoà was about to shout Thinh down and use foul language, which was his habit, when Thinh took a few steps into the middle of the circle where Dr. Đán was seated. He stared into Hoà's eyes and calmly said: "No one can order me around. If going to Thailand suits you, then it's **you** who should go, not me, not anyone else." He then turned to Đức Thanh: "And don't you dare to dispose of me in such a high-handed manner again!"

Thanh returned to his chair, took out his nail clippers and filed his nails, an ironic smile on his face. He had expressed his thoughts—and they were final. Phan Huy Đán could find nothing to say. He took the floor again to mumble his thanks for the meeting and by way of a graceful exit, touched his host on the shoulder and shook hands with each man present and said: "I understand. We won't rush anything, though. We have time to think about it. See you next time and meanwhile, don't bicker among yourselves. You and I are all friends, and Mr. Thanh here is a worthy man."

Đức Thanh did not fail to respond—however, not in words. He raised both arms, hands clasped, and shook them as if he were a politician running for office. Or more likely the winner in a primary acknowledging the acclaim of his fans. The political animal in him found satisfaction even in the meager accolade given him by his 'Chief' and despite the meeting being a dud, to him it was a successful accomplishment—he had acted as host to a political personality. Something Ngô Đình Diệm did not let him do, some other notability did.

Đức Thanh had another opportunity to repeat the performance—this time with a real celebrity—Prince Bửu Hội, the famed scientist. Bửu Hội came from Paris sometime in 1952 accompanied by Miss Ellen Hammer who later wrote *The Struggle for Indochina*.[31] Always on the lookout for political personae of all fibers, Đức Thanh must have been overjoyed to land this big fish! He organized a tea, also at his 23rd Street apartment, which while not as big as the one for Dr. Đán at Miss Bài's place, was more dignified if only because the personality was a real scientist and so far, not tarred with any political brush. Present at the tea were Miss Bài and her mother, the usual Đức Thanh group, the innocuous Thinh and Lâm, and my wife and myself.

There was no speech. The guests sat and talked quietly with their neighbors, not addressing an audience as Đức

---

31 Ellen J. Hammer, *Struggle for Indochina* (Stanford University Press, 1954).

Thanh would have expected. Bửu Hội modestly answered questions about Vietnam while Miss Hammer looked on. Otherwise, there was only small talk and the tea party—not a meeting—ended amicably.

11. A BEAUTIFUL CHAPTER OF MY LIFE

THE YEAR 1952 came to an end. It was full of events for my family, not the least of the being the birth of our youngest daughter, Muriel Josephine Bùi Mỹ-Nga. The Voice of America made a special recording to celebrate the occasion, an idea by our scriptwriter Sarah Newman that Mr. Pruett approved. She wrote a feature-length text that Mỹ-Nga's father translated and proudly announced her birth to anyone in the world who could understand Vietnamese. The VOA gave my family a tape of that broadcast as a keepsake, a departing souvenir, when we left the U.S. in 1956 to return to Vietnam.

The morning of the broadcast I was rather emotional. What with the rush of work in the office, another night-long "vigil" with Mr. Ngô, and the emotions brimming in my heart over announcing the birth on air, I was more dead than alive. This was a live show rather than a pre-recorded one because Sarah, an artist in her own right, wanted to polish her script to such an extent that we had no time to tape it.

When I went on air at 5 a.m. that morning, I had already

done the newscast and a live section with a colleague, but I was to present the feature alone. And do it I did. Not content to read just Sarah's script, I ad-libbed quite a bit, recited some lines of poetry I composed in the spur of the moment, even sang a few bars of English verses I invented on the spot. At one point, my eyes were blurred with fatigue so I couldn't make out the text I had translated myself. I remember it was this passage:

> *"The moonlight tonight shone bright high in the sky*
> *Don't cry, baby daughter; don't cry and go to sleep..."*

Sarah had written a lullaby that I turned into poetic Vietnamese that read:

> *Ánh trăng bạc rọi sáng trên nền trời cao,*
> *Nín ngủ, nín ngủ đi con ...*

However, I had no time to type in the accent marks to my Vietnamese script so when I reached the lullaby in my own language, my eyes couldn't make out the words. I was stuck but couldn't stop the broadcast whether I knew or not what I was to say next—I had to say something. By sheer force of habit, radio announcers feel the presence of their audience. We are on stage and there are no prompters because the script is in front of us, damn it! So, I read what I guessed the script said. Later, my own ears couldn't believe what I heard on the recording—it sounded like Cambodian or some toneless language!

Vietnamese is a five-tone language and if you don't use the correct tones, no one understands you. For example, if Cambodians speak Vietnamese, they can know every word but don't add the right tones, so their words sound like a piece of music where you take out all the notes. I was horrified to hear my voice reading the first Vietnamese verse in a monotone. But I pulled myself together for the second verse and read "Nín ngủ..." with a flourish, as if to compensate for that hapless first verse. Oh, my! I never in my life as a Voice of America announcer wished so much that morning that listeners in Vietnam did not pay any attention to what they heard, or better yet, had skipped the broadcast entirely, news commentary and all.

YET THE BIRTH of Muriel Bùi was worthy of commemoration, since she was the ***first*** child born of Vietnamese parents in the United States. Thus far, there were a handful of Vietnamese residents in America. but none was married to a Vietnamese spouse. In fact, Vietnam was all but unknown even at this late date. Americans could have a vague idea of Indochina—French Indochina—but had never heard of Vietnam. I did not blame them. Until a few years ago, we had been "Annamese" in English or *Annamites* as the French called us. The colonists didn't even allow the us to use our ancient name until March 1948 when they set up Vietnamese pro forma representations abroad; pro forma, for even then, the French, not the Vietnamese, determined Vietnam's foreign policies and ostensibly, Vietnamese ambassadors were no more than glamorized functionaries of the French Colonial Administration sent abroad. And that was normal, for even Prime Ministers from Nguyễn Văn Thinh down to the last one before Ngô Đình Diệm came to power were no more than high-salaried lackeys, so why should we expect 'Ambassadors' to be genuine? We knew it. Every Vietnamese knew it. Every Frenchman knew it. Only a few Americans knew it, but they did not interfere with France's 'internal affairs,' as their colonialism was termed.

WHAT WE DID not know was the birth of Muriel Mỹ-Nga, our youngest child, coincided—almost to the very first day of her life—with the prelude to Ngô Đình Diệm's rise to power. Nor did we know that our family would be literally dragged out of our quiet lives and willing or not, forced to enter battle, so to speak. It began as a mutual attraction between my family and Ngô Đình Diệm, telling us himself he never expected to create big problems for us to solve—not the least of them being money.

On the other hand, if things had been different, say he had ample financial means when he first arrived in the US, then we would never have met him. Đức Thanh would not have committed the error of asking for money and unwittingly eliminating himself from Ngô Đình Diệm's mental list of trustworthy collaborators.

As far as my family was concerned, it was fun to be with Mr. Ngô. It was a great consolation for us expatriates to have in him someone close who was not unlike a blood relation or a foster father as it were. The fact that our children called him 'Grandpa Maryknoll' without any urging on either side or *arrière pensée* [ulterior motive], was proof enough of our sincere attachment to him. It followed that neither money nor hard work was a problem for us: it was our filial duty, a pleasure, to care for our parents in their old age. This wasn't exactly the case with Mr. Ngô but the sentiments underlying our behavior with him were the same. And Ngô Đình Diệm appreciated us. He was not a stone. He was not cruel. On the contrary, he was a sensitive, warm-hearted, and loving man. If he were not so, our children would not intuitively feel they were loved. And had they been forced to call him 'grandfather,' they would have rebelled.

There was no question that we rendered a voluntary service to Ngô Đình Diệm the man, and not at all to the politician, whom we did not consider in the first place. If later we became politicized, if the politician slowly but surely took over, the fact remains that both were the same person and one did not replace, but rather, completed the other. Such was not the case for many politicians, and aspiring ones as well. That is why Ambassador Trần Văn Chương made me laugh years later, after Ngô Đình Diệm became President of the Republic, when the only reason Chương could think of underlying my family's close relationship with Diệm was FOOD! With a straight face, Chương demanded: "Did the President send for you because when he lived in America, Mrs. Văn cooked for him and fed him?" I think of how historian Barbara Tuchman wrote that Stillwell disparagingly referred to Chiang Kai-shek as 'Peanut' in his diaries. I think the good general did a grave injustice to the Generalissimo—nor did he know of the petty mind of Trần Văn Chương.

LOOKING BACK AT those months from July until the end of 1952, I feel like a beautiful chapter of my life and of my wife and children was written. We were not rich—on the contrary, we were heavily in debt—but happiness needed no money, at least in our case. With Mr. Ngô, we found meaning in our lives and we knew that we were doing a good thing for him. Despite my dislike for politics (or probably because of it), I did not see in Ngô Đình Diệm a future leader of Vietnam. I thought he was destined to go the way of unsuccessful revolutionaries who preceded him. Men like Cường Để, Phan Bội Châu, Phan Châu Trinh,[32] Nguyễn Thái Học,[33] and the like. Men of principles and courage; men who would rather die than compromise with the French colonialists and secure a phony independence for Vietnam. All Ngô Đình Diệm's past spoke loudly of this, which was why my wife and I deeply respected him. We thought he was not going to please the French and consequently he would stick to his own demands: True Independence, Genuine Freedom for Vietnam. And of course, he would never have that chance. Nothing in the U.S. policy vis-à-vis Indochina at that time induced us to think otherwise. We were proud to back a "loser" but one in the tradition of heroic patriots of Vietnamese history. Let them, the Đức Thanhs, the Trịnh Văn Chẩns, and the Nguyễn Văn Tâms, let them all flock to their own "winners!"[34]

Oh, my family! How I love you for going through all those years in America of trial and toil and quite a few of rejoicing! Remember that night, among many peaceful nights, when Mr. Ngô came home all tipsy because he had but a mouthful of whisky at a reception for Archbishop

32 Phan Châu Trinh (1872-1926) was a revolutionary and a Republican nationalist.

33 Nguyễn Thái Học (1902-1930) was the leader of Việt Nam Quốc Dân Đảng (Vietnam Nationalist Party) who was executed by the French after a failed revolt.

34 Nguyễn Văn Tâm (1893-1990) was Prime Minister of the State of Vietnam under Bảo Đại from June 1952 to December 1953.

Yu Pin—do you remember how he walked in the door? He stepped unevenly along our long corridor and sailed zigzagging to where we waited for him in the living room. He stumbled into the room and fell into his favorite armchair, laughing a bit more loudly than usual while excusing himself: "Pardon me, Mrs. Văn—tonight I had a drop of alcohol that certainly did not agree with me!" My beloved wife hurried into the kitchen and returned with a cup of scalding hot tea. And how much more loquacious and merry Mr. Ngô was that night—he who already talked and smoked nonstop!

Marie, the eldest, was only 11 then but she looked like a 14-year-old. Eighteen months of living in America had transformed her into a young woman long before her age. Without a doubt, our life in the U.S. was much harder than back in Vietnam despite the higher standard of living and all the comforts we never enjoyed before. For one thing, we had no parents nor relatives nearby to help us. Marie suddenly became a second mother to her younger brother and sisters. Like any typical Vietnamese woman, she immediately took cognizance of the new situation and willingly shouldered her new role in America, without anyone asking her to do so. Never once did she complain about the hard work or not having the free time or things that girls her age enjoyed in Vietnam or the U.S. She saw too well how her parents, let alone her young charges, wore old clothes which while not threadbare, didn't look too good and were just a touch above barely presentable. School, housework, cook, bathe and feed her younger brother and sisters, run errands, make a dozen trips a day to grocery stores. Then, school again as the days followed, like pages in a book.

Still, how beautiful life was overall! We were a tightly-knit family, topped by Grandpa Maryknoll who talked all night long keeping Dad up; and Mom busier a hundred times more with Ngô's guests and student visitors; and our little children were a lovely bunch, were they not? Remember how everyone slept in three beds squeezed into one room that swarmed with bedbugs left behind by the Russians who gave them to us? I had to get DDT to spray again and again before I finally eradicated them all. (By the way, DDT was also the nickname that Grandpa Maryknoll conferred upon Đức Thanh.)

Remember mom's bedroom always being dark because the tall building next door blocked all light? She had a double bed but almost always slept alone because Ông Ngô kept talking all night long to Dad. Against the wall was Muriel's cot, a first-month gift from Uncles Lâm and Thinh and other VOA members. Remember how quiet Muriel was—not a cry or a noise. She was bashful even as an infant, my Chinese Princess.

We loved our evening walks to the park. You children running over the clover carpet and even once finding a rare four-leaf clover, eating Uncle Thinh's treat of hot dogs and hamburgers. We borrowed a baby carriage from our neighbors, the Lanigans, for several months until we had saved enough money to buy our own straight-back but collapsible carriage. We pushed our Chinese Princess over those crisp autumn days bundled up in pink and white blankets. Sundays and holidays were spent mostly at Riverside Park enjoying its winding lanes and lush green shrubs. You children roamed around while I read, and Mom sat next to me on a bench facing the Hudson River mending clothes or just taking a welcome rest. The park was clean, passers-by were well-dressed and courteous. There was no such thing as fear, even at late hours when the warm weather kept us lingering outside on our benches, looking at the faraway lights of the Palisades Amusement Park across the river.

Nearing the end of 1952, our good friend Bùi Kiến Thành came down from Minnesota snow country and stayed with us. From then on, he shared every passing day with us and Mr. Ngô all the joy and sorrow, every moment of anger, happiness and excitement from all the precipitous events that piled up on us until Ngô Đình Diệm departed America. Soon afterward, Thành also left but until then, he was taking a Business Administration course at Columbia University, just a few blocks from our apartment. He had a room on campus but came to our place every free moment he had to share family life and the soirées at 111th Street, the "Ngô Đình Diệm salon" as it were. We also often had the company of Father Kiệm and a seminarian, Dominic Đỗ Văn Quý who took the photo of Mr. Ngô *en famille*: he in his favorite armchair surrounded by my family—the only family he had in the U.S. All the years later, each time my wife and I looked at the photograph, we see the smoke from Mr. Ngô's cigarette floating straight up to the ceiling and remember how he always leaned over to snuff out cigarettes, rubbing the glowing tip against the side of the ashtray until it fell off.

12. VISITORS

JANUARY 1953 WAS the beginning of a very exciting chapter in my family's life. Dominic was five years old then and I sent him to the neighborhood Ascension Church kindergarten, mostly to prepare for his First Communion next year and later on, first grade. Dominic proved to be a late sleeper and reluctant schoolboy even at that young age and he never grew out of it. Marie had to wake him up, not once, not twice, not three times—but a dozen times or more before he would sleepily sit up and get out of bed. Poor Marie wept so many times because struggling with her brother made her late to school herself! When Master Dominic was finally ready to leave the house, Marie had to drag him by the arm, trot them both to the school down the street and around the corner, almost running and out of breath to reach the school—after the bell had rung!

Grandpa Maryknoll used to tease Dominic: "Son, you will be a famous engineer on condition you work hard to acquire your degree. No school, no engineering, right?" And both the old man and the boy would laugh heartily while mock fighting kung-fu with against imaginary gangsters or highway robbers complete with dagger and mask. Dominic had bad teeth and despite rich food and milk, was skinny. Even years later, a photo of him at his first Holy Communion procession (taken by Trịnh Văn Chẩn) showed a smartly dressed Dominic wearing a dark blue suit with high collared shirt and arm band—but a thin, oh so thin neck! Mỹ-Châu on the other hand, was petite and plump, round of face and yet delicate of limb. Mỹ-Nga, just seven months old, was a reminder of her great grandmother (my maternal grandmother) with the same oval face and elongated, very oriental eyes. She much deserved the title of "Chinese Princess."

Many Vietnamese students continued to come to America via New York and my family continued the same routine of receiving and taking them to our home for a short stay before sending them on their way to schools throughout the United States. There were no memorable peculiarities concerning the students as they were mostly young men and women eager to learn, excited to see America, and all in all "good boys and girls," conscious of the difficult conditions back home and the sacrifices their parents made to enable them to study abroad. Quite a few of the students, moreover, were seminarians or priests and they were the last to cause trouble of any sort. None of them expressed the desire, for instance, to go to the other 'camp' of Đức Thanh and company and there was no smart aleck Lý Chánh Đức to show them how to misbehave.

Once in a while, the new arrivals had amusing experiences due to the language barrier and misunderstanding between French and English. One priest sailed to the U.S. and Father Kiệm and I went to meet him at the West 42nd Street pier. A customs officer going through his baggage questioned a suspicious-looking package wrapped in oil cloth with a label written in meticulous violet ink "AILMENT." The mystified officer pawed the package, weight it in his hand, and was about to ask for it to be opened when the priest pointed to the label, saying "Ailment", which succeeded only in puzzling the officer more.

I saw that our Vietnamese priest confused the French word "aliment" with its seeming English counterpart: ailment. I explained the mistake and proceeded to unwrap the package of a dozen or so *lạp xưởng*, the well known Chinese sausages that Vietnamese are fond of and that the priest thought was unavailable in the U.S. The officer had a good laugh and instead of disputing the admissibility of food, plants, or fruit and the like as was his responsibility, he waved us on. I am sure this sort of confusion was common to Frenchmen as well as French-educated people like us when first in contact with the Anglo-Saxon world. I made similar mistakes a few times myself in my first few months in New York. On one occasion at the Voice of America, writing on the worksheet covering each translation we made for the purpose of office control as to translator, time started and time finished, I had put down: "Achieved by Bùi Công Văn," etcetera. Later, to my chagrin, I learned that "*achevé*" [completed] in French does not translate at all to "achieved" in English.

VISITORS FROM HOME, as opposed to students, were quite a different story. Many if not most were politically-minded and did not travel on Father Jacques' scholarships but paid their own expenses. They were interested in talking to Ngô Đình Diệm or to make his acquaintance if they hadn't met him before. Visitors didn't realize they were in for a surprise as the man so highly spoken of was not a celebrity in the sense of being "glamorous" or otherwise "cleaned up for presentation to the public". Ngô Đình Diệm lived and worked in modest conditions, dressed almost shabbily, and was reticent when meeting new people. Even after the ice was broken and he was more loquacious and talked at length for his visitors' benefit, he never said anything nearly as what they hoped for or expected after travelling 10,000 miles to visit him. No, Bảo Đại did not invite Diệm to replace Prime Minister Trần Văn Hữu or anyone else. No, the French did not approach Diệm, and even if they had, his conception of and demands for Vietnamese independence had not changed one iota.

I well remember the two veterinarians from Vĩnh Long and Saigon who were fresh when introduced to Ngô Đình Diệm at 7 p.m. Tea and cigarettes. Two hours later, they took discrete glances at their watches. At 11 p.m., they openly stared at their watches. Past midnight, the vets' faces were ashen with exhaustion. I hurried to my wife's room, woke her up, and asked her to make a sandwich or something fast before the visitors collapsed. Food came and they ate with gusto, drank tea, and even smiled and nodded in concert when some words of Diệm's rambling reminiscences rang a bell in their mind about things and people in Vĩnh Long and South Vietnam. Fresh teapots kept coming in and laughter could be heard anew but that spurt of energy did not last very long.

Toward three in the morning, the veterinarians' eyes began to mutiny, if not their stomachs. Ngô Đình Diệm talked on, of course, but our doctors hardly followed him. They couldn't even look at their watches anymore. They would have given all their money to lay down right there and go to sleep. But more than good manners and knowing I had no room for them in my home, Mr. Ngô's lack of attention to them while he talked prevented them from doing what they wanted to do—make their escape. The pair yawned unendingly and I wondered how they stayed upright the rest of the evening—or rather, the early morning—when just at 7 a.m., Diệm looked at his watch and excused himself.

Another visit was Nghiêm Xuân Việt, younger brother of Nghiêm Xuân Thiện, a former governor of North Vietnam and predecessor to the then-Governor Nguyễn Hữu Trí. Việt was then working for the French Indochina Railway company and was visiting the U.S. for the first time. No doubt an admirer of Ngô Đình Diệm, Việt arrived at my place in the early evening and having been warned well in advance, was prepared for a long "audience" with the Patriot. He was younger than the two veterinarians yet after midnight, we knew he would not escape the night unscathed. Việt's color changed, his countenance became more ruffled, and he twisted and turned in his chair to no avail. The Patriot talked on, oblivious to his visitor's discomfiture.

Finally, at 7 a.m. and after 12 hours of straight talk, Việt's "audience" came to an end. Diệm snuffed out his final cigarette, looked at the first rays of dawn, then fresh as a daisy, apologized for taking up so much of the French Indochina Railways man's time, and excused himself. Now released, but hardly fit to return to his hotel, Việt relished the large bowl of corn flakes with banana slices with milk that my wife served him in the kitchen. "First time I ever enjoyed such a breakfast—this food is excellent," he exclaimed, much more himself now than a minute before. I offered another bowl, "It's a typical American breakfast. Would you have some more? You know, cereals are very nourishing."

Việt accepted a second helping with an undiminished appetite and then said goodbyes to me and my wife. Mr. Ngô meanwhile, had retired to his room and would not be seen again for at most a few hours. Two hours of rest were quite enough for him and in the nine months he lived with us at 111th Street and his unending nightly talks, I never saw him tired from so little sleep. Việt returned to Vietnam, and I never saw him again. I tried to telephone him twenty-one years later while on a visit to Saigon in summer 1974, but we didn't manage to meet. Perhaps I unconsciously was trying to keep intact in my mind the image of a younger Nghiêm Xuân Việt as he appeared that night in the company of the Patriot, one of the many pictures I cherished of my own younger days. Perhaps I did not wish to find an aged and wrinkled Việt who, like Dorian Gray, could stay young at heart and speak to me in a youthful voice while his true self might have become seedy and senile.

Among the visitors at this time in 1953, were Father Cao Văn Luận and Nguyễn Hữu Hanh. Father Luân was an enthusiastic supporter of Ngô Đình Diệm. After he first met Mr. Ngô at my apartment, he spent long hours with me walking in New York's Central Park, telling me how good Diệm was and how and why he was the last chance for Vietnam to become independent and free of French colonial domination. In his book entitled *Bên Giòng Lịch Sử* [Beside the Flow of History], Father Luận referred to when he met Diệm in New York but his original enthusiasm of two decades earlier was, alas, swept away by the fast current of history and into the sea.[35]

Nguyễn Hữu Hanh, many times Governor of the National Bank of Vietnam, former Finance Minister and currently an official of the World Bank in Washington, D.C., was a student at the École des Hautes Études Commerciales in Paris. Hanh counted himself as a nephew of Mr. Ngô, his father being a Ngô family friend living in Huế, the Ngô family's hometown and cradle of their ascendancy to many generations of high officialdom. Long before Hanh arrived in New York, Mr. Ngô had told me about Hanh's father and family and how Hanh had come to his house. He also especially recommended Hanh to me and indeed, we became fast friends.

The day Hanh arrived in America, I was on night shift at the VOA and after a whole night's talk with Mr. Ngô, Hanh and I took the subway from 111th Street down to 57th Street where the Voice offices were. After we breakfasted at a nearby eatery, I went to work while Hanh made his

35 Father Cao Văn Luận (1908-1986) would be the first Rector of the University of Huế founded in 1957. See Cao Văn Luận, *Bên giòng lịch sử, 1940-1965* (Saigon: Trí-Dũng, 1972).

way to his hotel for some much-welcome sleep.

Hanh was the only visitor I brought to meet the Đức Thanh group one night in a restaurant in Chinatown. Hanh had arrived from Paris where groups of young Vietnamese were supporting Ngô Đình Diệm as their true leader and last-hope to save Vietnam. I wanted Hanh to confront another group of young Vietnamese living in New York who worked at cross purposes with those in Paris. Or at least, give my friend an idea about those who in my judgment were French stooges on this side of the Atlantic. So, Hanh and I came uninvited and unannounced to the Chinese restaurant where they usually met. The group was unpleasantly surprised and did not fail to hide their feelings. We avoided any serious talk, however, and left soon after I made sure the group's faces and voices had been well memorized by Hanh in case their masters dispatched them to Paris to try to fool Ngô's young supporters in the French capital.

Hanh and I had a picture taken in my apartment with Ngô Đình Diệm, all the Bùi family except Muriel, Hanh, and Father Dominic Đỗ Văn Quý, the photographer. In those days, the French being so averse to Ngô Đình Diệm while the Americans played the French game, we deemed it useful to resort to camouflage to escape French censorship of our mail. Hanh rather childishly suggested he could address his letters to me as "Mr. Van Buick." A fabrication close enough and American-sounding enough to escape French suspicions. We corresponded thus for many months until Ngô Đình Diệm returned home in 1954 and Hanh very soon followed suit.

13. TẾT 1953

AS MORE VIETNAMESE in Paris in 1953 were urging Ngô Đình Diệm to come to France to work from there to influence the government for Vietnamese independence rather than waste his time in the United States where he hardly any substantial success and there was a stir and renewed antagonism among the opposing groups in New York.

The stir came first on the occasion of Tết in the year of the Serpent, or Chinese New Year 1953 which always comes later than the official or, as we still used the old phraseology, the Western New Year. (It's easy to remember that year of the Serpent thanks to the fact that our Chinese Princess was born in 1952, the year of the Dragon, which was immediately followed by the Year of the Serpent in the Chinese 12-animal cycle beginning with the Rat.)

What caused the Ambassador of the State of Vietnam in Washington, D.C., his Excellency Trần Văn Khá, to celebrate Tết 1953 more grandiosely than the preceding Tết of 1952 or the one in 1951 (for he was made ambassador as early or as late as 1950 in order to 'save face' for Bảo Đại who sulked in Đà Lạt instead of being in Saigon and acting as Chief of State for **two years** after the French signed with him the so-called March 8, 1948 agreement granting Vietnam 'full and complete independence.' In fact, the French had to 'perfect' and 'perfect again' the independence they granted the government of Bảo Đại until Ngô Đình Diệm came home and put an end to the game!)?

We did not know at that time, nor did we care, and in hindsight, it is easy to see why. The French were doing badly in Vietnam in both the military and political sense. Militarily, they were beaten almost everywhere and although the great battle of Điện Biên Phủ was still in the future, the initiative was already in the hands of the Việt Minh and the French had a bad time holding their own lines—and this, despite immense American aid, financial and military, which started to pour into the then First Indochina War as the Korean War flared up in June 1950.

Politically, the French situation was sliding from bad to worse in Vietnam. The Vietnamese had never stopped wanting independence from France and throughout almost a century they demanded, fought, and died for freedom from French colonial domination. The Việt Minh slogan of "Independence or Death" slogan bloomed everywhere after the French attacked Saigon and started the First Indochinese War. This was no empty demand that Communists used to deceive the people of Vietnam and "sell" them to the Russians or the Chinese. On the contrary, the rallying cry was and still is as it always was through the history of Vietnam interspersed with intermittent periods of independence and longer subjugation by foreign powers, the longest and most persistent of which was China, with centuries of Celestial Domination—the leitmotif going all the way from the very beginning to the end of the war recomforting, admonishing, and renewing courage and sacrifice in Vietnamese to continue fighting ever fiercer enemies—until victory was achieved.

THE FRENCH COLONIAL administration in Vietnam, and behind them a grandiloquent if short-sighted Charles de Gaulle drunk and obsessed with *La Grandeur Française,* so long humiliated by the Germans in the aftermath of the second World War, thought that France could easily recover her old Master's position in Vietnam. Speaking derogatorily of the Vietnamese independence movement the Việt Minh led at that time, the colonials slouched in their rattan chairs under fans sluggishly moving the air about, and quenching their thirst with tall glasses of Martel soda and dismissed any fear of the Việt Minh. France's young and starry-eyed newcomers from the *Métropole* contemptuously opined: "The Việt Minh—Pouff! They are nothing but a bunch of cowards. Shoot your gun in the air boys, and just the noise will make them disband and scatter like sparrows!"

If the First Indochinese War was started with a misconception held from the lowest soldier to commanding General of the Expeditionary Corps in Vietnam to win the war, the political side of the story was much worse. General Jacques-Philippe Leclerc, war hero and liberator of Paris, listened to lifelong 'Annamese' collaborators who had nothing to gain and everything to lose if Vietnam became independent. They counted on an elite formed and raised entirely in the French manner—to such an extent that they did not understand Vietnamese and spoke only French with their families—as the backbone of society. They launched a series of political setups nominally headed by Vietnamese of their choice who were nothing more than old colonial bureaucracies in disguise—old wine in new bottles. Of course, the French apparatus did not work. To no avail were all the so-called governments, all the freedoms granted piecemeal and perpetually to be 'perfected' and ameliorated in the hope of appeasing proud people awakened and aroused and demanding nothing less than their freedom. And the French, persuaded by their own henchmen, knew it.

Even the most contemptible sycophants ended up realizing that unless Vietnam could obtain **true** independence, the high positions they held and all the advantages and privileges under the protection of the French Expeditionary Corps, could not last. Therefore, a compromise was called for. Independence in the French Union as maintained and defended by France at the cost of so much treasure and blood, however, could never be diluted enough to satisfy the fiercely nationalistic aspirations of the Vietnamese people. Otherwise, the French colonialist perhaps rightly asked, what is the point of fighting in Vietnam and Indochina? France must maintain her prestige, or she would go down not only as a third-rate power in the eyes of the world and in her own eyes. The tug of war then went on indefinitely between Master and protégés. Each new 'advantage' that the French 'conceded' to the newly named Independent Government of the State of Vietnam had been wrenched from their tightly clenched fist. Each new government and Prime Minister, the heretofore yes-men altogether amenable to colonial interests, had to fight tooth and nail for each one of them.

The French consequently had to change horses periodically—and almost frantically as their situation in Vietnam worsened. After the first clumsy trials immediately after the war in the Pacific began in September 1945 in the wake of the Second World War, Vietnam had on one hand Hồ Chí Minh and the Sainteny Pact (March 6, 1946 Agreement allowing the French Army into Hanoi and Tonkin) and on the other hand, the well-meaning but ostrich-headed Doctor Nguyễn Văn Thinh[36] in Saigon whose hapless government of Autonomous Cochinchina that died stillborn with the demise of the poor doctor by suicide and was followed by a series of puppet governments. And such musical chairs ensued—the bane of Vietnam in those early years as Nguyễn Văn Xuân,[37] Lê Văn Hoạch,[38] and Trần Văn Hữu (Prime Minister in 1951-52 when my family and I left Saigon for America). Emperor Bảo Đại, who had always lurked in the background throughout this period, was France's trump

36 Nguyễn Văn Thinh (1888-1946), a medical doctor, was the first Prime Minister of the Autonomous Republic of Cochinchina from March to November 1946.

37 Nguyễn Văn Xuân (1892-1989), a general in the French army, was Prime Minister of the Autonomous Republic of Cochinchina from October 1947 to May 1948, and Provisional Prime Minister of the State of Vietnam's government under Bảo Đại from May 1948 to July 1949.

38 Lê Văn Hoạch (1896-1978), trained as a medical doctor, was Prime Minister of the Autonomous Republic of Cochinchina from November 1946 to September 1947.

card in her game in Vietnam. Sometimes he was gilded anew with the title of 'His Majesty' but without a throne or other times as 'Chief of State' with no more authority than when he was on the shabby throne in his decrepit Imperial Court in Huế.

That was why Bảo Đại sulked. He preferred to seclude himself in Đà Lạt and amuse himself with tiger hunts and elephant rides than be in Saigon going through the motions of a puppet chief of state. That was why two years after the Bảo Đại-Vincent Auriol Agreements when Vietnam was nominally master of its own house, the first few ambassadors were dispatched to 'represent' the country in capitals such as Paris, London, Rome, and Washington, D.C. The French conceded a 'face' to Vietnam, at least in the capitals that immediately recognized it after the March Agreements were signed.

That was why Ambassador Trần Văn Khá in Washington, D.C. began to stir from doing nothing after two years of diplomatic inertia. The occasion was Tết 1953. His Excellency came up from the capital to New York and paid a visit to the Vietnamese Unit of the Voice of America. That day, I was working the dayshift, translating with Chẩn, Quan, Miss Bài, and Lâm. I believe I was out somewhere when the ambassador entered our office. On my return, he was sitting with Mr. Pruett in his glass-walled cubicle near the window overlooking 57th Street, fourteen floors below. Khá was wearing traditional Vietnamese garb complete with dark-blue silk áo dài and turban. He talked with Mr. Pruett for a long while, but we could not hear them with the glass muffling all noise and besides, we were rushing through our translations for a recording session coming up.

Trần Văn Khá left the VOA most likely when my colleagues and I were in studios recording features for our next day's broadcast so, I didn't have a chance to talk to Khá or personally hear what he had to say. Mr. Pruett, out of deference to me who he used to qualify as his 'right-hand man,' i.e., the best translator and announcer he had, went out of his way to report to me the substance of his conversation with His Excellency, the Ambassador. Khá had personally extended a formal invitation to the Vietnamese staff at the VOA to attend the forthcoming Tết celebrations at the Embassy.

"Why should he come in person to invite us," I asked Mr. Pruett. Why did he come himself instead of sending an Embassy diplomat? Now, as I related in a previous chapter, Mr. Pruett was not exactly against Ngô Đình Diệm but neither was he for him. He also knew very well that at that time, Mr. Ngô was staying with me right in my Manhattan apartment. However, Ngô's residence was a taboo subject not mentioned by him or any Vietnamese employees (or Americans, for that matter) in my presence. Now that I think back on those days, it strikes me as exceedingly odd that everyone considered the matter secret or unfit for conversation—at least with me, the directly concerned party. There was a conspiracy of silence which included Mr. Pruett, a person I respected for integrity even if his moral or religious criteria did not always coincide with mine, and if in my hot-tempered way I sometimes gainsaid his managerial methods, it never meant that I was disrespectful of him or hated him. And he knew this well, too. Between him and me, the relationship was one of mutual respect and appreciation. Indeed, if this were not so, I frankly think I couldn't have lasted many months—let alone years—under his management. He was very appreciative of my work and never failed to praise me whenever the occasion warranted. Neither did he hold back from criticizing anyone in his missionary, one-direction judgment: for example, undiplomatically commenting on the work of our scriptwriter, Sarah Newman, which earned him her ever-lasting enmity.

Mr. Pruett didn't answer my question about Khá coming himself to the Voice offices. He immediately changed the subject and I soon forgot about the matter. However, the visit immediately roused a suspicion in my mind that the Ambassador might have intended to personally extend a cordial hand to me given his almost condescending gesture of making the trip to the VOA offices to personally invite us to his Tết spring celebrations. I thought he might want the gesture to be related to Ngô Đình Diệm, knowing he lived with me, and thus be looked upon favorably. Or he might have wanted to exercise some influence with the recalcitrant (of which I was one) with regard to the French and his government's policy and thus gain good points for his ambassadorial conduct. Indeed, if it were so, it would have been diplomacy on an infinitesimal scale, and I could not but smile at my own conceit.

My suspicion was not pure egocentrism, however, but shown to be well-founded. It happened that a few times earlier, Mr. Pruett pitted me against some young State

Department upstarts he disliked who came to the Voice from Washington, D.C. and spoke in favor of France's Indochina policy. On one of these occasions, I was rushing translations to make a recording session when I glimpsed Mr. Pruett stepping out of his cubicle preceded by a smartly dressed young man. He directed him toward me and as I stopped my furious typing and looked up, he gave me a discrete and unmistakable wink and said, pointing his chin at the young diplomat to be: "Here, I'd like you to meet Mr. So-and-so" then quickly excused himself, leaving me with the unwanted guest he usually dismissed by pleading a heavy workload. That is, he didn't often do this if his guest was less 'smart' and cocksure about their knowledge of things Vietnamese, French, or Indochinese.

Such was not our young man from Foggy Bottom. And Pruett judged that the guest deserved a tongue-lashing by a native of Vietnam, one whose hatred of French colonialism agreed with his. I had to resort to all possible and impossible control at my disposition to sustain a short conversation with the cockerel Mr. Pruett had dumped in my lap. The young man talked in a curious French (possibly acquired through some intensive course by Berlitz or the like) and proceeded to lecture me on the merits of a French management of Vietnam, a necessary step before my country could stand on her own feet. Despite the diminishing minutes I had to finish my translation before recording time, I enjoyed displaying an equal arrogance and uncouthness in giving back the same kind of 'lesson' my visitor gave me in (at least to him) perfect Parisian French, which intimidated him right from the start. He quickly took French leave, mumbling something in English, having decided that his French was not yet ready for combat, even if he believed his ideas and politics surely were.

My colleagues had a good time listening in while rushing through their own work and we had more laughs in the studio between the two recording sessions. Those were moments we enjoyed ourselves without in the least worrying if we inadvertently stepped on each other's toes. My archenemy, Đức Thanh and his second-in-command, Nguyễn Đình Hòa, by a curious arrangement with Mr. Pruett (unfair in my opinion), never worked on a daytime schedule from 9 to 6 like the rest of us. Chẩn, Quan and I each took turns working nightshifts while Miss Bài, understandably for safety reasons, never did. Lâm, the neutralist who often leaned on the side of his former sailor colleague, especially when a showdown took place, and he was afraid to face the music with them in private, likewise alternated day and night shifts. But he was an exclusive translator, meaning he neither prerecorded nor broadcast live because of a defect in his voice. That meant that up in the recording booth it was invariably me and the genuine "neutrals" of Miss Bài, Chẩn and Quan.

We, three men and a woman, recruited from Saigon to come to the U.S. to broadcast together in Vietnamese were all in the same boat. If anything, we should have been closer to each other than to 'outsiders.' A difference in temperament, however, and divergent outlooks kept us apart, and while not close friends we were at least not enemies. In the quarrel between me and the Đức Thanh group, my coworkers maintained a rigorous attitude of neutrality. As seen previously, Chẩn had his 'small' ambition and once even wormed his way into the antechamber of Prime Minister Trần Văn Hữu; he also kept a vague hopeful ember quietly smoldering in a corner of his heart, like charcoal burning under ash, of a post with Nguyễn Hữu Trí, the former Governor of Tonkin. Chẩn was not for the French either, like Đức Thanh's group, and was altogether harmless and gentle to the point of submissiveness.

On the other hand, Quan was a lone wolf, strictly working and saving for himself, and so avaricious that Chẩn, who shared an apartment with Quan, often complained of his roommate's stinginess. Politics for Quan were a waste of time and a luxury he did not care for and thought that if people knew this about him, he would be left alone.

Unfortunately for him, life is complicated and the most innocuous are likely to be the first victims. I was not sure if it was the hidden work of the Đức Thanh group in sowing dissension among us or Mr. Pruett's genuine disapproval of Lâm Chấn Quan, but the Voice of America was threatening to dismiss him at about this time. Like all our two-year contracts, his was about to expire. True, there was talk in the air of budget cutting and saving federal expenses and the infamous McCarthy Communist witch-hunting was gathering strength—but why was Quan alone threatened? Why not me or Miss Bài who were recruited under the exact same conditions as Quan? Why not Đức Thanh whose Vietnamese was antiquated and spoken with an unnatural American accent to boot?

What about Nguyễn Đình Hoà who held a student visa, not that of contracted worker like the rest of us? We were all mystified. And Quan was scared.

He certainly did not want to go back to Vietnam so one day he came to my home when Mr. Ngô was away at Lakewood and begged me to plead in his favor with Mr. Pruett "for you are his favorite and he is likely to approve whatever you suggest." My difficulty was in the person who would be dismissed in Quan's place: one of the Vietnamese staff must go. But I was not really in a position to influence Mr. Pruett and his superiors as Quan thought, and if I were, I'd have voted for Đức Thanh to go. First, because his Vietnamese was atrocious which led to his defensive attitude when he worked with me on nightshifts; and second, because he was the one to suffer the least among us, if go he must.[39] As a result, I did not intervene for Quan, and he was dismissed in April 1953.

I remember well those dark days of sudden and unexplained and random dismissals throughout different units of the Voice of America, falling like deadly axes to the

---

39 One night, while working with me on a newscast to be read on air by two men alternating, Đức Thanh took exception to my translation of the name of the then-Chinese Ambassador to the U.N., Dr. Chang Ting Fu. I correctly wrote *Tưởng Đình Phu,* as anyone reading a Vietnamese daily would know the name. Not Đức Thanh who did not read Vietnamese newspapers or checked his 'sure knowledge' of the language before criticizing me. For him, only Chiang Kai-shek's name could be rendered *Tưởng* because it was written as *Chiang* in English. Nguyễn Đình Hòa and his Chinese expertise was in the same category and persisted in using *Phun Sa* for jet aircraft because the Chinese use this in their newspapers. He once said that ALL Saigon's editors were ignoramuses who did not know how to write Vietnamese correctly. Birds of the same feather! (Au.)

right and left with victims, as far as I knew, being mostly if not exclusively Americans. Quan might have been the only 'alien' victim of the axes. The official explanation was 'To Save Money', but we all knew that the underlying reason for so many sudden layoffs came from the great fear that McCarthy stoked, his hate campaign being magnified day after day by interminable TV broadcasts and newspaper coverage of his melodramatic Congressional Hearings. All through the spacious offices and well-equipped studios of the Voice of America, a sense of panic hung in the heavy atmosphere that was almost breathable. The fear was so thick you could cut it like a karate chop.

Overall, the Vietnamese unit was immune from the axe. Except for Lâm Chấn Quan, none of us was threatened. The latter's case of forewarning followed by irrevocable dismissal, was a unique exception to the rule. Most of us did not really mind being sent back to Saigon—at least I was not. Two years of a 'hard life' in the U.S. was enough for me and my family.[40] Add to that the antagonism I unwittingly acquired from my political enemies, and the

---

40 Even in early July 1951 I had written home to friends complaining about all the 'hard work' I had to do to help my wife: domestic chores like sweeping, washing dishes, laundry which men never had to do in Vietnam. In one letter to a hometown friend whom I later offered a position at the Consulate General of Vietnam in Hong Kong I wrote: "you can hardly imagine that at 3 a.m. I was still sweeping up my apartment with a broom. My wife and kids were asleep, and I was finishing a household chore before taking the subway to my work that starts at 5 a.m." He wrote back: "I thought America was a paradise! The way you describe life over there discouraged me no end. I'd rather stay home then, and if offered a job such as yours, I'm sure I would decline it. Why, at least we have help! Even our wives can relax after the day in our so-called 'backward' Vietnam." (Au.)

'cold war' I had to fight willy-nilly, and the 'neutralist-but' attitudes of my own co-recruited colleagues including Miss Bài. Above all of this was a gnawing homesickness that I began to suffer as early as Christmas 1951 and I wrote movingly of this to Mr. Ngô in a "Greetings of the Season" card I sent him, which perhaps made him come to me in the first place. You will understand why sometimes I almost wished I were in Quan's shoes.[41]

41 I wrote Mr. Ngô that I wished to see him again if only because I was so homesick and he seemed to represent to me all that the true Vietnamese spirit (*Quốc Túy* or Nation's Substratum) required a gentleman (*quân tử*) to possess. I stressed that my wish did not mean anything political, and I remained absolutely apolitical. He did not reply nor show up until July 1, 1952. (Au.)

14. THE GOOD TIME

THE RENEWED AND aggravated antagonism between me and Đức Thanh group surfaced slowly but unmistakably soon after Tết 1953, or Spring of the Year of the Serpent. We had an uneventful Christmas but with Grandpa Maryknoll for company, the kids were enjoying themselves. Mr. Ngô and I had a new friend in Bùi Kiến Thành who had left Minneapolis, Minnesota to enroll in Columbia University in Manhattan. Thành was the eldest son of the famous Dr. Bùi Kiến Tín, of "Dr. Tín's Eucalyptus Oil" (Dầu Khuynh Diệp Bác sĩ Tín) that is very well known throughout Vietnam. If Vietnamese had an equivalent for a household word, it would be Dr. Tín's name, and not because of his political acumen. In fact, since time immemorial, we Vietnamese have relied on medicated oils like his eucalyptus mixture for a dozen minor pains and aches in the head, stomach, back, and more that are common to tropical climates especially because they are effective and inexpensive. Chinese medicated oil had been a household item in Vietnam for centuries before Dr. Tín's talent and initiative disputed the exclusive Chinese hold in Vietnam.

Bùi Kiến Thành lived on the Columbia campus a few

blocks from our home, but being busy with his studies, he at first did not visit us very often. During our second Christmas in America, we had the usual panoply of decorations and sweets essential for the enjoyment of the children. However, the most memorable item was our Christmas tree, taller than the one last year, and lavishly bedecked and twinkling with many-colored miniscule bulbs. After Christmas day, Mr. Ngô returned to his Maryknoll cell and we happened to have a long lull in our activities because no Vietnamese student or visitor came to New York. It was then that Thành profited from his university Christmas break to spend more time at our home and befriended our children. He was but twenty-two years old, more than a decade my junior, and he became 'Uncle Thành' to me and my wife as well as the children, from Marie on down to Muriel who already had begun to speak.

Uncle Thành arrived armed with quite an expensive movie camera he got as a gift and proceeded to film our apartment—in color! He needed a scenario or at least a scene with movement for his camera to record. We concocted the idea of a colorful self-propelled Christmas tree. I was to lay flat on the floor out of camera range and pull a string attached to the foot of the tree, move it slowly across the living room while the camera whirled away. I, Uncle Thành, and the kids toiled and sweated, rehearsed and performed, until the scene was recorded to the satisfaction of film director Thành. We proudly projected our first 'Technicolor' masterpiece many times and later, at gatherings of the students who flocked to our place during vacations, our 'Prix de Cannes' film was to give repeated encores. It was not the 'still life' we usually saw in camera photos, but a 'moving life' where only a tree moved by itself with no help from anyone although it was understood that a hidden person caused the movement.

STRING PULLER WAS precisely what I was suspected of being by our political opponents, obviously not meant as a compliment. As the Spring of the Year of the Serpent approached, Mr. Dư Phước Long, the newcomer who landed in our apartment several months before and went on to study in Naperville near Chicago, came back to visit and spend the holidays with us. He was soon joined by three students: Le Tuấn Anh, Nguyễn Văn Viên, and a third whose name I forget but whom we met for the first time. They were recommended to us by Father Jacques and their arrival was expected. Bùi Kiến Thành arrived from Columbia University almost next door, and Huỳnh Sanh Thông from Cornell University completed the reunion. We had a marvelous time, reminiscing of past Tết celebrations back home, the food we ate like *cành mai* (plum flowers) *cành đào* (peach flowers), *vạn thọ* (marigold), chrysanthemum, and the myriad incomparable pleasures we missed from being in the U.S. After remembering the past, we talked of the difficult present we were in, not because we cared much for anything, but because of our opponents who had once more joined ranks to bother us.

Ngô Đình Diệm was our undeclared leader. We meant to support to the hilt everything he stood for and in our modest ways and restricted means would carry out his ideal of Independence for Vietnam. Love of our fatherland was our only motivating force and we did not really care whether Diệm could seize power or not. All we wanted was to give the French hell! To unmask the Vietnamese 'traitor' bootlickers of French colonialists! We were politicized to a high degree to be sure, but we were more idealistic than practical-minded. Except for Dư Phước Long who had been involved and 'in it' long before us, we were all novices and never thought of using politics as a means for our own advancement.

It was the first time I had company that I could discuss strategy and tactics with for a change. Huỳnh Sanh Thông, of the trio Thông-Thái-Hiền of Ithaca, New York, came to meet with us for the first time. Bùi Kiến Thành as of now was untried and was not included in the list Ngô Đình Diệm wanted me to establish of his eventual collaborators—what our opponents called the "Black List." Still, Thành was enthusiastic and energetic and despite his youth, he was mature and devoted, and promised to be a precious comrade to us as well as a good friend. Next to him, Huỳnh Sanh Thông looked every bit the poet with tousled hair and untidy dress, and although undernourished, he was all smiles and his eyes shone with intelligence.

The opposite of Thông's appearance was Dư Phước Long who had gained weight after only a few months in America and seemed to like every bit of life here. He appreciated the American way of life so much that we got the impression he would rather **be** an American forthwith. He was cautious to such a degree in discussing maneuvers and tactics that he was in effect called a poltroon. As a joke of course, for he alone had been in battle with me, my wife, and daughter, Marie once when the General Association of Vietnamese Students launched its initial campaign in Đức Thanh's place in Greenwich Village. Nguyễn Văn Biện who years later returned to Vietnam and committed suicide in a fit of depression, was all fired up with ardor for battle and spoke vehemently of 'finishing them off!" But we could see that Bùi Kiến Thành was the 'Logician' *par excellence*. He was every bit the son of Quang Nam, the Province of Central Vietnam renown for critical minds and fierce spirit:

Quảng Nam hay cãi
Quảng Ngãi hay lo
Bình Định nằm co
Thừa Thiên nít hết!

The short stanza above describes the mentality of each province of Central Vietnam as inherent regional characteristics wherever in the world they may be. Quảng Nam has been celebrated by an illustrious son, the writer Phan Khôi who had a keen mind and undaunted courage. He was the leader of the Nhân Văn group and early in 1957 dared to openly criticize policies that had caused havoc in North Vietnam.

Our group pooled ideas and dissected our foes' every actual and potential moves. Their now defunct General Association was no problem, and the Vietnamese Catholic Students Association was a going concern, but Mr. Ngô wanted us to bring about the coordination of efforts. Besides Đỗ Vạn Lý who I had interviewed but a short moment at Miss Bài's home and who never showed up, I could think of no one reliable enough to add to our list. Thái and Hiền had been corresponding regularly, as did Thông, but their main concern was the Vietnamese Catholic Students' Association—not Ngô Đình Diệm.

Interspersed with merry-making and games were our 'seances' of intense *in camera* or closed-door discussions. We both worked and played until late at night and on the eve of the start of Tết and kept vigil for the stroke of midnight when we ushered in the Happy New Year of the Serpent. We made wishes to "Be wise like a serpent" according to ancient lore and until well into the small hours of the morning, we waxed poetic and in an inspiring moment, composed a sight-sentence Tang Dynasty style poem:

Một hai ba dở, bốn năm gàn,
Có đứa lùn-lùn lý sự ngang
Cọt-Ne ốm nhách, lù-xù tóc,
Náp-Bựa mập lù, bé tí gan,
Hùng Biện nhe răng đầu cắt cụt,
Đá Văn hĩnh mũi, đít mài sàn.
Khuya quá rồi bây! Thôi đi ngủ,
Để mai còn thức đón Xuân sang.

Each of us contributed one sentence, endeavoring to include each of our striking characteristics and making it as funny and memorable and as good as allowed by the strict rule of Tang poetry. A loose translation of our poem reads:

One two three, bad! Four five, hardheads!
A shortish fellow—oh, how well he reasons![42]

42 The second sentence describes Bùi Kiến Thành's physical and moral strong point: his logic was persistent and determined, not

The Cornell guy, skinny with tousled hair,
The Naper man, fat but having little bile[43]
The eloquent one sports a crew cut[44]
The verbose literary one, has trouser hems that sweep the floor[45]
It's late, guys! Let's go to sleep
To be fresh and gay tomorrow to salute Spring.

The opening line of the poem shows we were only five keeping vigil to ring in Tết. It is customary for Vietnamese to be humble, even derogatory, about themselves as a mark of humility. In poetry, the rule was always so, if not actually written in so many words. In fact, to praise yourself in poetry is unheard of. The stanzas contributed said of the five men present, three were "bad" while the fourth and fifth fellows were no better—and were *raisonneurs* (ratiocinators or logicians) to boot!

Thanks to this attempt at poetry, the five of us can easily be remembered from the mist of things past. I am especially grateful to the poem's "shortish fellow," Bùi Kiến Thành, for allowing me to use his office in an old

---

unlike that of the famous writer Phan Khôi. (Au.)

43 "having little bile" means 'poltroon.' The Vietnamese think cowards have small livers and little bile. It is similar to how the French blame all ailments or mishaps on their liver: "*Tout est de la faute du foie.*" (Au.)

44 A play on words: My Vietnamese name, Văn, means "literature" and I am also verbose so saying I am "Đá Văn is not complimentary. (Au.)

45 *Biện-hùng*: A play on words describing the man well. *Biện* was his name and combined with *hùng* translates to "eloquent"—which he indeed was. (Au.)

monastery in Hyères on the Côte D'Azur of France to write this memoir. More, I am particularly thankful to my host and good friend's prodigious memory that enabled his beautiful recitation of the poem five fellows composed on that New Year's Eve 23 years ago.

15. THE *SÛRETE´AMERICAINE*

AFTER THE GOOD time passed, some rough weather lay ahead for us. After the Tết celebrations were over and student visitors went back to their universities, I reluctantly resumed work at the Voice of America. The offices had recently moved to the Argonaut building on 224 West 57th Street, just on the other side of Broadway. Strangely, from the first day in the new location, I felt a stranger, colder atmosphere than was usual. From Mr. Pruett on down, the usual cordiality and friendly jokes that made life easier was conspicuously absent. It couldn't have been the presence of the Đức Thanh group, for as a rule, they never worked the dayshifts. What then?

Why the gloomy and unsmiling faces? Why the curt replies if I asked about something or other? My office mates were 'neutrals' at worst so even if my political opponents had succeeded in winning them over (which I doubted), they would not have shown such funereal countenances not just to me but among themselves also. What happened?

It was not customary in the Vietnamese Unit to discuss anything of a personal nature. So, everyone kept silent about the atmosphere and minded their own business. I was more mystified than worried or even anxious and it turned out that I did not have to wait too long to know the reason.

One early morning of a regular workday not long after Tết, I was summoned to a meeting in some mysterious higher-up's office. I left my translation unfinished and walked upstairs to the designated office. The office appeared even grimmer than the Vietnamese Unit's section as it was windowless and the five or six men there were all long-faced and somberly dressed. Behind a glass partition sat one man, no doubt the boss of the unit. I walked straight to him holding my convocation sheet in my hand but even after I presented myself, the boss did not look up or speak to me. He kept looking down at his desk although there was nothing in front of him.

I was almost angry, but I chose to sit down on a wooden chair facing him and controlling my nerves, looked straight into his eyes as he slowly raised his head to address me: "So, there is a split among you Vietnamese, is there not?" If anything, the man's first question was more obscure than I thought the whole affair was—whatever it might be. "What do you mean by 'split' and which Vietnamese do you speak of?" I asked.

My interrogator, if indeed he was one, did not elaborate. Without so much as a trace of surprises or even boredom, he called to one of the men sitting outside his cubicle who entered to deposit a dossier on the Boss's desk, lingering a bit at the door but not being asked to stay.

The Boss slowly opened the dossier and withdrew from it a single sheet that he didn't even glance at but curiously toyed with it, face down, so I couldn't not make out what was on it. A minute or two passed and I became very tense but remained silent, waiting for the other to speak first. Of course, I knew what he referred to with his curt phraseology about a split: among Vietnamese this could only be political and when I pretended ignorance, he did not have to waste time explaining and on that matter, we understood each other well.

However, whatever the paper the Boss was toying with, was something else. What could it be? A letter from France sent to me from one of Ngô Đình Diệm's supporters? If so, I would let out a sarcastic "Hallelujah!" for American-style democracy that intercepted private letters—no, it could not be that. Something pertaining to politics, no doubt, so Diệm naturally came to mind. I quickly reasoned with myself: Did the French succeed in convincing the U.S. Government to consider Mr. Ngô as *persona non* grata and thus force him to leave my apartment and return to Saigon? But if so, why me and not him, or somewhere else and not at the Voice of America's offices. Or could it be some bureau entirely different from the Voice?

My interlocutor did not deign to enlighten me. He seemed to enjoy delaying as long as possible, not apparently with the intention to induce me to speak first or as the French would say, *me tirer les vers du nez*—literally, to pull worms from my nose"—to get me to talk, worm out information from me. For he asked me no more questions at all, just sat there as if he had all the time in the world. After a long while, he finally told me the what and the why.

In a low, monotone voice he succinctly informed me that his office (which he did not name) had received an anonymous letter (which he did not produce so I had no idea if the paper he held was it or not) accusing Miss Bài and Lý Đức Lâm of something (he did not say), and the purpose of this convocation was simply to ask me whether I was the author of the letter. Naturally enough, I extended my hand and asked to see the letter that I presumed he was toying with. The Boss did not pass it to me, nor did he look for any other paper in the dossier that lay untouched. I was now irate and couldn't control my temper. I quickly stood up, seized my hat from the corner table, and in trembling staccato I blurted out:

"So, this is the reason! I am suspected of writing an anonymous letter! How can I answer your question if you won't even show me the letter?" The Boss didn't make a move, so I left his cubicle while throwing behind me: "No! I have never written anonymous letters in my life—I'm not a coward!"

None of the somberly dressed men in the outer room tried to stop me as I returned to my office some flights below, still trembling with indignation. No one in the Vietnamese Unit seemed surprised to see me come back in such a state. Now that I knew they surely knew something that I did not, they seemed to be watching me out of the corner of their eyes instead of pretending to be curious or even indifferent.

A conspiracy! Naturally, my thoughts turned to the Đức Thanh group. They, and only they, could be as low as to resort to anonymous letters. My contempt was so strong that I didn't think of asking any of them anything about the 'affair.' I slowly resumed my work and Mr. Pruett for once did not seem eager to mind whether we kept to his requirement of so many lines in so many minutes. The rest of the day passed in heavy silence and not even one word was exchanged between anyone in the room.

This incident was related to Mr. Ngô at home that night but all he said was *"Đức Thanh đức đồ!"* and we quickly changed the subject. Never once that night or any other night did we again refer to the 'affair." Later, I don't remember how or by whom, I learned that Miss Bài had also been summoned before me to the same office and returned, her eyes all red.

I had reason to be worried if only I were more realistic. It was the height of McCarthyism and the infamous Senator's nightly televised witch hunt was televised every day in lieu of the usual soap operas and government employees were being sacked left and right. I was a dreamer in the clouds so that even when dirty tricks were used to pull me down to earth like with the Boss, my enemies failed as I was ready to be sent back to Vietnam. If worse came to worse, all I had to do was resume some other trades I worked in the past, such as being an airline steward which I enjoyed doing for half a year before joining the U.S. Information Agency and hired to work for the Voice of America.

I had practical reasons to watch my step because

defamation such as what Senator McCarthy meted out day after day to his "fellow Americans" could very well be administered to me. An accusation of 'Communist' or 'Fellow Traveler' could bring about my outright dismissal and forced repatriation, it could subject me to endless interrogations. The Đức Thanh group had already given me a foretaste of interrogations, albeit done over a much lighter and nonsensical accusation.

My tempestuous nature had already brought trouble to my door but fortunately without me or my family ever realizing it. This happened during my early months in New York when Đức Thanh was friendly to us all and, particularly to me. I used to ride to work with him when he drove his car to work on nightshifts at the Voice. After work, we'd drive to his place down on 23rd Street and enjoy a breakfast of Chinese noodles that we enjoyed and sometimes he'd even drive to Chinatown for a meal.

Nightshifts had advantages that dayshifts did not. For, after only a few hours of work under no supervision, you could go home the rest of the day. Hoà used this scheme to pursue his studies until he graduated from New York University. Đức Thanh used it to take care of his import firm business. So, an early morning breakfast after work with friends was the equivalent of our habit in Saigon to enjoy a drink or two with friends after the day's work was over before we went home to rest. Only here in America, the routine was reversed: we didn't drink in the early morning, but we enjoyed breakfast and the all-day rest followed.

One such morning I went to Đức Thanh's place

accompanied by Marie and Dominic, for it was my day off and I decided to take the children for an early morning stroll. When we entered his building and were still walking along the short corridor leading to his apartment, we saw an older man lurching around near Đức Thanh's apartment. I should have paid attention but as usual, I ignored the man. More than anything, out of a sense of loyalty to a friend, I disliked the man who appeared to be spying on Đức Thanh's apartment if not trying to break in. I got irritated when the suspicious-looking man stopped us as we approached our friend's door. I didn't quite hear what he mumbled but impatiently said he was pestering us, and we weren't interested in what he had to say. Maybe I thought he was a shabby stranger trying to sell us something but anyway, I brushed him aside and when Đức Thanh opened the door, brought my children inside without mentioning the encounter.

Little did I realize I had committed a strong offense and the man in question was no less than an agent of some sort, an investigator for the FBI or CIA or similar! I found out about it the following morning when I arrived at work at 9 a.m., Mr. Pruett had a visitor with him in his office cubicle. I didn't pay any attention except think it was rather early for someone to have a business appointment. As compensation for leaving work before 6 p.m. in order to catch his bus to arrive at work earlier than the regulatory 9 a.m. this visit, whoever he was, must have arrived at about the same time.

About an hour later, while I was typing furiously as was my wont, the visitor exited the office followed by Mr.

Pruett who saw him to the door. On his return, he leaned over my desk and asked, "Mr. Văn, do you know who that man is?" When I shook my head, Mr. Pruett asked me to follow him to his office. There, I stood by his desk wondering what this was all about when my boss said: "That man came to see me about you." He paused and as I looked confused, went on: "Don't you remember? You saw him last night." The scene at Đức Thanh's corridor flashed into my mind. It was rather dark and there was no corridor light—no wonder I couldn't make out who it was. Today, in full daylight, the man looked younger and quite different from the seedy, shabbily dressed, old man I had a cursory glance at yesterday morning. Had he been disguised? Was this a cloak and dagger trick on me? Mr. Pruett explained but didn't shed much light on the mystery.

"He came to complain about your rude treatment yesterday. He said you were very arrogant and didn't answer a question he asked of you. He's a U.S. government investigator." As I remained dumbfounded, Mr. Pruett continued: "I told him you didn't know who he was and were no doubt concerned for your children. So, I think everything's all right and there will be no complaint against you."

I thanked Mr. Pruett and returned to my desk more perplexed than ever. I should have asked my supervisor what was a government investigator doing lurching about in the dark on the premises of a Vietnamese employee of the VOA? I should have been intrigued enough to ask if he knew if Đức Thanh was being investigated seeing he was at his apartment. And if so, why did the man ask me the question instead of asking Đức Thanh himself? Little did I know then the ways that FBI investigators went about their business. A few years later, agents investigated Huỳnh Sanh Thông and visited my home to ask about him. Of course, all I said on Thông's account was favorable, even exaggerated praise, so much so that it could mean an indirect rebuke to the FBI to pick on the least suspicious of men!

Back in 1953, I was too new to America to know about FBI agents and their investigations, and I was a little sorry I was rude to 'an old man.' As Mr. Pruett had given me his address, I wrote him a letter apologizing for my discourtesy when I mistook the agent for an importuning salesman. However, I also pointed out that had I known he was investigating a friend of mine, I would have firmly but politely told him to go to hell. I did not receive a reply to my letter. If Mr. Pruett got mad and kept that written proof of my 'arrogance' to use against me when the occasion arose, I would not and should not be surprised.

Back in Vietnam, we had been terrorized by secret police as well as regular police and people conceived an almost sacred kind of hatred for them. We found anything connected with "security" (i.e., secret) to be thoroughly contemptible. It is a trauma common to people living in fear because they are subjected to arbitrary arrest and out and out injustice. Such was the colonial police, secret or not. But not here in America, not in the U.S.A., or so I thought, that was why I went about my business unperturbed after this incident, or the more serious other time when Đức

Thanh or someone in his group was implicated. Come to think of it, it was strange that both times I had trouble with the *Sûreté Americaine* [the FBI] were connected with Đức Thanh: in the first case, he was the victim, so to speak; in the second instance, he or his accomplices were the originators.

Is there a 'dossier' for each individual living in the U.S.? Does such a thing exist in a great democracy like the U.S.A.? Or are dossiers the exclusive "privilege" for natives in colonized countries? I opted for negative answers to both questions and sincerely believed I was free in a free country where I could frankly and openly speak my mind without fear or hindrance. They say that ignorance is a blessing—and I was blessed.

For instance, one day about six months after our group recruited in Saigon had come to America, the Voice of America had us complete a form with routine questions like 'hair color' or 'race.' However, there was also a blank space reserved for our honest and uninhibited "impressions" of VOA after having worked in the U.S. for a certain time. I wrote: "Frankly, I think the Vietnamese translators and announcers for the VOA are mercenaries. We voice, parrot-like, ideas which are not our own. We render into our maternal tongue thoughts that are alien to how our people think. I, for one, do not think the **propaganda** as carried out by the Voice of America is effective. Still, we must earn our living and there is nothing we can do to change one iota in our jobs, so we are mercenaries." Mr. Pruett smiled when he read my impressions but didn't say anything before filing away my form along with those of my colleagues.

On another occasion, a Vietnamese acquaintance apparently had applied to the Voice and cited me as reference. I received a form where I was asked to state whether the applicant was "loyal to the Constitution of the United States." Of course, this was a routine question so unless the answer was "No", there was nothing to say. Not for me, though, so being contrary I wrote: "I am not sure if this man is loyal to the Constitution of Vietnam—if Vietnam has one—or not, so how can I be sure about his loyalty to the U.S. Constitution? Besides, I do not know if he has any idea about the Constitution of the U.S. I do not." To this day, I do not know whether as a result of my writing the applicant was turned down or was granted the job. Nor do I recall who he was either.

Thus, you could say I was inclined to take life and matters rather philosophically, if not fatalistically. We did not talk much about the Đức Thanh group's 'coup' against me. We soon forgot about it for in the following weeks, Ngô Đình Diệm received appeals from France and he had to decide whether to go there or stay in the U.S. Mr. Ngô absented himself from my home more often than usual and returned to his Maryknoll Seminary seclusion for this purpose. Meanwhile, we had to deal with the case of Đỗ Vạn Lý and some would-be collaborators of the cause.

IT WAS SOME time after New Year's Day that Đỗ Vạn Lý came to New York and entered into what was supposed to be a close relationship with Mr. Ngô and our group. He came to my home to meet with Thành and me, and occasionally with Mr. Ngô. After the reserved, if not unamicable first interview we had a while back at Miss Bài's apartment, I believe I had written him a few times about how kind Ngô Đình Diệm was to intervene with the FBI on his behalf thus saving him from trouble, and so on. I did this to dispel any bad thoughts he may have had toward Mr. Ngô who wanted Lý's cooperation. I correctly guessed that unless I told Lý of this assistance, no one else would—not Mr. Ngô, to be sure. Lý never wrote me back but when he came to my place that first time, he was a different man.

Lý warmly thanked me for all the trouble I took in relating all that Mr. Ngô had done for him and asked me to pass his thanks to his benefactor as he was not in New York at the time. Lý did not stay long in New York as each time he came up from Washington, D.C., it was for a day visit and he always returned to D.C. the same night. He never overnighted in my place as far as I can recall. Perhaps this was due to an unfavorable comment about Ngô Đình Diệm that my friend Huỳnh Sanh Thông had related to me, or our different temperaments, or simply because he and I didn't like each other much from the start so that despite all efforts to hide how we felt, our personal relationship was lukewarm, at best.

Đỗ Vạn Lý was thin, of medium height, and had a yellowish complexion. Although born and raised in South Vietnam, he affected a northern accent that poorly suited him. He was about my age but already had a long past of clandestine activities. Lý never spoke to us of his past, and it was actually Mr. Ngô who told us about Lý's involvement with the efforts of Prince Cường Để in Japan to liberate Vietnam from French colonial rule. For all I knew, Lý could have joined the prince's cause in Japan in 1940 after the Japanese first occupied Indochina with the connivance of the French.

Cường Để had gone to Japan early in the national resistance movement against French colonization of Vietnam but he did not accomplish anything of worth for the cause. The Japanese used him as a sort of 'scarecrow' against the French in Indochina and conveniently 'forgot' about him when they had obtained enough concessions. The prince lived in poor conditions in Japan until the end of his days and even when Japan occupied Indochina, they preferred Bảo Đại to him as the better pawn on their Southeast Asian Co-prosperity chessboard. In early 1940 Saigon had a recruitment office for Cường Để's efforts (likely financed by Japan) with the name of 'Agence S.V.P.' This could be translated as *'S'il Vous Plaît'* (Please Agency) or more appropriately, *'Servez Votre Patrie'* (Support Your Homeland Agency). It later entered my mind then that Đỗ Vạn Lý might have gone to Japan through the *Agence S.V.P.* around early 1940 when the Japanese first occupied Indochina.

I unwittingly ran into some of Đỗ Vạn Lý's mysterious past one day while searching for an opportunity to work abroad. A friend I had introduced to a Japanese company for work, Kiều Công Lập, told me of an organization that could smuggle young men out of Vietnam. Intrigued, I went with Lâp to the *Agence S.V.P.* where we were received by Trâm, a former classmate of ours. The company did not even look like a *bona fide* commercial enterprise lacking offices or typists. There was nothing except a glass-topped desk behind which sat Trâm wearing a brocade kimono.

Trâm gave me a sheet of paper and told me to write what he would dictate: "I, the undersigned, take the oath of eternal loyalty to Prince Cường Để—" My pen abruptly stopped moving when I looked up at Trâm and said: *"Mon vieux* [my old friend], all I want is to go abroad. I prefer France or Europe although Japan is fine with me since it's all you can do. But, to make me swear loyalty to a man I have never met in my life is rather...too much, don't you think?" Trâm silently took back my paper, tore it into pieces and tossed it in a wastebasket.

As an old hand at the game, Lý no doubt thought himself far superior to any of us who were novices in his eyes. His condescending observation about Ngô Đình Diệm's Catholicism was a telling trait but we were still too much the amateurs to know it. Lý's initial aloofness and reticence was part of his game for he wanted to be above everyone else except Mr. Ngô. When Lý's desired closeness to Diệm did not come about, he reluctantly but very cleverly stepped down one notch in familiarity with a possible new leader for Vietnam. He was playing a wait-and-see card: not entirely 'in' or 'out' of the Ngô clan at this juncture. Hence, the secrecy and air of mystery about him.

Lý had already started a group of his own in Washington, D.C with young idealistic students like Đỗ Trọng Chu, Trần Long, and some others. We in New York didn't know it then, but Lý kept them all on a tight leash and did not bring any of his group with him when making initial contact with us and also to meet Mr. Ngô. Lý always came and left Manhattan alone.

16. THE FAREWELL

IN THE MEANWHILE, life in New York for us took on a new, more accelerated turn. Our family was as good as submerged in Vietnamese political matters of the moment—a stretch of almost three months until Ngô Đình Diệm departed for France in early May 1953. The appeals from France became more urgent than ever and Mr. Ngô opted to head there. He started preparing and his stays at the Maryknoll Seminary at Lakewood or Ossining became longer than usual. Once he asked me to accompany him to Lakewood and to bring back to New York some papers to distribute to members of the Vietnamese Catholic Students Association.

When we arrived at the seminary, I thought I would accompany Mr. Ngô to his room and help him carry the papers downstairs but he stopped me at the foot of the stairs and said to wait for him. I waited a long time, all the while wondering why he should keep me out of his room like that. Was there something in the room he didn't want outsiders seeing? Maybe it was against seminary regulations to admit outsiders into the dormitory area. Did Mr. Ngô have a private room and not a cell in the regular dormitory? I was indulging in curiosity because of the long wait and I was also perplexed and a little vexed when Mr. Ngô abruptly stopped at the stairs as if I were about to intrude on his privacy.

Of course we had been to the seminary before. My wife and visited there a few times and on one occasion, we had brought along Miss Huỳnh Thị Xuân Yến, daughter of Mr. Huỳnh Minh-Ý whom Mr. Ngô counted as one of his staunch supporters in Vietnam. Mr. Ý was a notable in one of the Protestant congregations back home and, as things were at that time, it was remarkable that a Protestant should support a notable Catholic like Ngô Đình Diệm. Although both religious groups were Christian, they fiercely competed for followers and with Protestants being far in the minority, it was not unusual that they resented and tried to keep apart from the Catholics. Miss Yến was a music student in Minnesota and was visiting New York on her vacation.

On that occasion, Mr. Ngô, the talented amateur photographer, took a color photograph of my wife and Miss Yến walking hand in hand across the lawn of the Maryknoll Seminary. Mr. Ngô was very proud of this photo: the scenery was beautiful, the photographer's skill was excellent, and above all, Ms. Yến was captured as a graceful young girl in a green *áo dài*, the Vietnamese national dress. My friend, Huỳnh Sanh Thông saw that photograph and fell in love with the beautiful girl. He traveled to Minnesota to look her up and after a long courtship, during which Miss Yến wrestled with a bout of tuberculosis, the pair were married. Mrs. Thông was the younger sister of Mrs. Dư Phước Long, wife of the 'fat' man of Naperville when we made up that Tết poem for the Year of the Serpent. He was the one who asked me to deliver his letter to Ngô Đình Diệm all those years ago. Here was a case of marriage through political association, brought about by me and my wife showing the picture of Yến to Thông, and acting as unwitting go-betweens. I remember Mr. Ngô joking as he admired Yến as well as his photograph: "Look at this girl," he said jovially, "isn't she carrying something around her waist, under the *áo dài*? Is it hand grenades?"

The joke was told because throughout Vietnamese resistance to France's reoccupation of Vietnam, girls and women in Saigon sometimes smuggled grenades on their person to use against the French. So, at movie houses and theater entrances, policemen would search ladies' handbags for hidden weapons. It was reported that even Mrs. Ngô Đình Nhu was subjected to searches when she went to watch a movie. Of course, her husband was not yet the powerful man he became years later.

The Đức Thanh group's activities were reduced in scope around this time and after they launched their 'coup' against me about the anonymous letter affair, the battlefield lay quiet. Their attitudes and the latent feud did not change, however. On some occasions the two antagonistic groups met by chance in town and we each quickly went our separate ways. One time, Ngô Đình Diệm joined our groups for breakfast at a Chinatown restaurant. With him were the whole 'general staff' of his supporters present in New York namely Father Kiệm, Đỗ Vạn Lý, Nguyễn Thái, Huỳnh Sanh Thông, Bùi Kiến

Thành, and my family—complete with all the children. As we entered the restaurant, we saw Đức Thanh's group already seated at a table. It was the first time that Ngô Đình Diệm saw Đức Thanh since early 1951. We were rather tense. Considering the long, tumultuous feud between our groups, this confrontation was sudden, albeit fortuitous. We all trooped by without glancing at the other table and settled into one at the back of the restaurant that was already crowded at breakfast time.

We thought Mr. Ngô would ignore Đức Thanh and his group just as we were doing, but as soon as we all were seated, he got up and headed to the other table. We watched anxiously as Đức Thanh rose and went to meet Mr. Ngô halfway and both men moved to a bench against the wall, out of sight of either group. They talked for a short moment, then each returned to his table. I still vividly remember Mr. Ngô's last talk with Đức Thanh and this dim sum breakfast in Chinatown. How my table remained silent until Mr. Ngô had returned and the matter of the 'last encounter' was not mentioned at our meal nor ever again.

Nguyễn Đình Hòa, as we expected, celebrated Tết at Ambassador Trân Văn Khá's embassy in Washington, D.C. Hoà acted as if he were the leader of the 'loyal' students who attended the festivities. Besides his and Đức Thanh's group that belonged to the then-defunct General Association of Vietnamese Students, Hoà thought of himself as the Dean of Students (he was working toward a Ph.D. in education at NYU) and sported the Vietnamese male's national dress and turban for the occasion. Reportedly, Hoà also performed some 'religious' ritual before what the Alter of the Fatherland that the embassy had built for the occasion. All that hoopla, my group thought with anger, just for Trần Văn Khá to benefit the French!

Eventually, the day in May 1953 arrived when Ngô Đình Diệm would leave us and the U.S. for France. Perhaps the various groups of Vietnamese in Paris felt a mounting sense of urgency from the repercussions of successive setbacks in Indochina, and convinced Diệm that the time had come for him to come work with them on the other side of the Atlantic. Weeks before his departure, all Mr. Ngô's belongings had been gathered and brought to my New York home. Except for one suitcase and one briefcase that Mr. Ngô would take with him, everything he had accumulated during his three years in the U.S. were now with me—book, papers, some clothing, numerous personal items—and he asked me to send this heavy lot to him in France, care of a Mr. Tôn Thất Cẩn.[46]

---

46 All Ngô Đình Diệm's belongings were sent to him through a French shipping company in New York—but later than we wished due to lack of funds. I could not borrow a sum large enough to cover the cost until Father Jacques advanced me $300 from the Student Association funds. Periodically, he wrote asking me to refund the sum, but I could not repay him for three years, not until 1956, after I was named Consul General in Hong Kong. Mr. Ngô's portable short-wave radio was not working when he received it and he wrote to me to complain about it saying, "I don't have many valuable things and the radio is one of them. Frankly, I am sad to see it in such poor condition." I sent to France every personal item of Mr. Ngô except for one plastic briefcase with personal papers and his correspondence with Prince Cường Để in Tokyo. I kept the briefcase back because I thought the prince's letters were too precious to be sent by cargo. I personally handed those letters to Mr. Ngô in March 1956 when my family and I came to see him at the Independence Palace in Saigon. (Au.)

With Ngô Đình Diệm's departure imminent, there was a busy coming and going of well-wishers from Washington, D.C., Chicago, and other faraway places. Father Jacques arrived about the same time as Đỗ Trọng Chu. Đỗ Vạn Lý and Dư Phước Long came. Nguyễn Thái made it, but Huỳnh Sanh Thông did not. They all flocked to my apartment to say goodbye. Some came to my home for the first time after having already called on Ngô Đình Diệm at the Seminary like Đỗ Trọng Chu. He struck me as a gentle and likeable young man who was now at my house for the first time after visiting Diệm at Lakewood. He came as bearer of a message from Mr. Ngô and acquitted himself of his commission in a touching and memorable manner.

At this time, I was not in the best of health due to excessive loss of sleep and overwork and Mr. Ngô was concerned for me. After their talk and Chu was preparing to return to New York, Diệm gave him a paper on which he had written in Chinese characters JIN SENG and asked Chu to urge me to get it in Chinatown. Chu stressed how Mr. Ngô "worries about your poor state of health and insists that you go to Chinatown to buy it." As I pocketed the paper scrap, Chu gently repeated his message, which once more brought home to me what a good, caring, and sentimental friend to my family was Ngô Đình Diệm. he was no medical man yet in the tradition of old men of letters, Mr. Ngô wrote me a 'prescription'—in Chinese!—the lingua franca of Sino-Vietnamese apothecary shops. I never used my mentor's 'prescription' because ginseng was expensive and I overestimated my youthful strength, but also because Mr. Ngô's touching gesture and the way that Đỗ Trọng Chu delivered the message to me was in its way an already powerful psychological medicine.

After Father Jacques arrived at the apartment, in his usual precipitous way, he went straight to the telephone and started calling a dozen people before he finally came round to say hello to us all. I availed of his presence to bring up the matter of Lý Chánh Đức, the student turncoat who gave us plenty of headaches by joining the opposite camp and who continued to annoy our group no end. I suppose Father Jacques had tried to win Đức back to no avail and he considered Đức as lost to the enemy. When I asked point blank if any corrective measures could be applied, Father Jacques shook his head and sadly concluded, "There is nothing I can do."

Lý Chánh Đức and Nguyễn Văn Thơ were the only two turncoats who, as far as I knew, ever 'betrayed' Father Jacques, their personal benefactor. Both had obtained through the good priest not only their scholarships to study in America but travel expenses across the sea as well as occasional financial help. Father Jacques said of Dr. Thơ: "All I can say is that he was the one student to whom I devoted the most care and help, and yet..." He left his thought unfinished.

Lý Chánh Đức never accused Father Jacques of anything. His rebellion against the Catholic Students' association was because I caused him to lose face when I ordered him home after he brought two visiting female students to Hoà's apartment late at night when they had an early flight out the next morning. It was purely coincidental and could not be repaired because neither Đức nor I conceded fault. I hated the Đức Thanh group and their pro-French activities too much to let go my dislike; he, on the other hand, could not accept what he considered my high-handed way of ordering him to bring the girls back to my apartment. In politics, small incidents of a personal vein could, and did, bring important matters to an impasse. Thus, I was resigned to accept the loss of Lý Chánh Đức as did Father Jacques. As for Nguyễn Văn Thơ, the antagonism he conceived against the padre was violent. Tho could not find fault with him so could only fault him for his nervousness. Thơ's hatred for Father Jacques was the sole reason he joined the Đức Thanh group and unwittingly explained his own erratic behavior when he justified founding the General Association to "avoid being under the influence of a terrible priest." Thơ also divulged the padre's real name as "Houssa" and implied that he used the phony name of Jacques to hide his real name.

In the midst of all this hullabaloo, a real bombshell exploded in New York in the person of Cambodia's Prince Norodom Sihanouk. He had arrived from Paris and unexpectedly declared at a press conference that Cambodia was **not** independent, contrary to what the French claimed; that the French had deliberately deceived the world in this regard, and unless genuine independence was granted to his country without delay, he could not see how Cambodia could be saved. The prince's sensational declaration was carried on the front pages of all the important newspapers. The French didn't expect trouble coming from the quiet and docile quarter as the lackluster Sihanouk and his miniscule country.

For the Vietnamese, it was as if someone inferior to you, perhaps a younger brother, suddenly overtook you in the most important race of your life. If little Cambodia and its French-made king gathered enough courage to denounce France's treachery to the world, what would the bigger and more militant Vietnam do? Ever since September 1945, except for Hồ Chí Minh and the Việt Minh, no nationalist leader had issued such a declaration.

We felt as if we had been slapped in the face. The French who should be worried about the Vietnamese, on the contrary felt quite safe with Vietnam—except for the Việt Minh who were Communists anyway. At this juncture, who would belatedly emulate Sihanouk? What courageous leader would publicly announce the same truth—from the U.S.—and expose the French lie, like Sihanouk did?

Naturally, our eyes all turned to Ngô Đình Diệm. Diệm had been right here in New York long before Sihanouk arrived. He had a life-long history of resistance to French high-handed methods of colonization. Diệm was the only one—except Hồ Chí Minh—who could demand a status for Vietnam equivalent to India's in the British Commonwealth.

We were inexperienced and hotheaded and excited because Sihanouk had pulled his 'coup.' We wished our leader, Ngô Đình Diệm, would do the same or an even more sensational act! We would be overjoyed to see the French embarrassed and expose their bootlickers, sycophants, quislings, Đức Thanhs, and Nguyễn Văn Thơs! Let the sunshine enter the dark chamber that is Vietnam. Let Ngô

Đình Diệm speak up—our hero, our champion!

We spoke among ourselves and even got Father Jacques's approval: Yes, Mr. Ngô should speak up. One night, at the Maryknoll Seminary at Lakewood, with Father Jacques and all of us present, I asked Ngô Đình Diệm to make a similar declaration to the press. It was but a few days before his departure for France and I thought it would be good timing for his arrival in France would be heightened by front-page coverage if he made the same kind of denunciation as Sihanouk's now.

Ngô Đình Diệm's reaction, however, was as swift as it was unexpected. He brusquely turned to me and curtly responded with audibly suppressed anger: "This is my own business—you'd best leave it to me!" I was both surprised and disappointed. Almost shocked. Father Jacques, who sat next to Mr. Ngô, said not one word. An uneasy silence followed, and the matter was dropped.

For a very long time I pondered Ngô Đình Diệm's attitude that night: Why was he angry with me? Did I do something wrong? I was not satisfied with any rationalization I reached until several years later, after Ngô Đình Diệm became President of the Republic and I told my friend, Huỳnh Sanh Thông about Diệm's reaction to my proposal that night. Thông did not vote for Diệm and had joined with Nguyễn Tôn Hoàn to oppose my mentor.[47] Thông of course jumped at the chance to point

47 Nguyễn Tôn Hoàn (1917-2001), a medical doctor, political activist, leader of Đại Việt Quốc Dân Đảng (Greater Viet Nationalist Party), and (briefly) Deputy Prime Minister in 1964 in the government led by General Nguyễn Khánh.

out Diệm's "dictatorial behavior" and did his best to get me to turn my back on Diệm—to no avail.

In retrospect, it should be easy to see why Diệm reacted as he did at the time. He was about to leave the U.S. for France and had he made the kind of denunciation I asked for, the timing would not have been a good thing as I believed but instead, a very good excuse for France to slam her doors in Diệm's face. Sihanouk was nominally the Chief of State of Cambodia and had just left France when he pulled his trick. It was the opposite case with Ngô Đình Diệm who was a private Vietnamese citizen and heading **to** France. So, what seemed good sauce for the goose was not necessarily so for the gander. Not to mention **our** group's insistence and pressure, almost, to make this denouncement at a critical turning point in his political life. He had to decide if he should go down the path facing him. Events later proved that Diệm did make the correct choice, but I could now see how my urging got on his nerves and he had every reason to become angry with me. I still think Thông took it as a cheap shot by judging Diệm as "dictatorial"—and he used a narrow measuring rod to do it, too, à la Nguyễn Tôn Hoàn!

[NOTES ON THE JUXTAPOSITION OF TIME LAYERS: We are living, as it were, on different time layers which occasionally happen to mix into one in a flash! The past and present merged into one single layer tissue of existential time.

At the stroke of midnight tonight on April 4, 1978,

I lay in bed listening to the tolling of the bells of St. Louis Church, an early 10th century Church on the hill overlooking Hyères. The bells pealed out slowly, stroke by stroke, twelve rich bongs that were repeated one minute later. The old bells of St. Louis always ring twice, as if to say: I am e-t-e-r-n-a-l…

And with time, the juxtaposition of images: Pigeons fell off perches in their dwellings fixed by Time to merge into one ever-present tableau. I am staying in Hyères where realtors are holding Open Houses, inviting new and old potential clients to mix in a kind of Big Reunion, so to speak. People tumble in and out of homes for sale admiring amenities as if a search light shone on them … in a vivid technicolor continuity.

I saw a picture of Svay Rieng province (Cambodia) in September long ago, when high tides inundated every bit of low ground. My wife and I alight from the pedicab that brought us home from work. My beautiful wife, just 19, carefully negotiating the narrow wooden bridge submerged underwater, her *áo dài* rolled up and her calves exposed, almost blindly crossing the enlarged stream's roiling waters to reach home. Our place was on the second floor of a cement and granite house on top of a half-submerged first floor. The people living on the floor below us were Annamites—they were so *méchants* [evil]! We used to sit at a rattan table and chairs on our balcony to drink tea and admire the Black Virgin Mountain of Tây Ninh in the distance, towering above the immense plains that mirrored its trembling dark shadows ….]

IT WAS THE last night that Ngô Đình Diệm would spend at the Maryknoll Seminary so, together with Father Jacques, we all stayed until late at Lakewood, New Jersey. Mr. Ngô brought us to sit by a small pond on the grounds of Maryknoll House where we talked late into the night. Stars shone overhead and on the pond surface, we could see circle after circle of silvery water forming and radiating to the corners of the shore from fish snapping up insects. Finally, we had to leave, and we were quiet and feeling bittersweet to drive home together in Father Kiệm's battered Plymouth.

The next morning, Mr. Ngô came to spend his last day at my family's home at 111th Street in New York. Father Jacques took leave of Ngô Đình Diệm and drove back to Chicago. That night, the rest of us, except for Huỳnh Sanh Thông, kept vigil around Mr. Ngô. It was he who suggested that Father Kiệm telephone Đức Thành to pass along his farewell. It was a gesture of conciliation that Mr. Ngô initiated and although we all, the young ones, did not like the idea, we did not protest. Đức Thanh suggested a rally, a kind of get together but we did not agree. Mr. Ngô did not say anything, so we let the matter rest at that point.

ON DEPARTURE MORNING, the next day, we drove to Idlewild Airport in two cars: Ngô Đình Diệm and my entire family sat in Father Kiệm's battered Plymouth (it was Mr. Ngô's 'official car' for the duration of his stay in America). Following the Plymouth was Bùi Kiến Thành's second-hand car filled friends and supporters piled up like sardines: Đỗ Vạn Lý, Đỗ Trọng Chu, Nguyễn Thái, and Nguyễn Chí Hiền. Next to Hiền and squeezed between two male passengers was I believe Miss Linh, the sleepy-eyed sister of Miss Đẩu (the future Madame Bùi Kiến Thành), who was studying in New York staying at the International House and inseparable companion of Nguyễn Chí Hiền.

To our surprise, at Idlewild was Trịnh Văn Chẩn, who came alone to see Ngô Đình Diệm off. No one else was there, neither from the Đức Thanh group or the neutrals. If only we had said YES to Đức Thanh's suggestion last night of a rally, he certainly would have brought his entire staff for the 'rally'—and Nguyễn Đình Hoà would have had his great opportunity to perform! Hoà was quite a talented showman, even shedding tears as the plane took off if the scene warranted. Such a pity we didn't agree to the gathering.

Ngô Đình Diệm departing for France at Idlewild Airport
(New York, May 1953)

Standing: Mrs. Văn, Mr. Văn, Dư Phước Long

Seated: Ngô Đình Diệm, Father Trần Đình Kiệm

Note: The photographer was Bùi Kiến Thành

As it was, we were a happy chatting group moving about Mr. Ngô who was sitting for a bit. Thanks to good old Trịnh Văn Chẩn—our cameraman—we have a shot of Ngô Đình Diệm sitting and smiling all by himself in the foreground. His black briefcase was on his lap, his parted black hair was gleaming, and his dark brown suit was tidier than usual. Mr. Ngô's tie was replaced by a fancy one I gave him that morning after he called for help when his old tie refused to knot properly. Behind Mr. Ngô in the background were my wife, me to her right, and Đỗ Vạn Lý on her left. No one else among our group was in the snapshot.

And then a funny little 'accident' occurred. Trịnh Văn Chẩn wished to have a picture of himself with Mr. Ngô, perhaps the 'pièce de résistance' he aimed for in coming out to Idlewild this morning. He made the correct settings and handed the camera to me saying, "Just push the button," as he went to sit next to Mr. Ngo with a big smile on his face. I pushed the button, and a click was heard, and Chẩn happily looked forward to the souvenir shot with Diệm until ... he developed the film. Every frame on the roll was a masterpiece except when I "pushed the button" the photo was a complete failure. Chẩn was so chagrined that he didn't have a photo of himself with Ngô Đình Diệm and for a long time afterwards, he blamed me of deliberate 'sabotage' in order to eliminate him from Diệm's entourage.

As we stood at the windows watching the Air France Constellation taxiing on the runway towards takeoff, Đỗ Trọng Chu said: "Imagine, tonight the whole world will know that Ngô Đình Diệm is in France! Churchill will know it! Chiang Kai-shek will know it! ..." The shining silver plane was still on the runway, reflecting the morning's sunlight. In the distance, the plane looked small, like a baby whale on dry land. I thought: "Our Mr. Ngô is on that plane, perhaps thinking of us. In half a day or so, he will land in France and some Vietnamese will be at the airport to greet him, like we came here to say goodbye. Perhaps more people will be there than our numbers here. Still, to think like Đỗ Trọng Chu did that the "whole world" knows about Mr. Ngô's arrival in France, that powerful leaders like Churchill would know about Ngô is rather melodramatic. I doubt if Chiang Kai-shek even heard of Diệm." Even today I remember how that day I thought Chu's comment was childish and proved how unsophisticated we young people were. Đỗ Vạn Lý, despite his ten years or more with Cường Để in Japan and well ahead of us in politics, was no better. And we were soon to see him in action.

After Mr. Ngô's plane had disappeared to the east, we slowly and dejectedly headed home. It was an anticlimax after all the excitement, build-up, and rushing about which led to the farewell. We were left to ourselves to take care of our own. Whatever we did from then on would have to be don on our own. Guidance, if any, would be late in coming the same day. Nguyễn Thái returned to Ithaca, Lý and Chu headed to Washington, D.C., and the rest of us dispersed into New York City. For the first time after so many months, my family reverted to no students or visitors stopping for long or short stays, to me having no more all-night talks for a change, to being without

Grandpa Maryknoll.

We could not help but miss Ngô Đình Diệm, especially the children. Our living room which we turned into "His" room, was empty. "His" couch where he slept for so many months was now imprinted with his form—bent in the middle. We could not help but miss the sound of his voice and laughs, his cavorting with our little ones who asked about Mr. Ngô daily. Muriel was too little to talk to about Mr. Ngô, but we told Dominic and Mỹ-Châu that Grandpa Maryknoll would come back in a few weeks, which alas, caused them to begin looking forward to his arrival with fruit or toys in hand just like when he "came home" from periodic stays at the Maryknoll seminaries in Lakewood, NJ or Ossining, NY. Only Marie knew that Grandpa had gone to France for good, that he might return, but that was improbable. From then on, Bùi Kiến Thành became a part of our family. He came several times a week and often stayed for meals, and soon "Uncle Thành" replaced Mr. Ngô as a 'family member' in the house.

17. VISIT TO WASHINGTON, D.C.

THERE WAS A LULL after Ngô Đình Diệm's departure. We had some respite where my wife and I caught up on lost sleep and enjoyed our family life more than previously. Uncle Thành became more and more attached to us, as we were to him. Weekends were especially pleasant with him at our place. Sometimes, Father Kiệm came from Fordham University where he had a room on campus and drove us to the beach. We were fortunate to have Father Kiệm as a good friend for he helped us in every way possible and without him we could never have gone anywhere outside of New York City.

With all the long months that Mr. Ngô lived with us, we were kept very busy with his night 'vigils," his guests, and hosting students. After his departure, my wife, Marie, and I realized how worn down and exhausted we were: we could hardly move around like we did as a matter of course just a few weeks earlier; even energetic Marie was slower and somewhat sluggish. My wife and I concentrated more on caring for and enjoying our little ones. We all took it easy and finally got some much-deserved rest.

I remember well how long Father Kiệm had to wait each time he came down to take my family out. He would call in the morning, again in the afternoon, and yet we were barely ready. He usually sat and waited for hours and when we finally left the house, it was almost dusk. At first, Father Kiệm was a little impatient and would hurry us along, looking again and again at his watch. In the end, he got used to our rhythm (or lack of it) and he just sat and waited.

He usually drove us to Orchard Beach in uptown New York. This was a nice clean beach and as we always visited on weekdays, it was almost deserted. We had the locker room and all the beach to ourselves! A few times, he brought along Timothy, a little boy he knew, as playmate for Dominic and Mỹ-Châu. At other times on my days off, he brought me with him on his duty calls to hospitals to visit patients of his acquaintances and for whom he acted as confessor.

Uncle Thành brought us around in his second-hand car, too, but with his studies he was much busier than Father Kiệm and we had to wait for his vacation weeks to enjoy long rides out of town. Meanwhile, he spent evenings with us whenever he could, and most weekends. We would call Nguyễn Chí Hiền over on occasions, too, and if we had friends or visitors from out of town, Uncle Thành would be on hand to help us. On such occasions, Hiền was sought at whatever place he happened to live at the time. He was a 'big eater', so we always had to be prepared for his unusually large food consumption. Once, we had all finished our meal and nothing was left but plain rice. However, Hiền was not full yet and proceeded to put all the rice into his bowl—almost half a pot of rice!—and ate it all with only splashes of fish sauce, smacking his lips in appreciation. He was a 'big talker', too, and once late at night while we still lingered and chatted at the dinner table, a knock came from the other side of the wall from my neighbor next door. Instead of lowering his voice, my friend responded with a tremendous thud of a knock. In a minute, the angry neighbor was at my door to complain about noise at the late hour, but even more about Hiền's smack on the wall!

UNIVERSITY VACATION TIME rolled around again, and we were busy once more with students arriving in unending waves of two, three, or more young faces each school break. They availed themselves of the holidays to see New York while we lodged and fed them as best we could. We were already in debt and had been so for a long time, so a few more mouths to feed would not make too much difference. Most of the students were from outside New York state, but even in-state students like Huỳnh Sanh Thông and Nguyễn Thái were told by the Vietnamese Catholic Students Association that they could stay for a few days at our place, so they came. And more came.

It was fitting for the purpose that we succeeded in renting a large apartment with spacious rooms just one year ago in my mind, I always connected the birth of our youngest child, Mỹ-Nga, with Ngô Đình Diệm's coming to live with us and how it shaped future events in our lives. What we thought was a larger apartment for our family to enjoy was transformed into a lodging house for impoverished students in their first vacations in the U.S. The overwhelming majority of those who came to us were newcomers to America enjoying their first visit to New York City. Unfortunately, soon not only first-time visitors came to stay with us, but old-timers followed suit—especially fellows in our group involved with either the Association or Ngô Đình Diệm.

So, we had the unexpected spectacle of young men and women coming and going almost daily through the vacation months of 1953 and 1954. Their suitcases lined up along our long corridor and their multicolored clothing hung practically from the kitchen through to living and dining rooms.

The on-premises concierge was Mr. Corlett, a nice old man who lived on the first floor with his wife; they were so kind to us and always helped in any way they could. That first summer in 1953, however, they thought it prudent to give us a discreet warning. While a bit surprised, they were not worried by the succession of young 'guests' coming up to our apartment. At least, not until they noticed a strange man in a light-gray raincoat observing our apartment for several hours over many days from across the street. Mr. Corlett thought we were under surveillance and although he didn't think we were doing anything wrong, he suggested being careful since our 'guests' were evidently attracting attention.

My wife and I were a little frightened. For several days, I watched the man myself, the 'spy' or whatever he might be, and it was true that he watched my apartment windows from across the street, focusing on my apartment windows. I shrugged the observer off after a while, reasoning that if he were an FBI agent, he could have come up to ask us questions instead of conducting such showy spying maneuvers. I also tried to persuade the Corletts to see things my way and ignore the watcher, but one day the man disappeared. I still wonder who he was working for. Was it a Đức Thanh trick to wear down our nerves—a psychological war of sorts?

TOWARD AUGUST 1953, when the weather in New York was suffocating and the stream of students vising got thinner, I took a two-week vacation and drove to Washington, D.C. with Bùi Kiến Thành and my daughter, Marie. It was my first trip to the nation's capital. Thành's car looked solid enough and we piled our trunks in the back, not in the least worried about breakdowns. We jovially left New York with brave Thành at the wheel, driving through New Jersey to Pennsylvania on little-used old routes I insisted on so we could enjoy the scenery instead of major highways clogged with cars. We stopped when landscapes attracted us to thoroughly enjoy it and let the driver rest for a while. I recall inventing a stupid game that Thành and I foolishly thought was great fun.

We were moving along smoothly, crossing meadows and wheatfields and slowly climbing up steep hills, enjoying each mile of beautiful scenery. I suggested to Thành that each time we headed downhill after climbing a long slope bordered by spacious terrain, he should cut off the motor to save gas—so we'd kind of "float" down on air. Well, the motor got flooded on our second slide down the hill and it refused to start again at the foot of the next hill. We were at a loss, not knowing how to fix the car, so we could only sit in the heat and wait. Then, along came a farmer clanking along the road in his old pickup truck who stopped at our waving in distress. We explained the trouble and he gave a hearty laugh and an admonition: Never do that again! We had not only flooded the motor, but the car was running by itself—that is, with no control from the driver. If anything happened and the engine was off, Thành had no control over the car and couldn't easily turn the wheel. The kind farmer helped us get back on the road and we were relieved to have a close shave. But our troubles had just started.

At dusk, we were driving slowly along a deserted side road with dense foliage and pretty clearings when suddenly the car stopped with a jerk and a heavy thud underneath. We climbed out with darkness falling fast, thinking this time we're in trouble—and we were not wrong. The axle had broken. One end was resting on the ground, which meant the steering wheel was no longer connected. Indeed, we turned the steering wheel and it only spun freely in the night air. This was an unheard-of breakdown, and our only consolation was that it didn't happen on a crowded highway.

Unlike our previous stop which happened early in the afternoon, now we were broken down in the thickening darkness of night. We couldn't do anything but climb back into the car and wait—for what we did not know. It was unlikely that a fellow driver would happen along on such a deserted road. Farmers would have reached home hours before, and even if one came along at this late hour, what could he do about a broken axle and detached steering wheel? We were resigned that we'd have to spend the night in the 'forest' at the very spot where the car broke down, for we could not even push the car aside one inch.

Hours passed. We were depressed, hungry, and afraid. Owls hooted in tree branches all around us and we absolutely could not reach any other humans. The day's heat was gone and the three of us shivered as the small hours of the morning approached. We were too frightened, tired, and hungry to exchange many words between us. I lay across the back seat trying to while away the night and was able to nap a bit, waking just as dawn broke. The curtain of darkness receded as the morning dew spread across the green grass like a thin, misty carpet. Both Uncle Thành and Marie sat immobile in their seats like two petrified mummies. While I snored behind them, they didn't get a wink of sleep the whole night but were able to watch a school of young deer daintily cross the meadow toward some unseen creek or waterway in the hills.

Finally, when the dew had long dried up and the sun was high in the sky, our savior arrived. It was the inevitable farmer wearing a baseball cap who beamed a large smile at us with, "Good Morning, folks, what can I do for you?" He had a look at our broken axle, the disconnected steering wheel, blew a big cloud of country-tobacco smoke, and raised his huge paws in a sign of utter helplessness. We were miles from civilization, and he could not tow our broken-down carcass of a car!

He was a youthful farmer, full of vigorous goodwill. We did not have the strength to say no when he suggested getting under the car to try to fix what he could. Worming himself underneath, he began fumbling with the disabled axle while we watched from the side, helpless and discouraged. The young man stayed underneath for hours it seemed, without once complaining at the loss of work hours we cost him and for which we were as embarrassed as if we had forced him to repair the car.

He finally surfaced from under the car, sighed his capitulation, and said he would bring the axle to the nearest gas station or garage. The good farmer soon returned with a mechanic and after a few trips back and forth for parts, the car looked likely to run again. The morning was all but gone, the mechanic was paid and had returned to the garage, but the farmer would accept nothing from us to compensate for his devoting the entire morning to us. Thành and I would remember the good-hearted farmers of America farmers for a long, long time.

Back in the car, Uncle Thành took the wheel again, aged by an anxious night without sleep. Marie was tired but relieved we were continuing in the direction of Washington, D.C. I was privileged to have the whole back bench to myself and soon resumed my rickety nap. How long we traveled, I had no idea, when a rude bump and sudden stop threw me clean onto the car floor. I had scarcely opened my eyes when I heard Thành asking if I was hurt. I quickly reassured him I was fine but not before shouting a few insults at the car stopped just in front of ours. Barely awake, I thought that car was why I was hurled off my 'bed.'

It was otherwise: Poor Thành had fallen asleep and

rear-ended the car in front! The other driver approached, then after looking perfunctorily at his car's bumper, he just shook his head saying to Thành, "Nothing much," and left. I heard Thành happily mumbling: "Washingtonians are so civilized!" After the near-accident, we exhorted each other to stay as the roads were now full of cars as Washington was in sight.

Our first trip to the capital of the United States of America was an eventful one. Was that an omen of future events, fateful to us and to Vietnam? Washington would influence Vietnamese politics to such an extent that in the end, the U.S. took over and directly, if unwittingly, caused the tragic death of our good friend and Vietnam's leader. However, all this laid in our future and for the moment, the 'adopted' children, followers, and devoted supporters of Ngô Đình Diệm were blessedly ignorant of events to come.

WE SET OUT to have fun in the capital and fun we would have—at least that was what we thought. We quickly forgot the troubles we had *en route* and drove straight to Huỳnh Sanh Thông's apartment, which was in a cul-de-sac. This was a love nest as Thông and Yến had recently secretly married—not saying anything, having adopted the French philosophy of *"Pour vivre heureux, vivons cachés"* or "To live happily, lead a quiet life." This means embracing the quiet beauty of a life away from the spotlight.

It was our first reunion after the departure of Ngô Đình Diệm three months ago and Thông could boast of a brand-new wife who was not only pretty, but well versed in the culinary arts and entirely devoted to his whims, gastric or otherwise. Yến, as we have seen, was a typically South Vietnamese girl: not ambitious, self-effacing, and left all social and political chores to her 'trượng phu' or man of the house. She was grateful to me and my wife (if Thông was not) for unconsciously acting as 'go-betweens' when we showed Thông Mr. Ngô's very artistic photo of Yến and my wife. The fruitful issue of his photographic talent was their romance and newly joined lives. Thông and Yến fed us like kings and Thông royally acquitted his prerogatives as 'Collier in his Castle.'[48] For several days in succession, Yến treated us to seafood meals: a huge pile of live crabs she bought wholesale and kept in her bathtub!

We also had the company of a funny young fellow, Nguyễn Xuân Diên, whose sister, Nguyễn Thị Tuyết Mai, soon became Madame Nguyễn Thái. Diên was a romantic daredevil who, mandolin strapped to his shoulder, sang love songs under the window of his neighborhood Juliet, a young Korean housewife who, incidentally, was the very woman he later ended up 'separating' from her husband to making her his. Fortunately, no irate husband took revenge at this point in the story, the romantic fellow was only in hot pursuit of the lady. Only half joking, Thông would say: Diên, leave Yến alone—don't try to 'save' her the way you did the Korean woman!"

---

48 The French say, *"Le Charbonnier Est Roi Chez Lui,"* meaning even the lowly woodcutter who makes charcoal is master of his humble home. Typical French bourgeois thinking despite, or even because of, the French Revolution. As recently as March 1976, I dined with a French couple in Hyères where the conversation revolved around the same philosophy of the 'Charcoal Maker.' (Au.)

Thông had just been hired as teacher-translator for the Department of Defense, the same job Đỗ Vạn Lý had in Washington, to teach Vietnamese to advisers-to-be who, a short time later, went to Vietnam to beef up the extant American Military Mission in Saigon. They had the highest salaries in town for working Vietnamese, but while Lý lived in relative comfort and abundance, Thông spent his earnings as quickly as he could on restaurants and fancy food. He absolutely loved good food and relished the company of friends, be they true or not so true ones. For night revelries, we stayed late at Thông and Yến's home, sometimes listening to Diên plucking his mandolin or at other times enjoyed truly good music from Yến's skill at the piano.

For temporary lodging and sleeping quarters, Uncle Thành went somewhere else while Đỗ Vạn Lý brought Marie and her father to his secluded, air-conditioned bachelor's den. It was in a quiet neighborhood, miles away from most people, and for Lý, as far as possible from troublesome Vietnamese. We were the first intruders he ever allowed in his home for he meant to treat well the father and daughter who were the closest and most trusted of Ngô Đình Diệm's people—at least as far as Lý could make out. We never shared a meal with him, but when we were ready to leave Thông's late-night parties, he picked us up or Thanh drove us there and Lý did his very best to make us comfortable. In the heavy sticky heat of Washington summers, his air-conditioned rooms were indeed a blessing.

At the apartment, Lý introduced me to his few intimate

friends and coworkers for the 'cause': Trần Long was a young student, short in stature but long in idealism, and full of vitality; and Lý Việt Kiệm was a Cochinchinese from Sóc Trăng, whom Lý liked for his moderate political ambition while deploring his shallow knowledge and typical southern Vietnamese carelessness. There were a few unnamed and unseen others whom Lý promised to bring around but never did. It also seemed to me that for the first time, Lý opened himself more than ever by skipping his usual clam-like reticence and holding forth about everything he judged useful—but never about his past which then and to this day remains a closed book. Although he became loquacious and boastful as our conversations extended into the early hours of the morning, I felt a kind of barrier that prevented learning much about Lý's character despite many questions that burned in my head but were never asked. How did you come to join the Cường Để nationalist movement in Japan? What about the Hawaiian woman who helped you get to America? Did you marry her and then abandon her?

Throughout this period of unquestionably unique soirees that were never repeated, Lý and I contented ourselves with generalities and banalities. The only time I thought Lý showed himself more human, friendly in the real sense of the word, was when he warmly thanked me for taking an interest in him and 'hiring' him (*embauché*), so to speak. In the end, though, we finished by hating each other and although we maintained a rigidly amicable attitude, we knew we weren't exactly comrades in arms—or in anything else. Ngô Đình Diệm was the magic name that bound us together, and we continued to smile at each other while peace was safeguarded.

Unfortunately, peace between us was not to be maintained for long. For one thing, Đỗ Vạn Lý had the unpalatable urge to make any man he met his ally, inducting him into his personal army. Lý's detractors—and they were legion—say he deluded himself with the aptly named *'folie de grandeur'* [delusions of grandeur] mania into believing that he alone was capable of leadership. He wanted to turn the few young men he took under his wing into replicas of himself. And like a mother hen, Lý jealously guarded his chicks lest some 'outside' influence exert an unfavorable twist against him.

Another thing affecting our truce was that Lý's long-established and well-justified ability to attract enemies made him the bane of almost the entire Vietnamese community in Washington, D.C. No one I knew of spoke positively or even indifferently of him. Lý was the rare 'politician' who undauntedly acquired more and more opponents and fewer partisans by the day. Even those willing to accommodate Lý because they supported Ngô Đình Diệm like Dư Phước Long and Huỳnh Sanh Thông, conceived an almost sacred dislike for Lý. Trần Long ended their association by slamming his door in Lý's face and yelling, "You bastard!" or words to that effect.

Hence, a confrontation took place even on the day Thành, Marie, and I returned to New York. As a grandiose gesture by a self-proclaimed "Big Brother", Lý invited as many Vietnamese as he could reach to a big send-off for us at the Nanking Tea House in Chinatown. Most of those attending were not Lý supporters, and they enjoyed the black humor in knowing Lý had to deal with the moral ordeal of inviting 'enemies' to his gathering plus foot the bill on top! A few guests—and only a few—like Đỗ Trọng Chu were for Lý and were greatly embarrassed at what was to occur in the heat of ensuing exchanges between Lý and his guests. Curiously enough, Nguyễn Quí Anh, an embassy man was present at the tea party. Supporters of Ngô Đình Diệm distrusted him as we would find suspect any man or woman, Vietnamese or not, who worked for Ambassador Trần Văn Khá, and therefore indirectly for French interests in colonial Indochina.

Despite the seemingly cordial atmosphere Ly and the guests tried to maintain, barely camouflaged sarcastic digs could be heard floating through the room right from the beginning. With each new replenishment of hot water into teapots and steaming hot offerings of dim sum disappearing fast into appreciative and connoisseur stomachs, the comments exchanged became more biting and insulting. Mocking laughter and snorts were more clearly heard, almost appearing in the same rhythm as the savory morsels were inhaled. Lý was irked by the unfriendly atmosphere, and it showed in his thin face getting longer and longer and brusque behavior. Poor Lý! I could have even pitied him if he did not have such a striking capacity to bring thunderbolts down on his head! Apropos of something Lý said, which I had not the least interest but irritated me to no end, I committed a ridiculous gaffe.

Now, I had been drinking cup after steaming cup of a devilishly good *Hangzhou Yellow Huang Jiu,* a Chinese hot wine, and I tipsily thought myself in the clouds enough to respond to Lý's comment. I didn't refute him—no, I didn't even remember what he'd just said—I just outdid both Lý and Đức Thanh, the two biggest showoffs in Vietnam by boasting *outre mesure* [beyond measure] about myself.

"Mind you, boys!" I intoned with an exaggerated Oxford English accent that was more provoking than any regular Oxfordian or English speech. "You have here among you common mortals no less august a presence as **me**!" I said, thumping my chest, my necktie askew, and my forehead sweating. "Let me hear from any of you, including the First Secretary of the Embassy of France—oh, pardon the slip—of Vietnam," I said, jerking my chin at Nguyễn Quí Anh. At that moment, a memory flashed into my mind of calling the Embassy one day on some matter and Anh answering the phone in a very unnatural "Hulloo' that was the equal of my own farcical accent at this tea party. Of course, I meant everything as a joke, but being such a first-rate actor, I delivered my statements so naturally, without the trace of a smile, and fortified by heady *Huang Jiu* that my audience could only respond with a thick, heavy silence.

The party ended with a whimper and Đỗ Vạn Lý often reminded me about my boastful Oxford English accent. He had no other argument with me, then or later. Mao Tze-tung wisely said that "Revolution is no tea party." We were certainly not revolutionaries. We were a starry-eyed bunch of kids inadequately and ineffectively trying to oppose the French colonials and their sycophants in Vietnam. Some of us were more ambitious but we were basically just a bunch of kids—inexperienced, ludicrous, and immature despite all of us approaching middle age.

Back to New York Thành, Marie, and I drove, this time in safety to return to our work and studies. Our routines resumed their course and the months tediously advanced until at the end of 1953, the news came that the Voice of America offices and studios were moving from Manhattan to Washington, D.C. The move would be done in stages with the first to leave being anything unnecessary for the daily broadcasts and the last being the language units and personnel, which for us came in late 1954. Meanwhile, the battle of Điện Biên Phủ crowned the series of setbacks the French incurred in Vietnam and brought Ngô Đình Diệm to power and Pierre Mendès France to Geneva.

In the intervening months in New York, however, life was far from uneventful as Đức Thanh's group and himself still played tricks on us. Ngô Đình Diệm had been in France for seven months now and no word, no hope, not even the probability of his advisors and supporter's success came to us from across the ocean. No Churchillian nor Chiang Kai-shekian repercussions, to be sure, but no reaction whatsoever from the French political circle in Paris either. In my impetuous way, I wrote Mr. Ngô this 1953 Christmas message:

I know power per se was not and never had been your interest, but the country needs you and your leadership. Please pardon my presumption. I'm more impatient now than when you were here with us, if only because you are no longer present to give us a sense of purpose. I am not unaware of the tremendous obstacles you are bound to encounter in Paris, but please allow me to quote an ancient saying: 'Heroes can create appropriate circumstances as much as appropriate circumstances can, and did, create Heroes.' This, my dear Sir, comes from the bottom of my heart and without arrière pensée *[an ulterior motive] at all from me and mine."*

NGÔ ĐÌNH DIỆM did not acknowledge receipt of my letter nor write me throughout his stay in France, except for the few business missives I received in connection left behind in my home. My contact with Mr. Ngô became irregular and *Socialism,* the review that his brother Nhu edited (the only tenuous connection to home) and sent over monthly for distribution to students arrived more rarely, dwindling to one or two copies before it stopped altogether.

The *Problême Indochinois* [Indochinese Problem], in spite of military setbacks, was dormant in responsible French circles in Paris while in Saigon, Nguyễn Văn Tâm had some time ago taken over from Trần Văn Hữu, the former Prime Minister for the State of Vietnam. Ngô Đình Diệm laid waiting, inactive, and not a name being discussed. In America, the subject of Vietnam was as uninteresting as soccer scores in Brazil. Except for rare radio talk shows that only the initiated or the extremely bored could tune to, or people who needed to while away thirty minutes, or those with a particular interest in Indochina or Vietnam, the war "over there" could have been waged by "aliens" on a distant planet. There was a lull that was pregnant with an approaching thunderstorm, precursor of the devastating tornado that even then was brewing and gathering strength for battle in a godforsaken valley named Điện Biên Phủ.

During this lull, on one of the radio talk shows broadcast sporadically by the New York commercial networks, came the voice of—of all men—Mr. Nguyễn Đức Thanh! It was about 7 p.m. when the low sky was overcharged with thunderclouds and a threatening downpour kept New Yorkers indoors. I was fumbling with my radio dial, searching for nothing in particular, perhaps a little music to pass the time. Amid the jumble of commercial ads however came an announcement that "an authority on Vietnam, Mr. Nguyễn Đức Thanh, was about to discuss his country with our host." I was electrified. Turning the radio to full-blast, I ran to the telephone, knocking two chairs over in my haste, and rang up my good friend Bùi Kiến Thành at Columbia University. Fortunately, he was in, and he also became excited. Hung up and immediately glued my ear to my radio 'listening post.' I was all tense and worked up waiting for commercials to end so the interview with 'Đức đồ," Mr. Ngô's pejorative for Đức Thanh' could begin.

Not a good speaker under any circumstance, Đức Thanh hemmed and hawed and the interview came over garbled with atrociously accented English. Unexpectedly, the host took on the role of critic (and a caustic one at that) when Đức Thanh insisted that Vietnam was independent and that France had granted freedom to its colony as proclaimed, all vociferous protests to the contrary notwithstanding! Yes, I had heard Đức Thanh speak before but not at such length, and not on the air, to boot! It was shocking to me and also to the show's host. He asked his guest: "Are you Vietnamese?" to which the unworthy reply from an unworthy Vietnamese came: "I happened to be born there." There was no need to elaborate. A Frenchman could not have defended the French colonialists in Vietnam any better.

"I happened to be born there!" if we needed any proof that Đức Thanh and his group had sold out to the colonizers, this was it. How much did he get for speaking on this program? Perhaps not much or perhaps not a dime. Maybe he spoke his true convictions but why bother figuring out his reasoning. I recall thinking this interview was one of Đức Thanh's tricks—not the first nor the last—but it was a trivial and utterly insignificant defense of colonialism. We might as well save our breath and leave him and his group to the dogs!

But we were young then and life had not yet armed us with a suitable dose of cynicism. We felt insulted, betrayed, and dishonored. We trembled and seated with indignation for what was said. Thành and I compared notes and my young friend and I even went to the university's news room to have them make a copy of this speech for us. We didn't keep the tape though, judging it too poor in both content and quality to keep. The engineer who helped make the tape for us commented: "He said he ***happened*** to be born in Vietnam, as if he didn't care to be Vietnamese at all." As a result of what the engineer said, Thành and I put our doubts to the ide but in a sudden surge of scruples, we wanted to be fair: Đức Thanh fully deserved our doubts and he and his whole bunch of associates had been fairly judged and found wanting.

Another trick of Đức Thanh, or "Tricky Đức," —the nickname he got that was similar to that given to the highest-caliber machinator, "Tricky Dick" Nixon—many years later, was Đức Thanh's Vietnam Foundation, of which he was President. The first of its kind, a forerunner of half a dozen associations all purporting to have the interest of Vietnam to heart, was founded in early 1950 or 1951 and was supposedly already a going concern when I first arrived in the United States. As another example of the old malady of fanfarons, Đức Thanh used to carry calling cards displaying two titles:

Vietnam Foundation, President

&

Import-Exports Company, Ltd.

Vietnam Department, Manager

This was like the business cards a boaster was rumored to give out:

Mr. X. Y. Nguyen

Shook hands three times

with H.M. the Emperor

And neither was Đức Thanh's grandiloquence a joke, although the foundation was not his, title notwithstanding. No doubt he had sold the idea to some New York movie magnates as a place he could find refuge as he was in trouble with the FBI and the magnates could use it for income tax dodging purposes.

Đức Thanh once invited me to accompany him to an event at one of these bigwig's home and I accepted, taking Marie with me to see for the first time inside the home of a Manhattan millionaire. It was at a penthouse on the upper east side that greatly impressed us with chandeliers and silver cutlery, stiff shirts and bow ties, and servers with small white aprons and bonnets. Sadly, the soiree was a failure as far as the Vietnam Foundation's aim was concerned: even with Đức Thanh on its payroll working the crowd for the organization, he did not impress guests enough to bring in new members.

He did his best to behave like a red-blooded American, outdoing even himself when he told Marie her native *áo dài* was "in poor taste" for the evening. Near the close of the party, Marie offered to sing *Khúc Nhạc Ngày Xuân* (A Spring Day Melody)[49] her favorite Vietnamese song, as thanks to her hosts, something she was accustomed to doing from a very young age at such gatherings. Our American host and guests did not have a chance to respond before Đức Thanh and his cohorts Hòa, Linh, *et al.*, burst out laughing derisively instead of thanking Marie for the song. Such were Tricky Đức's antics which were often like his wheeling and dealing—on a small mean scale, after all.

For all his non-stop endeavors, Đức Thanh got what he deserved: silent contempt from his protégés who deserted him even before the end, and a philosophy to console them all in lieu of the political honors and wealth that Đức Thanh had once inspired in them and himself. One

49 This song by Văn Xứng began with the lyrics: *"Ngày trôi theo tháng giá mùa đông/Vàng bay theo lá úa ngoài song..."* (Au.)

of his disciples, a fellow named Thu, had the nerve to say that he had come out the better compared to 'poor Ngô Đình Diệm.' Later, in 1968 I had a conversation with Thu, five years after President Diệm was assassinated, when Thu pointed to himself and said: "If only Ngô Đình Diệm were President of the Vietnamese School (the U.S. Army's Language School at Monterey, California), which I am, instead of President of the Republic of Vietnam, he would still be alive today!" A rare gem of the Đức Thanh school of philosophy!

AMONG THE VISITORS coming to New York from Saigon during the second half of 1953 were two South Vietnamese: Hồ Quang Phước and Lê Thành Nghệ, who did not know Ngô Đình Diệm was in France and had come to call on him at my home. The pair drove a brand-new Ford that Nghệ had bought right upon landing in New York and walked up to 535 West 111 Street after ostentatiously alighting from the shiny car. They had a sort of *pilgrimage manque ´* (failed pilgrimage) being disappointed to only view the room Mr. Ngô occupied while staying with me. The news they brought from home pointed to the likelihood that Ngô Đình Diệm would be the next "Man of the Hour.' They said that Nguyễn Văn Tâm was doing badly as Prime Minister, and the French were considering a successor—Ngô Đình Diệm might be next. At least, that was my visitors' pious hope.

Lê Thành Nghệ was then distributor of Lederle Pharmaceutical products in Saigon and on two occasions I helped him with some translations at the company's New York offices. Hồ Quang Phước was a jovial *bon viveur,* a devil-may-care fellow as far as protocol was concerned, and always had *un bon mot* (witticism) ready when the occasion warranted it. Used to colonial Saigon's carefree and careless behaviors, Phước was impatient with America's lack of public urinals and once in Washington, D.C., I saw him do his thing right against the rear of a parked car, talking loudly all the while!

18. CORNELL AND BUFFALO

SOMETIME IN THE FALL of 1953, Bùi Kiến Thành and I, using a bit of my annual vacation days, drove to Buffalo University in upstate New York to hear a talk that a committee of Vietnamese students were giving to students and faculty. It was a long drive from the city, almost to the border of Canada, but Thành's car had been repaired and made good again after our horrendous breakdown experience in the summer. We left home in the evening, immediately after work and drove the whole night without stopping, except for short rests and coffee breaks. The car ran smoothly, so we enjoyed the landscape at dusk as a lingering sunset lit up miles and miles of beautiful upstate New York countryside.

There were promontories of dark rocky boulders, piled atop each other, each fantastically balanced like giant domino blocks roughly hewn from surrounding hills that suddenly loomed from curves in the winding roads. Sometimes, negotiating a curvy elbow in the road, we could hear a hidden spring murmuring as it meandered down a precipice carpeted with thick autumn leaves. Then the moon, bashful and pale in her nascent course, raced just ahead through thickets of branches and vines, as if daring us to catch up with her trailing ermine gown. We did mind our battered Dodge's age and did not exceed the prescribed speed limits. However, an accident did occur after we got lost and took a wrong turn. We made the wrong decision and instead of searching for an exit to get back on the right path, we stopped on a stretch of deserted highway to reverse directions. We had hardly reached the wet and sloping shoulder of the road when the rear wheels got hopelessly stuck in muddy grass. Try as might, the wheels spun futilely and soon, despair took over followed by panic. I left Thành at the wheel and went to post myself in the road, praying for a car to appear, but also to make sure no oncoming car crashed into our disabled Dodge, whose nose thrust well into one-fourth of the asphalt roadway.

A solitary car came alright but it was a police car, its roof lights whirling dizzyingly, and screeched to a halt three inches from me in the middle of the road. With my best smile, I bent down to explain to the officer what had happened to our car, but he did not smile back and instead stretched out his hand as if to push me away. I didn't really need to say anything for he knew at a glance what the trouble was. I had barely finished speaking when he jumped out of his car and lit a flare to place on the road just in front of our Dodge. After radioing back to his station, he redirected traffic which, thankfully, was not too heavy or too thick. After ten minutes, a tow truck arrived and two surly men hooked Thành's car onto the winch and in no time, the Dodge was pulled out of the mud for the cost of ten dollars.

The unsmiling police officer did not acknowledge our thanks but neither did he give us a ticket or reprimand us, which we appreciated. We were relieved to be back on the road and merge into the now heavier traffic to continue our interrupted trip north. Thành and I arrived in Buffalo just before dawn at the home of Father Phan, a priest sent to the U.S. for studies while attached to a local church. Nguyễn Xuân Diên, the romantic who romanced a Korean wife until she left her husband and whom I first met at the newlywed Thông and Yến's home, had a room in Father Phan's rectory. He made me and Thành comfortable so we could rest before the early afternoon talk that we had come for. Exhausted, Thành and I slept through until lunchtime.

The Buffalo University auditorium had been set up with the panel behind a large table, but the room was so huge and the students and professors present were so few that the room had an air of desolation and vague discouragement. At least that was my impression as I sat behind two rows of sparsely occupied chairs. There was a priest acting as coordinator and the panel was composed of Huỳnh Sanh Thông and Miss Nguyễn Minh Đẩu from Cornell University in Ithaca, my dear friend Thành who drove me up from New York, and a few other students whose names I've forgotten. The talk was on Vietnam but unlike later years, America of the mid-1950s did not have much interest in the country which explained the meager audience that afternoon. The group, despite being faculty and people who were more knowledgeable, were not informed enough on Vietnam and the few outsiders present knew even less. These were mostly old people who had never heard of the country and the best they could understand was the panel's patient and oft-repeated explanation of how France colonized the country and made it part of French Indochina.

The panel's presentation was rather lukewarm in tone and uninspiring in content. Speakers have to speak to the level of their audience, or before as fired up as with enthusiasm or brimming with goodwill they may be, after a while, they are reduced to giving elementary exposés and using tired clichés. Thành, for one, tried to inject humor and metaphors in his speech and the audience laughed their appreciation when he said that Vietnam was like a wagon being pulled and pushed by a locomotive (French) on a single track: it went this way and back; the other way and back; seemingly in motion but perpetually remaining in the same spot. When it was Miss Đẩu's turn to speak, she gave the many American women in the audience a picture of life for Vietnamese woman and explained how they did not 'compete' with men but 'completed' them. That was a clever play on words she made that was also appreciated by the audience. The presentation ended rather forlornly, but we were treated to meals at the university, had nice sleeping quarters on campus, and had the next few days free to sightsee or do whatever we wanted.

I have a clear recollection of our first night in Buffalo when the priest in charge of our group asked me how I like my food prepared. In the spur of the moment and for no particular reason, I remembered how a Filipino fellow in my hometown, Cần Thơ, answered years ago when the French were absolute masters in Vietnam, and no one spoke English except foreigners. He was one in a trio playing for Kim Thoa, a then-famous troupe singing *Cải Lương*, a popular form of Chinese opera blending Vietnamese folk songs, classical music, and dramatic speeches.

After such performance, most theater goers go to nearby restaurants to enjoy *Hủ Tiếu* (rice noodle soup). The Filipino band happened to come to the same restaurant my friends and I were at, and I was delighted to attentively eavesdrop to see if I could catch the meaning of their words as a measuring rod for the English that Vietnamese children are taught by French teachers. I was no more than eighteen then but knew that what we learned in the *lycée* was anything but usable. One of the musicians asked his friend almost the same question the priest asked me—"How do you like your meal prepared?"—and his friend answered: "As you like," which I understood, to my great pleasure. More than two decades later, the two moments joined in the present and I used the same wording I heard long ago to respond: "As you like." He smiled and said, "You sound like you're from a Shakespearian group" and when I looked startled for a moment, the priest clarified: "From the play, "As You Like It." Years later when I started to read and enjoy Marcel Proust, I remembered this incident as particularly illustrating to me what Proust described so beautifully in his *Remembrance of Things Past*.

It was during Thành's and my stay in Buffalo that I almost was caught up by the immigration police at the Canadian border. Our trip was rather tedious, so this was a hilarious incident for us. It happened the day Diên took us to see Niagara Falls from the Canadian side. We walked from one end of the bridge unhindered to leave the U.S. and when we reached the other end we would be in Canada where naturally, Canadian customs stopped us. Diên had his passport on him, so he was okay, but I had a problem. I had my passport, but my visa to work at VOA had long ago expired and it was the same story as my passport. (Vietnamese passports were purposefully issued with very short validity and could only be renewed from abroad with express permission from Saigon).

The Canadian Immigration officer held me back while allowing Diên to enter. Of course, Diên wouldn't leave me alone so we both walked back to the U.S side. En route, he was so worried lest I could be jailed for 'illegally staying in the U.S." that I told him, only half in jest, that if worse came to worse, I could stay on the bridge, and he'd have to bring food twice a day. Actually, I was angry with Custom's inconsiderate procedures and would have tried to play such a trick on them by daring them to arrest me or leave me stranded on the bridge were it not for Dien's obvious panic. I didn't tell him what I planned to do, and he walked on in despair, not knowing himself what to suggest to me.

I had no reason to be worried myself, for my delay in renewing either my passport or my visa was not from my negligence. It was entirely the Vietnamese government's idiotic validity rules and the no less irritating process my family had to undergo, in person, at the U.S Immigration Service office to have my family's visas extended. The Vietnamese Embassy instituted that we all come in personally and it was one day's round trip drive from New York if we had a car and if we could take a day off. The Voice of America, mindful of their schedule, took charge of our passports and mailed them to the Embassy in Washington, requesting renewals for the purpose of working with the U.S. Government's Information Agency. VOA had been handling it this way for several years for their Vietnamese employees without any hindrance and only recently did Miss Nguyễn Thị Dung, daughter of Nguyễn Đệ who was Bảo Đại's Chef de Cabinet and new First Secretary of the Embassy, require that we appear in person. Miss Dung returned our passports without renewals and I, for one, did not care to travel to Washington, D.C., at great inconvenience and cost, to comply with her display of newly acquired power.

As for the Immigration Service in New York, it was no 'service' at all, but each time our visas expired, it was deliberate humiliation and an unnecessary waste of time for my family of six to personally travel to apply for extensions—as if we were here privately instead of being brought over by the U.S. government. For me, I was highly irritated each time to be made to sit for hours at the desk of some officer doing nothing useful or necessary for the extension of visas. It was illogical for the U.S. government to have one of its agencies needing us here while another agency treated us as unwanted aliens here on visitor visas that they were required to periodically renew. We filled in no forms, answered no questions, just sitting there watching the surly face of the officer who seemed to be searching in vain for an excuse to reject our extension. And finally, after hours of waiting, the visa was reluctantly extended. Indeed, these long hours in the Immigration Office in New York stuck in my mind as a reminder in future to be in the

United States on no visas other than immigrant—so we would never again be treated as "undesirable aliens."

On that occasion at Niagara Falls, my visa had expired long ago without my going through the distasteful ordeal of renewing it. We could afford that "illegal" stay in the U.S., if any visitor could, simply because we weren't visitors at all. To be fair to the Canadian Immigration cop for turning me back, neither could I blame his American cousin for turning me away from reentering the U.S. if it came to that. They did their duty despite my papers being flagrantly improper. What I resented was the whole stupid business from the two agencies of the same government working at cross purposes to each other compounded by the Embassy of the State of Bảo Đại's Vietnam, whose arrogant daughter of a 'corrupt' henchman high-handedly demanding we personally appear to kowtow before her! I didn't care if I were put in jail or condemned to stay on the "No Man's Land" section of the International Bridge, shuttling back and forth between Canada and the U.S.

However, as I approached the American side, I thought better of being difficult. I remembered my wife and four children in New York and shrugged my shoulders in resignation before the U.S. Customs area and reassured Nguyễn Xuân Diên all would be all right. He was as afraid for me as he was for himself, such was Vietnamese psychology after years of French colonial intimidation that we feared being accused of any invention they wished or to be jailed just by association. If you are in the company of a criminal, you are bound to be one yourself, is it not? And the French arrested you first, leaving fanciful justice or injustice of your case to be determined later, if at all. I showed Diên my VOA pass, a respectable plastic-covered USG Employee Pass with my name and photo on it, saying: "This surely will serve in lieu of my 'no good' passport. Diên jumped at the idea, almost jubilant with relief. And the good old U.S. Customs cop smiled and waved me in and obviously preferred my right to be in the U.S. of my government pass to Diên's alien passport and visa. As they say, "When in Rome…."

On our return to New York, Thành and I detoured to Ithaca to drop off Miss Nguyễn Minh-Đẩu and Huỳnh Sanh Thông. The latter introduced us to his apartment which he shared with two roommates, Marjorie Weiner and a male American student—both absent the night we arrived.[50] We didn't meet them, but we saw their handiwork—or rather non-work, for together with Thông's help, their apartment was in such a state of dirtiness that no words could adequately describe it. I have yet to see a filthier apartment, especially the sink and pile of unwashed dishes filling it and stinking like carrion. The floor seemed to be a three-inch-thick pile of dirt caked into a slimy, malodorous carpet. And the beds hovering just above the unsavory damp rug, were jungles of pillows and sheets and blankets. A battlefield right after a skirmish when remnants of bloody encounters were not removed could not look any more distasteful.

We were not surprised to hear about the unorthodox

50 Marjorie Weiner's MA thesis is still a valuable study of the first two years of the Ngô Đình Diệm government. See "Government and Politics in South Vietnam, 1954-1956," MA thesis (Ithaca: Cornell University, 1960).

living style of the residents of this apartment. Marjorie would most naturally and without inhibition stretch out one of the beds and sleep until noon in her flimsiest night outfit (just a panty, to be precise) with her door ajar while the guys stepped in and out and around the apartment without discomfort. I was not to see Marjorie until much later, a not unpretty girl, but untidy from head to toe. Her light blue eyes were unwashed, and it was a real pity to see them cloudy, as if veiled by a thin mist, and the corners crusted with tiny lumps of dirt. Just a few years later, we were to meet her in Saigon, transformed into a totally different ripe fruit, so tantalizing a girl that the fairy tale image of Cinderella metamorphosed flashed into my head. Rosy-cheeked and gracious in every gesture, her curly locks fell in undulating golden waves over her shoulder, Marjorie was the picture of Madame Récamier in her salon,[51] especially when she received visitors every Wednesday and Thursday afternoon in her tastefully furnished apartment on Bà Huyện Thanh Quan Street. The Marjorie of her Cornell days in Ithaca was so unappetizing a young lady to Thông and his male roommate that everyone could coexist unperturbed.

Yet, each undiscovered beauty has her charms seen only by the eyes of her own 'Prince Charming', while the world around them whirls by, very much like the fable of "The Sleeping Beauty in the Woods" (*La Belle au bois dormant*). In the tale I know, the unlucky prince cannot awaken the princess for a very long time and suffers a

51 Juliette Récamier (1777-1849), a French socialite in the early 19th century, was known for her great beauty and her salon in Paris that attracted members of cultural and political elites.

near total nervous breakdown as a consequence. Thus, it was something of a shock for me and Thành to learn that, a few months after dropping them Thông and Miss Đẩu off, that Marjorie's 'prince' was a fellow Cornellian, our big-appetite and ever so affable Nguyễn Chí Hiền. Nevertheless, love being a conception rather than a reality was a Proustian definition of *l'amour* that I discovered and liked more and more with each passing day, and Hiền was much better off coming out the loser than succeeding in downing the sparrow with his arrow and getting what he so desperately wanted.[52]

I took the liberty here and in some other places to merge or amalgamate the present and the future, not through any impatience or lack of recognized methodological storytelling, but by a compelling sense of continuity and never ending even long after death. So present-past-future is nothing but eternity in a capsule, ready and colorful for whoever has a knowing eye to contemplate it.

On our way back to New York, we rendered Thông a service by carrying his books to New York and storing them in my apartment for the rest of his stay at Cornell University. We piled his books—and there were a great many of them as Thông was a bookworm—in the trunk of the Dodge and the back bench, overflowing on the car

---

52 In ancient Vietnam, the Emperor chose a husband for his beloved daughter by holding a sharp-shooting competition. On the appointed day, all pretenders received a royal arrow and bow from which in turn would try to bring down a sparrow released overhead. The successful candidate who hit the bird on the first try would be crowned as Royal Consort and his and the Princess' wedding, which would be the occasion for national celebration, especially for the Emperor's only child. (Au.)

floor as well. We came home by a longer, harder route than the regular turnpike where the traffic was always dense and there was no landscape to enjoy. We arrived at night the following day and toiled upstairs with load after heavy load of Thông's books. He would not take them away until over one year later, when the Voice of America had completely moved offices to Washington, D.C., and we with them.

19. AMERICANISMS

For the rest of the year 1953, Uncle Thành and my family grew more attached to each other than ever, especially in view of us leaving New York for good. We thought the transfer would come pretty soon, but as it happened, the Vietnamese Unit was among the last to go and I was in the last of the unit to leave the city.

During Christmas vacation that year, old and new friends came from out-of-state campuses to spend the holidays with us. Dư Phước Long came and so did Khương Hữu Điểu, a new friend studying engineering at M.I.T. in Cambridge, Massachusetts. Điểu was from Mỹ Tho, the delta province where I was born, and his father, Khương Hữu Lân owned a goldsmith's shop and a general goods store. I came to know his father when as a little boy, I accompanied my grandfather to town to order goods for our shop in a rural market district one kilometer from Mỹ Tho called Gò Cát. Điểu was too young to know me back then but when we discovered in New York that we were from the same Mỹ Tho province and that I visited his father's shops and storehouses, be became fast friends.

It was snowing hard on Christmas Eve as we trundled

down the subway to Rockefeller Center, bundled up in heavy coats and mufflers to see the unparalleled sight of the huge beautifully decorated Christmas tree, the ice-skating rink, the Promenade Anglaise, cafes, and illuminated alleys along the French bookstore. We admired the decorations along Fifth Avenue, the marquee lights of Radio City Music Hall, and St. Patrick's Cathedral, taking in all the marvels of New York and the richness of America. Long and Điểu were taking all this in for the first time and their admiring eyes reflected my own enjoyment at seeing it all myself in past years.

There was no *Réveillon* or flowing wine for us and although roast turkey was the main Christmas dish par excellence in America and most of the occidental world, we had only ordinary chicken on our morning-after table. For one thing, chicken cost less; for another, it always seemed to me that Alphonse Daudet's unforgettable *Les Trois Messes Basses* (The Three Low Masses) required a rustic setting of a village church, country folks, and a padre famished all year round being tempted by the thought of a golden brown roast turkey so he rushes through his Latin prayers—*Dominus vob—cum, et cum ---tu---o*—to get his masses over with. We missed all this in New York, and I missed my own Christmases of younger years, transposed, it was true, from the West but magically metamorphosed into Vietnamese pageantry and fitting snugly into our social life, Christian or not. Our Christmas eves were always big affairs with curried chicken and French bread along with assorted traditional Vietnamese tidbits, an indescribable delectation, especially after the six-hour fast prescribed by the Catholic Church until after Midnight Mass. My father, a talented amateur of traditional, music sometimes gathered his musician friends to reward us with a concert of classical music that lasted well after Réveillon and until the dawn of Christmas Day.

For my children, Christmas was a Western event for them for they had no other experience to compare it with. Except for Marie, the children had missed all the great celebrations in Vietnam like Tết and the Autumn Festival. But my wife and I didn't worry about that because we thought one day soon, we would be back home and the two, three, or even four years in the United States would be a pleasant and valuable experience for our whole family. How often in the past did I as a young husband (I married at just age twenty) and father of little children wish I could spend just one or two years abroad: be out of my country, visit far away places, preferably in Europe where I could acquire a higher degree of learning. Even just having been abroad would help me move to higher positions at any job I could get than never having been anywhere but in Indochina. Such was the situation in colonies that foreigners always got better jobs and treatment than natives. And natives who had been abroad were relatively better off than their compatriots who had never left the motherland. Not only did we suffer a lower—nay, a subaltern and out-and-out position of servitude vis-à-vis the French master race—we had to accept as superiors any non-Vietnamese subjects the French brought into their colonial Administration or commercial enterprises in our own country. They called us the 'Annamese' and the 'pacified Southerners' until 1945 and although the French conceded to our choosing "Vietnam" as our country's name—which was in fact older than France itself—nothing had changed with the departure of their armed forces and administrators.

Had I been a revolutionary, I would have joined the long list of our predecessors who gladly gave their lives for their fatherland and whose battle cry was simply, "Vietnam!" However, as just the bread-earner for my family, and realizing that nothing would change in the foreseeable future, all I hoped for at the time was a better life for them when I came home. Indeed, I tried to improve my education by enrolling at Fordham University when in New York, but the tuition and fees were too high to afford. My wife went to evening classic at the public high school but my only means to learn was through self-education. Self-taught men such as Phạm Quỳnh,[53] Nguyễn Phan Long,[54] and Trần Phạm Hộ, my wife's brother-in-law, served as good examples for me to emulate. My aim always remained to have a better life for my family once we returned to Vietnam after working for the Voice of America.

And now that Ngô Đình Diệm was in France, all hopes of his accession to power and a new life with justice, freedom and dignity for Vietnam dissipated into just hopeful dreams. I devoted myself anew to my family. All

---

53 Phạm Quỳnh (1892-1945), a cultural activist, writer, journalist, founding editor-in-chief of *Nam Phong* journal, and a Minister in the royal court at Huế.

54 Nguyễn Phan Long (1888-1960), a journalist, founder of *L'Écho Annamite*, deputy leader of the Constitutionalist Party, and Prime Minister in the State of Vietnam under Bảo Đại from January to April 1950.

the regular help my wife and I gave to the Vietnamese students who came to us in New York by Mr. Ngô continued but gone was the effervescence of militant nationalism and its unsettling consequences for my family. Nguyễn Đức Thanh and his clique were also quiescent, the old feud dormant, if only because the essential protagonist, Ngô Đình Diệm, was out of sight and there was little likelihood he would reappear on the scene as a hopeful leader or otherwise.

Thus, the year 1953 passed and the only news topic was McCarthyism and its most virulent development. One day, Dr. Melzer, our neighbor who long ago treated Mr. Ngô's backache, asked us to let Marie in on one of his client's children's groups for a performance of some kind. I was thinking of McCarthysim and declined, lest any complications resulted due to my position with the VOA, a federal government agency. Dr. Melzer took my response with chagrin, exclaiming: "I forgot the times we are living in now!"

My wife and I watched little Muriel grow up healthy and strong and because we expected to soon leave New York for Washington, D.C, Marie and mom took turns to sightsee or go to the movies as they had been too busy before catering to students and guests to even see the city for themselves. After school almost every weekday, mom went to her favorite neighborhood theater, the Nemo. She never watched so many movies in her life—and good ones too, like *Gone with the Wind,* which she saw three times! When mom was at the movies or food shopping, Marie watched her younger brother and sisters, cooked, washed, and did other household chores . Already in seventh grade, Marie would be thirteen in February but despite two years in America, her English was not yet good enough for her classes and she had to make extra efforts to keep up in her courses. Marie's father, despite being a translator, did not master his own English either, and often felt especially lost with American idioms and slang, which sometimes led to misunderstandings.

The Voice of America was then broadcasting a program of daily English lessons for the benefit of our listeners in Vietnam. As the best translator in the Vietnamese Unit, I was designated translator for a series of scripts written by some East European who may have been a linguist but not a good one for English. He recorded lessons that included many idioms and slang—a bad choice for beginners—which I translated to broadcast to Saigon. Typical American expressions such as, "It's raining cats and dogs," readily found their equivalent in Vietnamese, which colloquially was "*Trời mưa như cầm bình mà đổ*" [It's raining like water pouring out of a jar].

But idiomatic phrases like, "What do you know!' were difficult to match with their Vietnamese counterparts. Also foreign to Vietnamese listener-learners were references to well-known Americans who were unheard of in their country. For instance, Mrs. Pruett, who voiced female speakers for the broadcasts, when the script had someone ask her to sing, she retorted: "I'm no Dinah Shore!" For propaganda purposes it was perhaps right to introduce American singers to Vietnamese, but a bit far-fetched for the sake of teaching English. Both Mr. and Mrs. Pruett agreed with me, being Vietnamese-firsters themselves. Mr. Pruett also served as a male speaker in the lessons and his explanation—in Vietnamese—of each English sentence was excellent indeed from many years as a missionary in Vietnam. I was the M.C. or Master of the Class, who introduced the Pruetts as the English speakers, and according to the scripts, would joke or otherwise make the lessons enjoyable for listeners. The lessons fittingly enough began with the musical theme of the popular film, *The King and I*. As the music faded out, I gave my signature line in Vietnamese: "This is Bùi Công Văn speaking …"

These English lessons were very popular in Vietnam, no doubt because people were eager to learn English, but also because the Voice knew that it was not helpful to include other things besides straight propaganda, music, for example, or English lessons. We translator-announcers of the VOA used to consider ourselves 'mercenaries' although we didn't write that down in the "Opinions & Comments" section of a form the office told us to fill out. Hoà was quite envious that I was allowed to announce my name when introducing the VOA English lessons program and complained—to no avail—to Mr. Pruett that it was improper for an announcer to say his name on air. Indeed, we knew it was dangerous to attach our names to the political commentaries we all took part in reading for the broadcasts as most of the anti-communist commentaries were insulting to the Việt Minh and resistance in Vietnam. But the English lessons did not carry such propaganda.

Returning to my unfamiliarity with Americanisms and slang, one evening, Marie and I were in a grocery store near home on Broadway and after we had paid, I asked the cashier: "Could I have the slip to bring home to her mother?" I meant the 'slip" of paper, the receipt. The cashier maliciously rejoined: "What's her size? "I remember how Jewish shopkeepers in New York were not particularly nice to customers as a rule but were meaner to foreigners. Besides treating us as 'hungry Koreans,' they gave us bad-quality produce, overcharged us, and laughed behind our backs. One day in anger at my treatment, I walked away ignoring the few pennies of change for a slice of watermelon I knew the seller overcharged me. He called loudly after me: "Well, it's your money. Take it or leave it as you like." Another day in the subway, I greeted a white-collared clergyman with, "Good day, Father." He curled his lip and pointed to his wife sitting next to him: "And here's your 'Mother'!" Served me right for greeting a Protestant minister as a Roman Catholic priest. Good manners were not a prominent quality of New Yorkers, clergymen included. Bùi Văn Thinh related once how on the subway he'd given his seat to a lady standing near him but instead of thanking him, she almost shrieked: "Do you think I'm a disabled person or an invalid?!" There was no 'Women's Lib" movement here yet but what was *de rigueur* [obligatory] in the Paris Métro, for example, lost its charm on this side of the Atlantic. After being shamed many times for his courtesy, Thinh gave up his 'bad habit' but not before giving New Yorkers some elementary lessons in politeness: After giving his seat to a woman or older person who took it as a matter of course and no word of appreciation, Thinh bent slightly and shouted as if he was deaf: "WHAT DID YOU SAY? I CAN'T HEAR YOU."

The person would shout back, "Nothing, I didn't say a thing." "OH," Thinh stressed, I THOUGHT YOU SAID, 'THANK YOU'!" All around the little scene the crowd of tired and indifferent passengers pretended to be lost in their own world, but Thinh hoped the lesson in courtesy sunk into a few minds. Uncle Thinh, a man so nice that he was always badgered and taken advantage of by the likes of Nguyễn Đình Hoà, the well-learned but uneducated Ph.D. candidate, calmly concluded his tale: "However, New York is not America, believe me." I came to learn that indeed, it was not.

20. GRANT US FREEDOM AND JOY!

MY FAMILY AND I looked forward to leaving modern-day Babylon for Washington, D.C., capital of the U.S.A., where we hoped to see and enjoy the real America. Dominic was in school now, still a skinny boy with a long neck and the incorrigible habit of making Marie late for school, as usual. Mom was still catching her films at the Nemo theater and relaxing for a change after two and a half years away from home and overwork. Everyone in Vietnam had the support of family and even the poorest in Vietnam could find household help while in America, mom had only Marie. We thought we'd be in Washington by the New Year but the move didn't happen until late in 1954.

Tết 1954 was not celebrated at all, for soon after January, the news for the French in Vietnam was unfavorable and continued so for weeks and months to come. Military setbacks kept coming until they were crowned in late spring by the Battle of Điện Biên Phủ. For months on end, our daily VOA broadcasts almost exclusively reported events at Điện Biên Phủ. We became so familiar with the names of French defenders and personae, heroic or not and important or not, that repeating them day after day made our reporting almost clichéd. One nurse, Lt. Geneviève de Galard, 29, was singled out to be glorified day in and day out as the "Angel of Điện Biên Phủ." We announcers wound up hating her instead. If American policy was to support the French, we thought it could not do worse than this. Moreover, in the heat of the great battle where the fate of Vietnam was decided—the French made it so—what Vietnamese person, even a French stooge, could rejoice at a French victory?

The independence of Vietnam had such strong appeal to even the worst of her sons that when the hour of decision arrived, no Vietnamese person could remain indifferent, let alone wish that the fatherland would remain in its status quo as a foreign territory, any new name notwithstanding.

And finally, what had to come about arrived: France lost at Điện Biên Phủ!

The sensational end of the siege and the imminent end of an era of colonialism flashed around the world. VOA newscasts and commentaries, however, were inapt and almost disabled insofar as information and propaganda—or even misinformation—was concerned. For example, we gave out no news of the captured French survivors or the humiliation of the French armed might. What the whole world knew, VOA tried to keep from its Vietnamese listeners. The Republican Party then toed the French line and feared for their abandoning of the war. The U.S. government was afraid to offend France and so tried to play down the effects of the Great Defeat, perhaps more so than the French themselves. The VOA ignored the feverish maneuvers in Geneva, and we in America were none the wiser than our compatriots at home as far as the real news was concerned. Naturally, top secret plans such as Operation Vulture to rescue besieged French forces at Điện Biên Phủ that Eisenhower canceled at the last minute were no topics for commentary or news reporting. Because we lacked hard news, open secrets though they were for the rest of the world, we missed the sense of experiencing a historic moment when occurred and a fateful decision was made for our very future. And the future of the U.S. as well.

It did not mean that those were ordinary days in our VOA offices, however. A definite sense of urgency filled the air. Big shots we never met before busily came and went and the Vietnam Unit overnight became VOA's most important unit. Bosses of our Boss came over for prolonged subdued-voice discussions and when he exited his glass partition, he often wore an expression of deep concern.

It was in this atmosphere that Nguyễn Đình Hoà put on a show at VOA. Always a first-class actor, albeit unconscious of his talent, Hoà pretended enthusiasm for the Victory of Vietnam which caused no little amazement to the Big Shots—and later, his dismissal from the Voice. Hoà jumped up and down and shouted hurrahs for the victory at Điện Biên Phủ! Unrestrained in his sincere great joy at the defeat of the French, he displayed a rather puerile emotional outburst sprinkled with vulgarisms and plenty of foolishness—about himself. "So much the worse for the French!" he said. Perhaps Hoà overdid it in unconscious compensation for his hitherto pro-French attitude, or at least his lukewarm interest in real independence for

Vietnam. After all, he knew as well as anyone of us that the Embassy of the State of Bảo Đại's Vietnam in Washington, D.C. danced at the beck and call of the government of France. He only recently attended its Tết festival complete with the Fatherland's altar, national costume with turban and all. One of the American Big Wigs was shocked at Hoà's noisy celebration and whispered to me: "Why is Hoà showing such joy at the French defeat? Is he for the Việt Minh then?" My reply to such oversimplification could only state the obvious: "Certainly not," I said. "Any Vietnamese would be joyful at the prospect of his country's independence from the French."

My explanation did not satisfy the Big Wig, a Mr. Angus, if I remember correctly, nor did it please Mr. Hudson, a Lesser Boss. Less than a year later, Hòa was thanked for his services at a time that he badly needed the job. Sarah Newman told me that no matter how many times Hoà begged to be reinstated, his pleas were in vain. After a while, somehow, he was reintegrated to full-time employment and carried on at VOA, more wisely this time, until he received a Ph.D. in education and returned to Vietnam. He did so, however, only after trying unsuccessfully to become First Secretary of the Embassy of the Republic of Vietnam under Ambassador Trần Văn Chương of Ngô Đình Diệm's government.

From this period on until we left New York late in November 1954, events occurred so precipitously and dramatically that once again, they submerged our private lives. The Đức Thanh feud of old was as good as nonexistent as the wind had changed direction and with it, the flag and its holders. Not only did the old Đức Thanh company become indifferent, but an attempt at reconciliation, if not outright re-fraternizing with the 'turncoats', by chance ended with the opposite outcome with the supporters of Ngô Đình Diệm. I was going to have new enemies drawn from the ranks of my former comrades-in-arms. All this due to the unexpected accession to power of Ngô Đình Diệm in June 1954.

WITH THE FRENCH defeat at Điện Biên Phủ in May 1954, the Geneva Conference was convened. It was moving along hectically, if futilely, with John Foster Dulles playing his "Now you see me, now you don't" game when news of Ngô Đình Diệm being designated Premier by Emperor Bảo Đại came as a welcome surprise. Who pulled Bảo Đại's strings to put Diệm in power? We, his supporters and devoted followers, did not know and cared even less. We were sure that once in power, Diệm would at last put into practice everything he stood for all his life for the real independence of Vietnam. If anyone of our times could claim to be the leader to end the French game of perpetual domination, Ngô Đình Diệm indisputably was the man. How ever he came to power was immaterial to us, for he could force the hands of the powers concerned to let him carry out his life-long struggle for the independence of Vietnam to its successful conclusion. The hour was late, and if the powers concerned frustrated Diệm once more and forced him into oblivion, they had no one else to turn to except Hồ Chí Minh.

We anxiously followed news of developments that hot summer in New York when it was reported that

Ngô Đình Diệm obtained full power from Bảo Đại and returned to Vietnam. When news of developments came, it was not from Saigon but from Geneva where Mendès-France almost monopolized the conference first with his innocuous 'milk drinking' and then, as the hot days wore on, with his dramatic threat to resign as Premier of France if what was worked out was not signed by his mid-July deadline. The Geneva Agreements were signed.

We were in a state of perpetual anxiety, excitement, and bewilderment all rolled together as we knew nothing about developments at home. Then one night, I received a telegram from Dr. Bùi Kiến Tín, father of our family's good friend, Thành, who was studying at Columbia. Tín had been named Minister of Information in the newly-formed cabinet of Ngô Đình Diệm and asked the Vietnamese in New York and throughout the United States to stage an immediate and sensational protest against the partition of Vietnam as determined by the Geneva Accords.

It happened that my family and I were for once all alone that night in New York. We worried about the telegram: What shall we do? Who should we call first? Even the good doctor's son (Bùi Kiến Thành) was traveling somewhere outside the city. I placed a long-distance call to Father Jacques who responded in his usual nervous manner. He angrily said: "But this is no longer a student's show! We have a government which has ample means at its disposition. There is nothing we poor students could or should do!"

Undaunted, I asked the operator toward 2 a.m. to search for Thành at any telephone number I could think of. The operator was very kind indeed and sweetly spent long moments looking for him, finally locating him in Ithaca, New York. We didn't suspect at all that our young friend had been struck by Cupid's dart and the lovesick fellow had secretly gone to where his happiness lay: none other than the beautiful Miss Nguyễn Minh Đẩu had captured his heart, she who shared his causes, whom he met at the presentation in Buffalo—and we didn't suspect a thing! Happily, our 'lost' uncle was found and our MONUMENT 3-9499 telephone had never been so precious an instrument, not could any telephone operator have been nicer than the damsel who helped track down our 'lost uncle.'

Thành flew back to New York accompanied by Đẩu and all the fellows she could collect from Ithaca. More telephone calls were made so that many friends flocked to our apartment at 111th Street: Đỗ Vạn Lý, Đỗ Trọng Chu, Trần Long, and Nguyễn Văn Mừng came from up from Washington, D.C., bringing with them Huỳnh Văn Lang, a new comrade from Canada, who was visiting the U.S. for the first time. The days following were extremely busy as each of us tried his best to organize the demonstration. Lang painted slogans on homemade placards bought with our own meager money. We had no government funds! The Trần Văn Khá embassy in Washington, despite its new director in Saigon, did not even lift a little finger to help us. The very fact that Dr. Tín cabled us instead of the Embassy said enough about the measure of Khá's recalcitrancy that he brought it along from past to present. Father Jacques once more refused us any monetary help, rightly saying that his entire bank account could not advance us one cent. Of course, we kept the Đức Thanh group a 100-mile distance from our activities; we would not entertain even their moral support and definitely would not touch their money.

So, by improvised means and plenty of enthusiasm, we mobilized everyone we could outside of the Đức Thanh group. I asked all my neutral coworkers at the Voice of America, but none came from fear of McCarthy or the ghost of his dying campaign. Mr. Pruett, consistent with his disapproval of Ngô Đình Diệm, who he and everyone else except our camp judged would last no more than a few weeks, strongly advised me not to risk my job or stay in the U.S. by undertaking such a futile and unadvisable task. The beginnings of Ngô Đình Diệm were so unpromising that even if we had resorted to asking for help from Đức Thanh's group, they would have avoided us or turned us down. Prudence and savoir-faire have always been their forte. As Mr. Pruett pointed out, the risks were real enough and in these early hours of the fledgling Diệm government, no one could take the dangerous step of venturing an offense against not only the French but the Americans, too. No one, that is, except us who happily engaged ourselves in the task requested of us.

It also happened that a former colleague at USIS-Saigon named Nguyễn Kim Đính was on a tour of the United States and he chose to stay at my home as did Từ Ngọc Bích and Đinh Lê Ngoạn who similarly toured the U.S. in 1951. Although fresh from Saigon, Dinh was even more frightened of repercussions than my VOA co-workers. Not only did he disapprove of the protest we were organizing, but he was also prepared to leave my place the moment our demonstration ran into trouble. Like the others who bowed out, Đính thought the game was not worth the candle, that is, the reward didn't seem worth our efforts.[55] In the name of a vague 'friendship' because we once worked in the same office, Dinh invited himself in as my houseguest. Without the least scruple, he ate and drank and slept without repayment (while receiving per Diệm from USIS)—yet he made ready to jump ship if it threatened to sink—the rat! Years later, when he learned I was made Consul General in Hong Kong, all he could say was, "My goodness! Văn got rewarded that much just for going to a miserable demonstration!"

Huỳnh Văn Lang and the rest of our group remained with my family but Đỗ Vạn Lý, who already felt that his hour had arrived, went in with us in a big way. As he was perhaps the only fellow among us with a substantial wallet, he rented a hotel suite to serve as his headquarters for the duration of "the show." He registered at the hotel as "Dr. Đỗ Vạn Lý, Washington, D.C." And from then on, at least with anyone but our group, he presented himself as "Dr." and owner of a doctorate, no less.

While preparations were proceeding, except for Đỗ Vạn Lý, we worked and lived in my apartment. Lý did not deign to participate in such trivialities as painting or lettering placards and banners or mapping out roads to take for our coming march. He assumed the role of a

55 "Le jeu ne vaut pas la chandelle" translates to "the game is not worth the candle." A sentence used by French essayist **Michel de Montaigne** in 1580 alluding to gambling by candlelight: the cost for candles aren't worth potential winnings. (Au.)

statesman to be too concerned with 'important' matters to perform menial work. He would be the group's 'spokesman,' if not is leader. So, he shut himself away in his suite at a showy hotel on the East Side in front of the United Nations headquarters where the demonstration would take place.

I do not exactly recall why we set the demonstration for late afternoon into early evening instead of earlier in the day. Every one of us, except Đỗ Vạn Lý was present in the small park facing the U.N. My wife, children and even my smallest infant were there to support us. I could not take the day off from work, but in the evening when I arrived to join my family, I was so deeply touched that tears welled in my eyes to see my wife carrying a poster while my two little daughters had signs taped to their backs reading: PLEASE KEEP OUR COUNTRY WHOLE!" and "MY VIETNAM: UNDIVIDED AND INDEPENDENT!" Dominic carried a little sign with words painted in red, yellow, and green:

Though just a little boy
It's Vietnam I love.
It's my country, not a toy
Prayer to God above:
Grant us freedom and joy!"

He was the cutest little sign carrier I ever saw, and many passersby or curious onlookers stopped to take a picture of Dominic with his mini-protest sign.

The demonstration we put on was more in name than fact. No media came to take photographs to record the event or for us to send home to the Ministry of Information. Attendance was poor and as there were just a small number of us in the group, and the hour was late—all our efforts ended up in no big affair. Three or four banners, dexterously painted and lettered by the artistic hand of Huỳnh Văn Lang read:

DO NOT MAKE ANOTHER MUNICH

OF VIETNAM!

and

STOP THE COLONIALISTS FROM

CUTTING UP AND SELLING

OUT OUR MOTHERLAND

AFTER THEIR

INGLORIOUS

DEFEAT!

The 'show,' was a flop! Protests in America, and especially before the U.N. which had nothing to do with the Geneva Conference and ensuing partition of Vietnam, were not the huge anti-Vietnam protests they would become twenty years later. Perhaps we realized too well the weakness of our efforts and their utter futility. Maybe we didn't ourselves believe much in the appropriateness of the manifestation. Miss Bài and her mother came by to show their pity for our little children, probably silently thinking: "Politics!—that's where politics leads you, poor kids!" However, our group was enthusiastic, and we flocked into Đỗ Vạn Lý's hotel suite to rest our feet and watch his performance, for his turn had apparently come. Lý had typed up a press release while we were demonstration that read:

> (. . .) the statement said . . .
>
> (. . .) the Spokesman declared . . .
>
> Signed: Dr. Đỗ Vạn Lý

Lý called himself "Dr." for the first time and signed as our Spokesman so the "statement" belonged to him alone. Unfortunately for him, no press conference took place as not a single reporter showed up to Dr. Đỗ Vạn Lý's suite. These were expensive rooms, at least by our low-wage standards, and beautifully furnished. "Dr." Lý was smartly dressed and his politician's smile, no doubt practiced all afternoon before a mirror, could not have been more alluring. But the whole thing was a big FLOP! And Lý got depressed. The atmosphere in the suite was forlorn because Lý was depressed and more because we were all dead tired. The incongruous detail I vividly remember about that evening was a glimpse of and exhausted Miss Nguyễn Minh Đẩu napping in an adjoining room, the satin trousers that go with the Vietnamese *áo dài* outfit hanging neatly over the brass headboard so it wouldn't crease. This was not one of the rooms for public viewing or making speeches, so it was less expensively furnished than the main salon fancy enough for the esteemed "Dr." Lý. Outside in the corridor, my family stood patiently waiting for my USIS-Saigon comrades to travel home together with us. That night, part of the group decided to stay at the hotel while Huỳnh Văn

Lang joined us at our apartment. The following morning, out of town demonstrators all returned to their campuses and Lang spent a few more days with us in New York to resume his first visit to Manhattan that was so rudely interrupted by the hectic days following the telegram request from Saigon's Ministry of Information.

I cannot help but relive these days with mingled feelings of sadness and joy. Joy for our youth and utter devotion to country and for Ngô Đình Diệm and our friends. Sadness for our recognizing the too-obvious lack of reciprocity on the part of almost all of our so-called comrades—save for a single loyal and loving friend, Bùi Kiến Thành. Only two years later, when I and my family stopped in Vietnam on our way to Hong Kong to take up my diplomatic post as Consul for the Republic of Vietnam, I was shocked and extremely indignant to find a "new" and arrogant Huỳnh Văn Lang had been named Director General of the Office of Exchanges in Saigon.

He did not lift even a finger to help me get my money transferred, but instead directed me to see his secretary about my business. Incidentally, she was his wife and the same girl who Nguyễn Tư Bân grabbed and kissed in Times Square in 1952 after declaring that in America on New Year's Eve, men were free to kiss any woman they wanted at the stroke of midnight. The secretary returned to the office from some errand, undulating in her billowing silk *áo dài,* fingernails and a bright red and hair perfectly coiffed. I never did understand why, without even looking at me or asking why I was waiting for her, madame pointed her needle-sharp fingernail at the door and very unfemininely shouted at me: "Get out!"

However, my greater sadness came from the Boss, the Director General, who happily ate and slept without charge at my home in New York. If Mr. Huỳnh Văn Lang forgot many things, I did not. Even discussions we had those summer nights in 1954 are still fresh in my mind since for me, moments that I kept close to my heart never moved. Throughout my life, I was conscious that events condensed into one single mass, a kind of private movie reel of memories that I could replay without the least effort or incorporate new moments into a great universal eternity of never-ending days.

Uninvited houseguests, unwilling comrades, and even secret political opponents within our group were finally gone! We were left alone now with only our loyal friend, "Uncle" Bùi Kiến Thành. The Geneva Agreements gave refugees from North Vietnam a respite of 100 days to escape before the "curtain" fell on this hapless country of ours. This timetable fit snugly into our remaining days in New York when the Voice of America would also 'evacuate' the Vietnamese Unit to Washington, D.C. by late October 1954.

As the news from home was erratic, we did not have much to do or even worry about except a vague anxiety over ominous days ahead for Ngô Đình Diệm and for Vietnam as a whole. Like a prelude for the "TV war of the late sixties," all major television networks had reportage of events in Vietnam, especially fighting in Hanoi and the provinces, of the last days of the French, and the first days of the Việt Minh in power. My family now had a black and white TV set (we later gave it to Thông and Yến on our departure from America) and we carefully watched every evening news show at 8 p.m. One night, a ludicrously contrived news "report" was shown—to this day we don't know who was responsible for it: the Việt Minh who easily fooled U.S. reporters; or the journalists themselves who then and later during the bloody Buddhist demonstrations in Saigon in the early sixties, readily paid for faked shows to get *métrage* [footage].

What was aired that night was an unbelievable scene, sharply focused and with clear audio, of a CBS reporter interviewing a North Vietnamese peasant in his thatched hut while looking sinister in the background was obviously a Việt Minh cadre member. The exchange went like this:

Reporter: "Tell me, what is your impression of the new government's takeover?"

Peasant: "I would not know, I'm just a poor peasant..."

Reporter: "But please, you must feel something—"

Cadreman speaks to peasant in Vietnamese: "Don't be afraid, just do as I say..."

Peasant: "Yes, sir."

Cadreman in Vietnamese: "Start counting from one up—*Mau lên!* [Quick!]"

The camera was still recording while peasant and cadreman spoke, showing details of expressions and clearly capturing the conversation. The reporter was quiet at this time.

Cadreman speaks to the reporter in English: "Okay, I've convinced him to tell you his impressions now…"

Peasant: (slowly counting—anyone could see he wasn't giving an opinion): "Một, hai, ba, bốn, năm… [One, two, three, four, five]"

Cadreman: "He says he is extremely happy with the new government…"

Peasant: "Tám, chín, mười, mười một, mười hai… [Eight, nine, ten, eleven, twelve]"

Cadreman: "He is thankful to Hồ Chí Minh for…"

The put-up interview ended when the peasant had counted up to twenty. The reporter warmly thanked him and the cadreman then signed off: "This is X for CBS News somewhere near Hanoi. Good night."

The next day when I told Mr. Pruett about the report, he lamented the ignorance of American reporters, not so much about Vietnam and its situation, but on having no knowledge about the language on the part of Americans in general and reporters in particular. He immediately called CBS to complain, but no one seemed to be aware nor care they had been made to look foolish.

Like Mr. Pruett, I thought it was the cadreman who put the reporter on, and although it was shameful and irritating, it was also funny. In hindsight, however, I was inclined to call it a paid affair by the three in Vietnam so that the American public was the real gullible party in the matter. First, it was very rare in 1954 that a Việt Minh cadreman assigned to a rural location would be fluent in

English; second, the peasant may have been a fool and frightened of the cadreman, but his sharp sense of the ridiculous would not let him be easily cowed into making a public laughingstock of himself. To say that a peasant reciting numbers—in any language—was giving a political speech of sorts was more than unbelievable—it was sheer contempt. Or, it could have been quite a different matter if the peasant knew this interview was all make-believe and he was being paid for his acting skills.

Gullible or not, even ignorant or not, it was clear that American propaganda on a top network news show had been amateur work while directed by "backward" Việt Minh communists. It seemed to me a forerunner of sorts of the oncoming American war in Vietnam: generals and politicians based their efforts not on historical or political knowledge of the country but on preconceived western ideas and prejudices, ignoring glaring facts that even a cursory study of Vietnam's history would have exposed. In any event, the fake interview caused no waves and was soon forgotten.

The Ngô Đình Diệm government, struggling doggedly if seemingly hopelessly, for its survival was yet a problem in the making. With John Foster Dulles abandoning his "Massive Retaliation" threat and President Eisenhower one day playing up the Domino Theory then downplaying it the very next day,[56] plans had been made that if worse

56 °°°At a press conference President Eisenhower declared Vietnam as absolutely indispensable for the defense of Southeast Asia, it being the highest point of the 'Domino Theory.' However, in answering a reporter's question at a news conference a few days later, Eisenhower contradicted his previous statement. In effect, he said that Indochina

came to worst and the French abandoned an amputated but "saved" South Vietnam, the country would be taken over by the U.S. so that the partition of Vietnam would prove to be a blessing in disguise. This would not happen as we knew, because even if the French were not tenacious enough, as long as Diệm was in power, he would not let the U.S.—or any other power—take over. But all this was hidden from us so, blessedly ignorant, we went about our daily lives until at last in autumn 1954, we were to leave New York for America's capital city.

---

and Vietnam were not so important after all. Southeast Asia could be defended without Indochina securely in the Free World. (Au.)

21. LEAVING NEW YORK

PART OF OUR Voice of America unit had been transferred piecemeal long before it was our turn to leave New York. Even Mr. Pruett left before we did. As the day approached, we had to deal with trying to find a "taker" for our apartment who would agree to give us key money, a bonus equal to the $120 rent that we had to pay the rental agent when we moved in (a kind of extra fee to secure the lease or security). My family was very short of cash—an eternal problem, I know—and this taker had to be a compatriot as no foreigner would understand or pay key money except to an established agent.

Just a few weeks before, an incident with my pay highlighted my family's urgent financial situation: My usual fortnightly paycheck arrived but was erroneously made out to half my pay. I had to get Mr. Pruett's immediate intervention with Washington payroll to get the other half of the amount the same day or I couldn't pay my rent. My Boss offered to lend me the sum if there was any delay from Washington, but the check came right soon enough, thank goodness.

A student from Hanoi studying in New York,

Nguyễn Nhân, was interested in taking our apartment and promised my wife the key money we had paid the rental agent. However, when the key money was due, Nhân pleaded for extra time to get the money, despite our already arranging for him and his roommates to move in as soon as we left, then broke his word and disappeared. This left us on the appointed moving day with no choice but to leave the apartment for Nguyễn Nhân with no compensation for taking our hard-earned $120. This incident lived long in my wife's memory and Nguyễn Nhân became the epitome of the worst kind of Tonkinese or North Vietnamese deviousness and dishonesty.

INCONGRUOUSLY ENOUGH, IT was during this eventful transition period for Vietnam that the Voice of America assigned to our unit a long program featuring a famous protagonist of the Freedom Movement of Hungary. It was written as a musical feature with harpsichord, flute, and violin accompaniment in the background while the main character, the Poet-Minstrel exhorted his compatriots with chants and poems to fight for Hungary's freedom. I was assigned both translation and the voicing for the whole series, including poems and given the leading role of the Minstrel.

It took a long several months before the program recording was completed. As we went along, the previous day's recording was broadcast with this system continuing until the end. Our producer was a young American of Italian extraction named Joe Campanella. He became a very popular television actor but back then, he was an unassuming young man with musical and artistic talents.

Joe was responsible for choosing instrument music, blending it into the text along with the lyrical poetry. He did all this very well and was quite an agreeable fellow to work with, on top. Joe and I worked several months producing and recording together, even though Joe was not our regular producer and had been assigned to VOA on a temporary basis.

TOWARDS OCTOBER 1954, my family left New York. We had been given a government-paid ticket for an entire compartment on the train to Washington. The government also paid for moving vans to take our luggage, household effects, and furniture separately. Fortunately for the government, we had found a furnished apartment in Washington, D.C. so the moving costs did not cost the office too much.

We enjoyed this train ride enormously, leaving New York on a sunny day that was only slightly cold with the first chills of autumn. We boarded in late morning, unaware that the entire compartment was at our disposition. The privacy was wonderful and when the train started to move, we sat in our 'salon' facing a large picture window to enjoy the scenery passing by. We had large sofas that pulled out into beds and small felt-covered cots for our two little darlings. Marie and Dominic enjoyed the trip as much as their parents for they were old enough to appreciate traveling in "first-class" luxury. Mỹ-Châu and Mỹ-Nga were small yet, just four and two years of age, but they had plenty of goodies and toys to enjoy. We ordered drinks and food that came to us on a dining table covered with a spotless tablecloth and the best of cutlery. It was coincidental that traveling on VOA assignments had been first-rate both times for us, once from Saigon to New York and now from New York to Washington, D.C.

I remembered that the only uncomfortable travel assignment for VOA was flying courtesy of the U.S. Air Force to St. Louis, Missouri, in the company of a Korean colleague to interview some Vietnamese Air Force trainees that the French had sent over from Saigon. (This was in the early 1950s when the fledgling Vietnamese Army was newly formed under French tutelage after General Jean De Lattre de Tassigny urged it be created so Vietnam would have an army "to fight for your own country"). General Nguyễn Văn Hinh, son of former Prime Minister Nguyễn Văn Tâm, was the first Chief of Staff of the Vietnamese National Army and first Vietnamese in the French army to be promoted to general. Both father and son were French citizens.

The Korean fellow and I were distributed parachutes, the sight of which scared us out of our wits, and we sat on 'bucket seats' of hard cold steel. The cabin was windowless, just the regular Air Force type of plane that foreign correspondents routinely fly when covering wars. In St. Louis for two days, we had sleeping facilities in the B.O.Q. (Bachelor Officer Quarters) and ate at the Officers' Club. It was the first time I ever saw Vietnamese trainees in the U.S. They were sturdy young men from South Vietnam, sons of peasants and country people drafted into the army because they were too poor to buy a deferment. However, this was an opportunity for them to train abroad and except for eventual combat duties, it was a good thing for them. We spent the most enjoyable evening together at the base in St. Louis where they were stationed.

In later years, Vietnamese airmen came in throngs, but no one came to interview them, the novelty having worn off. I found it a touching experience that first time I kept them company that night: they were all unsophisticated young men from rice field origins, seeing the world for the first time, and so happy to have a compatriot in their midst some 10,000 miles away from home.

That night none of us expected that battles in our homeland would grow larger and larger and culminate in such fearful bombings that the tonnage surpassed even that of World War II and the Korean War. We didn't know which of those five or six young men were destined to reach higher stations in life and which would die young in fiery combat.

SOON AFTER OUR protest demonstration against the partition of Vietnam, the first batch of Vietnamese students and professionals went home from the U.S. led by Đỗ Vạn Lý. The group included Đỗ Trọng Chu, Trần Long, Nguyễn Văn Mừng (later the fiancée of Nguyễn Thị Quít of the first convention of Vietnamese Catholic Students Association in Chicago in 1952), Dư Phước Long, and Nguyễn Thái. Bùi Kiến Thành also flew back to Saigon on the same flight, but he did not belong in Đỗ Vạn Lý's scheme.

How the first flight came about, I don't know—I was kept ignorant of it. Suffice it to say that Đỗ Vạn Lý felt the time had come for him to "assume leadership" and act as spokesman for Ngô Đình Diệm's group—even the whole party—supporting him in the U.S.A. Naturally, I was the first person that Lý struck from his list. All efforts had been taken to keep his plots and maneuver secret. Not one person of the group that had frequented my home for the past two years; who had been cooperating with us; who ate, lived, shared worries as well as joys with us; and as recently as just a few days ago flocked into my home in New York for the protest in front of the UN headquarters—not one of them told me of their imminent return to Vietnam. Perhaps not too many of them were let in on the secret for "Dr." Lý always acted in secrecy. And even Trần Long—who broke from Lý, "sick and tired" of his high-handed methods and for regarding him as a traitor *(Việt gian)* who sold out his country's interests—even Long kept his mouth shut. Uncle Thành likely learned of the scheme too late to tell me in time, but anyway, he wasn't in New York. My family and I only learned of Đỗ Vạn Lý's feat the very day they came to New York to catch their plane to Vietnam via Paris.

It must have been a Sunday or a day off for me as I was at home doing nothing, so all of us were more than surprised to hear the doorbell ring. We didn't expect any of our group to return so quickly after these last hectic days of the protest demonstration. Neither did we expect any newcomers, either student or visitor, from Vietnam as we were always notified in advance of their arrival. Marie went to open the door and when Uncle Thành dejectedly made his way down our long unlit corridor to the living room (formerly Grandpa Maryknoll's bedroom), we heard her exclaim at once both sad and angry: "Oh, Uncle—I thought you would never come back!"

Thành didn't say a word, just silently walked in to drop down on the couch while heaving a long, tired sigh. My wife and I watched our friend in silence: we didn't have to speak because we knew. But we did not know all, nor enough of what was going on. There had been little peace for us since "Dr." Đỗ Vạn Lý stepped onto the stage.

Finally, Thành spoke up. He told us of ***their*** imminent departure today, of ***their*** conspiracy of silence, of ***their*** keeping me in the dark, and of ***their*** refusal to come by to say goodbye to us. The whole bunch of them, from "Dr." Đỗ Vạn Lý on down! "I'm the only one to come," Thành concluded, more depressed than even we were at this moment. We remained pensive for only a short moment knowing that time pressed him to be leaving and we had to hurriedly bid farewell to our good friend Uncle Thành, and wish him, his father, and especially Ngô Đình Diệm all the best. Thành had left his luggage with ***them,*** hurried 'home' to take leave of us, and now had to rush back to Idlewild to catch the flight with ***them***. He was the sole companion to walk down a lonely road to say goodbye to us before returning to Vietnam and the unknown. "Farewell, Uncle Thành!" We swallowed our tears. And our anger at **them** grew because we were left behind. Our only friend, Thành, was no longer with us.

WE WERE NOT exactly surprised at Đỗ Vạn Lý's behavior toward us. What we didn't understand was the attitude of the others who had frequented our place and worked closely with us like Nguyễn Thái, Đỗ Trọng Chu, Dư Phước Long to name but a few. Dư Phước Long, for instance, had no reason to turn against us and his behavior at the last minute told us much about his cowardly character, a 'small- livered' fellow as we correctly portrayed him in our Tết poem, spineless, a poltroon, and to top it all off, an opportunist of the first order since he only followed Ngô Đình Diệm out of calculation—he was not much above Đức Thanh's level as far as we were concerned. This character trait was soon proved to us when Long hurriedly left Saigon and Ngô Đình Diệm when he thought Diệm's ship was taking on water.

And Nguyễn Thái, an opportunist and bluffer of similar caliber as Dư Phước Long, I found Thái to be absolutely without scruple or principle of any sort. He used the Vietnamese Catholic Students' Association, Father Jacques, and me as stepping stones. Now that he thought he had reached a stone that would bring him to higher reaches, Thái did not stop to look back.

As for Đỗ Trọng Chu, a young man I judged more idealistic than the others, I was disappointed and sad to see him unreservedly and blindly follow "Dr." Lý. I used to have a lot of esteem for Chu, but because he left along with ***them,*** without even picking up the telephone to say goodbye, I held a long grudge against him. Nor did I see him again except for a short moment in Saigon when he was teaching at the Popular School and when on vacation in Bangkok in summer 1974 and visiting the Rose Garden cultural center, I couldn't not avoid a face-to-face encounter. His wife, the former Bà Mâu, came to my brother Minh's house to try to arrange a meeting but I hid and asked Minh to tell her I was out. My grudge was so long only because I had much more esteem for him than for, say, Nguyễn Văn Mừng and his wife, Quít.

It was no accident that I bought *Politics Has No Morals* by former President Herbert Hoover when I saw it in a Times Square bookstore. I bought it but never opened—the title alone was sufficient to remind me of my political enemies. Politics had never been in my veins: I was not made for it, nor had it tempted me. I was in politics solely because of the love my wife and I had for Ngô Đình Diệm who we came to know in America as a forlorn refugee, penniless, and friendless. Our children also loved him, calling him their grandfather, and we treated him as such and helped in any modest way we could. Meeting Diệm was an accident in our lives that brought us some bitterness but many joys, not the least of them being the friendship of our young but very mature and loyal Bùi Kiến Thành. Throughout the almost eight years I served under Ngô Đình Diệm in Hong Kong, I kept away from of Vietnamese politics where possible, which incidentally, kept me out of trouble. Not so for my young friend whom my children called "Uncle" in the Vietnamese way. Thành was dragged into it, to his disillusionment and disgust forced to play a thankless role until the end, was imprisoned for several years after the fall of the House of Ngô, until he was finally expatriated.

Fortunately for us, our futures lay hidden from us. The spotlight was not yet ready to shine on that corner of the stage where armored personnel carriers, bloodshed, military juntas, long-term jail sentences, and a major war using ultra-modern weapons and inventions were already being used. Yet, hidden from the sight of expectant spectator-actors, we mortal humans walk blindly on and unwittingly act our roles until the very end of our conscious lives.

22. ARRIVAL IN WASHINGTON, D.C.

Our train pulled into Union Station and Dư Phước Long was there to meet us. I had previously been staying in Washington at Long's home, reconnoitering the terrain, and preparing for my family's arrival. Long had recently returned to the U.S. from the homecoming arranged by Đỗ Vạn Lý and company. He stayed but a short time in Saigon after judging the situation untenable both for Ngô Đình Diệm and himself. He asked for and received a position as Secretary of the Embassy, now led by the government's new ambassador, Trần Văn Chương, whose daughter, the later infamous Madame Nhu, was the wife of Ngô Đình Diệm's brother. Besieged and alone in his Independence Palace residence, Diệm had granted Long this favor for his support and service thus far, believing he needed supporters to win French alliance over the religious sects and French-controlled armed forces standing against him. In any event, Long was not the only coward to jump a political ship before it sank. No less a personality than Trần Văn Đỗ, brother to Ambassador Chương and the first Foreign Minister representing Vietnam at the Geneva talks had panicked and resigned his ministry. However, Long not only ran fast but ran much farther away than anyone else. While Mr. Ngô may have granted Long his request for a job, he did not forget how Long had abandoned him when he seemed to be in trouble.

In my reconnoitering forays into Long's new neighborhood, I found a furnished townhouse at 805 Buchanan Street NW and leased it. The rent was $120 a month, the same as in New York but the house was more comfortable: there was a backyard with a bed of red roses and a front yard bordered with purple azaleas in their second bloom in late autumn.

While Long acted as host and benefactor as repayment for my family's two years of favors from my family, he left a sour taste in my mouth with his behavior. Long was not generous and exhibited every bad habit and poor taste of the *nouveau riche*. On top of this, it was important for him to impress me with his new diplomatic status, as if to laugh at my family's years of devotion to Ngô Đình Diệm when he did not even reward us but left us in the same position as when we first came to America.

Already, during the ten or so days I stayed with Long when I had to join the VOA staff prior to my family's arrival, I had a bad experience with Long's new arrogance and thin veneer of a 'bourgeois gentilhomme' while he decked himself out (s'*affubler*) in a bizarre notion of diplomatic garb. He did not miss the first opportunity to draw my attention to his car's diplomatic plates with the DPL lettering, which by coincidence, also were his initials! "Predestination, don't you think?" he asked. What infuriated me most was Long acting as if he were superior to me in every way, including his knowledge of

Americana. I never forgot the day when he took me for a ride in his new Chrysler or Mercury (which also required a long explanation as to his cleverness and new affluence in acquiring such a "high-class" automobile), Long stopped at a street corner and pointed to a procession of some high school boys and girls and announced: "Take a good look at the pretty majorettes leading the group. I'll bet you haven't seen that yet in America!" Imagine, I knew more of the U.S. having arrived a year before Long, who went straight to his Naperville, Illinois campus in the sticks, you could say, and who only recently had reappeared in Washington, D.C. Drunk with his new Embassy position and the luxury he thought no one of my standing could afford, Long really forgot himself! Slowly but surely, I learned the ways of politics and politicians and they taught me to always be on my guard, to hate politics more every day, and to get an overdose of cynicism that I could never dilute where professional do-gooders and politicians were concerned—especially the Vietnamese ones.

Dư Phước Long drove my family to our new home and it was about all he ever did to pay us back for our efforts and favors we voluntarily gifted him for two years. We settled down to our new life in the capital. Marie and Dominic went to the neighborhood parochial school and the parish was under the authority of Bishop McNamara. Mỹ-Châu and Mỹ-Nga (also nicknamed called "Lulu and Mumu") were old enough now to run upstairs and downstairs, explore the large basement, and play in both the front and backyards. The townhouse was comfortably furnished with old-style furniture and thick rugs and our front door had a two-toned doorbell that chimed gayly when someone rang it. There were three bedrooms in the house, and we gave Marie a smaller one overlooking Buchanan Street—the first time our eldest child ever had a private room of her own! Next to Marie was the master bedroom where Dad, Mom and the other children slept. Muriel's cot had been sent down from New York, about the only piece of future we ever owned in America. Dominic and Lulu shared a bed equal in size to ours as they would not hear of sleeping apart by themselves in the spare room at the back of the house.

Downstairs, the large living room had wall-to-wall carpeting with nice furnishings from the landlord and we bought a brand-new piano for Marie to learn to play. The television we also brought from New York occupied a central position in the bright and sunny room, which always had a vase of red roses Marie brought in from the back yard. Oh, how many times our family gathered around that television set, watching the news or soap operas in complete tranquility as we were no longer bothered with telephone calls, guests, or students from Vietnam. The children enjoyed their shows and each time a commercial featuring Bugs Bunny danced to a Canada Dry tune and stomping and flattening another rabbit that always got back up, the kids would laugh and applaud while crying out in Vietnamese: *Coi, coi! Nó đạp con ma!* (Look, look! He's kicking the ghost!)

Adjoining the living room was a spacious dining room with a large solid dining table of red oak. Eight or ten diners could easily sit there on crimson velvet high-back chairs while nearby, a large buffet with glass doors held dinner plates, glasses and cutlery. A lateral door in the dining room opened into a neat little kitchen that had two other doors opening to the back yard and the staircase with polished banisters leading upstairs. The basement was also fully furnished, but in a modern style, left behind we were told by the previous student occupant. A door opening to our nice backyard with its red rosebushes and hawthorns that bordered a small path leading straight to our garage which was really just a shed.

The novelty of the house with its "gardens," as we called our two yards with grass and flowers, its empty garage, and its tree-shaded street made us feel like we were in the countryside—how different it was from cosmopolitan New York with its 8 million souls. Psychologically, my wife and I divorced ourselves from our old life full of bitter memories and devoted ourselves to the happiness of our children and enjoying a new chapter in our lives. We enjoyed the absence of callers from the trade winds and felt a deep sense of respite as we recovered from the flood of uninvited houseguests, overseas students, and comrades we thought were staunch supporters of Mr. Ngô, but in fact were cold calculators who gave you the boot at their first chance.

For the first time since coming to the United States, I was able to accompany my children to and from school. One early winter afternoon, it snowed prematurely and hard. I had worked the nightshift, so I was free all morning and the rest of the day. As the flakes started to fall, lightly at first but quickly turning into a snowstorm with gusting winds, I began worrying about little Dominic whose school was about to release the children. I put on my overcoat and cap and quickly headed toward his school along streets already covered in deep and slippery snow, seeing everyone hurrying about, and shops turning on their lights for the evening. Dominic's school was closed and deserted but my little boy was nowhere in sight. Almost panicking, I searched around the school before slowly walking back home, hoping he had taken a different road home. I had almost passed a candy store when I looked in the window and who did I see but my Dominic sitting at the counter sucking a lollipop! Relieved but intrigued, as he sat all by himself in the store's semi-darkness, I quickly stepped in, held him fast, and asked why he came here instead of running home when snow started to fall. "I was walking home," Dominic answered, "when a nice old man gave me a dime and told me to buy myself a lollipop—so here I am, Dad. Don't worry, I'll finish it fast, and we can wait here for the snow to stop." So that's what we did. Mom and Marie laughed at our appearance when father and son reached home all covered with snow that quickly melted onto the carpet, "You two look like snowmen!" But they were relieved to see us, as they also had begun to worry about us.

Another day, a Sunday morning when it was sunny and it was hot outside, Dominic went to play with a couple of neighborhood kids named David and Allen. I started to get anxious when they were gone for too long a time. After I searched up and down the street, I stood impatiently waiting at the steps leading up to our front yard. Sweating profusely from the heat, I started cursing the naughty friends, two notoriously mischievous boys who broke our fence and climbed onto our garage roof, when from afar, I saw the trio walking my way. David and Allen ran away as fast as their short legs could go, leaving Dominic to walk home slowly and obviously afraid—he knew he was long overdue. My son excused himself and said his friends didn't want him to leave when he said he had to go home. "We were only playing at Roosevelt High School, dad, not too far away!" he said lamely and after my sharp admonition Dominic walked into the house chastised and dejected.

THE YEAR ENDED quietly for us, the family enjoying a quiet Christmas with a larger, more brilliantly decorated tree—happy to be undisturbed by unexpected guests. In contrast to the calm and cozy atmosphere at our home, the political atmosphere in the office as well as Vietnam was stormy. Ngô Đình Diệm's fledgling government was weathering the most severe typhoon in its short existence, and which blew hot and cold through the rest of 1954 and well into 1955. Each day, news from Saigon was full of mounting difficulties for poor Mr. Ngô, followed by what seemed to be insurmountable obstacles. The overwhelming consensus was that Ngô Đình Diệm could not survive this year let alone carry on to the next.

At the outset, Ngô Đình Diệm came home and took the reins under the worst of conditions. It was the general debacle in the wake of Điện Biên Phủ, immediately followed by the exodus of refugees from the communist-controlled North Vietnam. Named Premier by Bảo Đại, Diệm entered Saigon with nothing but a piece of paper bearing the signature of the Chief of State. He had no army, no money, no administration to call on. He had to build everything up from scratch. The French, in league with the religious sects of Cao Đài and Hòa Hảo plus the Bình Xuyên, not a sect but a group of former bandits, river pirates, and cutthroats that followed no one except themselves. In exchange for a monthly allowance of several million piasters, Bảo Đại had given them control of the police and they were doing their utmost to unseat Ngô Đình Diệm starting from the very first days he took over.

This was because Diệm did something no government before had done: he challenged the French, and indirectly Bảo Đại, by instituting changes to the country. To begin with, he ordered the closing of gambling casinos and bordellos that the Bình Xuyên ran (and from which monthly allowances were paid to Bảo Đại) at the same time they ran the police. And as Diệm had no authority whatever except the moral and nominal one of a Premier-designate, his order amounted to little more than a gesture. Still, it was a meaningful gesture, as reaction to it would prove beyond doubt if the new government of Vietnam was real or make-believe.

It went without saying that as far as the French and Bảo Đại were concerned, nothing was going to change: it would be business as usual. The problem remained a military one, as it has always been in the eyes of the French. They had lost the war, but still retained half of Vietnam and all the remaining Indianized countries of Indochina, namely Cambodia and Laos (or at least the greater part of Laos). The French Expeditionary Corps was still intact as Điện Biên Phủ was a peculiar case of bad judgment, an exception which did not necessarily prove the rule, and the Vietnamese armed forces were a growing concern. Moreover, the Americans were now committed to giving full military and economic aid and if necessary, would intervene in favor of the French since they no longer had a Korean war on their hands.

Ngô Đình Diệm could be a difficult man to deal with but there was no reason to give him all that he wanted: he had no police, no army, nor even a known political following strong enough to back up his demands. Apparently, Diệm had to play the game—or quit—and the consensus was that he had better play the game.

Dư Phước Long, the newly named Secretary of the Embassy, called me several times a day to discuss the 'unwise' moves by Ngô Đình Diệm. How was he going to back up his order about the vice dens if it was disobeyed, he asked. His own eyes had showed him that Diệm was a pathetic and lonely old man, friendless and powerless, rattling around in his Independence Palace—Long quit and practically fled from the country because of that image. He foresaw the imminent downfall of Diệm even before the man had assumed power. And now, this quixotic move shutting down the vice dens: "You'll see," Long predicted, "Ngô Đình Diệm will be the laughingstock of Vietnam!"

I faced this same kind of mute hostility at the VOA where Diệm was treated as an eccentric. Everybody, from Mr. Pruett down, looked at me with pitying eyes and never made any comment to me about Diệm's very important step to shut down the vice houses of Saigon. Morality could admittedly be a worthy cause, but who cared about morality when politics as such was the name of the game?

The hostility came firstly, from how each person, Vietnamese or American, felt about Ngô Đình Diệm. It was remarkable that Diệm, unlike any of the dozen or so personages the French put in leadership positions as part of the so-called Bảo Đại solution, was the only person capable of inspiring very strong feelings: on one hand, he had profound respect for the stand he took and obstinately maintained with regard to his conception of independence for Vietnam; or on the other hand, Diệm's ideas were dismissed as impractical, premature, or worse. No one felt indifferent about him. As I was Diệm's only staunch supporter present at the Voice, the sharp like or dislike for him was focused on me.

Theoretically, every Vietnamese or American of good will, supported freedom and independence for Vietnam. Even the most pro-French advocates of a 'necessary' transition period in which the Vietnamese people had to work hand-in-glove with the French before true independence could be obtained, even those fence-sitters or *attentistes* who could not or would not take a clear position on their own country's struggle for independence, did so not out of love for French colonialism, but because they felt (justifiably or not) that Vietnam was not ready to stand on her own feet, especially in the ideological conflict between the Free World and Communism.

In practical terms, however, nine years of warfare and political turmoil culminating in the partition of Vietnam left a bad taste in every citizen's mouth, so that the desire for independence was checked by a more urgent need for survival. Hence the cautious attitude toward strong men like Ngô Đình Diệm: he aroused more fear and uneasiness than hope and confidence. Adding to that his lack of real command of the power apparatus, Diệm was more irritating and presented a threat to those who had something to lose. Thus, at the Voice, I was on an infinitesimal scale at the receiving end of all the repercussions that Diệm's disturbing politics in Saigon were bringing about.

To the astonishment of all watchers, Ngô Đình Diệm survived his first crisis. The gambling dens and whorehouses were closed, and the expected revolt did not occur. But other storms were already brewing, more devastating than ever, just gathering strength and waiting for the right moment to blow away the unwanted Premier! The sects, the gangsters, and the army with French colonialists behind them would strike in concert and remove Diệm, once and for all. The detractors and enemies of Ngô Đình Diệm were so sure he could not last the first round that they just waited. So did Dư Phước Long. So did my colleagues in the Vietnamese Unit of the Voice of America.

I remained undaunted and went about my work as if nothing mattered. At Christmas, I sent through the regular U.S. mail a message of greetings in which my sole wish and ardent desire was to come home—not to serve his government in any capacity, but simply to be repatriated. I had had enough of living abroad and frankly, I was homesick. I didn't expect a reply and did not get one. Meanwhile, I had the pleasure and great consolation of seeing my good friend Trần Đức Nhuận who was visiting the U.S. on a U.S. Information Service-sponsored tour in November 1954.

Nhuận and I became close friends during the early 1950s. When I joined USIS and was in Saigon a few months before leaving for New York, he was the only South Vietnamese among the thirty or so translating staff who were all from the North. We took an immediate liking for each other. There was also an older Vietnamese man among the *personnel indigène,* to use the colonial expression for non-European employees, by the name of Cao Huấn Ngự. He was an eccentric tongue-lashing opium eater who did not hold back his insults regarding both the French and the Tonkinese staff. He was not a translator or of the generation and was not suitable to become real friends with Nhuận and me. Rather, he belonged to the rarified and shrinking circle of *désabusés* [the disillusioned] from an older generation hardened by frustrating conditions under colonialism into permanent cynics who took refuge in opium eating. As a result, although quite well educated, Ngự lived his life in the narcotic-induced clouds, oblivious of happenings in the real world.

Nhuận came to the U.S. after all other Vietnamese employees simply because he did not care to visit the U.S., even on a free tour. Nor was he a flatterer, so he did not push for rewards or vie for attention, perhaps proof in some way that it was no mystery why Americans in Saigon readily preferred Tonkinese over southern Cochinchinese, that is, ego boosters to the seemingly indifferent. So, that was how it came about that only after my family and I had to suffer through two years of uninvited guests from

Vietnam that I was finally reunited with a good friend from home.

It could be said that were if it was not for the prospect of seeing me again in Washington, D.C., Nhuận would have turned down his well-deserved tour of the United States. He was so looking forward to seeing me again that nothing else counted for him. He was a Vietnamese for whom no other country or other style of living could appeal strongly enough to lure him away from home for even a short duration. So, coupled with my gnawing homesickness, our mutually warm friendship was most welcome and refreshing in the otherwise dreary year end of 1954.

I will never forget the cloudy November afternoon and the shabby hotel that VOA had found for Nhuận. The inclement weather notwithstanding, sunshine was in our hearts as we joyfully walked arm in arm to the streetcar that would carry us to my home on Buchanan Street, uptown and just off Georgia Avenue. How sweet was the feeling of bringing my dear friend to my new home, unlike the countless others who had streamed into my apartment in New York! This was a treasured visitor, unlike other Vietnamese I had recently met in New York just before we moved to Washington. USIS-Saigon periodically sent groups of educators and functionaries from many regions of Vietnam, perhaps in preparation for the days to come when America would take charge of non-Communist South Vietnam in lieu of the French. One visitor I was pleased to see was a teacher from my Cần Thơ schoolboy days, Mr. Đậu. I brought him home so my wife could supply him with a true homecooked Vietnamese food after weeks on a diet of hot dogs and hamburgers and on his return to our hometown, never ceased to speak gratefully and fondly of us to my father. Another professor of mine from my college days came too, Mr. Trương Văn Di, but I missed seeing him before he was dispatched to his next stopover on his tightly scheduled tour of the U.S. There was a group of educators from central Vietnam of whom Mr. Huỳnh Hoà, father of Huỳnh Anh, a friend of friends of my daughter Marie, struck me as a typical functionary of Colonial Indochina—afraid of the French Master and quickly dismissing any 'political talk' likely to bring trouble to a long uneventful career secured and firmly attached to a status quo determined by the system—the French system of old; he would protest, "Oh, please stop this conversation on 'politics'" if I mentioned the Geneva Agreements and partition of Vietnam. I recall I insisted on a "real revolution in which Ngô Đình Diệm would carry out reforms, this being the last chance for Vietnam to escape communist control of the remaining half of the county," which scared Hoà no end, but he wanted to keep his boat sailing on calm seas. Unlike these and other visitors when my good friend, Trần Đức Nhuận, came, we relished discussing all subjects under the sun to our hearts' content. It was another classic case of: "A sweet rain during a drought/Old friends meet in foreign lands" [*Cửu hạn phùng cam vũ/Tha hương ngộ cố tri*].

Trần Đức Nhuận stayed with my family only one day before returning to his hotel to follow escorted tours before he was rushed out to other states according to a hackneyed overseas visitor program that USIS set up for visitors in the U.S. I did not see Nhuận again until several weeks later when he returned to Washington, D.C. prior to his departure for Saigon. Two days was hardly sufficient for the pair of us to reminisce about the good old day when we first became friends: the antics of Cao Huấn Ngự, our opium man who disbursed his daily ration of insults to the Tonkinese at exactly 9 a.m.; the group of disgruntled French male and female translators at USIS-Saigon unhappy to be put under my supervision, among whom, to my eternal regret, I did not detect a talented writer named Jean Hougron who many years later wrote a series of novels entitled *Les Nuits Indochinoises* [Indochinese nights]; and above all, the evenings Nhuận and I spent at the Quai Le Myre de Viler that was soon renamed *Bến Bạch Đằng* [*Bạch Đằng* Pier].

For several months from July 1950 to April 1951, each evening after work Nhuận and I, sometimes joined by others from the office, spent a few hours drinking beer and enjoying unexcelled Vietnamese delicacies at open-air eateries places along the quay that stretched from the *Pointe des Blagueurs* almost to the French Marina.[57] In retrospect, I realize this period was the only time that Nhuận and I really enjoyed our life in Saigon after the events of 1945,

57 Waterfront area from Pointe des Blagueurs (Joker's Point) to the French Marina was once a popular gathering spot for colonials and locals alike. Article and photos are in *Old Saigon Building of the Week: The Signal Mast - Saigoneer*: "...the headland next to the Signal Mast had acquired the popular name Pointe des Blagueurs ("Jokers' Point") and in the evenings many French expatriates would come here after dinner to watch the boats go by. From the 1920s onwards, the building at the foot of the flagpole was rented out to local entrepreneurs, who ran it as a bar." [Au.]

for soon afterward, I left my country and did not return.

Sitting there on the quay, a good breeze blowing in from the Saigon River, Nhuận and I contemplated the scenery of a hundred sampans moored nearby with its floating population, the hustle-bustle of the crowds on the boulevard, and the sunset on the far side of Thủ Thiêm, across the river where the Việt Minh had its redoubts and from where they periodically shot mortar shells into downtown Saigon. Our 'trademark' scene for these evenings was the French priest who faithfully passed by us every evening, cassock rolled up to mid-waist with a briefcase dangling from the handlebar of his cyclo, calling out to us from across the street, "Bonsoir Messieurs!" [Good evening, gentlemen!] We had barely sat at our table when the padre passed by, as if he watched from some spot for us to appear then he would signal his presence: cassock, bicycle and Bonsoir! In the long run, Nhuận and I watched for him in turn and would not order drinks until he had passed us, and the rituals performed. We called him '*l'Inévitable Père,* the Predictable Priest.

Imprinted in my memory is the picture of Nhuận on a November morning, walking by my side as we headed to Georgia Avenue to take the streetcar for downtown Washington. We had spent a sleepless night together at my home on Buchanan Street, talking far into the night and the approaching separation was painful. Neither of us knew when we would see each other again: Nhuận had already made up his mind to quit USIS as soon as possible (which he did one year later) and we did not have a chance to reunite while I stayed in the U.S. We walked up a small incline and I remember Nhuận's overcoat, beige and beltless, seemed to float around him, as if he was swimming against an invisible current.

In many ways, our friendship epitomized our separate lives ever since we first met and would likely be so for the foreseeable future. Ours was a close friendship of compatriots who destiny separated by tens of thousands of miles, occasionally to be reunited, and only for short durations. Nonetheless, separation only strengthened our great friendship. Besides periodic visits to Saigon throughout the years, we never had the chance to live in the same city again, and it seemed that the chances of ever seeing each other again would be even slimmer.

The year 1954 ended and despite the many memorable events forever sealing the fate of Vietnam, for my family, it was a relatively better year than previously. We had escaped the vicious circle of 'political' infighting—to which I said, "Good riddance!" I thought of how I never liked politics, but recognized that the fierce power struggle in Saigon was a constant reminder that no Vietnamese could ever truly ignore politics. Still, I pretended to be above it all and tranquilly enjoyed my family life.

23. A NEW ERA

IN 1955, HARDLY one year after we left New York, our peaceful life was completely transformed. Because Ngô Đình Diệm was no longer with us, we had the impression that we could revert to our carefree days. For one thing, we no longer had the succession of "houseguests"—students who arrived via New York en route to their universities who stayed with us; students already in the U.S. who came to the city for fun; visitors, either looking for Mr. Ngô who, if not staying in our home, took up a great part of our days and nights; or those 'friends' or 'friends of friends' or former colleagues who availed themselves of traditional Vietnamese hospitality by unscrupulously depositing their bags, baggage, and themselves at our place "for a few days' visit" to save on hotels. Besides, they told themselves, we were 'lucky' to be in America and were therefore 'richer' than them, so it was our duty to open our door to them. For another, Washington, D.C., although the capital of the U.S. did not attract Vietnamese visitors or students as much as did New York.

Now, my wife and I could leisurely watch our children grow up and devote our time to them. On an installment plan, we bought a piano so Marie could start her self-taught lessons; she got to be pretty good at playing her favorite piece, *The Green Cathedral.* Dominic, then seven, grew stronger and healthier, thanks to a comparatively more 'country' lifestyle away from a big city, his mischievous outings with David and Allen notwithstanding. My two girls, Mỹ-Châu and Mỹ-Nga, five and three years, were sturdy and rosy-cheeked babies. All in all, we enjoyed almost half a year of complete privacy, in contrast to our previous life in New York, and until we left America in early 1956, we were not bothered by unwanted guests or political happenings directly bearing on us. I remember well our long evenings *en famille* when Marie played the piano for us, the kids ran around, and my wife and I talked about our past adventures and our future hopes. I fully appreciated all the care and attention my wife showered on her family, being first and foremost a traditional Vietnamese housewife of those times. Our bathroom (we did not remove the "Incinerator" sign the former tenants put up) was the scene of many lovely mornings when I got ready to leave for work. Very much like Dominic, I prolonged my mornings in bed and took a long time over my morning ablutions and other *thủ tục* (procedures or routines), to use a favorite term of Tào Phước, another good friend of the same caliber as Nhuận, and of whom more will be said later. My wife, concerned I would be late for work, would repeatedly remind me of the time while I happily lounged in my half-full bathtub. She helped speed up my *thủ tục* and, as with a spoiled child, she would coax me out of the tub and rush me through a hasty breakfast in order to keep my unsyncopated time in step with an insensible clock everyone else operated on.

IN WASHINGTON, D.C., our unwanted guests were gratefully few and far between compared to New York. With the exception of Nhuận, I brought home only a few 'friend-guests' during our time in the capital city for dinner and a pleasurable evening chatting, or for a few nights. They were of my choosing and received our full and delighted attention.

A classmate from my boyhood days came: Valentin Thức came to the U.S. on a filmmaking scholarship and after some time in Hollywood, he came to visit, and I happily put him up for several days. Besides being a former classmate and playmate for many years in Cần Thơ during the early 1930s, he was also the son of my father's godfather and as such considered himself a close relative of ours according to the spiritual relationship observed by traditional Vietnamese Catholics. Valentin had been spoiled from his earliest days and although his parents' fortune had declined, he still behaved as if he were a millionaire's son. He never did any work with his hands, and I can still hear him asking my daughter one day: "Marie, would you wash this shirt for Uncle? Remember, rub soap well onto the collar." Marie obediently and politely complied, for she too was a Vietnamese daughter first and foremost who considered her filial duties not a pain in the neck, but a pleasure. One evening, before heading to Washington, D.C., he called long distance from Hollywood so I could speak to my younger brother, Bùi Công Lập, who was an officer on a ship weighing anchor in California. Lập did not make it to the east coast, his ship departing soon afterward, but to hear his voice across a continent after many years of separation was tantamount to having it straight from home.

On another occasion, Dr. Đặng Văn Chiêu, a doctor with the Army of the State of Vietnam on a visit to the U.S., came over for dinner. Chiêu was a classmate of mine when we both attended the Collège de Cần Thơ almost twenty years earlier. Another exceptional house guest came in August 1955—Đinh Văn Bân, also a former USIS-Saigon colleague. Bân came to join the staff of translators at the Voice of America and of this man, much has to be recounted later on.

Meanwhile, events in Saigon caught up with us and this time, I reacted to them with mixed feelings. At this time, Ngô Đình Diệm was in deep trouble with the sects, the French, and a new element—the army. He had no support whatever among the population, other than a lukewarm general feeling that he was an honest man who meant well, who tried his best to redress a terrible situation, and worked against insurmountable odds for the good of Vietnam. Being practical people, the Vietnamese realized too well that on one hand, the Việt Minh as a national independence coalition was victorious against a hated colonial regime and likely to keep resisting it as long as it stuck to its overworn trickery of the past. On the other hand, a Premier without an inch of military power in his hands, who was at the same time politically sabotaged by Bảo Đại's naming him head of a dying government and by the French who actually wielded power, was not a hopeful proposition. The feeling was that if Diệm must go down as victim of the colonialists and their henchmen, then nobody could do anything to help him. He would be a martyr, the first and only one throughout the shameful period known as the "Bảo Đại Solution." People would remember Diệm as an untainted nationalist, *simon-pure* in his intentions as well as his acts.[58] It would have been a well-deserved tribute to a man of indisputable integrity who had devoted his entire life to the cause of independence for Vietnam.

But no one expected Ngô Đình Diệm to win. Arrayed against him were the French who disposed of an Expeditionary Corps, somewhat humiliated by the defeat at Điện Biên Phủ, but fully armed with new ammunition and backing by an aroused America; an Army of the State of Vietnam which was Vietnamese only in name as its officers would obediently follow any order given them by General Ely, the French High Commissioner; the sects which without exception existed only by through payments ladled out to them by the same proponents of the Bảo Đại Solution. America had in Vietnam only President Eisenhower's personal representative, General J. Lawton Collins, who was also for the dismissal of Ngô Đình Diệm.

Such was the game. Such was the established order or whatever was left of it in the remaining half of Vietnam

58 "Simon-pure" means "genuine, pure, authentic, true," 1815, colloquial, from "the true Simon Pure" meaning "the genuine person or thing" (1795), from the name of a suitor impersonated by another character in a comedy, "A Bold Stroke for a Wife" (1717). English dramatist and actress Susannah Centlivre wrote the play where the real Simon Pure is treated as an impostor and is believed only after he has proven his identity. See: simon-pure | Etymology of simon-pure by etymonline. (Au.)

within a time limit of less than two years until 1956 when elections throughout Vietnam would decide upon its reunification. The French meant to stay. The sects meant to keep their respective fiefs and privileges. Bảo Đại meant to use Ngô Đình Diệm as a temporary card; and some even said the emperor expected Diệm to fall in order to demonstrate once and for all that he could not do better than his men or he himself could do.

The sects ganged up against the Diệm government, and despite willingly sharing power, they persisted in demanding his ouster. Trần Văn Đỗ resigned as Bảo Đại's Foreign Minister and representative for Vietnam at the Geneva Conference. The army generals, led by Nguyễn Văn Hinh, son of Nguyễn Văn Tâm, and currently Chief of Staff, demanded no less. From Paris, Bảo Đại cabled him to come over for new instructions. Even the famous stratagem known in Vietnam as "Điệu Hổ Ly Sơn" (Luring the Tiger to Leave his Mountain) meant taking away the strong man to leave the terrain open, did not apply in this circumstance as Ngô Đình Diệm was not much of a tiger, much less a strong man.

Everybody was against Diệm. Everybody, that is, except E. Lansdale, the famous "Ugly American, the Maverick of the CIA." With ample monetary means, Lansdale bought sects, men, Caodaists, Hoà Hảo, Nùngs, ammunitions and arms, Trình Minh Thế, et al., he maneuvered, cajoled, cheated, wheedled, and threatened. And he succeeded somewhat, mostly because money talked. The Hoà Hảo and Caodaists consented to entering the government; the Trình Minh Thế group agreed to enter Saigon on Ngô

Đình Diệm's side if ammunition and bags of money were provided; the fierce Nùng warriors would be mercenaries for whoever paid the most.

However, the army, the Bình Xuyên, and their French masters were not easily swayed. Not because they were any holier but simply because the reality of power—military, police, financial control, gambling and vice houses—was already in their hands and they would hold onto what they had. As La Fontaine said: 'A bird in hand is worth two in the bush" or *"Un tiens vaut mieux que deux tu l'auras."*

Washington, in the meantime, was undecided and unless it made its weight felt, the ball was up for grabs. Ngô Đình Diệm and his opponents faced each other, and both watched to see on which side the ball would fall. Lansdale coaxed Diệm into staying in Saigon instead of going to Paris and oblivion while the Bình Xuyên, spurred on by the French, started their attack on the government. The war was bloody but short as Ngô Đình Diệm held on. Ambassador Collins's recommendation that they replace Diệm had almost reached Washington when a telegram from Washington to the same effect reached Saigon. It was over. General Ely, the Army's chief of staff having abstained from unleashing the army, fled the country, and the remaining officers quickly acquiesced. Now it was ***their*** turn to serve Ngô Đình Diệm. Colonel (Big) Minh, later to become General Minh, chased the Bình Xuyên out of their strongholds and exterminated them at Rừng Sát (a tidal mangrove area) a few months later in October 1955. Having consolidated his power, Diệm opened a referendum in which the people would choose between him and Bảo Đại. With results being almost 100% in his favor (and questionable), Diệm declared Vietnam a Republic and himself as its first President.

A new era began. It was almost exclusively, the work of Lansdale: he decided to back Ngô Đình Diệm against the overwhelming majority of Americans then in Saigon; he was the one who 'found' Diệm alone and forlorn in his empty Independence Palace, deserted by his heretofore staunch supporters and surrounded by enemies; it was he who cabled Washington the first news of the defeat of the Bình Xuyên and thereby undid the "Dismiss Diêm" order.[59] For although Dulles was determined to save a "Free Vietnam" from communism, the whole of Washington, including Dulles, was no less determined to get rid of Diệm. Lansdale consequently merited his dissenters' caustic but accurate nickname of "Kingmaker."

WITH NGÔ ĐÌNH DIỆM solidly in power in Saigon, a plethora of his erstwhile lukewarm supporters flocked back in search of jobs with the new government. They would also make a 'pilgrimage' to Washington soon, among them a few who were among the original Ngô Đình Diệm group in New York and pay us a visit. Meanwhile we had in our home a new houseguest taken in by me and graciously accepted by my family. He was Đinh Văn Bân.

59 Recent scholarship has challenged this American-centric view about the rise of Ngô Đình Diệm as if it were all the work of Landsdale. See Edward Miller, *Misalliance: Ngo Dinh Diem, the United States, and the Fate of South Vietnam* (Cambridge, Mass: Harvard University Press, 2013).

Summer had passed by imperceptibly given our preoccupation with precipitous events in Vietnam. Marie, then fourteen, attended her last May Queen parade in grade school. She would soon enter high school and we scarcely had time to think about which school she would attend, nor how to pay for it. Dominic was seven and despite his unauthorized outings with Allen and David, he was not a bad boy. Mỹ-Châu and Mỹ-Nga, five and three, were constant companions to their mother, now that they could play in a backyard full of soft green grass and red roses and a front yard bordered with a bushy hedge. During the darkest days of Ngô Đình Diệm in Saigon, I had called on Bishop MacNamara of our diocese. He was attached to our parish's St. Gabriel's Church, and one evening, seeing me on the parochial school premises looking for Dominic, he invited me to his rectory for a chat. The old bishop was kind and well-disposed to learn about Vietnam and Ngô Đình Diệm, but there was not much he could do to help except offer his prayers.

For his part, Dư Phước Long at the Embassy was always on the lookout for news from home and continued to pester me with his incessant phone calls. As his dire predictions did not come true and Diệm triumphantly recovered from enemy attacks, Long's calls grew fewer and finally stopped. We hardly called on each other despite practically living a stone's throw from each other. Like a seasonal monsoon that blew hot and cold in turn, political happenings caught us, tossed us about, then released us to leave us once more, blissfully out of them. At least, I was personally happy to be out of the mess, still not terribly interested in politics. Little did I realize that my wife was secretly worrying about their future of our growing children and was discreetly taking measures, the effects of which I was soon to find out.

UNANNOUNCED THAT AUGUST arrived Đinh Văn Bân. At the Voice, we were routinely translating and recording as usual when in popped a familiar face—Bân, his face haggard, seemingly lost. Nobody in the office knew him, nor of him, so it was a surprise to be informed that USIS-Saigon had dispatched him as a new translator-announcer. I was the sole person to greet him as an old colleague and our mutual happiness was genuine. As Bân arrived unannounced, no one had gone to meet him at the airport as it should be, and we were at a loss ourselves as to why USIS-Saigon sent no telegram to announce his imminent arrival. Only long afterward did I learn the reason why.

Bân came to be known as a small-scale wheeler and dealer in the best sense: he was a resourceful and problem-solving fellow, a *debrouillard par excellence* who despite lack of education, had the savoir-faire to succeed wherever he worked in extracting the most profit and benefit and to eventually reach the top position available. Small-scale because he could not possibly aim too high yet; in later years when he had advanced enough in the world to be on a par with the powers-that-be and negotiating with ambassadors, generals, and prospective vice-premiers and ministers, Bân still lacked what is called 'sheer luck." At the time he first came over from Saigon, he was still a beginner in his inventive skills and his scale of necessity was much smaller. He profited from the fact that he got sent to work in America all by himself instead of getting himself into the group that came here within that first recruitment four years ago. He succeeded in convincing USIS-Saigon to leave his arrival date open so he could travel to as many countries of Europe as possible before finally ending up at the VOA desk. How could a telegram be sent, given his persuasion abilities?

Unaware of these little maneuvers of his, I took pity on the 'poor guy' and reproached USIS for giving him third-rate treatment, unlike my team that had been properly sent off and well received at Idlewild Airport. Since no one knew of Bân's arrangement with the Saigon office, I readily took him home that very afternoon—and he never left us until our own departure from the U.S. Bân became 'Uncle Bân' to my children and in the following six months that he stayed with us, my wife had a difficult time chasing after him each payday to collect his boarding fee for the house. Eternally penniless as he always spent his salary in advance, he could not resist the temptation of dressing up flamboyantly as he imagined Americans did and almost childishly parroting anything he thought sounded "Yankee." He had this addiction long before coming to the U.S. and already in Saigon was well known for his extravagances. All the paraphernalia and Americanisms of the early 1950s were displayed on his person: Manhattan shirt, striped nylon pants, Ray-Ban sunglasses .... Bân was a walking mannequin for American menswear, albeit a bit cheap and tasteless. He was only superficially sophisticated and trying to be on top as usual.

We gave Bân one of the two large bedrooms in the

back that looked out over the backyard. Marie had her own bedroom and we compressed ourselves into the other bedroom—me, my wife, Dominic, Lucie, and Muriel. Innocent and rather gullible, we took everything he said at face value and did not find it too inconvenient to have him among us. The first thing Bân did, just three days after arriving in America, was ask us to co-sign with him to buy a car on installments—a blood-red Bel Air Chevrolet. To Bân, this American model car was the supreme mark of his 'Americanism,' no doubt a dream he entertained for years.

Bân was completely dependent on me for his début at the Voice. He repaid me the best he could, and except for his embarrassing perennial arrears in the matter of boarding with us, he was in no way a bad friend. Being a practical, down-to-earth and no-nonsense kind of guy, Bân taught me a lot on how to cope with the harsh realities of the world. He was always agreeable and never refused to render any service we asked of him. Indeed, we thanked him for driving us anywhere we needed to go; and our children, deprived of their 'Maryknoll Grandpa' no doubt found in Uncle Bân a substitute relative to sometimes enliven their days. He served as my constant reminder of things practical, and it was due to him that many hours of overtime were earned through some weekend shifts. This was extra money I had never thought of that had of course been going to my other colleagues. What idiosyncrasies Bân had, I considered peccadillos, and never paid more than cursory attention to them. I even told my wife to be patient when he did his 'disappearing' act when his boarding fee was due.

THE HORN THAT I bought in Times Square on New Year's Eve 1952 had moved along with our things from New York to Washington and now stood on my desk at the VOA office. The first New Year of 1952 was marked in red pencil and was followed by successive years—1953, 1954, and now 1955—our first year in Washington, D.C. Soon I would inscribe 1956, a momentous year that saw the departure of Mr. W. A. Pruett, our Vietnamese Unit Chief.

It was toward the late fall of 1955 that Mr. Pruett, tired of his unrewarding work at the Voice of America, bid us all goodbye to return to his missionary work in Oklahoma City. His leaving us was a moving time that was not untainted by infighting and politics: petty politics of petty functionaries in a federal government setup.

Long before, in fact ever since I arrived in New York and through the dramatic events leading to the partition of Vietnam and its ensuing unsettling future, Mr. Pruett had always sincerely supported my country's independence and was openly anti-French, had been expressing his as yet undecided desire to leave the VOA. As his on-again, off-again pronouncements in this regard did not materialize into decisive action, no one thought he meant it. Whether Mr. Pruett had been pressured to quit by higher authorities at the Voice, I did not know for sure. However, I got the impression that he had been leaned on. For one thing, he was too strongly against French policies to please his bosses who worried what Senator McCarthy could do to them in his hunt for Communists in America. And I also suspected that he was secretly pro-Việt Minh, meaning pro-independent Vietnam. His antagonism toward Ngô Đình Diệm was not entirely motivated by being against Diệm's Catholicism: he simply did not see him as an effective leader for a truly independent Vietnam, or anything connected with the French was distasteful to him as that was still the case when Ngô Đình Diệm first received power through Bảo Đại.

Mr. Pruett certainly did not agree with John Foster Dulles's policy of supporting the French, and incidentally Ngô Đình Diệm, to the hilt. A veteran of thirty years' stay in Vietnam, he saw without bias the effect that colonialism had on the Vietnamese; and if he did not say it in so many words, his sympathy was all for the Việt Minh who he thought more 'independence fighters' than the northern Communists. During the policy meetings of top-ranking officials of the Voice, Mr. Pruett must have voiced many unpalatable opinions and he had undoubtedly felt their disgruntled remarks if not their blunt disapproval.

At the time of the much-vaunted exodus from North Vietnam and its blown-up campaign of 'voting with their feet,' Mr. Pruett had this to say concerning North Vietnamese refugees in the South: "Where shall they go next when general elections take place and the Việt Minh win?" His entire experience in Vietnam had been in the north, and he even spoke my language with a northern (Tonkinese) accent. If he had deep sympathy with all Vietnamese people, my unit chief certainly 'loved' the northerners a little more than their brothers in the south.

His superiors having consequently made life uncomfortable for Mr. Pruett at the Voice, it became more and more difficult for him to stay and work with the Vietnamese Unit, especially when, as the months passed, it became clear that Ngô Đình Diệm was not quitting and was daily consolidating his power. My boss did not hate Diệm, per se, but thoroughly condemned his accepting the blind and messianic anti-communist crusade that was U.S. policy. When the Vietnamese Unit Chief's departure was formally announced was when the petty politics of federal government employees came into play.

A farewell dinner party had been organized for Mr. Pruett. Knowing full well that the clashes that occurred periodically whenever I found or thought I found blatant injustice on my boss's part during our four years working together—they always ended amiably enough without me being pushed to the wall—Mr. Pruet's superiors concocted a scheme to humiliate him at his own farewell. No less a personage than Henry Hudson, then Deputy Director at the VOA, took me aside and whispered in my ear that I was designated to address the gathering short, give a farewell speech. Mr. Hudson did not have to recommend the kind of speech he preferred that I give. He supposed that I was all-out to "get" my chief, perhaps in revenge for his management. Hudson sprang this news on me only minutes before we entered the Chinese restaurant reserved for the party.

How well I remember that night! It had snowed so the streets were two-inches deep under an immaculate blanket. I wore my rubber shoe-covers and when I walked about the round tables in the large room giving a speech I composed as I walked, my wet rubber soles made a slop-

slop squishing sound and I left a trail of melting snow on the floor. The dinner was quick—too quick, as if the hosts were in a hurry to get home—if not to get rid of Pruett—and the party was nothing but a cursory gesture of dismissal instead of "Good Riddance!" I spoke pretty easily and well that night, inspired and stirred by my emotions:

Mr. Pruett, my friends:

It is an honor, and a pleasure, to address our good friend, Mr. Pruett, on behalf of Mr. Henry Hudson, and thank you for asking me to speak on this rather sad occasion, for Mr. Pruett is leaving us—for good.

In Asia, we the Chinese as well as the Vietnamese, according to the teachings of Confucius, give full respect to our Teacher who we place one knot higher than our own fathers. My friends, Mr. Pruett here deserves this respect. For 30 years, he taught our Christian compatriots in Vietnam and for four years he has been with us in the Vietnamese Unit at the Voice, lovingly teaching and guiding us. We sometimes clashed, but that is normal in a democratic country. Let no one construe that those light disagreements or even other more serious ones ended in unreconcilable viewpoints, unfriendliness, mutual dislike, nor hatred.

We disagreed, Mr. Pruett and I, on many things political and bureaucratic. But we wholeheartedly agreed on one essential thing: our intense dislike for French colonialism. Mind you, we never hated the people of France. What we hated was colonialism and its French version. Mr. Pruett and we all knew well what we were talking about: we both lived under it.

And now, allow me to bring a lighter touch to the evening.

Mr. Pruett, besides being our Teacher, was no less a friend to us. He interested himself in our personal welfare and called on us when we were sick. If you will permit me to mutilate a Confucian saying about the King-Teacher-Father hierarchic order of devotion that every son must observe, I will loosely apply this teaching to friendship in general and recite my version 'Friends' *which is* Quân Sư Phụ *in Vietnamese and* Bạn Hữu *in Cantonese, as I see some Chinese colleagues are here to honor Mr. Pruett tonight:*

'One day of being friends

Half a day of being friends

Friends we must remain:

(The length of time does not determine if ours is a profound or light friendship.)

So, Goodbye, Friend Pruett! As the French, who I admire culturally but despise politically, say: "Partir, c'est mourir un peu" *or* "To leave is to die a little." *Dear Mr. Pruett, a part of you and of us dies a little with your departure. Come back to us as soon as the 'weather' permits.*

Deafening applause—a warm appreciation of my impromptu speech which I thought had some eloquence and was especially witty and to the point. Mr. Pruett was visibly touched, and he made his thanks to me and the entire room while almost choking with emotion. However, one person did not like my speech: Mr. Hudson. A few days afterwards, he personally stopped at my office and ominously said: "I did not expect you to give that kind of a speech—I do ***not*** like people to let me down!"

Contrary to Mr. Hudson, our scriptwriter, Sarah Newman, was all happiness. The dear soul had seen Hudson assign me the role of after-dinner speaker and was dreading I might comply with an embarrassing or even insulting 'coup de grace' to Pruett and his tenure as our boss. After the farewell dinner broke up, Mr. Pruett kindly drove Sarah and me back to our homes. I was never to see him again.

ONE POLITICAL FALLOUT from the ascendancy of Ngô Đình Diệm was the so-called leader of the Đại Việt [Great Vietnam] Party, Nguyễn Tôn Hoàn, whom I had met in Hanoi in 1950. He came to Washington in late 1955, vainly trying to wrench Mr. Ngô from the American embrace. Smartly dressed and in his mid-thirties, Hoàn was a handsome man. He immediately found a friend and follower in, guess who, Huỳnh Sanh Thông, our very own friend of such recent times but now openly and angrily opposing Ngô Đình Diệm. Of course, there was an explanation for this.

When I saw Thông last in late 1954 prior to moving down to Washington, D.C., he was packing up for an imminent trip to Vietnam. He had received a telegram to join the Đỗ Vạn Lý group that had returned to Saigon a few months earlier. Very soon, however, Thông was unpacking as a second telegram arrived countermanding the first, leaving him at a loss to what was happening at home and why. No further telegram or communication arrived. After months of vicissitude, Ngô Dình Diệm recovered and consolidated his government but still nothing was heard from Đỗ Vạn Lý or anyone else. Thông slowly turned bitter as his anger grew. We remained staunch friends but did not discuss this curious episode. In his spare time, Thông taught my wife English and after my family and I were more settled in Washington, we merrily headed out to a pizza joint to consume a lot of beer together. Nonetheless, he remained tight-lipped on the subject of Ngô Đình Diệm.

It was after I was introduced to Nguyễn Tôn Hoàn that I fully understood how angry Thông had been with the telegram episode. Hoàn did not mince words in his opinion of Ngô Đình Diệm and *The Washington Post* had printed Thông's first "Letters to the Editor" condemning and ridiculing Diệm. Thông had repaid Đỗ Vạn Lý and incidentally, Ngô Đình Diệm, in kind and with a vengeance. I fully sympathized with my friend, although I could not stomach Hoàn's politics as I too, had been let down by Lý and his disciples, if the few who followed him in flying to Saigon in mid-1954 could be described as such. As for Hoàn, he mistakenly thought that my criticism of Diệm's government, especially his ambassador in Washington, had put me squarely in his own compound. He did not realize his error until few months later on returning from France he complained that despite his urging, I did not write him while he was there. "You're still a Diệmist," he said bitterly, "and I thought you did not like him!" I did not reply but thought that being called a 'Diệmist' was a thousand times better than being a "Hoànist." At least Mr. Ngô had fought his enemies and won whereas Nguyễn Tôn Hoàn had been collaborating with Bảo Đại all along.

By consorting with Nguyễn Tôn Hoàn, Thông drew the attention and ire of the U.S. government. Ngô Đình Diệm had already acquired strong lobby support, so working against him, even verbally, could be dangerous. The FBI began to investigate Thông and sent agents to my home to inquire about him. I told them in no uncertain terms that they were barking up the wrong tree and as far as I could ascertain, Thông had been and still was a strong supporter of Ngô Đình Diệm. The agents left without further ado, but as Thông's especially well-written "Potemkin" 'Letters to the Editor' of the Washington Post, it was no surprise that soon afterward, he lost his job with the Defense Department. I did not learn about this until 1956 after I had left the U.S. Remnants of McCarthyism still were in America and Thông became one of its victims., ironically, because he followed Đỗ Vạn Lý!

To replace Mr. Pruett, VOA brought in Dale Purtle, a young man who was uncouth in appearance but highly educated, versatile, and a linguist of sorts. We hit it off and remained friends for many years, even after I left the U.S. With Pruett no longer on the scene, the atmosphere in the Vietnamese Unit relaxed overnight. Constant irritation used to be our daily ration in the office as Pruett watched us closely. Almost simultaneously with our completing a translation or some other work, another job was handed out, gently but firmly. With Purtle, we reverted to our Saigon-style work pattern, that is, we worked at a leisurely pace and except for recording or broadcast sessions that of course stayed strictly on schedule, we were free to handle our daily translation workload as we saw fit. As a result, there was no 'stock' of translated scripts ready to draw on so despite our operation being rather a 'hand-to-mouth' affair, this happy time obtained until my departure from the Voice of America.

I have alluded to the plethora of busybodies who flocked to Washington from Saigon after the rise and secured positioning of Ngô Đình Diệm at the top of Vietnam's power pyramid. Hardly a day passed without at least one visitor either in town or calling on the VOA's Vietnam Unit. These people were new adepts, either newly recruited or old turncoats reshaped into ardent and vociferous "Diệm's men." Most were civil servants of one kind or another, a few were province governors, but none were military. There was Võ Lăng, a rather new name to me, who was supposedly a close collaborator of Mr. Ngô although I had never heard of him before. It was rumored that Lăng came to Washington to promote a "National Revolution Movement" through a paper of the same name that appeared daily in Saigon; but the contents of the paper made us extremely discouraged about the very 'revolution' the movement purported to tout.

And ever ready to contradict us, at least in the sole matter of early accomplishments of the government, was Nguyễn Đình Hoà. Dr. Hoà unashamedly praised everything pertaining to the government of Ngô Đình Diệm, which he had now given the hackneyed title of 'National Leader.' Whereas before Mr. Ngô's ascendancy, Hoà had labeled him an uncultured man of little political acumen, but Diệm had now metamorphosed into a "perfect, perfect, just perfect" leader. My irritation at Hoà's too frequent reference to a perfect Mr. Ngô grew so much that one day, it burst into a rather violent verbal duel during which Hoà threw at me: "Yeah, I know, Mr. Diệm should not forget his *Bát Cơm Phiếu Mẫu!*[60] Of all people, Hoà was needling me about being left behind by not only Mr. Ngô who supposedly owed me a debt, but also by Hoà's whole gang who now enjoyed high positions and mocked me from Saigon, this same gang that not many years ago so fiercely opposed the Đức-Thanh group. I was not untouched by this smarting blow. It was true that, like Thông, I felt forgotten; but unlike Thông, my sole desire was to go home and live a peaceful life in my now peaceful Vietnam and I actually wrote to Mr. Ngô to ask for just that. Sick and tired of the opportunism of the so-called elite of Vietnam, of which Dr. Hoà was a prime example, I shrugged his arrow off with: "Don't ever deduce from your own thinking what is on my mind. You and I are not of the timbre." As far as I was concerned, Hoà was just another busybody.

Little did I realize then that I was absolutely correct. Unknown to me, Hoà had been courting Ambassador Trần Văn Chương for a Secretary of Embassy position and Chương had apparently transmitted his approval of Hoà's petition to Saigon. In fact, Hoà was already preparing himself to become a diplomat by buying himself a brand-new black Chevy sedan. One evening he even gave me a ride in it to the Pentagon where he would give a talk on Vietnam to a military audience on a par with two other

---

60 "Bát Cơm Phiếu Mẫu" literally translates to "Mother Phieu's rice bowl" from a story in the *History of the Three Kingdoms: China.* One of the protagonists, Hàn Tín, rose to become the First Minister at the court of Lưu Bang when the ruler defeated his enemies and ascended the throne. In his youth, Hàn Tín had been so poor that every day he had to beg for his bowl of rice from Mother Phiếu. Hàn Tín did not forget her kindness after he became powerful. (Au.)

diplomats, one speaking for Cambodia and the other for Laos. Hoà must have been laughing under his hat that evening to see me so blithely unaware of his imminent success. Yet at the same time, my not knowing his secret was what determined Hoà to hurt me to the quick and refer to his own reward whereas I was dangling, left in the lurch by my mentor.

MORE HURTING, HOWEVER, were two other troublemakers who arrived toward year's end: Nguyễn Thái and Đỗ Vạn Lý. Nguyễn Thái was of the original Thông-Thái-Hiền trio from Cornell University in Ithaca; 'Dr.' Đỗ Vạn Lý, of course, was the one who led his whole gang back to Vietnam to get government positions. Thái dropped by Buchanan Street one evening and stayed late crowing about his success in Saigon. He was now the Director of Vietnam Press, known and respected as being one of close collaborators on President Diệm's plans for Vietnam's future. No, he did not know if the President had received my letter. Yes, 'Dr.' Đỗ Vạn Lý was in the U.S., but exactly where, he did not know. And yes, we are all very happy in Saigon.

I rang Dư Phước Long up who was surprised at my call, but eager to give me the latest news. He supposed I was mad because 'my' gang, now riding high, had turned against me and stressed that all my efforts had earned me nothing from an ungrateful Ngô Đình Diệm. Oh, and as a matter of fact, even he, Dư Phước Long, was already a diplomat! Thus, he was pleased to inform me that 'Dr.' Đỗ Vạn Lý was that very evening dining with Ambassador Chương and if I called Ly there, I would certainly catch him. Which I did—Lý had an account to settle with me!

Đỗ Vạn Lý was all gracious when he answered the telephone: "Yes, I was very busy, much too busy. Yes, of course: here is my hotel telephone number and address. Tonight? Ah, er, why don't you . . . ? Very well, and by the way, I have this . . . very interesting thing to give you. Oh, no, of course not—please come right over—." Đỗ Vạn Lý wasn't at all eager to see me, his politeness notwithstanding. He knew he had to settle an account with me and dreaded it. All the way back to his hotel that night Lý must have been cursing the bad genie that leaked his whereabouts to me. And he needed some kind of protection against my wrath!

When I entered his hotel room that night, a few hours after my call to him, I found Ly flanked by an Embassy man, Phạm Đặng Tài. Lý smilingly received me and quickly produced a small envelope to pass to me. A quick glance at the handwriting on it told me it was from Mr. Ngô himself. I pocketed the envelope and turned to Lý. I lost no time in telling him point blank how disgusting it was for him to have led the group from Washington to New York and back to Saigon without a word of goodbye to me. Was he afraid I would interfere with his acceding to a position of some sort in the Ngô Đình Diệm government? To my avalanche of angry words, Lý could only present a blank face that became paler as I jumped up, brandishing Mr. Ngô's letter in his face and shouted: "And why didn't you deliver this letter to me? Why did you keep it in your pocket and not even ask someone to give it to me? Why?" As I spoke, my anger mounted and I took a few steps forward which made Lý think I was about to strike him as he tried to push back even farther into his seat. I glanced at the Embassy man sitting next to Lý and saw that Phạm Đặng Tài's face was even paler than Lý's and the whole scene struck me as too ridiculous. I shrugged and stalked out without another word. I was not to see Đỗ Vạn Lý again for seven years when a similar scene, although more violent, repeated itself.

The next morning, I was amused to read in the columns of the Washington Post the following denial from the Embassy of Vietnam:

"The Embassy of Vietnam hereby denies all declarations made by Đỗ Vạn Lý to the effect that he was here as a "personal representative of President Ngô Đình Diệm." H.E. Trần Văn Chương categorically refutes all such allegations and Đỗ Vạn Lý is no more nor less than an *imposter.*"

24. "THINK OF YOUR KIDS"

THE YEAR 1956 BEGAN routinely enough with a Vietnamese New Year's party at the Embassy of the Republic of Vietnam. This was the first embassy party I ever attended—unenthusiastically. His Excellency, Trần Văn Chương, a man of very short stature but very long ambition, already considered himself equal to if not superior to President Ngô Đình Diệm. He had no photograph of Diệm in his office, but he did have a portrait of his wife daintily displayed on top of a piano. There used to be a huge painting of Bảo Đại on the wall just above the head of the Ambassador when he sat at his desk but with the former Emperor's dethronement, the painting was removed and nothing put in its place on the wall. This fact alone augured poorly for both for Ambassador Trần Văn Chương and Ngô Đình Diệm's Presidency. I thought to myself: If a man such as Chương is allowed to represent Vietnam and its President, then he should represent his wife, Bảo Đại's defunct State of Vietnam, and a musical-chairs President—in that order.

I already had, on two occasions, the opportunity to see Ambassador Chương at close range and get a clearer picture of the man himself. The first occasion was when

I interviewed him for the Voice of America. Bảo Đại's painting was then hanging on the wall and throughout our interview the Ambassador insisted that His Majesty remained very high in his esteem. He boasted of his relationship to the ex-Emperor and left no doubt in my mind that he had little respect for Ngô Đình Diệm. The term 'imposter' that he later used for Đỗ Vạn Lý must have been present in his mind when he spoke about the President in our interview. That much was clear to me.

On another occasion, Chương invited me and Mr. Pruett to a dinner at the Embassy where it was manifested to me that His Excellency was henpecked. Madame Chương presided over the evening and her small-statured husband looked his part: a junior partner at the beck and call of Madame L'Ambassadeur. No wonder ***her*** portrait was displayed in his office in lieu of that of President Ngô Đình Diệm. Francis Cunningham, Jr. was one of the other guests at the dinner and no mention at all was made of either the President or of Vietnam. Much was discussed about Madam Chương's title as she was then a member of the French Union Council. I remember well how the conversation on that subject developed: everything turned around Madame, of course, and we concluded by agreeing that the title, 'Madame Le Conseiller' fit her best, to which she gave an approving nod. We should have stood and bowed several times to her, Japanese-style, and our *savoir-vivre* [etiquette] would have been judged complete. Diệm's brother and his wife, the Ngô Đình Nhus, at that time were still an unknown quantity and there was no thought of connecting the Ambassador's behavior to the *Eminence Grise* in Saigon.

This reverence for ex-Monarchy explained why such incongruities as remnants of the *ancient régime,* staunch Francophiles and unashamed supporters of French colonialism in Vietnam, Miss Elizabeth Đệ, daughter of the former Cabinet Chief of Bảo Đại, or Henry Trần, son of the former Ambassador Trần Văn Khá, still held responsible positions in Ambassador Chương's embassy. Why Mr. and Mrs. Chương themselves were such remnants: they were French citizens of the same caliber as Nguyễn Văn Tâm and Trần Văn Hữu, one notch higher than Trần Văn Khá, for instance. And all this, at a time when the Ngô Đình Diệm government spoke of bringing about a "National Revolution!"

SOON AFTER TẾT in February 1956, I was invited to the Embassy for a personal chat with the Ambassador. Under Madame Trần Văn Chương's portrait, the Ambassador asked me if I had any university degree. To my negative reply, he continued: "Not because I attach any importance to such degrees. Why, President Diệm himself has no university degree whatever!" An oblique denigration cast against his president. What I didn't know was that Mr. Ngô had asked his Ambassador to contact me for a possible job at the embassy! After some verbal roundabout, Ambassador Chương asked me what kind of position I would like to hold. Without any hesitation I answered:

"Pardon my frank reply to your frank question. I do not give two hoots to a position in your embassy. But if it were an order from President Ngô Đình Diệm, I would like nothing less than the position of a *conseiller*" [counselor].

"Please explain yourself."

"There isn't much to explain. You know what I mean." I didn't want to underline too much my play on words, thinking back to the ambassador's dinner with Lý the other night. Instead, I continued:

"Of course. The function of a *conseiller* is to advise. On many things, such as how to get rid of the servants of colonialism."

Mr. Ambassador was not amused. He reverted to my 'lack of education' as I told him I had no university degree. Gently enough, Chương boasted of his own brilliance—contrasting himself not just to my own little self, but clearly to what the President lacked. Ngô Đình Diệm had no university degree, nor did he hold any government position higher than a province governorship whereas Ambassador Chương had been a famous lawyer in addition to serving as Foreign Minister in Trần Trọng Kim's cabinet. Why all this boasting if not to indirectly refute President Diệm himself as well as his cablegram concerning me. Then Chương ridiculously asked if Mr. Ngô appreciated me because my wife used to feed him! Some Ambassador!

The Ambassador decided to turn to the question of Nguyễn Đình Hòa whom he insisted he wanted to employ. He let me understand that I somehow prevented Dr. Hòa from being admitted to Chương's embassy as he had been turned down—by the President himself. I knew nothing of this: of Hòa's application or his being rejected. A few days later, Hòa himself got Sarah Newman to ask me point blank whether I was reporting to Ngô Đình Diệm about his application to the post of secretary of the Embassy. I simply told Sarah that the President did not have to hear from me—he could make his own decision and if by any chance Hòa had already been engaged—which was not the case—then the ambassador should not remain silent. He could insist on hiring anyone he chose to work under him. Either that or he should resign. He chose to ask me instead—what importance I was given all of a sudden!

Ambassador Trần Văn Chương did cable Saigon, not about Dr. Hòa, but regarding his interview with me where he told them that **he** had turned me down. This was his way of paying President Diệm back for refusing Hòa's petition. I believe that if by chance the President insisted that he take me in, Chương would have resigned. Saigon's reply to the Ambassador's cable with another query: "Shall Mr. Bùi Công Văn accept the position of Head of Mission in Hong Kong?" I did not get to read this cable as the Ambassador asked me the question, but first summarizing it to such an extent that I could not understand what its meaning really was. For Chương omitted the words, "Head of Mission" and he asked if I would serve ***at*** the mission in Hong Kong.

Asking no further questions, I left to go home and discuss this odd meeting with Uncle Bân, writing down the question: "What is the ***nature*** of the position in Hong Kong?" Bân was more excited than me—he saw an opening. He talked all night to me about the chance I could be something like a diplomat and I should not turn the offer down! The following day when I asked the question to the Ambassador, Chương gave a big laugh, and only then did he consent to tell me that I was to be the Consul and there was no such thing as the 'nature' of any position. He had just deliberately and gratuitously poked fun at me: had he just given me the information straight in the first place, I wouldn't have needed to come back to the Embassy. I abruptly ended the interview and as I walked out, Chương called out after me: "I have to give Saigon your reply: Yes or No?"

FOR SEVERAL DAYS, I deliberated with myself and my family: Shall I accept or not? Until then, I had no idea that Vietnam had any kind of representation in Hong Kong, and I thought I was unprepared to assume the position of Head of Mission so some training was needed to precede such an important post. Little did I know that no matter how high your position in partitioned Vietnam, in the South all you needed was a combination of savoir-vivre and savoir-faire which involved a lot of back-bending and little know-how, if any.

At home, Uncle Bân came on full-strength. He spared no effort in convincing me that the offer was the best for me and especially for my family to accept. He reasoned: "Why, if this offer came to me, I would accept without blinking an eye! Ngô Đình Diệm owed you a debt and now he pays it: let him pay. Give him the pleasure. Give your family a break." And so on.

I remained undecided that day with Bân and for several days after. My wife never said a word one way or another. All our children, including Marie, were too young or too innocent to know. My strongest desire as always was to come home—as a private citizen. I wasn't tempted with a career in politics as it frightened me: it gave me the uneasy feeling that I was going to sell my soul.

Whether or not Bân spoke to Gilbert Newbold, chief of the Thai Unit, I did not know, but several days later 'Uncle' Gil advised me: "Văn, think of your kids." He was right: I had not thought of them. As they were young, I did not see the need to earn more money as we were happy enough as we were. In Vietnam, if we returned, I could have a good position given my work experience in America, and we would not want. I never thought of "letting Mr. Ngô pay me back" as Bân had urged. All I wanted was to live in my own country and I was naïve enough to think that outside of any government position, I could influence the President to do some good for the country. It was offensive, even repulsive, to suggest to me as Bân did, that I would have plenty of opportunities to 'make money' in Hong Kong. "How?" I asked Bân who could only give a hearty laugh at my pitiful ignorance but was kind enough to reply: "Aiiee! You'll see how later . . . when you're there."

Some advice also came from an unexpected source: Vietnam. I received a letter from home in which it was reported that my brother Lập's father-in-law, a physician, had commented that if the rumor that I was a good friend of President Diệm was true, then I would be really nuts to stay there in the United States.

None of this unsolicited advice influenced me one way or another. All I cared about was going home. Which led to the next item on my list of worries: how to earn a decent living in Saigon. Hypothetically, I could avoid politics and get a job in the commercial world, but I wasn't too sure I was good at that. To work again for USIS was unattractive enough a thought to abandon it forthwith. I would be better off staying with the Voice of America here in Washington. To play it safe, I finally decided to accept the offer, then once back in Saigon again, we'll see. If worse came to worst, I could always give Hong Kong a try and come back to VOA as a last resort. Having made up my mind, I immediately took the step to discuss my thoughts with Dale Purtle, who reassured me that my last recourse would be available to me.

When I gave Ambassador Chương my acceptance, he congratulated me but also reminded me of advice he never offered me: "You see? As I told you, it would be better for you to ask Saigon for a position as Head of Mission than working here at my embassy." I mentally raised my brows when he implied that he had suggested the above and that I applied for the position—but neither was true! Yet I did not say anything and instead thanked him. I had one other request when Saigon urged the Ambassador to dispatch me immediately to Hong Kong to take charge of the consulate: I asked to borrow a small sum of $60 from the Embassy's emergency funds. My family was again short of cash.

In hindsight, I can now see why I reluctantly accepted the post of Consul in Hong Kong. The determining factor, above everything else, was the immediate and urgent need of money for we were perennially in debt. Most embarrassingly, I still owed Đỗ Vạn Lý money he had lent me, unasked, when we were still on good terms, and

I needed cash to expedite Mr. Ngô's baggage to him in France. And last September, when I took Marie to register her at the Holy Name High School in Takoma Park in uptown Washington, D.C., I realized how much money I would soon need for my children. It was dark when I introduced her to the Mother Superior, and father and daughter were both tired after a long day. I had to plead with the good nun to admit Marie on a special reduced-fee cale, payable on installments. She agreed, which relieved us, but the experience weighed heavily on my mind. So much so that when Uncle Gil at VOA advised me to 'Think of your kids,' a bell rung in my head echoing from that evening when daughter and father sat in the Holy Name school's parlor while dusk gathered outside.

PREPARATIONS FOR OUR departure progressed apace. Bân was all enthusiasm and happily helped shop for clothes and it seemed thousands of other necessities. As a mark of unequalled esteem, we gave our TV set to Thông, which greatly irritated Bân who silently felt we were neglecting—after all, he was the only one of the Vietnamese group to stay behind with me while all the others rushed back home with Nguyễn Đình Hoà's group. To console him, I said that when in Hong Kong I would think of a way to bring him over to work with me. He was delighted to hear that and exclaimed: "Ah, as for that, we'll see—we'll see!"

Very rapidly, the day arrived to depart from Washington's National Airport for Saigon. It was early March 1956, and we were due in Saigon in a few days, no later than my birthday on March 7. The entire Vietnam

Unit of the Voice of America came to the airport to see us off, including Dr. Hoà who showed no outward sign of dislike of me. However, on the keepsake copy of Thoreau's *Walden Pond* that my colleagues at VOA had given to me, Hoà sarcastically wrote:

Tiếng Nói Hoa-Kỳ Thừa Âm Hưởng,
Cộng-Hoà Nam Việt Góp Anh Tài

Literally, this translated to:

[Your] reputation is felt at the VOA,
While your talent is donated to the Republic of South Vietnam.

But it could be more subtly translated as;

Lo, a vacancy left at the Voice,
Ah, the Republic in South Vietnam gleans talent!

And this subtlety counted: Hoà's mockery transpired through outwardly kind and congratulatory words. Such is the manner in which Vietnamese poets of the old school poked at those they wanted to ridicule. On two occasions, Nguyễn Đình Hoà thought I was too dull to see through his clever tongue-in-cheek insults. The first occasion being his reference to Mr. Ngô's *Bát Cơm Phiếu Mẫu*. (Not for nothing did he get a *Docteur ès-lettres* –a PhD!)

For the record, I should reiterate here that I didn't think Dr. Hoà was a high-caliber scoundrel. After all, there are different kinds of SOBs: some are dangerous while others are not. The latter SOBs are mostly annoying and quickly range themselves on the winning side, as Dr. Hoà himself demonstrated many times.

Again, for the record, I mention the poem I wrote in the traditional Tang Dynasty style of poetry honoring Nguyễn Đình Hoà's wedding in New York City.

Hữu duyên ngàn dặm cũng đưa sang
Tấn Tấn từ đây gá nghĩa vàng.
Nữu Ước ngày nay vui họp mặt,
Hà Thành thuở ấy thắm đôi đàng.
Trai thanh phong nhã trang tài tuấn,
Gái lịch yêu kiều bực đảm đang.
Đừng bảo Ông Tơ còn hủ lậu:
Tàu bay, biển cả, ổng đi càn!

There was absolutely no *arrière-pensée* [ulterior motive] whatsoever in my poem of congratulations and praise for the newlyweds. A free translation reads:

Destined to be together but kept apart by thousands of miles,
Two good families will henceforth be joined
As you happily reunite today in New York
After such a sad separation long ago in Hanoi.
The groom is handsome and talented
And his bride is lovely and accomplished!
Don't think the Old Silk Man is behind the times:[61]
He knows all about jet planes and ocean liners!

---

61 Old Silk Man: In Chinese mythology, every couple on earth are predestined to be husband and wife. The god in charge of matrimonial union was an old man whose heavenly job was to weave together two silk ropes, each representing the Yin (male) and Yang (female) element of individuals on earth. When completed, no one could separate his rope. In Sino-Vietnamese literature the god is called *Ông Tơ* or "Old Silk Man." (Au.)

Nguyễn Đình Hòa and I, after all, could have been friends were it not for the unbridgeable gap in our approach to life. We both appreciated Vietnamese literature and he did not seem to look down upon me although I did not have one-tenth of Hoa's university training. Once again, politics was the cause of our dissent.

25. GOING HOME

AT NATIONAL AIRPORT that afternoon, my family and I said goodbye to many friends and a number of foes who came to see us off. It was almost five years to the day that we left Vietnam, we were going home. As the plane took off on the first leg toward the Pacific coast, I felt born again, in a way almost rising from the dead. My dream of coming home had at last come true! My loving wife, who had suffered through five years of hard work, worries, and perpetual penury deserved a break. My children's lives would be different from the only one they knew, especially for Marie. She had to carry many responsibilities and chores and cared for her brother and sisters without enough money for her schooling, not to mention decent clothing and small personal pleasures. After all, she was fifteen now and no longer a little girl. I had been living in the clouds for too long: it was my nature to pay little attention to the practical side of life and in the old Vietnamese tradition, it was my prerogative as husband and father in the old Vietnam's tradition, to leave all household worries and cares to my wife. I was born too late: I should have lived at least one century earlier.

Ruminating on these remorseful thoughts, I touched

my wife's hand where she sat next to me at the window seat and we turned to watch our children, their faces beaming with joy and so happy in their new outfits. Dominic was smartly dressed in a light blue suit while Lucie and Muriel were resplendent in twin green and canary-yellow dresses, clothing my children had never enjoyed before.

Our four-engine airplane (jet planes had not arrived yet) carried us to the west coast and we were actually going around the globe but this time closing the other half of the circle and coming back to our point of departure five years earlier. The plane had touched down somewhere in the Midwest to change crews and then continued to San Francisco. In the sun's slanting afternoon rays, I watched our little girls playing and reminisced: Lucie had been an infant of eight months only when we brought her to the U.S. and now she was six; Muriel did not even exist then and will see Vietnam for the first time at age three; and my boy, Dominic, who happily sang on the Constellation flight from Saigon to Paris for French Union councilors in his cute but correct Vietnamese, was now a young boy of eight and no longer singing in his mother tongue. Marie, our eldest child, matured before her age for carrying quite a load on her shoulders for five long years. What did she think now, looking out the window into miles of empty space? Was she expecting a happier life, lighter loads on her young shoulders? Or dared she think of a different life from the one she had lived, a far superior life, perhaps even one of luxury? She would not know what lay ahead and neither did her parents: we all had to wait and see. Suffice it to say that we were happy to see our children happily enjoying the flight: something new and a change to daily routines, even for children who had no idea what we were heading into. When the plane started its descent to San Francisco, I woke from my solitary thinking and dreaming, Thoreau's Walden Pond lying unread in my lap.

At San Francisco Airport, a Pan American Air Clipper was waiting to take us on the last leg of the trip home. As we took off at night, we were provided berths to sleep in, unlike our Air France Constellation flight out five years ago when we had to sleep semi-upright in our seats and only Mỹ-Châu could stretch out in a tiny little hammock dangling overhead. We landed in Honolulu at eight in the morning and since we had to spend almost the whole day there until our flight that night, Pan Am offered us the option to rest at a hotel or take a sightseeing tour of the island. We chose the tour and much enjoyed the beauty of the island, even visiting some pineapple farms and their canning operations.

Once again on the plane that night, we headed continually westward with stopovers at Guam and Wake Island and landed at Clark Airfield in the Philippines the next afternoon. We were almost home! My wife and I felt our chests starting to fill with tumultuous mixed feelings. Already the unbearable heat reminded us so poignantly of the heat in Saigon itself. Hurry, Iron Bird! Go faster to take us home!

Just a few hours later, Tân Sơn Nhứt airport looked terribly sad and forlorn to me. I did not have time to analyze this strange feeling but shepherded my family through customs and police lines to the exit gate where, out of the waiting crowd stepped the most wonderful sight of Bùi Kiến Thành and his wife, Đẩu to bid us welcome!

Was I dreaming or imagining things? Did I actually hear my name being called out? YES, I DID! Uncle Thành stepped up, shook hands, then out of his mouth came: "My God! What are you coming home for?!" As I was still a little shocked to see him, he added: "...and with your whole family, too. . . !" As husband and wife shepherded us to their car and ferried us away, I glanced back at the crowd at the gate and at Tân Sơn Nhứt overall and that same forlorn, an indescribably sad feeling still registered with me—why? Was it because I had been so used to the brilliance, even the grandiosity of things American that in comparison, good old Vietnam looked so run down? Why did Uncle Thành's greeting seem so discouraging to me? Did I have a downhearted feeling because of the physical aspect of a Vietnam revisited after five eventful years, or was it something psychological, or even an omen?

I didn't have the heart to go deep into it as the dusty road took us away from the airport while the late afternoon sun fiercely beat down. Thành didn't live too far from Tân Sơn Nhứt and as there were few cars or people on the roads, we soon pulled into his courtyard. We stepped out onto a lawn with pebbled lanes and drooping chrysanthemums that invoked the same sadness which to me hung, powdered and invisible like pollen in the air. Something only people with allergies felt while the rest of the world passed by immune and indifferent.

On a long table on the front verandah of Thành and Đẩu's villa, a banquet awaited us: all the Vietnamese delicacies you could think of tempting us that ranged from *chả giò* to *nem* and *chả lụa* interspersed with *rau húng* and *lá quế* (fresh green herbs and vegetables) and so much more all crowned by two respectably-sized whiskey bottles. My good friend and his wife meant to treat us to a feast for the first thing to enjoy back home: delicacies drenched in good old fragrant but quite pungent *nước mắm!*

My family all sat around the table and while happy to enjoy the feast, were mostly going through the motions. We were all physically exhausted from the very long trip home and I felt oddly mentally depressed. Our hosts had already had their lunch, so they prepared this banquet especially for us. So, we smiled and chatted, but also hurried through the meal while Thành and Đẩu looked on. The children showed signs of sleepiness and were directed to rest in an adjoining room. With only adults in the room, I told Uncle Thành about my assignment to Hong Kong. This immediately relieved him of his worries: he was afraid that I had brought my family home for nothing, perhaps even punishment, and had worried so much for our sake.

I learned then that conditions in South Vietnam were far from settled in the countryside despite recent victories over the sects and President Diệm's decisive control over Saigon and provincial capitals. Thành brought out a batch of pictures he took in Bến Tre during a recent visit: The Việt Minh had displayed beheaded cadavers and mutilated bodies of peasants in village marketplaces as a lesson to anyone who thought they were no longer in control. With sad eyes and a small shrug of his shoulders, Thành said:

I'd like to show these to the President to prove to him that it's far from quiet in the Delta.

This was the first element of uncertainty that I got straight from a trusted friend, and it weighed heavily on my mind, although I did not comment one way or another. Nor did I tell Thành of my intention to stay and live in Saigon if conditions were good rather than going on to Hong Kong and take up my assignment there. Apparently, there was no need for me to tell him this because my mind was already half made up: we would have to go. Unaware of the thoughts swirling in my head, Thành quietly told me to have a rest before he drove me to the Ministry of Foreign Affairs to see what they had in store for me before moving on to my Hong Kong post.

While we rested, a surprise visitor arrived: Marjorie Weiner, the ugly duckling from Huỳnh Sanh Thông's days at Ithaca! A familiar old face now transformed into a quite presentable (and no longer dirty) young lady. Marjorie entered the room and hugged me (which we had never done in the U.S.), but we were in Saigon after all, and Marjorie did take a lot after Saigon's French manners. Besides, her joy at seeing old friends was quite genuine. We had such a nice chat.

Around 5 p.m., Thành drove me down to Rue Alexandre de Rhodes where the Ministry of Foreign Affairs had its offices. He led me to the office of Nguyễn Hữu Chí, Chief of Staff for Vũ Văn Mẫu, the Foreign Secretary. Chí was surprised to see me for I did not cable the Ministry of my arrival (thinking that the Washington Embassy would do it), but they had reserved rooms for me at the Hotel

Catinat on *Rue* Tự Do. As the Secretary was not there, Thành brought me back to his home and moved all of my family to the hotel that night.

It was our first look at downtown Saigon since our return. Somewhat cheered after settling into our rooms at the hotel, I telephoned my father at his office in the Industrial and Commercial Bank. His voice sounded hoarse almost beyond recognition, but when he realized he was speaking to his son—at home in Vietnam—his voice became as I remembered it, but at the same time bewildered and jubilant. He immediately sent a telegram to the family and my parents-in-laws. Auntie Ba, my wife's sister, came up to Saigon the next day and kept my wife company until we left for Hong Kong.

Early morning the next day, the first thing I did was take my family for a ***real*** breakfast at the Café Nguyễn Thị Trước on Boulevard Bonard (later renamed Lê Lợi Boulevard). It was renowned for its *Hủ Tiếu (*rice noodle soup) where diners dipped a crusty golden pâté of minced pork into the delicious broth, well-seasoned with the best Phú Quốc fish sauce, and generously peppered with scarlet slices of bird's-eye chili. The good old café was overcrowded, as always, and we enjoyed our soup tremendously.

The next step on our agenda this first full day back in Vietnam was, of course, to visit our former house in Gia Định, a nearby suburb. We took a "matchbox car" for this trip and it was hilarious fun riding in this homely contraption of a carriage. The children sat in the front next to the driver who managed the lone horse. I wondered if

Muriel at age three would remember this first and only opportunity to ride in a matchbox car again. Marie sat next to her sisters with Dominic squeezed in between them while Mom and Dad brought up the rear of the box, dangling their feet as the horse kept to a steady trot. Thống Nhứt Boulevard, Rue Massiges, Đa kao, Cầu Bông Bridge crossing a small brook into Gia Định itself, the Lê Văn Duyệt Tomb and Temple, the Bà Chiểu Market, the Gia Định Church, onto Quai Doceuil, then home at last.

What a surprise for the house residents when we arrived unannounced and unexpected! Here was our house, looking exactly the same as when we left it five years ago. Our grandparents thought they were dreaming when they saw us—but no, we were real—and quickly called for the rest of the family to come. crowded around us. My brothers and sister: Uncle Minh, still a bachelor; Uncle Hiền, already married and living with his family; Uncle Lập, still on the high seas or in France; Cousin Xuân, son of Fourth Auntie; and dear Dì Tám, mom's eighth sister who had been keeping house for us during these past long years.

Bùi family outside Hotel Catinat, Saigon, before leaving for Hong Kong (Summer 1956)

Dominic Nghiệp and Lucie Mỹ-Châu at Sở Thú (Botanical Garden & Zoo) in Saigon before leaving for Hong Kong (Summer 1956)

We made such a commotion we made! The whole neighborhood came round to see us, exclaiming their wonder at seeing our healthy children now grown up and marveling at our newest addition "Made in the U.S.A"—Muriel Bùi Mỹ-Nga!" When my grandma realized that we were not home to stay but would soon be off again to Hong Kong she was visibly shaken. Why, Hong Kong was to her as unreachable as the moon! And we didn't even have any luggage! Home for us was not Vietnam, but some faraway land again and this first night after so many years away, would not see us at home with her. Oh, my beloved Grandma, how could I soothe your heartbreak and help you understand why just barely reunited with you I seemed eager to leave again? Was it fate or my own volition? Could I not, for your sake say, "Yes, I will stay home!" I hadn't seen President Ngô Đình Diệm yet but when I did, could I not tell him: "Thank you, Sir, but I'd rather stay home with my grandmother?"

Life seldom, if ever, had offered us anything so clearcut and easy to determine when we had gone through our lives almost blindfolded, taking what at the moment seemed to us the best of two or several possible paths. I had already made up my mind to go to Hong Kong. The independence so dear to the Vietnamese, for which I fought in my own way and suffered the consequences—was all that true or an illusion? Was Vietnam truly independent? Did we not depend on the U.S. for our very existence as the non-Communist half of Vietnam?

This first day back in Vietnam, after seeing our old home and beloved family, we returned to the Hotel Catinat where, in due time, Auntie Ba, Dì Tám, and Dì Cúc came and stayed with us for the rest of our time in Saigon. I also made the necessary telephone calls to the Independence Palace for an appointment to call on the President and word was sent back that an official car would come for us that evening for an audience with our President Ngô Đình Diệm.

I left word for my wife to prepare the family and when the official car arrived, we would all go together and then I went for a stroll. However, while I was out, Marie mistakenly thought I had gone to the Palace to see Mr. Ngô without her or the rest of the family! She waited for my return for a long while, but when I did not appear, Marie took it upon herself to join me "there" at the palace. She walked all the way to the palace and told the guard at the gates that she wanted to enter because "my father is in there talking to the President." After checking and learning from the guard that the President was busy and had no one in audience with him, Marie was incredulous. She could do nothing else, however, then walk back to the hotel, very much let down and depressed. Only when she saw me there did she believe the guard. Shortly afterward, the government car arrived, and we all piled in, the children happy to soon see their 'Maryknoll Grandpa' again.

It was about eight in the evening, all the streetlights were lit, and traffic was scarce. The car drove us through the gates and up to the Palace entrance just like we were guests of honor. Our six-member family walked in past the astonished faces of the Palace guards. They stood at attention, not because they were saluting us (as we'd like to think), but because they were supposed to hold that rigid military stance no matter who passed through the front gates of the Palace.

We walked on thick carpets and saw chandeliers, high ceilings, and followed a splendid stairway that led us up one flight to the President's office and living quarters. The rococo Independence Palace had been built by the first French Admiralty after they took over the southern part of Vietnam that they baptized Cochinchina. More than 80 years had elapsed since the Palace was built and now the very first Vietnamese to occupy the building was Ngô Đình Diệm, the first President of the Republic of Vietnam! I also realized the honor given my family to be invited to enter the Independence Palace. I held my wife's hand as we walked up the stairway, flanked by my children, and in my mind circled the thought: "This is real . . . this is not a dream." The French who 'owned' us as well as our country ever since I was a child, had really vacated their palace, the symbol of their sovereignty over us. Soon, hopefully, they would all be gone!

On the landing, we proceeded to a huge reception room richly decorated and luxuriously furnished with plush armchairs, polished wooden tables holding Vietnamese *objets d'art* [art objects]. On the walls hung giant colorful and exquisite lacquered panels. We waited, our morale high, our senses very impressed, and our hearts extremely proud of the man in control of all of this, in control of our Vietnam and our destinies. We sat silently, awed and expectant, when almost noiselessly, through a side door entered our good friend and our children's Maryknoll

Grandpa, President Ngô Đình Diệm.

We all stood up, although Marie had to help her brother and sisters to do so as they only knew the man before them as their Grandpa who they played with just a few years back. Mr. Ngô gave us a happy smile, waved us to sit down and without shaking hands, took up his seat on a long canapé opposite us and asked his first question: "Ah, so you are just back?"

Here was the man who lived so close to us for many months in New York now transformed into the President of Vietnam. There were no perceptible changes, even the little standoffishness he affected; this was normal to us because the head of state and a Confucian must observe before all else a minimum of prescribed formality, even vis-à-vis his own children. We settled into a long and sometimes intimate conversation with Mr. Ngô who once in a while reverted to his familiar jokes. For our part, we happily smiled but kept a strict protocol and did not allow ourselves to joke back or otherwise be disrespectful. Mr. Ngô called me "*Ông*" as of old, and I had yet to address him as "Mr. President." I did not find continuing the old appellation we used of "Ông Ngô" as discourteous nor did he show any sign of disapproval.

As far as his calling us home now instead of earlier, Mr. Ngô had this to say: Yes, he had received my Christmas 1955 letter (he received daily delivery of all personal mail, safely and meticulously ranged in a sealed box), but I must have known that it was not safe for me and especially for my family to return to Vietnam earlier. Besides, his policy had always been to never call people back: if he did, they might not like it back here and on top of that, could disagree with the work assigned and consequently blame their President. No, anyone who chose to return to contribute his efforts to this government did so at his own discretion. Let him say such and the government will cover his repatriation as Đỗ Vạn Lý and the others had come home at their request. The lone exception was me and my family, Mr. Ngô concluded. He created a job he deemed suitable for me and brought us home at a time he found propitious. My wife and I were deeply touched and thanked him profusely yet knew that our words could never fully express our love and appreciation for his consideration. Ngô Đình Diệm, however did not let the occasion pass without referring rather bitterly to Dư Phước Long who had deserted him at the height of his crisis with a rebellious Army and the Bình Xuyên: "If Mr. Long had not insisted on leaving Saigon in a hurry, then I have no doubt that today he would be made a consul somewhere!"

The younger children had begun to slumber so one after the other, we laid them down on the settee to sleep while our conversation continued. So far, Marie had not exchanged one word with the President, but she alone of my children stayed awake through the long monologue Ngô Đình Diệm shared with us. Our presence that night was an extraordinary event for the Independence Palace, but a certain detail makes it more memorable. While Mr. Ngô talked on, we sat listening to him pretty much as we did years ago in our New York apartment that was beyond modest when compared to this splendid presidential sitting room. From the corner of my eye, a pink shadow suddenly appeared from a side door on the left. It came nearer, walked past behind the President's back, and disappeared behind a door on the right without missing a single one of Diệm's visitors in the piercing stare from a pair of truculent eyes under arched China-ink eyebrows. The shadow and searching look belonged to a lady in a pink *aó dài,* and despite passing by like a hot breeze, we knew it was no other than Madame Ngô Đình Nhu, Mr. Ngô's sister-in-law. The colloquial Vietnamese comment would be: "*Còn ai trồng khoai đất này?*" [Who else could it be but her Ladyship!].

Indeed, the pink shadow was the wife of the President's brother, the only Lady-in-Residence. We had never seen her before, but there could be no mistake who she was. Specifically, it was how she acted, walking by authoritatively, if furtively, her feminine curiosity, and obvious questions: Who could these people be, this group from nowhere, with a woman in it to boot! And the President himself receiving them as if they belonged to the prestigious Ngô clan. Indeed, it was the daughter of the diminutive Ambassador Trần Văn Chương in Washington, D.C.

Our audience with Mr. Ngô took several hours and when it ended near midnight (not a record by Diệm's standard), I passed him the black leather portfolio containing his correspondence with Prince Cường Để which I did not send along with his other luggage to Paris. The President appreciated my safeguarding these papers for hand-written letters by the late Prince were of invaluable historical value. My family then took leave of Mr. Ngô, and me carrying little Muriel in my arms, we walked slowly out of the audience room, Domonic and Lucie sleepily leaning on us and we walked down the staircase as if in a dream. This first interview with the President was also our last one in which Ngô Đình Diệm kept some of his former bonhomie and so much of the seemingly ancient pre-Presidential days' atmosphere obtained. It was also the last time Marie and our sleepy children saw their "Maryknoll Grandfather." Although at the time none of us expected it to be so, this is what came to be, and until his death, Mr. Ngô never saw again the children he played with and brought for walks in Riverside Park.

My wife and I came back to see the President several times prior to departing for Hong Kong twelve days later. Unlike the first and only time he received in a formal room, for all the other visits we were always admitted informally into his private chamber on the same floor. And in none of the visits, not even the first, did I ever mention I might want to stay in Saigon so that a job could, as he said, be "created" that suited my abilities, preferably in the private sector. I had the gut feeling that it was unrealistic to go back to our pre-American experience and resume our lives as if there were no five-year gap, Geneva, or especially Ngô Đình Diệm in between. Besides, as Uncle Thành tried hard to point out to the President and his entourage, things were far from as rosy as they believed.

THE ROUND OF official calls, to my Foreign Minister boss, Vũ Văn Mẫu, on the finance Minister as he would approve an advance on my salary from the Ministry of Foreign Affairs (our perennial lack of funds!), on the

Ministry of Finance whose Director General, Ngô Trọng Hiếu, who was a fat, loquacious man very much on the ascendancy; on the Exchange Office, whose director, Huỳnh Văn Lang was no stranger to us—he was the 'artist in residence' who painted the anti-partition protest rally at the U.N. in New York who rather than helping me, had his vainglorious secretary showing me the door—I had to work through all that crap and more, the *corvée* or drudgery that petty people required me to work through. Phew! I signed with relief when the last form was signed and stamped, and I could devote my time, energy, and happiness entirely to my friends and loved ones.

My friends always came ahead of my loved ones and relatives. Uncle Thành discreetly stepped back to give me space to meet up with old friends that he knew I would enjoy seeing. First on my list was Trân Đức Nhuận, who at the time lived with his wife at Cô Bắc Street, not far from Cầu Ông Lãnh Market. My wife and I lost no time calling on the Nhuậns who were rendered almost speechless when we knocked at their apartment door at dusk. We had come home unannounced except to Uncle Thành, so my friend could hardly believe his eyes. Until I left for Hong Kong, not a single day passed without our meeting at least once a day, revisiting all our favorite spots we frequented five years ago. Many changes had taken place and Bến [Pier] Bạch Đằng no longer had its open-air eating center, but our high spirits meant there was no end to our mutual enjoyment at being together after such a long time.

Nhuận introduced me to an old acquaintance, Trân Thọ Phước, then working for Air Vietnam. I had passing knowledge of him who one day came with Trần Văn Khê to the British Information Service where I used to work. Many years had passed since that day but a friend of Nhuận could only be a friend of mine, so Phước and I sealed our friendship that day. He was lean and always dressed in jacket and tie, walking reproof to me and Nhuận who some days sported flamboyant shirts and on others, more subdued Hawaiian shirts. We patronized almost all the gourmet restaurants of the day and as there was no curfew, rare were the nights when we left before closing time in the small hours of the rising dawn. In the Sino-Vietnamese tradition, one of the rare happinesses in life is to talk with friends so we did not waste a moment. And if the amount of whiskey or brandy consumed should cause some brows to frown, let it be said that:

> *Tửu Phùng Tri Kỷ Thiên Bôi Thiểu!*
> *Thoại Bất Đầu Cơ Bán Cú Đa!*[62]
>
> *Friends sharing a thousand cups of wine is nothing!*
> *But even half a word with incompatible folks is too much!*

And miracle of miracles! By almost an astronomical coincidence, a good friend from when we three all worked at Air France, Nguyễn Văn Ba, chose to return to Saigon on the exact days that I was present! I had been away for five years in America while Ba had moved to France for several years where he instructed the lovely hostesses of the Union Aéromaritime de Transport (UAT) in Paris.

They say that orbit-bound comets do not return to

---

62 These verses are from a poem by Ouyang Xiu [Vietnamese: Âu Dương Tu] (1007-1072).

the same spot in the universe during their path through infinite space for decades or even tens of decades. Yet one did return during the blessed year of our lord 1956. Ba's being in Saigon when I was there was an event no astrologer foretold and was not likely to repeat itself soon, if ever.

So, the three of us tilted 'a thousand cups' so many times that I almost forgot my assignment to be Ngô Đình Diệm's man in Hong Kong. Ba's UAT headquarters was in Khánh Hội, just across from the Arroyo Chinois, whose blackish waters washed down the smelly viscosities that fishmongers daily tossed out from Cầu Ông Lãnh Market. The current brought the water under the high-arches of Cầu Mống or Rainbow Bridge and out past the Pointe des Blagueurs, to the melancholic but uncluttered Saigon River. My two friends' days were taken up by office work and although we pointedly made up for this loss with lunch-and-siesta midday breaks, we never had enough time to be together. Indeed, we had the same spirit of *bỉnh chúc dạ du* [hold a candle for a stroll at night] as described so picturesquely by Tang Dynasty poets Du Fu [Vietnamese: Đỗ Phủ (712-770)] and Li Bai [Lý Bạch (701-762)]. When it was necessary to

> *Light up our Torches/And play at night,*
> *Since days were too short/For good old friends to consort*

The old days that we could not enjoy, being born too late, despite trying hard to recapture them for ourselves, communism and other -isms notwithstanding.

MY FATHER WAS then working in Saigon, living with

my Auntie Four or Cô Tư in her thatch-hut home on stilts in the swampland of Xóm Chiếu, not far from the Rainbow Bridge. Our paternal house in Cần Thơ was cared for by my stepmother, and as soon as possible, the whole family would move to Saigon. My wife's sister, Dì Ba, and her younger half-sister, Dì Cúc, came to stay with us at the Hotel Catinat for the duration of our stay in Vietnam. Her godmother, Mrs. Jean Lambert Cần, whose husband taught me English at a time when the French colonial masters would not hear of any Annamite as much as pronounce one word of English—and thus launched me into a career and exodus to America—also came to see us. The sweet old thing could not imagine why, coming from the U.S.A., we did not bring back gold bullion in our suitcases! The old folks' idea of the wealth in America!

We were busy in our few days in Saigon. My wife had her hair permed in the modern style, left in the dust was her old-fashioned style of hair pulled straight back into a low bun; she went on shopping sprees also, for essentials as well as fun things. I diligently worked to squeeze in more time with my friends while Father Kiệm, who was so helpful to us in New York and was now back in Vietnam, piloted my children through the sights and smells of Saigon while Marie spent time with her young auntie Dì Cúc and old girlfriends from Gia Định. Except for Marie, none of the younger children would ever see Saigon again. Finally, our holiday was to end when word came from the Independence Palace that I was overdue at my Hong Kong post. Our departure had been fixed for March 20, 1956.

26. AN IDEALIST IN HONG KONG

AT 6 A.M. ON the appointed day, Phước came to see us off on behalf of Air Vietnam. This was more than just a business call for Air Vietnam, perhaps then working in tandem with Air France, had some tenuous connection with our flight. Nonetheless, as was his wont, Phước found it more 'orthodox' to combine pleasure with business. And in this case, friendship was an intense pleasure for him. To calm his professional conscience, so to speak.

We had no cars from the Foreign Ministry but two from Air Vietnam which took us to the airport. It was not a tearful separation as we were filled with happiness and excitement. Nguyễn Thái, then Director General of Vietnam Press, came to shake my hand; I didn't think it was for professional reasons but could have been for some public relations stunt for himself. Sensing perhaps a Presidential stream of favor and influence pointing in my direction, it would be good politics for him to befriend anew an old 'friend', unlike the blockheaded Huỳnh Văn Lang.

While my wife took charge of our numerous relatives

who had flocked to Tân Sơn Nhứt airport for our 'triumphant' departure, I had time to consider with Phước a plan for more frequent get-togethers over the coming months. We conceived then of a short stay in Đà Lạt, a combination of pleasure and business so the two of us could be together to enjoy the wonderful landscape of high plateaus. This plan was realized sooner than expected, just a few weeks later.

The two-hour flight to Hong Kong was uneventful and our Super Constellation landed in Kowloon at the old Kai Tak Airport, a jut of rocky land hewn from the hills. The airport was so narrow and small that the airplane had to descend almost to sea level before it could slowly fly in to gently touch the runway as if it were some light-footed giant bird alighting on this piece of mainland China just in front of the famous Lion Rock mountain Taxiing in, the plane accidentally cut one of the cables on the poles level with its wings but fortunately, no harm was done. When the airplane stopped and the door yawned open to let in a whip of hot air, I felt a familiar sense of déjà vu: I had landed many times at this same Kai Tak airport six years earlier when I flew for Air Vietnam. The first time I ever visited Hong Kong was on the eve of Chinese New Year, 1950, when both sides of Victoria Harbor were bedecked with red-and-yellow star flags of Communist China.

At the foot of the stairs to meet us stood François Lê Quang Nhã, the outgoing Consul of Vietnam whom I was replacing. We shook hands and Nha let me and my family pass like ordinary tourists through the lines for health, police, and customs. I did not know any better to protest, and as a matter of fact, until I reached Saigon, I had not known that a Vietnamese consulate even existed in Hong Kong. Back in Washington, D.C., I had vaguely imagined having to build a brand-new consulate from scratch, hardly knowing the right financial and practical ropes to pull but ever confident at somehow, "a government should have ample means," as Father Jacques said at the time of our Anti-Partition Demonstration in New York.

Lê Quang Nhã was a short, ultra-active little man, very French in approach (he was a French citizen) and had surprisingly good English. Nhã had been dismissed by President Diệm and if he put me through a humiliating procedure in the ungentle hands of Hong Kong customs and police satrap—a harmless enough measure of revenge on the hated Ngô Đình Diệm government—it was not too bad after all. I innocently shepherded my family through the entire process, all the while beaming a green diplomat's smile, at peace with himself and the world.

Admitted into Hong Kong at last, I unceremoniously led my family out of the terminal, all of us blinking in the glare of the midday sun. A barrage of reporters surrounded us, and I answered their questions, all the time holding hands with Dominic who was also smartly dressed and looking in every way a diplomat's son in his own right. No, I told the reporters, I was a private citizen; this was my very first job not only in diplomacy but in any capacity in government—French or Vietnamese. No, I had no plan whatever concerning the future: all depended on President Ngô Đình Diệm; and yes, I did love Hong Kong a lot as I had visited this British Crown Colony many times in the past,

FRANÇOIS LE QUANG NHÃ took the whole family, not to a hotel to freshen up, not to ***his*** consulate which was on Hong Kong Island across the harbor, but straight to the Tien Hong Lau restaurant, well known for its 'Beggar's Chicken.' Nhã entertained us and when the lunch was over, he had his driver named Chan, a lean Chinese who was tall and nervous, bring us to the Miramar Hotel where we would stay in rooms reserved for us for the next ten days or so while he evacuated his residence on the top of the Peak.

Each day, I crossed the harbor from Kowloon on a car ferry to go to work at the Consulate on Queen's Road Central on Hong Kong Island, officially known as Victoria City. The Consulate as set up by Nhã in 1954, looked more like a commercial office than anything else, straight out of a catalogue for the typical small-cubicle "offices" that small merchants rented then in the crowded island. It had the virtue of being larger than most of the same office type and rang: L-shaped and boxed in between a row of elevator doors on one side and a Chinese merchant's cubicle-office on the other; its five-room stretch housed rooms for a Consul, Vice-Consul, Personal Assistant, and Reading Room all labeled in black letters on smoked glass; a long counter in the chancellery separated the inner offices in the far back for the Consul, Vice-Consul, and Personal Assistant and the Reading Room in the front; public access was through the lone entrance door on the opposite end.

The Reading Room was negligently kept with stacks of books and magazines strewn about; it also smelled faintly of fish as the room also served as dining room where the staff took their meals at noon. The room was the rendezvous place for Vietnamese residents who found it a convenient place to stop and rest their feet while occasionally glancing at the papers and reviews. The windows gave onto Queen's Road meaning that hellish traffic noise invaded this very poor choice for a Reading Room! I took an intense dislike of this room from the outset and quickly had it cleaned up, waiting for the transfer of the entire Consulate to another location more to my taste.

My staff, all picked by my predecessor, consisted of Mrs. Eileen King, an older English lady who was slender and gaunt of face, conservative in outlook and manners, but very efficient and devoted. The Personal Assistant was Nguyễn Văn Tiến, a fortyish Vietnamese who had lived all his life in Shanghai where his Shanghainese wife and children still lived, and whom Tiến periodically chatted with long-distance on the Consulate's telephone. He was our '*chancelier*' or chancellor, a kind of secretary to the Consul tasked with screening, sorting, and preparing the many daily applications for visas, notarizing, and the like for the Consul's approval. Phạm Văn Cúc was a young North Vietnamese, also married to a Cantonese wife, who was Secretary of the Chancellery and helped with miscellaneous bookkeeping. Last was a very smart young Chinese named Wong, whose position was technically Office Boy, but who was given an array of jack-of-all-trade tasks from carrying twice-weekly diplomatic pouches to Kai Tak Airport to preparing fragrant cups of tea for visitors to the Consul, in between paying petty cash for various office supplies.

This reduced staff of four was all locally hired. No one from any Ministry, or even Saigon, worked here at the Consulate in any capacity. It had been rumored that François Lê Quang Nhã set it up this way to keep his affairs away from too close scrutiny by Saigon. It was also one of the reasons for his dismissal. It certainly looked easy given this arrangement to keep the Foreign Affairs Ministry in the dark so long as all paperwork was properly taken care of.

I was an absolute ignoramus at Consulate work and told François so, to his delight and asked him to initiate me into this bewildering mess and show me a way to sort it out. A classmate of mine at Petrus Ký Lycée who was then Secretary General at the Ministry, asked me to "go easy" on Nhã, which I did, giving him all the time to settle his business prior to his leaving Hong Kong for good. However, Nhã gave me nothing by way of real instruction, let alone initiation. Instead, he just furtively came and went who knows where, talked in low tones with Mrs. King or Tiến just out of earshot, and otherwise wound up his affairs which had nothing to do with official business. All he gave me was a heap of typewritten papers he prepared himself, stating to his satisfaction that all the existing stocks of passports, fiscal stamps, bank accounts and the like that I was to sign as "accepted as true and correct." I did so without any means to check the numbers, for no control was easy or even feasible on my part, except for bank statements which Nhã never was involved with anyway. Then, François Lê Quang Nhã disappeared from the scene without even a little "Au revoir."

The Consulate had two 'extra' employees on the payroll, also local hires, whose work had only the most tenuous connection with the mission to Hong Kong. Mr. Trương Anh Mẫn was a sixty-odd year-old journalist who worked half a day on his Chinese-language newspaper and a few hours producing the Consulate's translation and summary of the daily Chinese press to send to Saion. Mrs. Võ Thị Diệu Viên, called Miss Hoa, an author (Gió Bấc) in her own right who was married to a Chinese, but in the fashion of artists, kept her maiden name preceded by 'Miss.' Miss Hoa then, had nothing to do except help Mr. Mẫn put together a magazine in Vietnamese that was mimeographed and 'published' by the Consulate. This was sent once every few months to the few residents in Hong Kong, not so much by way of information or even propaganda, but because it was the fashion for each Mission abroad to publish such as magazine. Since the Vietnamese colony on the island was about the tiniest in the world—and incidentally, the easiest group of Vietnamese expatriates to deal with having adopted the Chinese attitude of live and let live—and the outgoing Consul did not worry overmuch about them as he certainly had other things in mind than their welfare or the Vietnamese government of Ngô Đình Diệm whom he secretly despised.

Miss Hoa and the old Truong Anh Mẫn were then, rightly considered as 'extra' personnel, and didn't much care that they were treated and paid as such. Interestingly, this pair developed into my closest collaborators at the Consulate, to the amazement of the remaining staff who had been conditioned to treat them poorly by François Lê Quang Nhã. Both were paid even less than Wong, the office boy, but since they had almost nothing to do with the proper work of the Consulate, they could not remonstrate without risk of losing even their meager salaries. Life in Hong Kong was not exactly easy.

From the first day I set foot in the Consulate, everyone was grim-faced and uneasy. I knew nothing about running a government Mission and openly acknowledged my lack of training. Why, François Lê Quang Nhã and Pham Khao Rậu (then Consul in Singapore) were both trained at the French Consulate General in Hong Kong for several months prior to assuming their respective posts. Not being given any training, I 'democratically' invited all present to teach me and contribute their utmost to help me do a good job. For I meant to do a good job and would not accept perfunctory performance that was so entrenched in Vietnamese functionaries.

I emphasized that I would not hear of any customary 'Tea Money' paid under the table for any service rendered at this Consulate. The former Consul, I noted, had "perhaps wrongly" been accused of such bribes and even "selling his signature" for hard cash. François Lê Quang Nhã and his family were the products of France and the few selected to privileged posts selected few privileged with the French era: of which his father, the Chef de Province (*Đốc Phủ Sứ*) during French colonial rule, Lê Quang Hổ; his uncle, Lê Văn Hoạch, the first Vietnamese of French citizenship ever made Premier of the Separatist Government of Cochinchina; another uncle, a technical support officer (*Agent Technique)*, Lê Quang Nghị; and of course, François Lê Quang Nhã himself. I knew it was said that Nha, perhaps sensing his impending end with the ascendancy of Ngô Đình Diệm and the consequent demise of the French era, had been preparing in all haste a 'nest egg' before he was obliged to leave the Hong Kong Consulship and Vietnam for good.

I raised my 'innocent' (i.e., unsophisticated and starry-eyed idealistic) voice against such practices as may have been tolerated in the past and declared that we all would walk a new path from now on. I promised, without ever suspecting how unrealistic such a promise was, that I would demand and obtain a raise in salaries for everyone in order to help them live decently and abandon the bad habits of the past in the Consulate. The staff listened to my speech, eyes downcast and with long faces. None of them made a comment. They knew the realities of life even if I did not, just as I confessed to not knowing how to run a Consulate. In Hong Kong, bribes and corruption were an institution, a way of life.

No staff member approved of my sincere if hopelessly unrealistic pep talk. None, that is, except for the two 'extra' hands, Mr. Trương Anh Mẫn and Miss Võ Thị Diệu Viên, alias Miss Hoa. Only these two faces had smiles and shining eyes, their heads slightly nodding. They were, in all appearances, the neglected minority, the 'outsiders' in a highly lucrative and exclusive oligarchy. And then I arrived, like a proverbial downpour in the midst of a prolonged drought: "*Đang cơn nắng hạn gặp mưa rào!*" Or a refreshing southerly wind amid a hectic summer:

"May gặp nồm Nam cơn gió thoảng
Đàn ta, ta gảy khúc Nam nghe..."[63]

Luckily the southern breeze blows by,
Let's pluck our southern song on our guitar!

These two could not but welcome my new approach. Having already noticed how Miss Hoa had been looked down upon by her office colleagues, I made it a point to give her a ride in the consular car with me every day after work. The office boy, rude with everyone and doubly so with her, could hardly control his trembling hands to open the car door for me and slam it shut after she took her seat. While crossing the harbor on the vehicular ferry I had plenty of time to inquire about the kind of work and 'bad habits' of the past at the consulate and was amply instructed by Miss Hoa day after day after day.

As for the old man, Trương Anh Mẫn, we lunched together almost every day either at some restaurant in town or, more often because of its proximity, at the Dim Sum tea shop at the top of our building that did a flourishing business. Little by little I learned that the old man was a revolutionary, expatriated for over 30 years, and whose great uncle, Mr. Nguyễn Thượng Hiền, was a follower and closest collaborator of our famous revolutionary Phan Bội Châu.[64] Mẫn himself left Vietnam at 18, immediately after he passed an examination in the classics to achieve the title Cử Nhân in the old royal system, this being the

63 These verses are from a poem titled "Vào Hè» (The arrival of summer) by Dương Bá Trạc (1884-1944).

64 Nguyễn Thượng Hiền (1865?-1925) was a Vietnamese scholar-gentry and anti-colonial revolutionary activist.

last one of his era as from then on, education became French-programmed and directed. Mẫn stayed with Phan Bội Châu and his great uncle in China near the Hangzhou Lake (a site of renowned beauty where Nixon was brought during his first visit to China in 1972), in Japan, back to Canton in China, and lastly, in Hong Kong.

I also learned that during Ngô Đình Diệm's short stay in Hong Kong in 1947, when he was consulting with and urging Bảo Đại to refuse the diverse French offers at the time that were tantamount to making him a puppet for colonialism, he became friends with Mẫn and on many occasions, they visited mainland China together. Thus, I made a new sympathetic friend, and we were seen together almost daily, to the exasperation of those that Francois Lê Quang Nhã left behind.

VERY QUICKLY, THE consensus of the 'left-behind' group as voiced behind my back by Phạm Văn Cúc, was that I was a perfect ignoramus. Not knowing my grade, not sophisticated enough to be a Consul, I was, on top of that, hopelessly 'reactionary'. What was the point of being Head of Mission, or working at a consulate for that matter, if corruption was to be avoided? Only an incurable 'reactionary' or a shameless liar, could preach such a line of conduct—in Hong Kong, of all places! They all proceeded to ignore me, but also kept an eye on me for improbable poking into their dealings, and continued exactly as if Francois Lê Quang Nhã were still in control.

The Consul and Mrs. Bùi Công Văn, Hong Kong (1957)

Mrs. Bùi Công Văn and Governor of Hong Kong Sir Alexander Grantham at a reception (2/22/1957)

Governor of Hong Kong Sir Robin Black and Mrs. Black are with Mr. & Mrs. Bùi Công Văn (1958 or 1959)

Group photo of a diplomatic corps at national dress party, with Bùi Công Văn standing in the back, fourth from left and Mrs. Bui seated second from right (around 1962)

Already, back in Saigon earlier in March while my family and I were still at the Hotel Catinat, many well-wishers called on me. Some just hinted at 'assistance,' but Đỗ Văn Cửu, a cousin on my stepmother's side, found it normal to enlighten me in the ways of 'making progress' in the well-established ways of the world. After not too much beating about the bush, he took the straight line as the shortest route from one point to another and said: "You'll be rich in no time in Hong Kong," and added as Đinh Văn Bân had warned me, "you'll see, you'll see!" To which, vexed by Cuu's taking it for granted that I belonged to the same school of thought, I indignantly replied: "But you're barking at the wrong tree, poor dog! Not Me! If Ngô Đình Diệm were bad enough to have me doing his job in Hong Kong the way you said, then I'm afraid he would not be President for long!" Cửu was dumbfounded and never brought up the subject again, quickly leaving me to my backward notions.

At the dinner party I gave my first week in Hong Kong for all the Vietnamese residents, I publicly explained changes to the Consulate in the same vein and tone as I did my staff. They received my speech very well, although some of them confided to me that it was easier said than done. And my confession of both ignorance and a sincere desire to 'serve' each and every one of them was a bit off beat! Most of the residents were conservative and as such, did not accept a public servant to be literally their servant. One successful businessman told me about his response to consulate visa expediter Phạm Văn Cúc's opinion of my consulship: "The Consul may be a perfect ignoramus as you think, but one thing he does know is to give you the boot!"

The first thing I did, in line with my policy, was to suppress what was called the "Overtime System." Since the Mission was established in early 1954, a system was instituted where any visa applicant had to pay an extra fee with the misnomer "Over Time" because if this were so, it should be paid to the home government, not the applicant. Created at first to secure a 'supplement to salary' by Francois in order to give his subordinate some bones to share among the group while he wheeled and dealed all by himself with big business and merchants. This system taxed only those applicants who wanted their 'visas expedited' somehow, and mostly because they applied on a weekend when the Consulate, like any other office in town, was closed.

Arbitrarily calculated—'fixed' is a better word—the 'over time' was collected throughout the week and amounted from several hundred to several thousand Hong Kong dollars. Francois divided this sum with everyone except Mẫn and Miss Hoa. For fairness' sake, Francois gave himself the lion's share, of course. For me, the astonishing thing in this system was that applicants never complained and were more than willing to pay. In fact, they insisted on paying, knowing full well that it was by far the lesser of two evils: either they paid a relatedly small sum and got their visa 'sped up,' or they might wait for weeks to be told that "Saigon has no word on your application yet."

At first, I refused to take Francois's lion share which by right became mine, and let the staff divide it up as they saw fit. This delighted the gang as the addition of my/ Francois's share was by no means negligible. However, I very soon put an end to the system altogether, promising to have all their salaries jacked up and I immediately wrote to the Ministry to that effect. As the weeks passed without even an acknowledgement of my request and no reply whatever to my reminders, the payday tension almost physically mounted and then spread over to every day. Realizing the meagerness of their pay, I relented and allowed them to make a reasonable charge (about one-tenth of the highest amount on record—and strictly on weekends when 'over time' meant what it said, like for big companies whose shipping manifest needed to be visaed in a hurry. Needless to say, staff found means and tricky ways to devise the highest 'reasonable' charges possible and I did not have the time nor energy to impose personal control over it.

What further changed my staff was forcing them to let Mr. Mẫn and Miss Hoa to have a part of the cake. If, I pointed out, Saigon made it necessary for you to charge the public 'over-time' to compensate for your low salaries, then Mr. Mẫn and Miss Hoa who have lower salaries than yours must also receive their share. Thus, the 'over-time system' continued, although slightly corrected.

Overtime was not the main disease at the consulate, though. For instance, Nguyễn Văn Tiến who oversaw passport visas, could make ten times his salary by doing nothing but what he was supposed to do. The Chinese came to his house and literally begged him to let himself be bribed. I had the ugly choice of either replacing him (but then, who would be the *Simon-Pure* to take his place without also taking bribes?) or, also unlikely, to keep such a close watch on him that he wouldn't receive anyone having any business with the Consulate at his private home.

"There is nothing you can do about it," said Dr. Francois Sun, a Vietnamese dental surgeon, long established in Hong Kong, who befriended me almost the first week I was in town. His Chinese name of Sun Tsung Tak, for convenience's sake, was but the translation of his Vietnamese name, Thân Trọng Đức of the well-known Thân Trọng clan of Huế in Central Vietnam, a scion of which was no other than Madame Trần Văn Chương, née Thân Thị Nam Trân, wife of the Ambassador to Washington, D.C. Francois continued, "If you control Tiến or anyone else, you will end up paralyzing your Consulate. The staff will continue taking bribes and you will be blamed for any delay—whether or not you caused it by not signing the visa. Believe me, the fault will be all yours! Don't be such a fool and be called anti-Chinese! As a matter of fact, not taking bribes in this town is the worst anti-'Sinoism' imaginable. Everybody does it, from the Governor or Hong Kong on down."

Little by little, I learned my lessons. And although Dr. Sun tried to impress me with the 'troubles' I could incur if Tiến, for one, was dismissed, I was not worried about it when I decided to keep him. It was the glaring realities of life, which up to date, I refused to see. I was soon to learn more painful lessons much more serious and pregnant with dire consequences for both Ngô Đình Diệm and Vietnam, or at least the remaining 'free' half of the country.

IN THE MEANTIME, after ten days or so in the Miramar Hotel in Kowloon, word came to us that the former Consul had vacated his house on the Peak. This area was the secluded spot comprising the highest hilltops on Hong Kong Island, directly behind Government House and overlooking downtown Victoria City. This was ***the*** prime residence for every Hong Kong snob. To own or even rent a house on 'The Peak' was to belong to the exclusive club of the 'Nobles' of Hong Kong. All dignitaries, money-ennobled or knighted by the Court of St. James for whatever reason, had to have their abode on The Peak. It once was a 'No Chinese Admitted' place on a par with the Shanghai parks of old, although no mention of dogs was made, during the heyday of British colonization prior to Pearl Harbor. Since then, however, many a Chinese, Sir this and the Honorable that, or simply a Mr. Millionaire, shared The Peak with white aristocracy. Francois Le Quang Nhã rented a house at mid-level Peak Road, at the end of a winding road cut into the side of a rugged hill.

My family quickly moved in and the same headaches with the Vietnamese personnel at the Consulate repeated themselves at the residence with the existing Chinese staff. The standard household staff for every well-to-do family in Hong Kong consisted of a Number One Boy, a kind of butler who supposedly supervised all the domestics, a driver, a cook, and a wash amah. Wong, the Number One, had been stealing left and right from François to get kickbacks while ordering supplies or just siphoning off the stocks of food and liquor. He also had heard of my 'innocence' in diplomacy and expected to bleed me white when we moved in, but his arrogance brought me to a quick decision: dismissal on the spot. A few days later, Wong jumped me at the Consulate and when the police were summoned, the two Chinese officers took ***his*** side, teaching me in a gentlemanly way another lesson on "anti-'Sinoism.'"

For the first time, my family enjoyed decent housing. Marie, then 15, was old enough to appreciate it more than her brother and sisters and she wrote home: "I enjoy living under the Vietnamese flag." Indeed, a huge yellow flag with three red stripes flew over the house at the top of a solid pole. Nearby, on the other side of the hill, flew the U.S. and the Dutch flags. It was not exactly Embassy Row but Foreign Missions, too, not only enjoyed snobbism but promoted it, at least in the British Crown Colony of Hong Kong.

To see my family moving in, modestly dressed and still more modestly baggage, the Chinese household staff shrewdly appraised our value in terms of dollars and also prestige. Hence, the Number One's arrogance after I dismissed him on sight, however, the remaining servants didn't behave any more realistically. And my habit of saying, "Thank You," to them for any service, rapidly reestablished the confidence so much so that my wife, afraid lest they take advantage of us, had to remind me several times that "We are no longer in the United States!" Ah, how much more did I have to learn to cope with the

East? Or should I say, with the different words of East and West? Corruption, however, was a sin committed aplenty but not condoned by the West and the Westernized Asians on their way to decolonization and statehood. And I was very much one of their most innocent idealists.

In 1956, I was not alone in this trend toward idealism. Many were, from President Ngô Đình Diệm on down, affected by an unjustified optimism, inspired not by a judicious analysis of the situation present and future, but almost fatalistically by a certainty of success. A 'mystical' sense of perhaps divine mission pervaded the Independence Palace to seep through layers of supernaturally disposed souls present here and there throughout the government apparatus, and emanating as it were on the peaceful waves of the South China Sea toward diplomatic representations in this neighborly part of Southeast and Northeast Asia.

Realities, and political realities at that, dissuaded these goggle-eyed idealist-optimists—if not President Diệm himself—soon enough, but the year 1956 was definitely the highest point of Ngô Đình Diệm's ascendancy and career. Coupled with his recent victories over the sects, the rebellious Army, Bảo Đại, and the French themselves, was his untarnished reputation of a life-long integrity and incorruptibility. It was unthinkable to have corruption in the government, and while communism was the chief enemy, it was yet dormant (the deadline of a July 1956 General Election as agreed to at Geneva and the Agreement itself, being dead), it was not the pressing problem of the day. Publications around that time straight-facedly wrote that corruption "no longer existed" under Ngô Đình Diệm.

The same spirit prevailed in my little world, at least as far as I was personally concerned, and I quixotically continued with my private anti-corruption crusade. Part of this reform-minded effort, itself faithful to the spirit if not the letter of the 'National Revolution' at home, was my concern for the underdog. One evening, a visitor calling on us at the Miramar Hotel during our first week in Hong Kong told us that Francois Lê Quang Nhã's consulate was pretty much a 'private concern' run by and for the former consul with only the strictest number of employees. As a case in point, my visitor recounted his situation: jobless and on the verge of starving in cosmopolitan Hong Kong, he told how he came repeatedly to the consulate not for any handout but for the lowliest job of office boy, which he would have taken even as second to Wong, the Chinese office boy: "Mind you, Mr. Consul," my visitor pointed at his chest, "after all, ***I am*** a Vietnamese citizen!" I decided to hire him forthwith and told him to present himself at the chancellery the next morning. His name was Nguyễn Van Nhu and was put in charge of the numerous visitors from home who, with the passing days, found their way more and more often to the British Crown Colony. Until our departure from Hong Kong and well after, Nhu was the busiest member of the Consulate, as he was indispensable to every Vietnamese visitor, high or low, who without exception, monopolized him from arrival to departure. It was the beginning of a tiresome 'fame' our Consulate acquired which, during later years, developed into a "Free and Easy Visa Dispensing Office", where applicants for visas to travel abroad—and especially to Europe—were told by the Home Ministry: "Go to Hong Kong: the Consul there will grant you exit visas for any country you want."

Groping my way along almost alone, I gradually imposed on the staff the notion that the 'Revolution' was genuine, and they came around to seeing things my way, or they at least realized it was worse than useless to resist. However, little work had been done as far as the Consulate's daily routine chores were concerned. Besides passport visas that had been approved by Saigon and were delivered as a matter of course, there were the trickiest visas to grant on commercial invoices. Any firm dealing with Saigon had to submit pro-forma and definitive invoices for consular approval certifying that "the merchandise concerned were correctly priced according to current market quotations." Not counting the unfeasible control of whether the merchandise invoiced in fact corresponded both in quality and quantity with actual shipments. The long-established method practiced in Hong Kong was to ship a certain amount of goods of a certain quality from one Chinese firm in Hong Kong to another firm in Saigon (also Chinese most of the time) with any kind of paperwork having little to do with its correctness. To ask the Consul to certify papers' authenticity was tantamount to offering him an open road to collect time-honored 'Tea Money.' There was the sheer herculean task of checking hundreds of invoices, each bearing thousands of items against daily fluctuating market commodity quotations. With the Cold War then going full swing, the problem of distinguishing which merchandise was Communist-made and which were not via a Certificate of Origin authenticity was as thin as the paper on which it was printed. Apparently, this was deemed an impossible task to do honestly or conscientiously: it could not be done—period—so it was not done. I was amazed to see the invoices piling up daily on my desk, untouched. Every two days, I stored them away to make room for another pile and the rumor had it that I was "negotiating a way for kickbacks" before I finally would sign them. The plain fact was that I was at a loss of what to do and found no one to help me out. Should I return them all and thus stop trade between Hong Kong and Saigon, the main reason this Consulate existed in the first place? Or could it be done some other less cumbersome way with, say, no visas needed at all? Why should the Consul sign anything he knew nothing about?

After ten days or so, I determined that a solution had to be found or I might as well resign, for even the Governor of Hong Kong could not keep his job if he somehow interfered with the 'free trade' between the Colony and the outside world. Even Hanoi already had begun trading with Hong Kong. Some friends who meant well whispered into my ears that if money had no odor, it had even less of a smell in Hong Kong. Why should I break my heart over such an obvious modus vivendi?

I must have some help, I thought, a trusted man. A person from the Ministry if possible and preferably someone I knew well to at least do the paperwork, the cumbersome checking of stated commodities against stated prices. I could not blindly sign any paper like Francois Lê Quang Nhã did—it was said he even signed heaps of blank invoices in advance (for a fee of course) for firms to fill out later at their leisure. And it was said that he was dismissed for that, too. Yet, no one at the Ministry told me about how to proceed, what pitfalls to avoid, what help I could get. I had to figure this all out by ear, without notes or instruction, and bear the consequences.

Paper invoices piling up notwithstanding, I wrote the Foreign Affairs Ministry and stated my problem, asking for a trusted man to help. In the meantime, my diplomatic activities went on as they must, and diplomacy consisted mainly of receiving, entertaining, and seeing off our home government VIPs. During my tenure in Hong Kong, the first of them all (and of the highest caliber to boot), was Nguyễn Hữu Châu, then Secretary to the Presidency. In him, I unexpectedly found help, if only because anyone less influential than him would have left me facing piles of invoices and mounting grudges from Hong Kong's commercial world.

Nguyễn Hữu Châu, aside from his privileged position of Minister to the Presidency and thus the closest advisor to President Ngô Đình Diệm, was also the husband of Madame Ngô Đình Nhu's sister whom he was divorcing. Mr. Châu was awaiting a presidential pronouncement on his case (since it involved the Ngô family), but he remained very much an 'in' person and could be the most powerful man in government after Diệm's brother Nhu and his wife. I banked on this fact for some advice and was impatiently looking forward to the day he arrived.

The Hong Kong government dispatched the Director of Foreign Trade, a Mr. Barlow, to Kai Tak Airport to meet H.E. Nguyễn Hữu Châu. I arrived early and was at the airport restaurant having a drink when Mr. Barlow appeared. In my clumsy haste to stand and shake his proffered hand, I knocked over a chair and profusely apologized as he bent down to right the chair. He unceremoniously led me, hand on my arm, to the Immigration and Customs counter where we stood waiting for the plane from Saigon to arrive.

Too new to the trade to even know—and no one at the Consulate so much as suggested it to me—that a person of Mr. Châu's rank should be welcomed in the VIP room at the airport. Mr. Barlow, no doubt looking in vain for me there before he found me at the restaurant, was diplomatic enough to take the matter in hand. As soon as the airplane taxied to the tarmac a few yards from the immigration counter, we both stepped out to meet Mr. Châu. Barlow took his passport and "whipped" the minister through the immigration line in a jiffy and we rode to town in the Consulate's official car. It should have been obvious to me, but even then, it somehow was not, that this was how I should have been welcomed to Hong Kong as representative of the Republic of Vietnam. More so than His Excellency, who after all was but a visitor passing through Hong Kong. Instead, François Lê Quang Nhã deliberately left me unmet, unwelcomed, and unceremoniously inching my way through immigration lines like any tourist—and with my family in tow! But no matter. I was preoccupied with my problems at work and anyway, VIPs as well as protocol interested me little. That arrival day, I was looking at my job with different eyes, with an artist's outlook, a poet's approach to a scenic post which, as President Diệm himself explained to me, "I assigned you there because I knew Hong Kong would please you with its beautiful landscape."

VIP welcoming rituals observed or not, I quickly set things on my own unorthodox and slightly eccentric step. Nguyễn Hữu Châu was taken straight to the Chinese Tea House on top of my Consulate's building—Lê Quang Nhã's example was not lost on his novice!—and after sampling the tasty dim sum from steaming bamboo containers that pretty Chinese servers carried around the room on trays suspended by straps, dangling before their half-full moon chests, chanting their wares all the while, the minister asked for and got a conducted tour of the Tiger Balm Mansion, a 'marvel' he had heard so much about and a must when in Hong Kong. Ironically, I was conducting the tour despite never having visited the mansion myself. It was an ugly piece of chinoiserie, baroque, and childishly shaped and colored; it had the aggravating fault of being too vast, too stretched out on level after level of man-made rocks and streams.

The tour took several hours, and reverting to my own ways when bored or unwilling to comply overmuch, I preached tiredness and let his excellency explore for himself the intricacies of a concrete and cement 'Buddhist Hell' complete with its "Ten Penal Gates." Mr. Châu had hardly gotten half-way through, however, when I called up from below and pointed out to him a Chinese vendor of noodles and Fukien vermicelli soup whose mobile kitchen cart was parked against a jutting false rock shaded by a panoply of green bamboo and banana leaves. The minister nodded his assent and good humoredly accepted his bowl of vermicelli while I had already started shoveling mine into my hungry mouth. Any VIPs expecting diplomatic treatment from me were doomed to exasperation.

Mr. Châu's good mood helped me present my problem to him and he promised to "send over to your Consulate whomever you name for the job you have in mind." I was much relieved to obtain his word and to this day, I still think back with unsuppressed merriment to my first "diplomatic gaffe" that put an end to my vexing problem. Mr. Châu's word had power and the excellent result of seconding Huỳnh Văn Tư from the Economic Affairs Ministry to the Foreign Affairs Ministry and dispatched post-haste to Hong Kong. The icing on my cake was this expert was a good boyhood friend from Mỹ Phong village, famed for its flower cultivation. Tư helped me sort out the accumulated invoices in no time and at least on paper, I could without qualms certify the invoice quotations as "true and correct" and state there was "neither over- nor underpriced," providing that the merchandise shipped could be verified accordingly which thankfully, was not my responsibility!

But it was two long months before Tư arrived, 60 miserable days in which I struggled single-handedly against a well-entrenched modus operandi. Soon, I asked for and obtained a Mr. Sư from the Ministry, but even fortified with helpers, Consulate personnel could barely attend to decent and honest work. Until 'my men' arrived, I was like Wong, the shrewd Office Boy who combined several jobs from code-deciphering to bookkeeping and party-arranging, a jack-of-all-trades forced to cope unaided with constantly shifting demands. Many were the nights when I had to stay behind and struggle with the code-book in order to read a ciphered telegram from the Ministry (a job Francois Lê Quang Nhã did himself after training and years of practice—local personnel having nothing to do with this) and then, to bring the book home and work until early morning to encode an urgent reply.

Hardly had I been somewhat relieved of my workload and constant preoccupations when K.C. Leong, a Pepsi-Cola tycoon, owner of The Peak residence rented to the Consulate, sent word that the lease had expired, and we had to move out. A month of house-hunting ensued and finally in June, we moved to a brand-new villa at 11 Perkins Road, Jardine's Lookout. Here we settled down and spent the best years of our stay in Hong Kong until the debacle began in late 1962 that culminated in the precipitous fall and killing of President Ngô Đình Diệm in 1963. We had thus a respite of almost seven years in which to, as Uncle Gil said, "think of our children", and indeed, it was about time to think of them and their neglected education.

After over two months of waiting, Marie was admitted to the Maryknoll High School run by the Maryknoll Sisters, in Kowloon where she went early every morning, crossing the harbor on the Star Ferry. Chan, the driver brought Marie to and from the Star Ferry Dock Yard every day and then right afterwards, took Dominic (8) and Mỹ-Châu (6) to Royden House, a private school on the Hong Kong side, and fetched them in the afternoon. In between, he was free to retire for the day if we had no party to attend or stayed over several times a week for late dinners or other official functions.

Bùi Công Văn gives speech wearing national costume on the occasion of the Republic of Vietnam's National Day (October 10, unknown year)

Mail from Vietnam addressed to the Mission in Hong Kong

Muriel Mỹ-Nga and Lucie Mỹ-Châu in Hong Kong on National Day with ceramic dish of Diem's image on table (October 10, 1960)

27. FRIENDSHIPS

ALL IN ALL, these Hong Kong years were hectic and unceasingly bothersome in one way or another, but we surmounted most difficulties by keeping President Diệm in mind, knowing well how much more difficult his own task was we willed ourselves to do our best to repay his kindness and trust in us. The first year for my wife and I would set the pace for the rest of our Mission to Hong Kong. This time left many a poignant as well as pleasant memory in our lives and by chance, was also the best year of the Ngô Đình Diệm administration. We were not without many years of happy life, for next to being home in Vietnam, Hong Kong was the best place to live and work. For one thing, it was so close to Saigon that we were practically home and a first opportunity to go home hardly six months after assuming my post presented itself in late summer when Vice President Nixon visited Saigon.

I was to convey a very special shipment of fireworks hastily ordered from Macao and carried that same day to Saigon in time for that night's celebration of Nixon's arrival. Air France had removed six rows of seats from a special plane for the trip as fireworks or firearms or ammunition are not allowed in passenger cabins: I flew home alone, with no other passengers and only the crew as companions. When the plane landed at Tân Sơn Nhứt at dusk and a Foreign Affairs Ministry official took charge of the shipment, I quickly disappeared into the crowds and incognito, enjoyed two days visiting with family and friends. For now, I considered my job as exclusively being in Hong Kong, not in Saigon, and was not squeamish in getting lost for a few short days from my work and headaches. A sort of R&R for diplomats abroad, although in reverse, and rightly so.

It was the same evening of my arrival that I went to see my father for the first time at Cô Tư's (Auntie Four) house on stilts over the swamp waters of Xóm Chiếu, near Khánh Hội. I did not see him in March on our return from the U.S. for lack of time (although at Huỳnh Sanh Thông's request, I did go visit ***his*** father at the latter's apartment). In the twilight of that summer evening, Cô Tư's house seemed so tiny and poor and my father who was resting on a bamboo-framed bed looked so emaciated and haggard that I was touched when he hastily got up to receive me as if I were some important caller. I made up my mind to do the utmost and move him out of this pauper-like abode. It struck me then to look back in time and saw in my mind's eye our paternal house as it was 20 years ago in 1936 when I received my Diploma of Higher Primary Education and graduated from Cần Thơ College (a high school). We were far better off then than in these years: my father much enjoying his life, I was in the prime of youth, and we both along with my younger brothers, had been living wonderful years.

This was the first in a series of regular trips home from Hong Kong. I'd visit family and whenever possible snatch my good friends Nhuận, Phước, and Lương away from whatever work they were doing. For my sake, they gladly skipped their noon siestas and thus was born the habit of getting together on my visits and intensely enjoying every minute together. It was as if we unconsciously all knew we were in our homeland on borrowed time that could be ended overnight, no one knew when.

It was thus that on the third and last evening together in Saigon, my friends were waiting for me at Đồng Quê restaurant, a countryside eating place far from the city when I was detained in the Independence Palace by one of the interminable "sessions" of President Diệm. The hours passed and the President kept talking. Eight, nine, ten o'clock … the eleventh hour was approaching. A thing that had never happened before came to pass when "in audience" with the President. I stood up in the middle of his monologue and without further ado, told him that "my friends" had been waiting for me ever since seven that evening. I excused myself and left—to the astonishment of both Diệm and a captain attached to his private service who remembered filling my glass of wine—a unique "never heard of" instance according to all who knew where the President treated a caller with wine—mass wine—the only alcoholic beverage in his possession. Rather than keeping my friends even longer that evening, I apologized and left. A thing, they said, which had never been done before—almost a discourtesy to the President. The fact that I did it, and got away with it, greatly enhanced my "prestige" in the eyes of the Palace denizens.

1956 was the last year in which President Diệm was still fresh from his victories over the remnants of colonialism and not yet besieged anew by new opposition, the least of which was not the Communist's fledgling campaign culminating in the National Liberation Front,[65] had time enough to prolong, so to speak, his private soirees with me *en tête a tête* [face to face]. One night, in the midst of one of his "sessions" with me, Ông Ngô picked up his telephone and told the Vice President, Nguyễn Ngọc Thơ, to "wait for the Consul who, from here, will stop at your place and the two of you will talk things out together." Diệm meant from my periodic reports to him on problems I had to solve in Hong Kong and the subject was the economic trade between the colony and Saigon. As was Diệm's habit, he kept talking on and on and forgot all about his phone call to the Vice President. When I finally left the Independence Palace and was driven to Thơ's residence, it was three in the morning! The poor man had not dared to call back and countermand the President's order or excuse himself by simply leaving a note for the doorman to tell me to see him the next day. Instead, he was in his wrinkled pajamas and yawning ferociously when I was shown in.

---

65 The National Liberation Front for South Vietnam (NLF) was to be founded in December 1960 as a cover for North Vietnam's leadership of the communist insurgency in the South.

Bùi Công Văn with other officials in Saigon 4/27/61

Vietnamese heads of mission deplane in Saigon for a Ministerial meeting called by President Diem (Bùi Công Văn is in the foreground, to the left of the man holding a white hat) (1961)

IN THE FALL, the first conference of Heads of Missions was called to take place at the Foreign Affairs Ministry and be chaired by the Foreign Secretary, Mr. Vũ Văn Mẫu. It too, was to be the first and last conference in which, still afire with energy and yet undiluted realism, I vehemently spoke up, stating my problems, preaching reform and improvements, and otherwise annoyed other more sophisticated—that is to say, cynical—colleagues.

Trần Văn Chương, Ambassador to the U.S., and especially Ngô Đình Luyện (a younger brother of Diệm) behaved as if they were above all the rest. They talked nonsensically and curtly, verbally looking down on all at the conference, the Foreign Minister included. The Ngô Đình Diệm government in later years was accused of being a "family oligarchy" and rightly so, but back in 1956 when it still rode high on the general esteem of the public, we at the conference were given a bitter sample of this in the "misdemeanor" of Chương and Luyện. Four years later, when the second Conference of Heads of Missions convened in the thick of a mounting crisis (the Liberation Front had started its guerilla movement and already had some victories to their credit), I kept my mouth shut. Let the Chươngs and the Luyệns talk to their hearts' content, I told myself.

In the Diệm administration, I was perhaps the lone exception to the general practice for cabinet members and the lowest of functionaries alike: everyone had to deal with, and follow the orders of, the Political Advisor to the President, Mr. Ngô Đình Nhu. I had never once been inside the Adviser's office except toward the end of the government and in circumstances both exasperating and ludicrous. Until then, I had only been in touch with the President and the Foreign Minister as far as my Mission in Hong Kong was concerned.

Neither had I been called home for consultations, perhaps because I found enough opportunities of my own to come home, but primarily because it was soon a well-established procedure to let the President deal with me on any failings—if he so desired. At least for the early years of the presidency, when Diệm found the time and mood to talk to me, the result was to revive in a way the friendly, intimate atmosphere of his exile years in New York, a rather particular relationship which was misinterpreted as favoritism and worse. Political enemies did not wait long to start a whispering campaign against me, even while it was Ngô Đình Diệm himself who repeated many of those accusations to me!

BACK IN HONG KONG, the first national day of the Republic of Vietnam was celebrated on October 26, 1956. It was the day, one year ago, when the results of the Election-Referendum struck Bảo Đại from the position of Head of State of Vietnam and proclaimed Ngô Đình Diệm President of the Republic. We gave a reception at the Repulse Bay Hotel where Governor Alexander Grantham replied to my toast to "Her Majesty, Queen Elizabeth the Second" by raising his champagne glass to "President Ngô Đình Diệm of the Republic of Vietnam." All Hong Kong was present, The Republic was nascent, all prospects looked good, and the future seemed assured. The Geneva-prescribed date of July 1956 for Reunification Elections had passed, unobserved and forgotten.[66] From now on, at least for the many partisans of Ngô Đình Diệm, there was no reason to doubt the survival or even the prosperity of the Republic. We had every reason to go on, optimistically building from an undisputed leadership to progress toward unlimited possibilities.

Our home life also visibly improved. We were happy at Jardine's Hill, as the neighborhood was called in Chinese. Against the background of a ridge of hills stretching from Diamond Hill to as far as Repulse Bay, our villa proudly flew its red and yellow flag. The house's fortunes for many years went up and down according to the fluctuations of the Diệm government back in Vietnam. Despite its hasty construction for commercial purposes rather than a more solid architectural style than a homeowner would like, the house's layout was modern, simple, and comfortable. With three bedrooms and a spare room upstairs, our villa boasted a large living room, a sunny and bright study, and a Chinese style dining room which was rather small. Our front verandah was spacious, and cars could drop visitors off right at the front door under the children's bedroom which protruded out front, like a beige Domino block supported on two round columns that extended from the mid-level of the spacious building and front yard.

Chrysanthemum, *thược dược* (dahlias), and various seasonal flowers adorned the front yard carefully tended by a gardener, while in the back yard, my wife enjoyed her

66 The Ngô Đình Diệm government protested in vain against the division of Vietnam and did not sign the Geneva Agreements, which were essentially an agreement between the communist and French governments.

small garden of lettuce, Vietnamese vegetables, and chili peppers. Dominic started keeping fish and birds and even white mice which procreated apace and one day escaped in tiny files through mom's vegetable rows. Canaries gave us hours of delightful birdsong and sometimes, I taped and played back recordings of their own chirps to get them to respond, not recognizing their own melodies.

Muriel was only four and still too young to go to school so often, I took her to downtown Hong Kong, or Wan Chai, and treated her to wonton soup and noodles—she called such outings with me "an adventure." Soon, Dominic was a young student at St. Joseph's primary school, renowned for its strict discipline and high standards of education. While Marie continued her studies at Maryknoll High School in Kowloon, Mỹ-Châu went to the Maryknoll Primary School on the Hong Kong side. Resplendent in their uniforms, the children nowadays belonged to the so-called "high-class" of the colony and Dominic's schoolmates bore names like Lobo, of the famous god dealer family from nearby Macao.

On the mountain behind our home was a winding trail cut out of the rock of Mount Butler called "Sir Cecil's Ride" that led from the villa all the way to Repulse Bay miles away on the other side of the mountain. We often strolled this route *en famille,* accompanied by our dogs Lassie and Lucky. On the hillside, green with pine groves and sprinkled with red and white wildflowers, we sometimes stopped to let Lucky lap from a pool of water overflowing from a nearby spring, or he would plop down right in the water cool off in the heat of the summer. Dominic had school friends Wai-Yi (nicknamed 'Shrimp) and his brother Shin who lived nearby and the pair frequently took off with two brothers who frequently visited at the villa and kept our children company. They never tired of adventuring on Sir Cecil's Ride and "getting lost" in the maze of shrubs and trees and paths that led to 'ancient ruins' which to the young ones, took on the appearance of castles in misty virgin forests.

In December, a telegram arrived from the Presidential Palace inquiring if we could locate "a certain Mr. Trương Anh Mẫn, publisher, whose address was somewhere in Hong Kong." It seems President Diệm remembered his old friend from nine years ago in Hong Kong and wanted to get in touch. Apparently, his Foreign Affairs Ministry did not know or felt he could not inform the president that Mr. Mẫn was working at the Hong Kong Consulate and there was no need to search for him. Perhaps the Ministry did not know if the man even existed, although his name appeared on payroll the Consulate submitted every month to accounting.

To my reply that Mr. Mẫn was one of the Consulate's employees, the President quickly sent an invitation for his friend to come visit him and an order for me to accompany him home. Both of us happily complied and once more I was on a flight to return to Saigon—the third time in less than one year at my post. For Trương Anh Mẫn this was a sentimental trip as he had never been to South Vietnam and our travel date of December 28 was particularly coincidental as it was on this same date 30-odd years ago that Mẫn left Hanoi for China and had never come back.

Thus, on the flight home, Mẫn was inspired to compose a poem commemorating a historically significant trip for him that marked almost half a century in the struggle against French colonialism in which he played his own small part:

> *"Hôm nay hăm-tám tháng Đề Xàm,*
> *Bỏ nước ra đi vẫn nhớ ngày...*
> *Trời Nam mừng nỗi mây mưa tạnh,*
> *Đất Bắc riêng thương gió bụi đầy...*
> *...Tri ân ghi tạc tấm lòng này."*[67]

As soon as the airplane touched down on the runway at Tân Sơn Nhứt airport, Trương Anh Mẫn was so overwhelmed by strong emotions that he began to sob while tears ran down his cheeks. I reached over and patted his shoulder and both of remained wordless until the aircraft stopped. When the doors were opened to let in an avalanche of hot air, Mẫn was composed enough to smile and comment on Saigon's weather. We were met by a Palace official sent by the President to meet us, and he told us to go straight to Independence Palace as the President was waiting for us.

How familiar the Presidential Palace looked to me! I had been in and out of it often during the past ten months, and it seemed I knew by heart every nook and cranny of it—at least the second floor where Mr. Ngô had established his

67 Only part of the poem is given due to my faulty recollection. Mẫn spoke of leaving 30 years ago and returning today on the same December 28 date; his joy to see the South at peace; his sorrow and pity for the North still in agony; and gives thanks (to the President) for a gesture he will never forget. (Au.)

living quarters. Mẫn and I were immediately brought up to the President in his private rooms where with shining eyes, Diệm looked straight at Trương Anh Mẫn's face. He very seldom did this: in fact, I never saw him look anyone straight in the face. Even during hours of talking with me, it was only rarely that he obliquely rested his eyes on me and then only for a split second. The President looked at his old friend as if trying to read the changes in the face of a man he had befriended so many years ago. Diệm remained seated in his armchair, extended a hand for Mẫn to shake, and his first words of greeting were the same as what he said to my family last March when we first came home from the U.S., "Ah, so you've just arrived home!"

The President was visibly touched at seeing his friend, although his words and manner did not show it. This was one of many occasions when he summoned Mẫn or me to Saigon for nothing more than "just a talk." At least in this year of 1956, Diệm could afford to give way to his personal feelings and prove his faithfulness and loyalty to his friends. He did so in his Confucian manner, not with words, not even with gestures which Westerners, for instance, could interpret as expressing his deep feelings.

It was Diệm's very summoning us, that he wanted us brought straight to the Palace to see him, the absence of any official motive or even political significance in sending for us—all this belied his outwardly cold and detached manner. Diệm followed the Confucian code of behavior for a mandarin, the 'father' of the people who, even as he loved his children dearly, would rather leave the physical manifestations of that love to their mother while adopting a stern attitude toward them, Mr. Ngô similarly conducted himself towards his official wards—the people of Vietnam.

Needless to say, Trương Anh Mẫn, a scholar of the old Confucian school himself, understood Diệm's behavior and appreciated every detail of it. One could safely state that Mẫn found in Ngô Đình Diệm the reward so long overdue for his long revolutionary life, although subdued in the manner of *Văn Thân* rebels[68] or the life and activities with Phan Bôi Châu[69] and later Cường Để. Although neither the first nor the second group succeeded in driving the French from Vietnam, nor survived their revolutionist careers to see an independent Vietnam with their own eyes, it was by their tradition and example that Diệm carried their struggle to a successful conclusion. Mẫn rightly saw in the President's act a recognition of his heroes' and his own sacrifices for the nation. Hence, the historical significance of this trip for Mẫn and the sentimental gesture from Ngô Đình Diệm, his friend and President.

The President invited all surviving followers of Phan Bội Châu and Cường Để to a commemoration ceremony that he sponsored where Trương Anh Mẫn was the main celebrant. Attending the ceremony from my own family were Đỗ Văn Ý (Uncle Eight on my stepmother's side) whom Cường Để sent to study in Germany and Jean Lambert Cẩn, my wife's godfather, who in his youth

68 Văn Thân was a popular movement during 1865-1884 in central Vietnam led by scholars to support the Vietnamese monarchy and oppose the French.

69 Phan Bội Châu (1867-1940) was one of the most prominent anticolonial revolutionaries in early 20th century Vietnam.

followed Cường Để and studied engineering in England and consequently taught me English at a time when all Saigon's elite was Francophone.

Ngô Đình Diệm, who made me Head of Mission to Hong Kong because he knew I "would appreciate the scenic beauty" of the island; who remembered Trương Anh Mẫn and cabled me directly to locate Mẫn, despite a Foreign Affairs Ministry that could, if asked, immediately inform him where the man could be found in the maze of Hong Kong publishing houses—that side of President Diệm is unknown to most people and needs to be stressed here. This same Ngô Đình Diệm could not be but a kind, loyal, and sentimental friend. It was not, at the outset, our political acumen nor our administrative know-how that decided Diệm to place my family where he did. On the contrary, knowing us very well, he preferred to have us out of the country where politics and politicians would exasperate us in no time, resulting in us having to leave Vietnam as a result.

His calling us home was, at least in this first year of our Hong Kong Mission, entirely for sentimental reasons, and we responded to it accordingly. I did not have to be told twice to distinguish between Ngô Đình Diệm the President and Diệm the man. And if, in later years, I was so many times on the verge of quitting my post in disgust, it was this redeeming feeling about Diệm in the early days that kept me in the job.

After several soirées with the President and Mẫn in the former's private --quarters—so simple it was almost a monk's cell—I clearly felt the itch to see my good friends Nhuận, Phước, and Lương on the other side of the ramparts of the Independence Palace. I was lucky to have Mẫn occupy Mr. Ngô's attention in the Presidential Summons that came every night during this prolonged visit home.

My friends ignored their families when I was in Saigon (at least Nhuận and Phước did). "Families," they claimed, "we have them every day; but who knows how long or how often we can be with **you**?" Our friendship was and still is a kind of *Đào Viên Kết Nghĩa,* the kind described in the *Story of the Three Kingdoms* wherein three friends vowed eternal friendship under a blossoming peach tree—outmoded, impractical, but warm and as durable as matrimonial ties (or maybe more so). We never tired of seeing each other and we enjoyed every minute of being together, whether in their homes or at a thousand dining and drinking spots in and out of town.

This time, Air Vietnam, no doubt at Phước's prodding, offered me free tickets for a trip to Đà Lạt. Of course, Phước served as my 'guide' and rather than make our habitual rounds of Saigon's restaurants and tea shops, the two of us took off on a memorable three-day visit to the high plateau. I had never been to Đà Lạt before and visiting the beautiful place in the company of my good friend added to the pleasure of being in the famous hill resort. We took rooms at the Langbian Palace[70] which was the premier hotel then, and visited waterfalls and hillside trails while soaking up the artistic dreamy atmosphere of the town.

70 Renovated and renamed in 1995 as Đà Lạt Palace Heritage Hotel. (Au.)

When we returned to Saigon, sad news awaited me. On a visit to my old home in Gia Định, I learned that my grandmother was not well but thought it was not serious until one night she came to my place from a visit to the dentist who suspected she might have cancer, not a toothache. I was alarmed and quickly arranged to bring her to Hong Kong, cutting short my stay in Saigon and leaving Trương Anh Mẫn behind. Oh, how poignant that flight to Hong Kong was! The only flight we ever took together—and the first flight ever for my grandmother. On takeoff, I watched her carefully to see if the new experience adversely affected her in any way, but she was all right. Then I held her hand tightly, trying to communicate silently all the love I had for her. She was happy, smiled all the time, so perhaps the novelty of the flight contributed to her temporary feeling of comfort. She enjoyed her meal, which relieved me but also was so touching I was almost in tears. Here was my grandmother who took the place of my mother who died when I was barely six months old! She it was who bottle-fed me from that day on, mourning her only daughter, who raised me in her home until I was six years old when my father took me away to school with both of us crying inconsolable tears on being parted; whom I never missed seeing her at least once a year except for the five-year stretch I was in America, and now we were reunited but for how long? She it was who, when I fell in love, accepted my loved one as hers long before she became her granddaughter-in-law; who shared all our happiness and sorrow; who raised our children and loved them as much as she did me; who chose the name of Dominic Nghiệp for my son whom she spoiled from the day he was born; who bathed and dressed him in clean clothes in a daily ritual of carrying him piggy-back to the gate of our house on the Quai Doçueil in Gia Định to await my return from work. Now, my grandmother was sitting next to me on her first flight to an island as unknown and strange as her disease. I could not love her enough. Yet I had been neglecting my grandmother, my very own mother, in my pursuit of happiness, for some slippery and dubious thing called 'the future.'

28. IN SHACKLES RATHER THAN FREE

LIFE MUST GO ON, and so it did. Back at the Jardine's Lookout villa, the joy of reuniting with my wife and children for a time postponed my anxiety about grandmother's state. The Christmas tree still stood in the corner, the canaries still sang, the children were preparing for New Year's Eve celebrations, and our household resounded in joyful celebration. We had so much happiness in one year and so many changes in our lives that one or two unexpected bad luck events had to count among them, as our Confucian-Buddhist-Taoist tradition had it. Optimism rose again in me, nonetheless, and we confidently ended 1956, hoping for bright days ahead. That night, the first time my grandmother was ever reunited with my family under one roof, we were reminiscing about the last five years of separation when she called Dominic to her side and asked: Nghiệp, child, do you remember the song you used to sing any time your papa returned from a trip abroad. Do you remember the goodies he brought the family like apples, grapes, and sugar cubes?" He could not recollect what his great-grandmother was talking about, so she told him he used to sing a certain song:

Bôm, nho, xá-lị, cục đường,
Đem về thắt gióng cho nàng đi buôn!

This was not the correct song: *Bôm, nho, xá-lị* [apples, grapes, and guava (ổi xá-lị)] were the fruits Dominic enjoyed so much but he had mixed up the second verse with a lullaby!

We brought grandmother to our family physician, Dr. Rodrigues, who after many tests, determined to our sorrow that she had cancer of the mouth. There was nothing medicine could do for her except medicines to relieve her pain, acupuncture, and the like. We did all of that and even a good neighbor, Mr. Lư Hoà, recommended a good Chinese acupuncturist doctor whose treatment quickly relieved grandmother of much of her pain.

TÊT 1957 ARRIVED. This was the first Têt we really celebrated in an independent Vietnam. Remembering how previous lunar celebrations had been falsely managed by the Washington Embassy as a cover for French colonialism, with 'Fatherland Altar' and all, we made our a simple but genuine and significant celebration. Among the Vietnamese gathering at our Jardine's Lookout residence's First Day of Spring festivity was Bishop Hoàng Văn Đoàn, a refugee from Bắc Ninh, North Vietnam, who gave us a recital of traditional songs and poems. We rejoiced at the thought that this Spring Festival was the first when Vietnam enjoyed true independence and we were thankful to Ngô Đình Diệm, who accomplished it.

From our vantage point, we stood far from the

difficulties President Diệm faced at home and we were oblivious to the precarious situation that South Vietnam was really in. Like Californians who live unconcernedly above the Great Fault running deep under their feet, both President Diệm and the South Vietnamese were to be reminded of their borrowed safety by periodic rumblings and quakes—the telltale signals of an impending political eruption.

Such a quake came soon enough just four months into the year. In April, when the President inaugurated an agricultural fair in Ban Mê Thuột in the Central Highlands, a malcontent opened fire on him with submachine gun as Diệm led the official procession into the fair. Fortunately, the gun jammed after the first bullet hit the Minister of Agriculture in the shoulder and the would-be assassin was arrested, punched, kicked, and nearly launched on the spot. My friend Uncle Thành's father, Dr. Bùi Kiến Tín, was in the presidential group as he was the presidential physician. Had the gun not jammed, no one in the group would have survived. As it was, however, President Diệm was 'miraculously' saved, which went far in contributing to the myth of his 'divine mission,' something that he himself came to believe over the years.

This first of a series of rumblings that were felt, violently during the years, was quickly forgotten. And who was there, close enough to Ngô Đình Diệm yet far enough from his entourage like Uncle Thành (who was now in some finance-banking representation in New York) to give a metaphorically tug at his sleeve and say: "Listen, Mr. President, can you hear what I hear? Let's be careful of the danger!" A year before, Thành had shown me photographs of villagers killed by the Việt cộng in Bến Tre Province and had meant to show them to Diệm to alert him to all not being as good as he thought. But could he do this? And if he did, what good would come of it?

For this spring, emissaries from Political Advisor Ngô Đình Nhu came to try and urge me to 'go along' with their scheme of making money for the coffers of the Party. I was to 'collaborate' from Hong Kong by signing all the invoices submitted to the Consulate for commercial visas without regard to their correctness as I insisted on doing since I took over from the former consul. By doing this, I would help those merchants who worked for the Party to get their calculated extra margin of interest which went to the Party's coffers and thus serve the cause.

This confirmation of the 'power behind the throne' of the Nhu faction both discouraged and disillusioned me. I refused to play ball, and the emissaries went home never to return again. I went on checking commercial invoices as usual but soon noticed a visible shrinking of their volume. At the same time, shipping manifests presented the same volume of trade as in previous months and kept on increasing as time passed. Apparently, ***they*** bypassed the Consulate, and word had been put out to the Hong Kong merchants to ignore consular visas. Official remonstrances on my part were likewise ignored.

In addition, Ngô Trọng Hiếu who was now Vietnam's diplomatic representative in Phnom Penh, Cambodia, came in person to Hong Kong to plead for my 'cooperation' with ***his*** financial political project. The authority behind the project, Hiếu assured me, was also Ngô Đình Nhu. When I asked for a written confirmation of what he told me that was signed by Nhu himself, Hiếu laughed in my face: "Why would you refuse to work for the cause, you who are in politics yourself?" He told me in no uncertain terms that such a letter of confirmation would only be dreamed up by an apolitical animal like me. To which I heartily agreed and reiterated my refusal to 'cooperate.'

Months later, when the coup d'etat against Prince Norodom Sihanouk failed and Ngô Trọng Hiếu became *persona non grata* to his court, the mysterious political purpose explained another disillusion for me. I began to consider my mission as purely against 'dirty businesses,' reasoning that if I could do nothing to stop them in Hong Kong, I could at least indirectly expose them by refusing to sign the invoices. Naivete! Doubt! An uneasy feeling of bad things to come for President Ngô Đình Diệm if this trend was not checked. A beginning, too, of detachment itself, the fruit of an overwhelming sense of futility in whatever effort at correctness, let alone reform of the grandiloquent 'national revolution.'

Once disillusionment set in, creeping cynicism was not too far off. Outwardly I did not show anything but in my heart, I secretly pondered this gnawing question: Should I expose 'them' to President Diệm with proof and irrefutable argument and demand immediate reform not only in my Hong Kong Mission but throughout Vietnam's government machine? Or should I do as I felt while submitting my resignation knowing my action would be tantamount to a direct attack on the presidential family and consequently displease Diệm? Would it be useful to quit? Or would it only bring misery to my family? Was I 'important' enough, apart from a nonpolitical friendship with the President, to somehow influence things and change people with my resignation? Obviously not.

"Vivre d'abord, philosopher ensuite" [Live first, philosophize later], French commonsense returned to me with a vengeance. If left alone, I would still live in my own kind of clouds far away from political and plain realities. For me, living meant losing myself in literature and poetry, and visiting friends, and talk, and music. So far, I had been working just for enough to sustain my family. Never had I thought of a dubious future that required increasing physical and material needs, as if one could live 'not by bread alone.' Reality opened my eyes fast enough.

My father was in dire need of a decent home to live in, as all his life savings were not enough to buy even a modest abode. One day my wife came to my office to plead with me to help my father: she said if I didn't, his living conditions would deteriorate and jeopardize his health. I knew we didn't have any money in our bank account and without hesitation 'borrowed' a large sum from Consulate funds and immediately sent it to my father.

On another occasion, I was able to buy my wife a present for the first time in 18 years of married life. This came about when my wife stopped at the office on her way to accompany the wives of Saigon officials in Hong Kong for their usual shopping sprees. I had been oblivious to her long months of 'humiliation' having to walk alongside those ladies—spouses of members of Congress and high officials, ladies in Madame Nhu's Women's solidarity Movement *(Phong trào Phụ Nữ Liên Đới)*, and similar—resplendent in their silk national dress and diamond and precious gem jewelry while she was plainly dressed. Compared to the Saigon butterflies, my wife's 'poor' outfit and total absence of gems on her person was living proof of her husband's integrity. However, incorruptibility was not a respectable (i.e., valuable) commodity. It ensued that my wife's 'shabby' appearance reflected on my poor diplomacy. The ladies showed they were embarrassed to be seen with her, which in turn humiliated my wife.

Once the delicate problem was explained to me, I withdrew the entire balance of my bank account for my wife to buy the *very first pair of diamond earrings* I ever offered her as a gift. In a flash, the memory surfaced of our penniless days in New York when we had to take ridiculously petty loans from good old Chẩn for our daily food, while contracting heavy long-term debts for Mr. Ngô's cause. My wife's face beaming with joy as she left my office moved me to tears. She was relieved from a humiliation she had to bear for so long!

If nothing else taught me to climb down from my cuckoo land, it was the benefit to my wife and children for the very position I occupied, thanks to Mr. Ngô. I should have been born many centuries ago, when values and the meaning of life were measured on a different scale, not gauged in terms of diamonds, dollars, or sterling. A dichotomy was tearing my heart apart. While I was faithful to my outdated conception of a 'gentleman,' I was constantly drawn back to reality. A poem I composed at that time reflected my inner state of well-preserved integrity:

Kỷ Niệm Một Năm Hương Cảng

Ngày này năm ngoái tớ sang đây:
Theo thói thường tình: Bước dặm mây![71]
Gang thép vướng chân mùi tục lụy,[72]
Đá vàng kết cánh nghĩa vơi đầy.[73]
'Thương nữ tri vong quốc hận,'[7475]

71 Vietnamese poetry, Tang Dynasty style, takes after the Chinese model and uses classical sayings and references aplenty. "Bước dặm mây": In the old days, a successful candidate at the Imperial Exams was elevated with great pomp and ceremony to the rank of Mandarin. He was metaphorically 'walking on the Cloud's stairway.' And his achievement was congratulated with cries of "Great Success!" (Au.)

72 The Vietnamese colloquial saying is: *"Miệng nhà quan có gang có thép"* meaning "an official's word is like cast iron and steel" that conveys the idea of his oppressive power of the populace; references to "*gang* and *thép*" implies self-mockery as if saying: "Ah, you're a mandarin now!" At the same time, a gentleman scholar, free by nature and artistic by inspiration, found his official duties bound by whimsical royal decrees and batted about with court maneuverings so that many a shackled scholar longed for his freedom lost. (Au.)

73 Stone and gold (Đá vàng) refers to the idea that a wise man can discriminate between two minerals to know which has value or not; here, the wise man is Ngô Đình Diệm who picked me out of the stone-like collection of 'servants of colonialism' deaf to the appeal of their fatherland and made with me a pact of eternal friendship. (Au.)

74 Flower girls refusing statelessness: there is a story that a Vietnamese envoy to China was given women to entertain him but he they declared to his face: "We will not sing for a man who has lost his country. We are ashamed for his statelessness!" Moral: even prostitutes feel shame when their country is lost to foreign domination. (Au.)

75 It is not clear where Mr. Bùi Công Văn's story of the Vietnamese envoy above came from, but *'Thương nữ **bất** tri vong quốc hận,'* is a line from a famous poem by the Tang Dynasty poet Du Mu (Vietnamese: Đỗ Mục, 803-853). In contrast to the "flower girls" in Mr. Bùi Công

Anh hùng há để dạ riêng tây?[76]
Tạ lòng người cũ ơn tri ngộ :
Báo đền nợ nước phận râu mày.

The First Anniversary in Hong Kong

I came today, a year ago, to this place:
Ordinarily, I'd be congratulated with 'Great Success!'
But alas! I'm in shackles rather than free,
To an old friend nevertheless, loyal I must be.
Why, even flower girls don't resent statelessness,
Should a Man, then, care for his own interest?
In appreciation of an old friend's esteem:
I am here to serve my country with all steam.

I was nevertheless bothered by the practical side of life, and not least by the so-called 'diplomatic' side of my work which required a presentable appearance. They say that when in Rome, do as the Romans do. I was in a post-Điện Biên Phủ, pre-Dollar era of a half Vietnam that was too much inclined toward material comfort and unwisely thought that under an omnipotent American umbrella, the only worthy occupation was how to get rich quick. A race toward the highest mark of distinction, as it were, of possessing the latest gadgets, the most expensive Mercedes Benz, the largest diamonds….

Văn's story, Du Mu expressed sadness when he heard those girls sing the song "Hou Ting Hua" [Vietnamese: Hậu Đình Hoa], which suggested to him that they seemed indifferent about the loss of their country.

76 "*Anh hùng*" translates to a man with solid (Confucian) principles, a gentleman, an honest man, and a good civil servant, in contrast to "tiểu nhân," the 'little' man. (Au.)

A constant gnawing in my heart turned my Hong Kong days into a sad exile. Not quite impervious to the precarious balance in which South Vietnam was preserved as a non-communist Republic, I did not feel sure, however, that my 'special' friendship with the President could influenced him to jettison his malevolent entourage—especially the Eminence Grise of Ngô Đình Nhu and his wife, his father-in-law Ambassador Trần Văn Chương in Washington, D.C., and their henchmen. My quixotic efforts at waging revolutionary war from Hong Kong was just that—idealistic.

Meanwhile, my grandmother who I brought to live with us in Hong Kong, saw her cancer turn from bad to worse when palliative acupuncture and neither Oriental nor Occidental medicines did little to relieve her pain. With each passing day, her already bony physique grew more emaciated, and her appetite was as good as gone. Sensing her imminent departure from this world, she reluctantly but firmly asked to be brought home to die. To my wife was given the heart-breaking task of accompanying grandmother back to Vietnam. Feeble and suffering constant pain in her mouth, she said goodbye to us all while tears flowed.

She left in September but had three more months before death ended her suffering, but she kept it from us. Courageous as she always was, my grandmother led us to think that she was not really hurting too badly: she swallowed her pain and rarely showed it to those around her. However, after she left Hong Kong, alone and thinking about her and missing her as much as I did when as a little boy, I spent my summer vacation with her in Gò Cát, Mỹ Tho, but had to return me to my father in Cần Thơ to return to school. I cried inconsolably long after her departure.

Without my wife, our Jardine's Lookout house was empty of her spirit. One weekend afternoon, just back from our walk on Sir Cecil's Ride, the children and I lay about relaxing in the large living room. A dog barked somewhere out in the hills and the breeze shook banana leaves along a shortcut between the Indonesian Consul's house one door away from us. Listening to my girls squabbling in their play I thought to myself: My children won't remain Vietnamese for long. Already their main language is English and unless I bring them back to Vietnam, they will forget the little Vietnamese they know. I'd like to encourage them to speak nothing but their mother tongue at home as they get quite enough English in school. So, I took out a tape recorder and unknown to them, I recorded all their talk. I thought to keep the tape for some future day when they were grown up and play it back for them to reminisce about just one afternoon of their youth in Hong Kong.

I went on becoming more and more depressed. My work was tedious, and my thoughts were demoralizing. My wife had returned some time ago and as I listened to her recounting how a fortune teller in Saigon read her palm, I became more listless than ever as the woman told her: In the near future, you will have two great mourning experiences." She advised me to try to forget it all and get away from my work and I heeded her and cabled the Foreign Ministry for permission to take a vacation in Japan.

The reply came quickly: "PERMISSION GRANTED. BY PRESIDENTIAL ORDER. HOWEVER, YOU ARE TO REPORT TO SAIGON BEFORE GOING TO JAPAN."

I was perplexed. Why 'report to Saigon' first instead of leaving from Hong Kong which is already halfway to Japan? Did anything important arise in Vietnam? I was soon to find out although my interview with Vũ Văn Mẫu, the Foreign Secretary, did not enlighten me in the least. There was nothing Mẫu wanted me for, he said, and as it stated in the cable, it was President Diệm who asked me to come home.

Thus, I was in a state of anxiety that I met with the President the same night I arrived in Saigon. Contrary to all expectations, Diệm did not have anything special to discuss or ask of me--at least, he did not say so. His first words to me were: "Ah, so you are going to Japan." Not a question. Not an exclamation. Just a matter of fact statement. Relieved, I sat back and spent the evening listening to his ramblings, saying very little myself, and consuming lots of tea. As South Vietnam was quiet, he seemed relaxed and enjoying his conversation, reminding me much of the Ông Ngô of his evenings in New York. In hindsight, though, it seems he had a purpose in calling me back prior to my vacation. Perhaps he did not want to let me go, but in his way, he preferred to tell me so in person but changed his mind when he saw me. Whatever the reason, it was considerate of President Diệm to treat me in this delicate manner.

The next morning, I went to Gia Định to see Grandmother. She had deteriorated so much that I hardly recognized her. My auntie Cô Tư was directly nursing her, helping, and loving her in every way possible. In the half darkness of the old house, my grandmother lay on her bed, emaciated to the bone, her malignant wound on her lower jaw reaching down to her throat. She could hardly swallow her food and spoke hoarsely, wincing painfully with each word. Finish! Finish! I thought inside. There was nothing to do but wait for the end but the sooner the better because her pain was unendurable. Would morphine shots help? I wanted to stay and weep but my grandmother could not stand that. My sorrow augmented her pain rather than the other way around. She held my hand and said her last words to me: "Go on and rest in Japan, my son. Do not linger here. I will be alright. Cô Tư will help me . . ." So, I left, still unbelieving that that would be the last time I saw her. It was early December 1957.

The next morning, I was on board an Air France Super Constellation to Japan. From my window seat, I looked down at a patch of dark-green forest miles under me, perhaps in the central highlands of Vietnam. In a gap between one copse and the next, deer were visible, tiny and agile, running happily about. Slowly relaxing from all my anxieties, I helped myself to sake that I was served and fell asleep.

Bùi Văn Thinh (no relation), our Ambassador to Japan, had me brought directly to the embassy in advance of a splendid dinner that night *en famille.* First, however, I insisted on time to relax in the privacy of my hotel room, and he let me go. A few days in Tokyo, then I took a train to Nikko in search of volcanic landscapes and more restfulness. In the late hours of the next evening, while in my room, the telephone jangled. It was the embassy, relaying to me the sad news that my grandmother had died!

I rushed home but when my plane landed the next day, grandmother's funeral had already taken place. She was brought to our village of Bình Phong, Mỹ Tho, to be buried on land belonging to my uncle Hai Ngự. It seemed that due to delays in transmission, the telegram had reached me in Japan too late to attend the funeral. I could only go to my village afterwards, accompanied by my father and my wife, the first time I ever returned to my boyhood village after the events of September 1945, twelve years earlier. A car took us early the next morning to Gò Cát, my little hometown, two kilometers from Mỹ Tho. From there, we had to walk on dikes and paths across rice fields and bamboo groves to reach Uncle Hai Ngự's estate where Grandmother was buried. My dear grandmother's plot was new, so it was just a mound of earth in front of the tomb of Auntie Sáu Hương, my Uncle Hai Ngự's younger sister. At this place, twelve years ago, grandmother and grandfather, my wife and my children hid from the French troops in 1945. Here, at the same spot where grandmother's tomb was located, our little Marie and Tuyên, her younger brother who died, played in the calm moments between raids. Here also, back in time, I played as a little boy with Uncle Hai Ngự's children—my cousins Sáu Nhu, Bảy Khiêm, Tám Ngự. And now, it was a mound of earth with my beloved grandmother under it. Goodbye, grandmother. She was 75.

News of our coming home to the village spread rapidly by word of mouth and soon Uncle Hai Ngự's house was filled with relatives and friends. My grandfather, then 77 years old, walked unsteadily down the bamboo-rimmed pathway towards us. He spied us from afar and tears began streaming down his wrinkled cheeks. "Oh, my son! My son! Where is your grandma?!" Uncle Hai Ngự quickly brought us inside and the circle of relatives closed in around us. Tears and more tears. Home-made rice alcohol called 'chum' was served to drown our sorrows. In the hangar, a shed where rice was beaten to its required whiteness, stood auntie Dì Sáu. I came over and leaned on her shoulder to lament my loss.

When it was three in the afternoon, we had to hurry out of the village as no one knew what would happen when darkness took us over. My father was particularly worried, and I was pulled from the crying circle. Back on the road, still dazed with emotions, I was almost oblivious of the dangers lurking in the bush. A Việt Minh ambush could materialize at any moment and I, an official of the hated Ngô Đình Diệm government, a regime they already called "Mỹ-Diệm" meaning "U.S.-Diệm" could easily be kidnapped on the spot. Nonetheless, I stopped any time I saw a man on the road, inquiring: "Sir, do you remember me?" This was so rash because it was a badly kept secret that the countryside was riddled with Việt Minh, the Resistance Movement, which was now termed "Việt Cộng." Already, skirmishes occurred, and these little engagements signaled growing guerilla activity throughout the delta. We were yet to be alarmed and from the President on down, it was still business as usual. The

Cần Lao Party grew apace, as did the power of Mr. and Mrs. Ngô Đình Nhu.

The prediction of my wife's fortune teller came true soon enough, for in early March 1958, my grandfather followed his wife to the grave. After his funeral, we lingered around in Mỹ Tho city where a cousin of ours lived, chị Ba Kiểu. I had the pleasure of returning to the same city not long afterward to introduce my friend, Bùi Kiến Thành, to the beautiful area. Along the way we passed the Bến Lức and Tân An bridges where Thành and I observed guard pots mounted on the slopes of either ends of the bridges. Decidedly, this was not as peaceful a time as the government would have the people believe. To get a better idea of the situation, we ventured out from chị Ba Kiểu's house to the outskirts, toward Vinh Trà Pagoda, Cầu Di bridge, and yonder, past the Cao Đài Temple on the road to Bến Tranh. Our trip was uneventful, but this was more luck than established security.

Back to Saigon we went, stopping over at Cai Lậy, a renowned Việt Minh stronghold, for its proximity to the Plain of Reeds (Đồng Tháp Mười). There was a strong appeal for expatriates like us, in the villages and small towns of countryside Vietnam. Thành had just come home from his tour of duty in New York, a mission he did not like, and was preparing to settle down and work in the private sector well away from politics and government circles. We took refreshments in a café at the marketplace and were pretty frightened by the truculent faces we saw there. Anyone could be Việt Minh for all we knew and if they wanted to take us into the bush, they could do it openly, with no chance of our being rescued. Prudence prodded us to leave the café instead of lingering, but we still strolled among the hawker stands in the market. When Uncle Thành aimed his camera at a young *bì cuốn* (spring rolls) vendor, the girl protested: "Did you have my permission to take my picture!?" she made a gesture, as if she would hide her face from the camera, and slightly turned her back to us. We desisted because after all, East and West are so different: In New York, a girl would be flattered to be photographed but in Vietnam or many parts of Asia, it is an affront. Or would it be? Perhaps it is only a matter of the social manner in our approach. Deep down, a beautiful woman wants to be admired—in the East or in the West—but whereas a wolf whistle is accepted in one part of the world, it is not good manners in the other part.

29. BLACK SMOKE

"IN THE MIDST OF LIFE THERE IS DEATH, AND IN THE MIDST OF DEATH THERE IS LIFE." I read this thought in a book that my wife's godfather gave me. It described a scene in which a football match was progressing when a funeral passed by, and the captain ordered the players to stop until it passed—a sign of respect for the dead. Should they have stopped? Or, with life and death being but two sides of one coin, should they go on playing? Jesus said, "Unless the grain dies, the young shoot cannot grow." The book was in my grandparents' house in Gò Cát, Mỹ Tho, that was burned down by French troops and their partisans in October 1945.

The thought came to me, in this second year of my Mission to Hong Kong. I did try to snuff the old candle out, thereby echoing whatever revolution President Ngô Đình Diệm was supposedly starting with his government at home and put a new light to this representation of his abroad. However, the light refused to die down and kept on emitting black smoke, itself a reflection of what was going on in Vietnam. Since 'life' here refused to die, then 'death' was already germinating in it like a worm, nascent and growing more virulent as time passed in the heart of this red apple, shiny and appetizing to all onlookers. For revolution, or to be more to the point, reform is not a solitary game. It takes two to play. Already, the First Conference of Heads of Mission that October 1956, the foreign Secretary Vũ Văn Mẫu gave a veiled warning to the government at home when he quoted from *The Tale of Kiều*: *"Sao cho trong ấm thì ngoài mới êm"* (If it is not good inside, don't expect it to be better outside).[77]

Yes, it was futile and pointless to 'rationalize'—a term used at the conference—the work being carried out by our diplomatic missions abroad, if the mess continued unchecked at home, perpetrated by the very entourage of President Diệm. Besides, problems and discouragement resulting from my dealings with both the government at home and the consulate in Hong Kong, I was constantly irritated by what I called the 'colonial spirit' of the crown colony. Despite the overwhelming presence of Communist China at the island's threshold, the island remained in face as well as in name, a "British colony." The white man, hardened by a century of British domination in the Far East, still was very much the 'Superman' in his overseas territory. Except in occasional riots such as the one in early 1956 when white people had been indiscriminately terrorized (the Swiss Consul's wife was burned to death when a mob overturned her car) and jolted out of their usual complacency, the ordinary train of life for the white man in this colony was not too different from the way it was fifteen years earlier, prior to the Japanese occupation in 1941. The usual Chinese kowtow still obtained, every priority was

77 See Nguyễn Du, Huỳnh Sanh Thông, and Alexander Woodside, *The Tale of Kiều*, 78.

still given to white skin, and most exasperatingly, the same treatment, the same discrimination, and the same color-consciousness prevailed in the consular corps as well.

One day, on the occasion of some ceremonial opening I had been invited to, I arrived at the site where the Chinese traffic policeman stopped my car—which was flying the Vietnamese national flag and had diplomatic plates—while waving ahead any consular car with a white man in it to the main entrance. I got so mad I told Chan, the driver, to step on the gas and "run over the damn cop" if he did not get out of the way. Of course, Chan being Chinese himself, was scared and just waited. I refused to budge so a long line of entering cars was thus held up. I took one cigarette, lit it, and tried to relax by quietly smoking in my seat. After two puffs, I saw from the corner of my eye the khaki-uniformed shadow of the policeman approach and say something to Chan. Now, I spoke Cantonese and I became even angrier that he had ordered the driver to pull over to one side of the road while asking, "What country is that Consul from?"

I got out of the car, pointed a shaking finger into the policeman's face, and told him in Cantonese to 'Get lost!' I shouted at the top of my voice: "You damn police dog, why should you be afraid of the white man and treat me, a fellow Asian—let alone a Consul—in such a manner. No wonder the white man shits on your face!" I got back in slamming the door but instead of going ahead, I told Chan to return me to the office. I thought of complaining to the governor of Hong Kong but after I cooled off, I realized the ridiculousness of the whole damn thing. I did not complain, but neither did I forgive nor forget.

Another time, at the Jockey Club, white guards at the entrance of the hippodrome took me for an ordinary Chinese and used foul language. Outraged, I shouted back: "Look here, if you don't apologize, I will kill you on the spot!" The captain of the guards came over and, believing I was Chinese, said in English: "Kill a policeman? I would arrest you for that!" I thrust both hands straight at him and said in the same language, "Well, handcuff me then." To which he said meekly: 'Ah, how well you speak English." That was his way of apologizing as I understood it. I shrugged the apology off and walked away. To this day, I still think he took me for a Chinese Communist. I wonder why.

All these little incidents and thought patterns got on my nerves and I was constantly morose. My reports home—political, economic, administrative—received little response. In fact, the Office of Political Advisory, headed by Ngô Đình Nhu but run by Dr. Trần Kim Tuyến, took over what was the proper domain of the Foreign Affairs Ministry. The latter assumed only tenuous administrative responsibilities in regard to its representations abroad. I found this out almost accidentally when an economic report I wrote—stamped "Secret and Confidential"—concerning the dumping being practiced by Communist China on the Hong Kong consumer market was printed *in extenso* on the front page of a Saigon daily. Alarmed, I asked Vũ Văn Mẫu why my report was printed in full. "Don't ask me," Mẫu laughed, "ask the Office of the Political Adviser," pointing in the direction of the Independence Palace.

The only time the Foreign Affairs Ministry took matters in hand, following one of my reports, was at the beginning of my assuming office in early 1956, and it must have bene seriously reprimanded, for the Ministry never again exercised its authority over me. Instead, it served as a mailbox for whatever reports it received from missions abroad and transmitted them to whatever ministry they concerned. Those in turn, forwarded them to the Political Adviser's office for their decision and action, if any.

It was an affair of several tens of thousands of medals bearing the likeness of President Diệm, ordered by the then Minister for Information, Trần Chánh Thành, to be made in Hong Kong by a Chinese firm and distributed to the Information cadremen who were supposed to work in the countryside as Agit-Prop agents— terminology for Agitation and Propaganda, working at cross-purposes with the same Việt Cộng teams throughout the delta. As the invoice presented to me for a visa amounted to hundreds of thousands of Hong Kong dollars, I pointed out to the Foreign Secretary that such a large sum of foreign currency could be saved if the medals were made in Saigon, which was not impossible.

Vũ Văn Mẫu gave me high praise for the initiative, in fact, officially writing to me that "This is the first time the Ministry ever got a report disclosing what must have been happening as a matter of course for years in Hong Kong in collusion with the "Merchant Crooks" at home". Consequently, the medal order was scrapped in addition to the Foreign Secretary's authority (nosiness) over the matter. As for my consular interference, short of having me replaced, which Nhu's henchmen and later Minister Nguyễn Đình Thuần tried to do without success—I could be circumvented by not submitting any more commercial invoices to me. And that is what the Political Adviser's office did.

This same usurpation of authority applied to the Vice President and Secretary of Economic Affairs, Nguyễn Ngọc Thơ. Customs fell under his jurisdiction, and I complained many times to him in person about the irregular practices condoned by customs in allowing entry to merchandise not certified by my Consulate. Each time, Thơ also pointed in the direction of the Independence Palace, which was all that was needed for a comprehensive reply. "All emanates from the 'Old Man' in there," meaning President Diệm. Of course, it was understood that the 'Old Man' had nothing to do with it, but it was taboo to mention the names of Diệm''s younger brothers, be it Nhu in Saigon, Cẩn in Huế, or even Luyện in London. Real power needed no name.

We were preparing to move the Consulate to another building and had to wait almost two years before the new Chartered Bank Building was finished and we could sign a five-year lease, and the move date was fixed. Tết was approaching and my wife and I requested and received permission to come home for a New Year celebration. We left a few days before the actual consulate move took place, during the Chinese New Year's holidays, when every business office and bank in town was closed.

IT WAS THE first Tết my wife and I celebrated at home ever since leaving Vietnam for the United States nine years ago. We were heading home, just the two of us, leaving the children in Hong Kong with their Auntie Dì Tám, who was on the Consulate payroll as a clerk in my effort to keep an eye on Tiến and his dealings with Chinese visa applicants.

What a sentimental journey home we had! Tết being what it is in Vietnam, we were doubly happy to celebrate it with our parents and friends in our homeland after so many years abroad. After spending the closing days of the Old Year in the lunar calendar with my father, brothers, sisters, and friends in Saigon, my wife and I drove down to Cần Thơ to ring in the New Year with my wife's parents and relatives. Auntie Dì Năm's husband, Dượng Năm, a taxi driver, used his own cab to drive us to Cần Thơ. We had a joyful trip as along the way from Saigon, passing each town and marketplace, we saw decorations and the whole countryside bustling about in a festive mood.

In Cần Thơ, we landed first at Auntie Dì Ba's place, on Trần Thanh Cân Street, before we moved on to my wife's parents' home near the church and next to my paternal house where I grew up. For three days, it was the biggest and grandest Tết we had ever celebrated. Monseigneur Nguyễn Văn Bình, now Archbishop if Saigon, was the parish priest at Cần Thơ then. We attended mass and heard his homily. We had all manner of rejoicing, all kinds of goodies imaginable for our traditional Tết that year. When we sadly had to depart, it was Long, the young student who met us in Paris in 1951 and now worked for the National Bank of Vietnam, who got a ride back to Saigon with us. Like the many Tết celebrations we missed while in the U.S., we had not seen Long for many years, so we enjoyed a most agreeable journey catching up on our lives all the way back to the capital.

We arrived in Saigon to learn that during the Tết holidays a large-scale Việt Cộng attack had taken place in Tây Ninh province in southeast Vietnam. It was blamed on the unpreparedness of the Army which had given leave permission to too many soldiers. It was the beginning of much more serious attacks to come but we were too confident to worry about it. The 'peace' which obtained since July 1954 was already something of the past and South Vietnam remained blissfully unaware while the insurgency was gathering its strength.

THE NEW CONSULATE of the Republic of Vietnam on the 13th floor of the Chartered Bank Building on Hong Kong island was a brand-new office that overlooked Queen's Road Central. Our national flag could be seen flying from the roof from as far away as the Peak about a mile away. The Consulate's location, arrangement, and layout better suited the consular functions than the previous one. There were better inner offices for me and my secretary, Mrs. King, as well as Mr. Tư.

The physical aspect of my mission in Hong Kong changed, but its moral one hardly did. I had to content myself with whatever it was, whether I liked it or not. The alternative would be resigning and even that would not change one iota of anything. I had thought I could serve President Ngô Đình Diệm better by staying on the job. After all, I could still help the Vietnamese travelers prevented from doing so by the Interior Affairs Ministry in Saigon. And, thin as the chance would be, if worse came to worst, I could denounce the ill-doings of Diệm's entourage. I decided that 'late and little' was still better than 'never and nothing.'

I still felt dejected, however, and a sense of helplessness overtook me. I sincerely considered myself as a good for nothing *(vaurien)* and did not hesitate to say so to my staff. Often, I availed myself of occasions when they were all together to tell them: "I am no different from the monkey you see performing in some Shantung troupe putting on a show in the marketplace to get you to buy their medicine. The man in charge pulls the rope attached to the animal's neck and sure enough, the monkey performs a cute somersault. So do I react to Saigon pulling my strings, me dressed in my red hat and yellow coat in our national colors that represent my 'glamorous' title and position. But I can't somersault on my own: the string-puller is the President, of course, yet sometimes I wonder if he really is the only one doing the pulling . . ."

It was in this self-mocking mood that I composed this poem:

TỰ MẮNG

Cũng thừa vai vóc kém chi ai,
Bốn chục tuổi rồi hổ mặt trai :
Tế thế an bang đành chẳng đạt,
Tê gia tu tánh cũng vô tài.
Thạnh-dốn, Ba-lê qua đủ cả,
Sài Gòn, Hương-Cảng mặt càng chai.
Gan lì thử hỏi thằng tôi nhá,
Phù du kiếp sống ngắn hay dài?

SELF-MOCKERY

Head high, shoulders strong, I am second to none,
Yet at forty, how ashamed a man am I:
Granted, it's not for me to save the world or nation,
But neither can I be master of myself or family.
I've been through Washington and Paris and
Showed my jaded face in Saigon and Hong Kong.
I'm not joking my friends, let me ask myself:
Is it long or short, this ephemeral existence of mine?

Bishop Hoàng Văn Đoàn, perhaps sympathizing with my lot, wrote a poem to refute my downcast feelings and urged me to take heart. I cannot recall his poem, which is a pity as he passed away in the early 1960s, and was a very sympathetic man, a poet clothed as a clergyman. It was he who brought joy to ***all*** our gatherings in Hong Kong as he never hesitated to sing or recite poetry to entertain the Vietnamese community in Hong Kong whenever we met for whatever occasion.

My complaint about President Diệm's entourage was not without grounds, for as in early 1959, without asking for my consent, the Foreign Ministry sent a cable to the effect that a certain Nguyễn Đình Hiếu was accredited to my Consulate as an official from the Foreign Affairs Ministry. The cable even stated the date of arrival in the colony. I protested: it was my strong feeling that whoever the minister wanted to send to work under me should first be known and approved by me. A long reply came back that I had to accept the man and that was the last word to me from the Ministry, once more reiterating the date of his arrival.

Almost on the heels of the Foreign Ministry telegram, Nguyễn Đình Hiếu arrived at my office the next day. I gently told him that I could not accept him as a matter of principle and not that I had anything against him. Hiếu begged and pleaded to no avail. I told him to stay in the hotel and wait until I returned from Saigon where I would clear this matter with the Ministry then expressly forbade him from entering the Consulate during my absence.

I went home but Hiếu showed up there that night after dinner. More pleading and begging, more promises of complete submission and unsurpassed devotion, then he memorably said this: "You are well known for your gentleman's attitude in habitually helping the 'underdog' and I hope I can bank on that. Rather than flock to the 'strong and powerful' of the day, as do the little men or tiểu nhân, as a quân tử (gentleman) you prefer to take the side of the weak and oppressed."

His words smacked so much of the professional sycophant, so reeking of shameless flattery that I felt more chagrined than offended to listen to him. I took time to explain to Hiếu why it was impossible for me or for any head of mission for that matter to take on an employee he neither knows nor wants. Little did I know or even suspect that Hiếu was forced on me by the Political Adviser's office, the same office that published my 'Secret and Confidential' report about merchant visa manipulation in a Saigon daily paper. If I were Hiếu, I wouldn't need to be told twice to go back to Vietnam: Why would anyone insist so much on being taken on unless he was in desperate need of a job—which was not the case? And going to such lengths in pleading for me to change my mind about him? When I finally cut short Hiếu's lamentations and sent him back to his hotel, he let me understand that he would not return to the Ministry unless ordered to do so.

Incensed, I flew to Saigon and confronted Foreign Ministry Secretary Vũ Văn Mẫu who only then admitted the man was recommended to him (read: *ordered*) by no less an authority than Dr. Tuyến, Director of the Political Advisory Office and right-hand man to Ngô Đình Nhu, the President's brother. The Secretary fully sympathized with me but there was nothing he could do other than point out that Nguyễn Đình Hiếu was no stranger to me, being the elder brother of Nguyễn Đình Hoà whose 'American Ph.D.' Mẫu looked down upon. (Hoà had been Dean of the Faculty of Belles Lettres of Saigon University for a while until President Diệm got wind of it and remembering what Hoà did to him in New York, unceremoniously dismissed him.) Now his brother who just happened to be a protégé of Doctor Tuyến was dumped on me!

Protégé or not, I did not go along peacefully. I went to see the President. So far, I had always been quickly admitted to Diệm's rooms any time I came home from Hong Kong and was either called in or asked to see him. This time things were different. I had to wait for hours on end. Pleading a tight schedule, the officer in charge kept me hour after hour in the waiting room. When finally shown into Diệm's office many hours and cups of tea later, I found an irritable president. He avoided my problem for a while, telling me instead accusations "people" heaped on me like corruption, nepotism, and non-cooperation. What people, Diệm never said ("All I heard is from 'people' in general); Please, an example of nepotism ("I can't name any particular deed"); Did he mean non-cooperation with the Political Adviser's Office? ("No, certainly not.")

The President was evasive and almost reluctant to even say that much so I came to the point: Hiếu, elder brother of Nguyễn Đình Hoà, unknown and unwanted by me, will not work at the Hong Kong Consulate against my will. Diệm seemed to know Hiếu was Hoà's brother as he did not comment on this fact when I expected him to be surprised and displeased. In the end, when I left the President, it was agreed that Nguyễn Đình Hiếu would not be accredited to Hong Kong. I had removed another thorn from my flesh. This episode was another reason to make me a stranger to my government and, subtly, to Ngô Đình Diệm himself. My last interview with my friend and mentor, delayed beyond reasonable excuse, was but a sample of more of the same and worse to come in future relations between me and Diệm. The President was surrounded by men loyal to Nhu and Tuyến. They could keep anyone from seeing the President, as I was soon to find out.

30. OPERATION "CELESTINE"

MEANWHILE, WE HAD the pleasure of the company of our devoted friend Uncle Bùi Kiến Thành. Instead of Nguyễn Đình Hoà's brother, we had Thành staying with us for several months—what lovely consolation! His visit was also very fortuitous as K. K. Tse, Director for the Far East Division of American International Underwriters (AIU) asked me to recommend a Vietnamese who could be trained to manage its Saigon branch. Who had better qualifications than Thành who was already fluent in American English!

Thành arrived in late summer and lived with us at Jardine's Lookout. For several months, he and I relived our New York days and sadly recognized that we were no longer enthusiastic believers in Ngô Đình Diệm as we now had many doubts. For one thing, Thành had been gently pushed out of Diệm's government. Not because "Uncle BK" (as he was known at AIU) cared two hoots about a government position but because being prudent and perspicacious, he saw long before many others the contradictions and built-in weaknesses of the administration. Thành had been solicited and welcomed by the President and Brother Nhu but as time went on, and as his frank ideas often displeased more than flattered, his 'audiences' with the powerful became few and far between.

For me, it was a godsent pleasure to be reunited with Thành. From the first day he arrived at Kai Tak airport until his departure several months of hard training later, it was a constant relief BK brought me either in the tedious but exasperating work at the Consulate or in the entertainments required as part of my job to diverse visitors from Saigon: government officials, members of congress, big businessmen, and more self-important people.

One of these visitors was Dương Văn Minh ("Big Minh"), then a malcontent general who, rumor had it, might one day pull a coup d'etat against President Diệm. Big Minh landed at Kai Tak one afternoon in summer 1959. I met him as protocol prescribed and brought him to the Peninsular Hotel and as he thanked me on my leaving matter-of-factly said: "À votre service, mon général." This was just a polite way to say, "Don't mention it" and it was the French style to address him by his title preceded by "my," it wasn't nothing to get excited about. At least that was what I thought before Big Minh surprisingly rejoined: "Oh, but not yet—not yet!"

Minh's misunderstanding was a giveaway of his secret intentions. The rumor was well-founded after all. It would be confirmed and executed four years later with a little connivance on the part of the CIA. I laughed over Minh's rejoining that afternoon and even then, I thought Big Minh was not the kind of leader likely to do much good. I believed if a choice was necessary between, say, Ngô Đình

Nhu and any of his generals, it would be the lesser evil to have Nhu.

The same evening at the Tai Tung Restaurant on Des Voeux Road, Uncle BK and I entertained General Big Minh and Nguyễn Hữu Hanh who happened to be on the same plane as the General from Saigon. In the alluring atmosphere of this high-class Chinese dining place, sequestered in a private room, after many *kampei* with the tongue-loosening yellow wine, General Minh spoke of his finding the situation in South Vietnam bad in a military and political sense. Alluding to the self-centered and incestuous power machinery that fed on itself exclusive of anyone outside the 'entourage', I pointed to my chest and like Louis XIV, said: "L'État, c'est moi" [I am the State]. I had no inkling whether the General understood, appreciated, or found my pronouncement too cryptic as he made no comment. Maybe the General is thick-eared, I thought, or concerned enough to hide his feelings so I didn't pursue the matter. Except the next day, when asking a favor of me for a trivial purchase of some Hong Kong commodity or the like, General Minh referred to my statement at the restaurant: "You ***can*** do it, for you said, 'L'État, C'est Vous'" [the State is you]. He was more thick-eared or more devious than I thought, to turn this against me—and for such trivia! I replied: "Forget it, General, it was just a drunken proposition."

WE HAD THE pleasure of bringing my father and my wife's parents to Hong Kong for a visit. They stayed with us for three months and only my father returned earlier as he had his job at the bank. We had feasts, boating trips, excursions, and otherwise had a wonderful time with our parents. My wife and I considered this the high point of our career in Hong Kong, for filial duty required that children must love their parents and care for them in their old age. I even asked our good neighbor, Mr. Lư Hoà, to secure an exquisite pleasure for my father-in-law (highly appreciated by a Vietnamese connoisseur but perhaps repugnant to Westerners) of a dinner of dog meat enjoyed at his farm in a secluded area on the road to Aberdeen. The British 'Protection Against Cruelty to Animals' societies on the Island would never hear of it.

At Deep Water Bay, Big Wave Beach, the New Territories, the Tai Pak and Sea Palace...we took our parents to visit all the famous spots of Hong Kong and Kowloon. My wife and I remained forever grateful to President Ngô Đình Diệm, our Ông Ngô, for this chance to accomplish our filial duties towards our parents. And by sheer coincidence, he also gave me the chance to see my grandmother just before her passing.

MEANWHILE, WHAT DR. TUYẾN could not do openly and straightforwardly, he did by hook and by crook. The Nguyễn Đình Hiếu affair had died down a while back and I completely forgot about it until one day a coded telegram advised me of the impending arrival of a 'secret agent' who, CIA-like, would work in my officer undercover as a consular official. The secret mission was code-named 'Operation Celestine', which was very James Bond-like and had a story that goes back a while.

On a previous visit to President Diệm I had reported that Hanoi was establishing a commercial representative position on Hong Kong. The office was at the China Bank two doors down the road from the Consulate. Intrigued, Diệm asked me if it was possible to "lure the man away to our side—to freedom." Like any anti-communist, Diệm took it for granted that given the opportunity, Communist officials abroad would defect. The Hanoi man was Bùi Khôn, and whether it was a coincidence or not, his name seemed to be a reflection of my own, the Saigon man. Ironically, I called myself *Bùi Dại* which meant "Bui, the idiot" as opposed to Hanoi man's "Bui, the intelligent (Khôn)." In official functions I often saw Khôn from a distance and it would have been easy to just walk over and shake hands. I submitted a request to do just this to the president and was waiting for permission. It was in connection with this matter that Dr. Tuyến's telegram arrived, apparently with presidential benediction and respectably code-named 'Operation Celestine.'

I had in mind a civilized meeting between two Vietnamese representatives of two parts of the same Vietnam, but Saigon's idea was entirely different and so disingenuous to my way of diplomacy (I was allergic to anything related to the secret police), I did not protest lest I be accused of 'sabotaging a secret operation.' I said to myself: "Okay, so much the better than you want to take control of the matter from me." I didn't like the way Diệm hinted of the plan to me, anyway. I didn't trust turncoats and Trần Chánh Thành was one of them—I had my doubts that Diệm and the Political Adviser could most blindly trust him.

Đỗ Sỹ Kiệm was the Hong Kong man for 'Operation

Celestine." He was a Tonkinese of suspicious appearance, about thirty years of age, with a sickly pale complexion and furtive gait. Everything about him spoke of the typical although novice secret agent. His effete manner of walking about and discretely eyeing people around him suggested a queer on the lookout for a partner. I would have given him three months on the job and if I could not stomach him, then home he would go, Operation Celestine or not. Dr. Tuyến furnished Kiệm with a two-way radio transmitter-receiver that he installed somewhere at his lodgings. I heard about it, did not like it one bit, but reported the information with no comment.

The year 1959 progressed until one day at lunch, I complained to Dr. Francois Sun, my dentist friend: "I have been in Hong Kong too long," which clearly reflected my feelings about my job. Francois and I had a Hong Kong lawyer as companion at lunch that day. When he retorted that "four years in the colony was not too long," I told him that it was one-tenth of my life so far! "Ah," he said, "if you see things that way, then there is nothing more I can say." Too long for me, indeed. I longed for a transfer somewhere just to change the atmosphere of intrigue and secret operations. I was glad President Diệm did not promote the Mission to Consulate General level, for if he did so, I would become Doyen of the Consular Corps, which was an extra unwanted charge on top of the work headaches I already suffered.

MY CHILDREN WERE doing well, meanwhile. Marie had graduated from high school and would enter Rivier College in Nashua, New Hampshire. Dominic was doing well at St. Joseph's and Lucie and Muriel were at Maryknoll Sister's Primary School both on the Hong Kong side. I was becoming more and more discouraged with my work and President Diệm was less and less accessible to me when I came to Saigon for a visit. On top of all of this was sadness that Uncle Thành was returning to Vietnam having completed his AIU training. He left in early 1960, leaving behind Lucky, the dog he intended to bring home for his young son, Bùi Kiến Thế, but couldn't conveniently accommodate on board the airplane.

Tết passed and one day, coming home from work, I was told that Đỗ Sỹ Kiệm came to see my wife and bluntly extorted money under the usual pretext of 'fund-raising for the Party.' A veiled threat of some sort had been hinted at and she had to tell me about it. So, here it was, Operation Celestine! Celestine indeed. I returned to my office and spent many hours alone, thinking. It was time for me to leave Hong Kong—and President Ngô Đình Diệm. Things had reached the point of no return for me, and I was bitterly reproaching myself for accepting this position. I should have stayed in America or stayed in Vietnam once back home like my friends Nhuận, Phước, and Lương. Again, I thought how politics was not for me and never had been. President Diệm's portrait on my desk: it was the same picture the seminarist Đỗ Văn Quý took when he was with us in New York. The picture had not changed, but Diệm had—he was no longer the man I once knew and loved. Now, he was the President of Vietnam with his own family, which to my mind he had placed above country. I could not understand nor approve of it—and I resented this. Words came back to me, not from the Ngô

Đình Diệm of old which was a thing of the past, but of Ngô Đình Cẩn, his brother, the 'Viceroy' of Huế. When I refused to cooperate with men purporting to work for in his same old 'fund-raising' ploy, Cẩn supposedly threatened: "That Văn! Wait 'til he shows up in Huế and see how I deal with him!" Is this story true or false? How would anyone know?

I FLEW BACK to Vietnam in March 1960 and it the saddest homecoming I ever had. Sure that I would not have easy access to President Diệm, I asked Uncle Thành to approach his father, Dr. Bùi Kiến Tín, to help me, for he alone as private physician to President Diệm could let him know without hindrance that I urgently needed to see him. He did this and told me to come to the Palace early the next morning. There, I faced the same rituals: sitting in the waiting room, sometimes crowded with people of all sizes and calibers, in uniform or civilian dress, where they drank cup after cup of tea, just like you. Sometimes you saw the President walk by in the corridor and the whole crowd—you along with the rest if you didn't feel like an outsider—reverently stood up with head bowed. Diệm passed the crowd like a gust of wind, glancing quickly at you as if was wondering why you were all there.

At other times, you are alone in the waiting room, forlornly observing the guard on duty who did not speak to you unless you asked him something. You wait and wait for hours, looking out at the same scene: lawn, marine flagpole, iron gates, lamp posts, Công Lý street skirting the Palace front is, then the spacious but traffic-jammed Thống Nhứt or Union Boulevard with the Cathedral jutting out at its rear, all red-bricked and vaguely reminiscent of colonial overlordship.

Gone were the early days when like in the fall of 1956, Trương Anh Mẫn and I were shown into President Diệm's office straight from Tân Sơn Nhứt Airport. True, times had changed: Now I had nothing to report except how I was faring, how big my children had grown, had I yet started "the book you propose to write"? No, now I had problems I needed the President to solve for me. Patience, man, I told myself: it's one day in the "Life of Ivan Văn!"[78] Just one more day. Today.

I remembered the time, not long ago, when I had to sit for hours in this same waiting room, along with no one else to dispute priority with, not a single word from the guard on why I had to wait so long. My friends. Nhuận, Phước, and Lương were waiting for me at home, and I had been at the Palace since 4:00 pm. The night advanced to seven then seven-thirty and I decided then that I'd had enough of waiting that day! Without a word, I got up and walked out. Võ Văn Hải, private secretary to the president, materialized from nowhere (had he been watching me all these hours from a hidden chair?) He stopped me and on learning I had a dinner appointment with friends, he said aghast: "You must be joking! You can't be serious! Look, you are waiting for THE PRESIDENT! What friends of yours could be as important as THE PRESIDENT?!"

---

78 By evoking Solzhenitsyn's Denisovich who was a prisoner in Stalin's Gulag, the author hinted at his deep frustration and boredom. See Alexander Solzhenitsyn, *One Day in the Life of Ivan Denisovich*, trans. Ralph Parker (New York: Dutton, 1963).

I said nothing and silently walked on, down the stairs, and out. I overheard Võ Văn Hải telling the officer on duty to "Report to the President that Mister Consul had some urgent business and could not wait." Was it all a pretense? Was Diệm really that busy? Did he keep me waiting in a demonstration of power? And that was the last time I waited.

AT LAST, PRESIDENT DIỆM received me. At first, he listened to my story with a non-committal attitude. Then, he slowly observed: "But Đỗ Sỹ Kiệm (the agent heading Operation Celestine in Hong Kong) saw your wife in the privacy of your home. There was no one to witness what he said—only Mrs. Văn's words." I was incensed. I stood up, choked with emotions: "Mr. President, do you take me for a liar?" Tears brimming in my eyes, I went on: "If you do not trust me, then why do you keep me in my post?" I was offering my resignation with vengeance. Blunt and loud.

Diệm did not accept it, however. When he spoke again, I knew what was on his mind. "They told me", invoking the same anonymous 'They,' "that Mrs. Văn took bribes from the Chinese." I rejoined: "Suppose she did. Is that a reason for your brother's man to go and extort money from her? Is it right?" The president paled. He looked offended when he said: "Mr. Văn, remember that I am the president. Respect my prestige." Precisely because you are the President, I was inhibited whenever I wanted to report anything in connection with your … family. I was inhibited for the same worry about your prestige.

An uneasy silence descended. President Diệm relented,

nonetheless. His expression changed and he was no longer angry. After a lengthy silence, when he told me to go see "Mister Political Adviser" my reaction was brusque: "I do not have to see anyone but you. You are the President!"

Diệm laughed at this. No doubt, he had never heard such a reply from anyone because without exception, no one had the temerity to refuse to see Ngô Đình Nhu. On the contrary, everyone considered it a great favor to be able to see him. This was made clear when the President next said in an almost paternal tone: "I have never met anyone as **strange** as you are. Why, in this government, you are the only one who does not want to see the Political Adviser." Then, his tone became even softer and kinder, as if cajoling me: "Go and see Nhu. He alone knows his business. I do not."

Upon this note, we departed still friends. Yet I had the impression this was the last interview I would have with my friend and president. Looking at him a last time I felt: *Here is the same Ngô Đình Diệm I knew. He may have changed but deep down, he remains my friend. I will stay on in my post because of him.* When I held the door for Diệm to pass out of the room, he came so close that his clothes brushed me. I could not know that this was the last time he was ever that close to me.

Võ Văn Hải arranged my interview with Diệm's brother, Ngô Đình Nhu. It was the first and only time I saw him. My wife and I had received Nhu and his wife a few times when they passed through Hong Kong and treated them to dinner at the Aberdeen floating restaurants or the like, but I had nothing to do with him officially. I never saw him in Saigon in or out of his office, nor even had any idea even where his office was located. Võ Văn Hải had to direct me there.

In the antechamber to Nhu's office, Minister for Information, Trần Chánh Thành, had been patiently waiting long before I arrived. We both waited some more in silence. There was no guard on duty here and the room, on the same floor as the Presidential living quarters but on the right side, seemed darker, quieter, and somehow sadder and more dismal.

Once in a while, a girl bobbed her head out of a door that she opened and shut, allowing a split second to peep at those who were waiting there. She could have been a secretary or a servant for all I knew. The atmosphere was less 'official' than in the presidential antechamber yet seemed more somber and vaguely suggesting a 'cloak and dagger' milieu (but perhaps I imagined this). At length, Trần Chánh Thành, who had been tight-lipped so far, leaned across in his chair and whispered to me (the room seeming to encourage soft tones and tiptoeing) that I could go into Nhu's office first. He had no pressing business and could wait. I thanked him and waited some more.

Finally, the door to Nhu's office and the same girl who checked on us invited me in. I walked through a soundproofed padded door into a rectangular room (also soundproofed with padding from floor to ceiling), slightly larger than the one the President used to receive me in. This room was air-conditioned (Diệm's was not), filing cabinets against a wall and a long desk with gadgets here and there where Nhu awaited me. This inner office gave me 'the creeps' like a CIA inner office and the man in the office could be a lean, diminutive Allen Dulles. But my imagination and auto-suggestion could run wild.

Ngô Đình Nhu did not move from his seat nor offer a hand to shake. All he said was, "Please sit down." I felt like I was in a psychoanalyst's office. I broke the heavy atmosphere as if I were the patient and spoke first (almost facetiously addressing Nhu as 'Doctor'): I gave him a resume of what Đỗ Sỹ Kiệm had been doing in Hong Kong, culminating in his threatening my wife. I did not mention Dr. Tuyến or anyone else. This took about five minutes, but Nhu did not once stop me nor ask any questions. He must know about his men by heart. Then he said, his voice warmer than I expected: "Please give me in writing a report of what you just told me... (a short pause) ... so I can 'liquidate' the matter." I nodded consent and stood up. There was no small talk, no civility of any sort in a cold, clinical, and efficient meeting. I might have been talking to a surgeon. The whole thing took less than fifteen minutes. I stepped out of Nhu's office to a deserted antechamber. Trần Chánh Thành was no longer there.

Leaving the Presidential Palace, I went back to Nguyễn Hữu Hanh's residence on top of the National Bank Building where I stopped anytime I came to Saigon, I sat at one of the small desks in his children's study room and started typing my report. Incidentally, Mrs. Hanh had just gifted me a Vietnamese-keyed Olivetti portable typewriter which I 'inaugurated' with this memorable report. I started the report in French: "Monsieur le Conseiller Politique et Cher Monsieur," trying to make up—at least on paper—

what civility was lacking between Nhu and me at our meeting. As I typed, however, I could not help thinking it was odd, odd and ridiculous, that no one dared to call the Political Adviser by his name. No one ever addressed him as "Dear Mr. Nhu." Should I start it now? My opening in French of 'Dear Mr. Political Adviser and Dear Sir' sounded almost sarcastic, even to my ear. Nonetheless, I kept it and continued typing my two-page report. I put in a nutshell what I told him that morning, adding a few newly inspired adjectives such as 'omnipotent' and 'Public Enemy Number One.' There was no conclusion. It had been understood that **he** will 'liquidate' it.

I telephoned Võ Văn Hải who was eager to have my report. He at once gave me a rendezvous at the Café La Pagode, next to the Air Vietnam office on the corner of Lê Thánh Tôn and Tự Do streets. Hai was to personally bring the report to Nhu. I was not—repeat NOT—to see Ngô Đình Nhu or anyone else anymore! Irritated, I thought, I have had enough.

At La Pagode, Hải pocketed the report I handed him in an open envelope. I knew he was eager to read it as he was very much against the Dr. Tuyến group. This was an affair he could use to sap the group's strength. Hai left at once and I remained at the café, thinking about things over several cups of coffee. In the report I had requested a transfer to some other post as I felt I had been in Hong Kong too long. I did not demand any disciplinary measure against the 'secret agent' knowing full well he was Dr. Tuyến's man who was in turn Ngô Đình Nhu's man. A rush of being sick and tired of this whole business overcame me: of Vietnam under the U.S. umbrella, of Saigon-style government and politics, of Võ Văn Hải and Political Advisor Ngô Đình Nhu. The only redeeming shadow, although faint and tired, was Ngô Đình Diệm but he was kept inaccessible behind the ramparts of Independence Palace. I did not realize how close my thoughts were to the truth.

I must get away from Saigon, I know. I could not find it in my heart to go see my friends Nhuận, Phước or Lương who did not know I was in town. This was a special trip, and I lost no time in seeing the President first. I borrowed Hanh's car and drove up to Đà Lạt. I stayed at his ranch-farm near Tung Nghĩa, 25 kilometers from Đà Lạt. Hứa Xiêu had his own ranch nearby and I often drove up to see him but this time, I mostly shut myself in at Hanh's place, listening to short wave broadcasts from Far East network-Tokyo, drank plenty of whiskey, and fell asleep early. It was like I was recovering from shock. This was my second trip to Đà Lạt but unlike the first one with Phước, I was lonely, depressed, and despondent.

After a few days, I drove down to Nha Trang taking the Belle Vue Hill route. The beautiful landscape I had not seen before cheered me up a bit. Chàm [Champa] ruins, towers of dark brown laterite, some still standing but others half-fallen as if decapitated by a giant sword in centuries past. Riceland and meadows studded both sides of the winding road where an irrigation canal meandered, grass blades poking out of its limpid water. I stopped to rest in the shade of a Chàm tower, the overhang reeking of bat droppings, I thought of the valiant Chàm people who once ruled this land. They had their families, kings, and temples before Vietnamese invaders from the north slowly but inexorably pushed them out. We usurped their land piecemeal, tricked them by giving a princess to their king in return for two large provinces, attacked them, and finally exterminated them.

In Nha Trang, in the Hotel du Beau Rivage run by a Frenchman, I met Trần Lý Thích, the VOA man in Okinawa and his 'Russian' wife and their son. Thích had left for Okinawa one week before my family and I departed for New York in 1951. That evening, Thích and I drank whiskey at a bar frequented by American advisers who even then, already were coming in great numbers. One of them, a major, was all happiness when he found out we both spoke English. He was particularly annoyed by a Vietnamese 'secret agent' he pointed out who he claimed could make life for him uncomfortable by his reports to the government. How uncomfortable, we asked? Not uncomfortable, really, the major admitted: he loved it in Nha Trang and it would be a pity if he couldn't stay. "Ah", I thought, "so Dr. Tuyến's men were here, too!" I glanced at the man he pointed out lolling at the bar counter, whispering something into a bar girl's ear.

By pure coincidence, before leaving Đà Lạt for Nha Trang, a cabinet maker at Tùng Nghĩa gave me a handwritten introduction to his brother who worked in the city as a plainclothes policeman. I had nonchalantly pocketed the letter and forgotten all about it. Suddenly remembering it, I showed the man at the bar the envelope and asked, "Do you happen to know this man?" Surprised but pleased, he answered, "Sure I do. That's me."

Thereupon, without being invited, the man walked over to our table where the major also sat, read his brother's letter, then ordered a round of drinks for everyone. I could see that the American major was pleased. Confident that the agent did not understand English, he purposely annoyed him with frequent verbal shows of 'friendship' by speaking English with Thích and me, his new friends.

31. WHO'S AFRAID OF WINTER?

BACK IN HONG KONG, I was still in the same languishing mood despite being relieved that Đỗ Sỹ Kiệm was gone—lock, stock, and barrel. Ngô Đình Nhu did 'liquidate' Kiệm after all, yet I didn't doubt that another Kiệm would show up in the future. I deliberately stayed away from the office and had papers brought to Jardine's Lookout for my signature. It was late March and the weather was fresh. I enjoyed my family; many fish, birds, and dogs in the house, and walks on Sir Cecil's Ride trail. In a poetic mood, I had the following poem composed as a reply to Trương Anh Mẫn's birthday wishes to me:

Đông Tây chưa gặp bạn bằng ông,
Kể từ thân mật tại Hồng Kông.
Cách mệnh bôn ba, tâm vẫn sĩ,
Phú Cường, lận đận, thủy như chung.
Sớm tối luận bàn cơ đất nước,
Trẻ già kiên quyết mệnh non sông.
Năm lần mùng Bảy kim ô mọc:
Xuân tái lai rồi, há sợ Đông?

I have yet to have such a good friend as you, East or West,
Ever since we met in Hong Kong.[79]
Revolutionary and expatriate, you remain a scholar,
Rich or poor, you are constant like a star.
Morning and evening we two discussed our country's lot
One old man and one young one, our blood is equally hot.
Five times, my Golden Eagle rose up:
Spring has returned: Who's afraid of Winter?[80]

SOONER THAN I expected, a second conference of Heads of Mission was called in July 1960, and I reluctantly came home. The conference's aim was to impress our ambassadors abroad with the good results the government had achieved at home so they could spread the good news to their posts. The great success at the moment was Prosperity Zones [*Khu Trù Mật*], named for the establishment of secure land zones where people could safely cultivate and prosper.

The conference was held at Independence Palace,

79 A 'scholar' in the Confucian sense is a *quân tử* or gentleman who is noble both in spirit and action, whether rich or poor. (Au.)

80 Golden Eagle: Classical literature metaphorically compared the sun to an Eagle or Hawk, the bird appearing golden in the rays of the sun. For example, in the epic poem Kiều, Nguyễn Du described a sunset as: "The Raven had been swallowed up by the Westerly Hill," meaning the sun had been hidden by the Westerly Hill. The sun is referred to as the Raven that set in the West. If it was sunrise, the description would be "the Raven emerging from an Easterly Hill." Mẫn was saying that the 'sun of my birthday has risen five times' meaning that Trương Anh Mẫn had congratulated me five times on my diplomatic anniversaries, the first being on March 7, 1956. (Au.)

not the Ministry for Foreign Affairs as in 1958. It had a ceremonial opening with President Diệm presiding over the first session. Pomp and pageantry. The ministers were in full attendance and also present were military members, resplendent in their brass. It was a big show.

Heads of Mission were almost all present. With the lone exception of Đỗ Vạn Lý, who had not attended the first conference either, everyone was there. New faces included Đặng Đức Khôi, Chargé d'affaires in Bangkok instead of Mai Văn Hàm who had long ago resigned; Trần Hữu Phương, Chargé d'affaires in Bonn, a subsidiary to Ambassador Luyện's Embassy in London; Nguyễn Văn Hiếu, brother of Nguyễn Văn Thiệu, a future President of Vietnam, Consul General in Jakarta.

Vũ Văn Mẫu presided over the working sessions which lasted ten days. Nguyễn Hữu Châu was gone. Ministers, each in turn, took the rostrum and 'lectured' heads of mission on their respective ministerial work and projects.

However, all was in vain—the spirit was gone! The whole event was a display of non-existent enthusiasm with presenters going through the motions of emphatically explaining, presenting, defending, and even obliquely criticizing their own work or other ministers. I listened to an interminable monologue of Ambassador Ngô Đình Luyện to the United Kingdom with only one ear, the other being distracted by wooden clogs clacking on a concrete floor somewhere outside the conference room. I did not retain, nor did I understand, one single word of Luyện's exposé. Ambassador Chương to the United States criticized President Diệm in veiled terms, too full of himself to let the opportunity pass without drawing a balance in his favor. Perhaps he was dreaming of becoming president soon. Still, I did not speak up and on the fourth day or so, Vũ Văn Mẫu called on me from the rostrum: "And Mr. Hong Kong, don't you have anything to say?" I firmly responded: "Not one thing."

It was almost a relief to have a break from the suffocating atmosphere of the conference room when Heads of Mission were taken on a tour of Prosperity Zones in the Mekong Delta. We all boarded planes to Sóc Trăng, then helicoptered to Vị Thanh, where Architect Ngô Viết Thụ had constructed a full-size model of a Prosperity Village for us. It was a hastily put-up display, as rough and incomplete as a badly done maquette. Constructions and one or two bridges arched in the oriental style were half finished, and traces of cement showed. Part of a thatched hospital had two rooms: one room had a young woman lying in a bed with a blanket across her stomach. It was so transparently a mockup that the 'patient' herself could not help smiling, turning her face to the earth wall. The other room was empty. Rows of small houses with palm-leaf roofs, freshly-built for us, were half occupied with 'residents' told to pretend they dwelt there just like the 'patient' was admitted to the hospital. And the plowed earth all around, still steaming in the early sunlight, was a telltale sign of work hastily done on orders from higher ups. It was the precursor of the Potemkin 'Strategic Hamlets' and 'New Life Villages' of later years where the same kind of put-up shows were hastily done for the benefit of the President and his entourage.

The ambassadors were conducted through several pieces of similarly prepared terrain and none of them really finished. It could be called 'a going concern.' It was patchwork grafted onto some existing houses and here and there we could see bushes of red and green chili peppers fruiting. I picked some of these and tasted them—they were real and spicy! My impression was that once the ambassadors were gone and the show over with, many of the home dwellers would return to wherever they were ordered to come from, and the rows of houses would be more than half empty.

When our conducted tour was finished and we returned to a communal room, I had the pleasure of finding there an old college friend, Lương Vinh Hiển, who had become a teacher. He had been roused from bed and driven post-haste from Cần Thơ to Vị Thanh to join a group of similarly awoken teachers brought there to impress the visitors from Saigon. Hiển approached my chair from behind and tapped my shoulder and that was how I knew he was there. Delighted to meet again, the pair of us sat together and talked in low tones while the head of the Prosperity Zone gave a lecture from an improvised platform. What a wonderful meeting with an old friend!

Part of the conference had us visit Huế, Pleiku and Ban Mê Thuột. On the eve of my departure for Huế my father stopped by, perturbed because he remembered my telling him of Ngô Đình Cẩn's threat should I ever show my face in his territory. He asked if it was wise for me to go and only reluctantly left after I assured him there would be no mishaps.

In Huế, we were treated to a formal visit to President Diệm's paternal home where Ngô Đình Cẩn lived with his aged mother. Phạm Khắc Hy, then Ambassador to France, led the delegation to the bed of the old lady. She spoke in a feeble voice and Hy, presented our respect and good wishes on behalf of the delegation. Ngô Đình Cẩn, however, was nowhere to be seen. After this was a succession of dinners at the Province chief's residence; a select few were invited by General Trần Văn Đôn, military commander for the region, for a semi-private soirée on flower boats drifting down the Perfume River [sông Hương]; and one or two tours of developed agricultural grounds.

Up in the highlands in Ban Mê Thuột and Pleiku it rained and the road in places became as slippery as if it had been greased. The same shows and same 'models' of this and that, groups of Montagnard children in classes led by Vietnamese teachers, and acres of red clay loosened by the downpour that landowners splashed across, carrying the esteemed Heads of Mission from one show to the next.

It was a pleasure when the group was finally driven down a road to a military airstrip where a plane waited to take us back to Saigon. Emerging from a dense forest, we stopped at a restaurant by the wayside for refreshments. The surprise was that the owner was no other than Cáp Văn Trang, a fellow Cần Thơ-man. He was no less surprised to see me in the midst of the wilderness. After a life of activity in commercial and industrial enterprises, Trang had retired to this lost corner where only hunters and stray travelers stopped for food and drink.

The conference that began with a bang ended with

a whimper. President Diệm thought that showing his ambassadors these 'accomplishments' would strengthen their dwindling optimism about his government's efforts, but the contrary must have been produced. Not one mission head was fooled by what he saw, and they all returned to their posts, perhaps hoping never to be called back again.

On the last day of the conference, President Diệm gave a talk to the entire Diplomatic Corps. The members listened (or pretended to listen) for over an hour as he rambled on and on as usual and when he was finished Diệm rapidly headed to his offices. He suddenly stopped on his way and motioned to Trân Văn Dĩnh, saying, "Mr. Dĩnh, follow me!" A few steps further, he signaled to Hà Vĩnh Phương who stepped out of the crowd and quickened his steps to follow the President, his back somehow half-bent, as if too awed to walk upright or too afraid to be judged insolent if he did so. It was a sad scene. I never forgot the show unwittingly put on by the Hà Vĩnh Phương and Trần Văn Dĩnh as the typical sycophants of the court of Ngô Đình Diệm.

NOVEMBER 11, 1960, a day like another in the year. In the late morning, a telegram came from the Ministry, laconically telling us about a coup d'etat by elements of the army. The fact that the telegram was sent at all spoke well of the news as otherwise, we would not have been informed. We were waiting for further news when in the afternoon, I received a telephone call from Tokyo. It was Ambassador Bùi Văn Thinh, asking if the coup had been successful. His tone was that of a man anxious to see the coup succeed, not the other way around. Perhaps taking me for a like-minded person, Thinh said that in Japan he heard that Ngô Đình Diệm had been deposed and the army was in control—was this true or not? He sounded disappointed when I told him we had no such news in Hong Kong. The night passed without any more updates until the next morning, November 12, when the Ministry sent a long telegram with details: A limited revolt by discontented elements of the Paratroopers had been put down and President Ngô Đình Diệm was in control. Repeat, it was the work of separate elements, not of the Vietnamese Army as such. I was reading the telegram with relief when I was told that the British Chargé d'affaires in Saigon wanted to see me. When he was shown in, he said he unfortunately was on vacation in Hong Kong when the 'coup' in Saigon took place and was anxious to learn of the latest developments. I told him the contents of the latest telegram and invited him to stay in my office as further developments came in, if any. He did. After a few hours of no news, I invited him to Jardine's Hill to have a drink with me by way celebration. He was very much relieved to have no bad news and happily accepted.

It was an abortive coup. What happened revealed a grave state of discontent not limited to a few elements in the Army. A few weeks before had appeared the Caravelle Manifesto by some intellectuals, among them Trần Văn Đỗ, the former Foreign Minister who represented the Diệm government at Geneva, trying to warn Diệm of a deteriorating situation prevailing in Vietnam.

We had thought that the government might adopt

new policies aimed at redressing the situation. Nguyễn Đình Thuần, then an ascending star in the government sky, a Secretary to the Presidency, declared that 'There would be a total recast of the government." As a result, however, a few so-called 'Super-ministries' were created with new 'Super-ministers' including Ngô Trọng Hiếu as Minister of Civic Action; and Đặng Đức Khôi until then an unknown element under the skirts of Dr. Tuyến. General disappointment: no hope of improvement could be entertained with such superficial and ill-advised changes. Dr. Tuyến and Ngô Đình Nhu remained at the same pinnacle of central power as before. This was the impression we had from Hong Kong.

Like most of Ngô Đình Diệm's former supporters, we had long been disappointed with the Nhus who we thought were usurping the President's power. We, too, wanted some real changes, if only to eliminate the bad influences on the government such as Dr. Tuyến. We did not want Ngô Đình Diệm replaced simply because there was no one we thought capable of taking his place. The support we still had for the President was lukewarm, conditional to the changes we no longer believed could be brought about.

Nguyễn Thái, for one, had left Saigon and turned against Diệm. From the U.S., he wrote the book, *Is South Vietnam Viable?* a copy of which was lent to me by Stanley Karnow, then a Hong Kong reporter for *The Saturday Evening Post*.[81] And Thái kept sending tracts and pamphlets to me denouncing the Diệm government.

81 Nguyễn Thái, *Is South Vietnam Viable?* (Manila: Carmelo & Bauermann, 1962).

32. A MALARIA-SUFFERER STUCK IN DELIRIUM

THE YEAR 1961 began with news from Vietnam's new "Strategic Hamlets" project dominating the news. Reams of printed documents concerning the project poured in with every incoming diplomatic pouch. The Consulate was asked to have The Strategic Hamlets propagandized in the Hong Kong news media. Judging the matter entirely uninteresting to the public, I just filed them away.

We were going through a worse period when confidence in the success of the Diệm government diminished with the passing days so that over the months even its very survival was in doubt. Life, for us in the colony, was reduced to a waiting game. We waited for further developments we felt were bound to come—if not with the government, then against it.

Politically, I was like a malaria-sufferer stuck in delirium, seeing and feeling through misty layers. There was no hope left, not unlike the last days of my grandmother's illness, where my love for Ngô Đình Diệm was tempered and diluted by the dangerous and exasperating antics of his brothers. This caused a war in my own heart, tearing it, gnawing at it, shifting my loyalty one day to this side and the other side the next day.

Professionally, there was nothing I cared about any longer. Invitations and official Hong Kong government functions whose attendance were a "must" for the consular corps were indifferently declined and ignored. Who cares about his outhouse's appearance when fire threatens his very bedchamber? Personally, as was my artistic wont, I took refuge in the little routine rounds of my daily private life, finding in them eventual sources of creative work I planned to do at some future date. I would more attentively observe the Jardine Hill house and its surroundings, making mental notes of details and colors. I would store them away: our children's birthday celebrations with their little friends, kids like the Pakistani Trade Commissioner Abdul Rab's cute baby-doll daughter, the American Army's man in Hong Kong, Colonel Shoemaker, who was our neighbor, ponytail wagging 'Blondie', and the brothers Shin and 'Shrimp' Wai Yee Lin.

The daily noontime waiting for Dominic at the foot of the cable car station in front of the Chinese supermarket was also a high point of the day. I sat in the car and observed colorful throngs going up to the funicular car that brought them up the steep hill to the Peak or, when Mỹ-Châu and Mỹ-Nga were with us having been fetched first by the driver, we stepped out to buy a popsicle or two from the store. Finally, Dominic in his St. Joseph's School white uniform detached from his group of chatting and horse-playing boys heading downhill and joined us. The car pulled out, climbed the Peak Road over to Queen's Road East, took a right along a long barracks, stopped at a crossroad traffic island where the Chinese policeman performed his usual ballet and hand signals, turned right again on King's Road East where the crowds were so dense I always imagined it was an ocean of humanity (a replica of teeming China in miniature), made another right turn up Tai Hang Road with St. Paul's Hospital on our right where my dad had a short stay from a slight illness, and Dominic had to have many glass slivers removed from his legs after a mishap filling a glass vial with firecracker gunpowder, until a final left turn brought us to Perkins Road and home.

It was in this 'I-Couldn't-care less' mood that I read the news of Vice-President Lyndon B. Johnson's stop in Hong Kong on his way home to the U.S. after an official visit to Vietnam on behalf of President John F. Kennedy. A year or two earlier, I would have gotten in touch with the American Consulate General and met the Vice-President. I felt it my duty to meet official representatives of foreign governments on their way to or from an official visit to Vietnam and although it wasn't a requirement, I always found time to perform the duty. There was more reason: I also felt to befriend American representatives. American help to Vietnam was appreciated—until it degenerated into a blatant and heavy-handed interference.

With Johnson's arrival, however, my stay-away rule was observed. I found it amusing to read in the *Hong Kong Tiger Standard* that the Vice-President shopped in town and bought no less than three dozen tailored shirts. The

British Colony certainly deserved its reputation as **the** shopping paradise of the East, after all.

However, the memorable event for me was the unexpected visit of His Excellency 'Dr.' Đỗ Vạn Lý. Steve Markbreiter, a British architect working in Hong Kong was married to Ly's sister-in-law, Tuyết Nguyệt. Steve and I were good friends, and he announced Lý's arrival as a matter of course. Neither Steve nor his wife knew of Lý's and my ancient antagonism which, even to me, seemed like an antediluvian remnant of a far-away Washington past. I was prepared to forget everything and meet Lý on friendly terms.

It was late September 1961 and Hong Kong weather being what it was, it might as well have been mid-August. Đỗ Vạn Lý was brought to my Jardine's Lookout house, accompanied by Steve and Tuyết Nguyệt. Lý gingerly stepped into my home, cautiously studying my attitude, and only relaxed when he was assured by my frank and open-arms reception. We drove in two cars to dinner, having separated Lý from the Markbreiters, my wife and I took him to Aberdeen for a reunion dinner at the Sea Palace floating restaurant. There was no mishap then, nor was there any hint of old enmity in the following days. A few more outings, to Steve's country residence and other eating places, and the wound might have been forgotten.

Until one day, incensed by what I thought was a well-meaning gesture on my part produced a terrible result and our patched-up amity was blown sky high. I had long kept mental track of the debt I owed Đỗ Vạn Lý for his financial help prior to returning to Vietnam in 1954 in dispatching Ngô Đình Diệm's baggage to France. Now was my chance to pay Lý back because I truly appreciated his help and meant to sincerely thank him. I telephoned him and insisted that he come to see me but alone. Little did I know that asking him to come alone alarmed him: he came reluctantly but with his wife and Tuyết Nguyệt in tow.

Lý entered my office at the Consulate, and I don't recall how the misunderstanding occurred. I began by invoking the financial debt I owed him, the amount of which neither of us remembered, but I said I would pay it back generously, several times the amount. In the course of my preliminary speech something happened, either in my unwitting harsh tone when invoking the unpleasant past or in his facial or otherwise disagreeable reaction, the goodwill was destroyed and the old animosity rearing up surprised us both. A quarrel began: subdued tones grew into a shouting match that was easily overheard from outside my thinly partitioned office. The door burst open and like an unraveling bolt of multicolored silk in flew Tuyết Nguyệt and Lý's wife, the latter being especially hysterical. She stood between Lý and me, brandishing her bony arms as if to protect her husband from my assault and vociferously insulted me. Poor Lý, cowed and somewhat reassured by the presence of his wife, he just stared at her. I was at the same time indignant and disgusted and was repeating in French: *"C'est dègoûtant! C'est dègoûtant!"* [Disgusting!] This made Lý's wife jump around like a mad dog, heaping more gutter vocabulary on me then turning to drag her husband out.

She did not leave before glancing at the open checkbook on my desk and from which I said I had prepared a check for what I owed Lý. She stretched out her hand, palm open, and demanded: "Now, how about the check!" I smiled contemptuously, closed the checkbook, and ignored her. Only then did Madame Lý rush out towing her husband behind her. What a woman! I decided that she had the upbringing of a fishmonger—quite a match for Đỗ Vạn Lý! Tuyết Nguyệt had stayed behind after the Lýs left and tried to calm me down by rubbing my chest, saying: "Now, now…don't be angry" as if I were her little son.

Of course, Lý and his wife never showed up again. And, as if on purpose, the day I left for Saigon. The afternoon of the blowup, I attended the Indonesian Independence Day reception, my mind still bogged down by the unhappy incident between me and Lý. I could find no consolation in the milling crowd of the reception, so I made a snap decision to go to Vietnam. For no reason whatsoever.

I SPENT THREE WEEKS on this trip home, a strictly private visit. I made a personal stop to see President Diệm, inquiring about his safety and health after the coup of last November, and commending his welfare—which was also the National Welfare—to the providential care of God. The President seemed tired and aloof. It could have been official business, but he also seemed withdrawn, a closed book from which I read neither Diệm's political or his own thoughts. I did not realize it then, but it was the last time I saw him. We said almost cold goodbyes: he, absorbed in his inward thoughts and I, unenthusiastic as ever to experience the treadmill of Palace protocol to see him another time during my stay

It was also the last time I was in the Independence Palace as it stood for in less than six months, it suffered air bombardment and while reconstruction was undertaken, Ngô Đình Diệm and his brother Nhu and family moved into the Gia Long Palace. I didn't feel that I had come back home at all. In hindsight, it seems Diệm's fate was bound to the Admiralty Palace, the symbol of French dominion over an ancient Vietnam where Diệm was first and only leader able to recover from the French. With a little imagination, it might parallel the historical "Ma Yuan Bronze Column" which the famous Chinese general raised in colonized Giao Chỉ in 47 A.D. This was a region of north Vietnam ruled by various dynasties whose defeat of Vietnamese heroines, the Trung Sisters, led to Vietnam's loss of independence: *"Đồng trụ chiết, Giao Chỉ diệt"* (If this bronze column falls, Giao Chi is destroyed).

Determined to get away from Hong Kong for a while I asked my father to take a leave of absence from his work and the two of us went up to Đà Lạt for a vacation Father borrowed the house of Hứa Phùng Chân, a rich rice merchant he knew, for our stay in the mountainous resort. Up there, for ten days, father and son enjoyed the best vacation we ever had. The house was a beautiful villa all the way downhill from the residence of the mayor of Đà Lạt, Trần Văn Phước. The mayor often joined us for outings in the peaceful hills and merrymaking in town. Peaceful in appearance, it seemed at night, any time I turned on the radio, Việt Cộng broadcasts echoed loud and clear, as if their studio was based in Đà Lạt itself.

It was during this stay in the highlands that I met again two of the many young students who used to come to my apartment in uptown Manhattan: Lê Tuấn Anh who was present with Biện the night we celebrated composing a poem (Biện committed suicide after he returned to Vietnam); and Nguyễn Tư Bân, the 'little fellow' who kissed a sailor's girlfriend in Times Square on New Year's Eve 1952 "because custom lets you and the girls don't mind." Bân married the very same secretary of Huỳnh Văn Lang who had shown me the door when I applied for a transfer of funds to Hong Kong in 1958.

Oblivious to the present and its realities, I lazed around Đà Lạt until we had to return to Saigon in mid-October to hear about the Taylor Mission, a state of emergency declared by Vietnam after Việt Cộng attacks stepped up in the countryside. Still the Emergency was more something on paper than a reality. The Saigonese went about their daily lives unconcerned and even the government seemed to minimize the seriousness of the situation, its going along with the American alarm was more of a gesture than a cognizance of reality. Unconcerned also, I took along with me to Hong Kong two young Vietnamese ladies who were participating in the upcoming International Fashion Show: an Air Vietnam hostess and the singer, Bích Chiêu.

Back in the colony, I learned that Đỗ Vạn Lý told Steve and Tuyết Nguyệt Markbreiter his concern that I was trying to harm him and my sudden trip to Saigon was to report on Lý to President Diệm. What a peanut-brain Lý was!

MY WIFE AND I were attending a dinner at the home

of the Indian Commissioner to Hong Kong, B. P. Adarkar when word came that a lone Air Force pilot had strafed and bombed the Independence Palace that morning. It was a stifling hot February night. The dinner was abruptly terminated, and we left with apologies, walking home as he lived around the corner from us. We turned on the shortwave radio to try to catch what we could of news from Saigon. The next morning, we got a telegram from the ministry informing us that President Ngô Đình Diệm was safe. Only Ngô Đình Nhu's wife had been wounded and the attack was the job of a lone pilot. Here we go again, I thought: It's always the lone discontented member of an otherwise completely loyal Army.

Thus, the year 1962 began badly enough, but as if it was not enough of a headache for us in Hong Kong to handle, almost on the heels of the Palace bombing came the Hoàng Thi Thơ Performance Troupe of singers and dancers.[82] First Võ Văn Hải then Huỳnh Văn Lang sent me urgent confidential letters to keep an eye on Hoàng Thi Thơ. His coming trip to Hong Kong was a disguised 'artistic' tour when the real purpose was to transfer dollars out of Vietnam, and I was to submit a full report on Thơ's trip.

Meanwhile, before Thơ's needs came those of Madame Ngô Đình Nhu. One afternoon she landed at Kai Tak airport completely transformed. She was no longer the haughty First Lady I used to hate with all my heart. Instead, she was now the 'poor victim' of an assassination attempt from which God gave her a respite. "They aimed at us,"

82 Hoàng Thi Thơ (1928-2001) was a popular song composer.

she exclaimed, 'They wanted to kill me and my husband!" She paused for breath then rushed on: "They knew well we lived in the right wing of the Palace. They deliberately tried to bomb us out of existence!"

We were told that fortunately, Madame Nhu escaped with minor bruises from falling through a gap that a bomb had cratered on the ground floor. Her husband escaped unscathed and unfortunately, the real victim in the attack was the nursemaid who cared for Nhu's baby. She said the servant was the real death they wanted to inflict on the Nhu family, to frighten her family. When we inquired about the health of President Diệm, her voice became bitter: "Oh him! No, he is all right; not even scratched! Only us—after all, **we** were the ones they were after, not him".

We brought Madame Nhu to the Repulse Bay Hotel and there, once the door to her room was closed, the Political Adviser's wife pulled up her trouser legs to show us the bruises she had. They were bad enough. She had come to Hong Kong to shop for a new wardrobe, for all her clothes had been burned. Her husband's too, she added. However, she refused to shop for the President's clothing claiming they were untouched from the bombing. A minor detail perhaps, but it said a lot about her consideration—high or low—for Ngô Đình Diệm.

HOÀNG THI THƠ arrived soon after. His theatrical and music hall troupe of a dozen lassies and twist-master boys gave a series of performances at the Municipal Theater which had been newly built at the Townhall compound. Because of the national character they gave to their performances, the Consulate had no choice but to help them every way we could. This we did, which contributed to their success in Hong Kong until a scandal happened.

For the seamy side of this tour was not artistic performances as such, but a cloak to allow Hoàng Thi Thơ to transfer dollars abroad--$40,000 strong! I got wind of this through the Hong Kong grapevine but could not lay my hand on any proof, the island being a free port that knew no such thing as foreign currency control. Still, forty-thousand dollars—ticket sales notwithstanding—Thơ said he could not pay the Shamrock Hotel where his troupe were occupying no less than a dozen rooms!

At first, Thơ thought he could bluff his way to the Consulate's coffers for his hotel expenses. He told me that his troupe had not only been authorized, but encouraged by the Political Adviser to give performances in Hong Kong and Japan as a political measure aimed at propagandizing Vietnam abroad. As such, it was the Consulate's duty to come to Tho's rescue. I sent a cable to Võ Văn Hải for corroboration, which alarmed Hải. Unknown to me, it seemed that a cold war was developing between the sides of the President and his Political Adviser.

Very much reminiscent of the Lê Kings and Trịnh Lords' rivalry under the Later Lê dynasty, each camp served its own master where the Nhu camp took precedence, like the Trịnh Lords of old. Võ Văn Hải would want me to handle the matter as secretly as possible and once I had proof in hand, send him the final report which would allow him to destroy the Nhu camp's evildoers. Hải must have been cursing me from his cage-like office in the Independence

Palace. No answer came to my cable, so I did not find any proof to send Hoàng Thi Thơ to hell either. I ignored his pleadings and promises, telling him no to his face that no Political Adviser would be able to force me to disburse government funds against my better judgment. And he was a liar: no one had ever succeeded in scaring me with an "order" from a so-called "order" from Ngô Đình Nhu who, by the way, had never sent Thơ on such an errand.

After ten days, the Shamrock Hotel manager came to see me, for Thơ still had not paid for his rooms yet. I told him not to worry: if worse came to worst, I would pay the hotel myself then sue Thơ, which calmed the manager who returned to his hotel to wait. The waiting game lasted another week during which I had Thơ's Chinese associates in Hong Kong summoned to my office for separate interviews. Each of them confirmed to me that Thơ came for the dollar transfer, but he did not need their service for that, and they only helped in the music-hall business for commercial interest. With the associates' permission, I taped out conversations with the plan to send the tapes to Saigon but changed my mind on realizing the lack of hard evidence. After all, I mentally shrugged my shoulders, what use was it to catch a small thief when the whole house was going to burn to the ground?

In the end, Thơ paid up his hotel bill after all and Võ Văn Hải wrote to urge me to submit my report, and disgusted with the whole affair, I wrote down whatever flimsy episode Hải could use in his report and I asked my wife to bring it home, for it was as good as lost if sent by diplomatic pouch which was no problem for Dr. Tuyến to access. Then, I took off to Thailand for a holiday in Bangkok. The whole thing seemed childishly harmless enough until we realized that this infighting between the brothers' two camps and with the ascendancy of Nhu's camp from that moment until the tragic end, President Diệm's side was losing ground—Huỳnh Van Lang lost his position as Director General of the Office of Exchange and Võ Văn Hải remained Personal Secretary to a president gradually losing power. The final outcome was a conspiracy aided by a little push from the CIA that tossed the baby out along with the dirty bathwater.

HONG KONG AT that time was experiencing a severe drought. Water was rationed to such an extent that people had to fill jerrycans of sea water for washing purposes and collect drops from air-conditioners for drinking and watering gardens. We had already moved from Perkins Road after our lease ended to a small villa at 89 Repulse Bay Road on a slope of a hill overlooking Repulse Bay Beach. Up there the wind blew fiercely all day and night, and I called where we lived "Wuthering Heights." Psychologically speaking, the villa was a suitable dwelling for the last stormy passage of our career in Hong Kong, a pale reflection of what was developing with galloping speed in Saigon.

It was physically stormy at the house also. The first 'welcome' to the peak we received was Typhoon Mary, who like an angry girl, tore up our plants, uprooted trees, and hurled rocks hard enough to break our two-inch thick front door glass. Mary's sisters followed her almost regularly and if they brought water aplenty to a thirsty and dehydrated Hong Kong, they also wrought havoc on the outdoors of the entire island and its residents.

Political madness in Saigon went on unchecked and with the accelerating American interference in the war under the guise of "support," ridiculous reports of goings-on reached Hong Kong like US-trained guerilla operations, American advisory teams being attached to different levels of government, military, and civilian operations. All this left us bewildered: it should be logical that the people best suited to fight Vietnamese communists were Nationalist Vietnamese and that no other race—not the white race, at any rate—could teach Vietnamese what we had to teach Americans in the first place.

Not to be surpassed by the Americans who were new to the game after all, Great Britain had her Thompson Team advising Ngô Đình Diệm how to fight guerillas and win people over! A Vietnamese saying about funerals goes: "*Nhiều thầy rã đám thối ma*" which literally means: "Too many bonzes are good only for poor funeral planning and rotting corpses." It's a macabre but down to earth Vietnamese rendering of the western proverb: "Too many cooks spoil the broth." We in Hong Kong weren't exactly hopeful of a brilliant outcome of the war now raging more fiercely with each passing day.

I took another pleasure trip to Taiwan and returned in time for Vietnam's national day on October 26, 1962. It was by now routine for the Consulate to celebrate the day with a reception at the Repulse Bay Hotel followed by a big party in the evening at the residence for the Vietnamese community. The celebration this year was made special by the presence of Uncle Bùi Kiến Thành who stopped over after some business in Japan and an eccentric engineer, Nguyễn Văn Diên, who contributed such large and colorful banners bearing slogans and good wishes they could be seen far down from even Repulse Bay beach.

The Vietnamese community's attendance was also more numerous and more enthusiastic than in previous years. For one thing, the festival atmosphere was more attractive thanks to Diên's artistic talents. For another, I dressed up for the first time in traditional costume and turban and moved about the crowd flanked by Uncle Thành and my eccentric friend Diên. A third exceptional treat for the celebration came courtesy of Air Vietnam that flew in fresh and fragrant that day a veritable feast of Vietnamese delicacies: *chả giò* (eggrolls), *bì cuốn* (spring rolls), *bánh hỏi, nem chua, chả lụa, bánh bò* and more all accompanied by *nước mắm ớt, đọt mọt, đọt sộp, lá cách,* and all. It was never truer that day than you win the hearts and minds of people through their palate than a thousand flowery speeches!

33. A MAD RACE TO PERDITION

ANOTHER YEAR PASSED and 1963 began. This was my family's eighth year in Hong Kong. Soon after Tết, the battle of Ấp Bắc took placed, a fierce encounter the outcome of which was not a victory for the republic, and which augured more and bloodier battles to come. By then, however, it was the political side of the problem that bothered us and not so much the military side.

Like a seriously ill patient waiting for a major surgical operation, Vietnam laid almost unconcerned on her sickbed, contenting herself with palliatives like medicated oil or rubbing alcohol. There was no more hope for a major reform. All that the November 11th coup had brought was the creation of "super ministries," the introduction of old faces with new power, and of all things, the strengthening of Dr. Tuyến's dubious operational apparatus. The Independence Palace bombing was as good as forgotten—a mosquito's bite, as it were.

I had made up my mind to stay put in Hong Kong for a while for, on my last trip home to Saigon, friends and relatives had advised me to refrain, if possible, from exposing myself too much in the capital where Dr. Tuyến's henchmen were practically taking the law into their hands and 'accidents' might happen. After the Hoàng Thi Thơ affair, I still had more reason to be more cautious. Besides, it tired me in advance when I thought of going back to Saigon: the long, arduous waiting if I wanted to see the President, the "nothing new, every thing's okay, ask the Palace not me" attitude from the Vice President and each ministry on down.

My wife and I decided to bring our parents over for a second visit to Hong Kong. My father and my wife's parents arrived in March and my father stayed longer than planned because of a slight operation he had for a cyst. My parents-in-laws stayed much longer and only returned home in July. Auntie Dì Tám had returned to Saigon from her stay with us and my sister, Cô Bảy, had been living with us since July 1960. We did not know it then, but this visit to Hong Kong was to be our last reunion with our parents.

In mid-April while my father was still with us, the first Buddhist incident occurred in Huế. We did not pay much attention to it while negotiations and recriminations were going on and even news of the shooting victims was minimized. After my father returned to Saigon, however, the Buddhist affairs became ***the*** Problem of the Day.

Negotiations between Vice President Thơ and the Buddhist hierarchy produced a conciliatory communiqué and my father jubilantly wrote us that the affair was settled. Nothing was farther from the truth for in June came the suicide by fire of Bonze Thích Quảng Đức, transforming an internal Vietnamese problem into a matter of international proportions. South and Southeast Asia raised their protests and even in commercial-minded Hong Kong, some Buddhist clergy and societies lodged written protests that promised more confrontations.

I recalled how long-drawn out and forcible the 'fundraising' campaigns for the 25th or Silver Anniversary celebrations of the Bishopric of Mgr. Ngô Đình Thục, President Diệm's elder brother. This had been going on for almost a year and people in every walk of life in Vietnam had been "asked" (sometimes threateningly), by cadremen and busybodies of all imaginable organizations to contribute funds. The more prosperous merchants were practically blackmailed into 'donating' large sums, while those holding more lucrative government posts competed on who could bring in the largest contributions. Perhaps they sensed an opportunity for advancement but more likely, it was to maintain a beneficial status quo for themselves.

Going hand in hand with such financial overzealousness was the no less damaging 'religious' fervor that on Celebration Day bedecked the whole city of Huế in Vatican white and yellow flags. When the Buddhists commemoration of Buddha's birthday took place in May, however, Huế authorities found it proper to forbid the flying of Buddhist flags. Hence, the cause for the first Incident of the Flags.

It became clear to me then, that the whole mess had its root in Bishop Thục's 25-year anniversary. Had it been reduced to a reasonably correct size, both physically and morally, excesses would not have been committed. As it was, matters unfortunately and inexorably flowed down its course and still to come was the extra push that sent the car rolling more rapidly to the waiting precipice.

MEANWHILE, MARIE RETURNED from the U.S., having received her B.A. from Rivier College in New Hampshire. The day of her arrival, the whole family went to greet her at Kai Tak airport. Reporters got wind of my presence, but refused to believe that I was only there to meet my daughter. They kept watch on me to see what my secret VIP was as whoever it was must be connected to the Buddhist affair in Vietnam. They were all disappointed that it was just Marie, after all, but all the while, they kept bombarding me with questions when I had no details to offer them about the sorry business.

From July onward, Vietnam was on a mad race to perdition beginning with a mimeographed set of instructions from the Office of the Political Advisor sent post-haste to all diplomatic representations abroad. It was revealed that Ngô Đình Nhu was the new absolute power of the entire government. He refuted in harsh terms all concessions President Diệm had made with the Buddhist hierarchy and practically condemned Diệm for his actions. Nhu implied a new policy, clearly set, to follow in dealing with the Buddhists and put them back in their proper place. The 'Republican Youth' was to be the Praetorian Army of Ngô Đình Nhu. As their leader, Nhu would take things in hand and all past conciliation with the Buddhists was as good as null and void.

A cold sweat ran down my back when I fully digested all this. Unmistakably clear, even then, was that the Ngô family had reached the "point of no return." They either came out victorious against all odds or they would go down, ignominiously defeated. Coupled with a total absence of Presidential orders, these new instructions emanating from Nhu's office were tantamount to a palace coup. Ngô Đình Diệm had been as good as deposed by his own brother. It had been accomplished not with guns but by a slap in the face!

New instructions came pouring in with each diplomatic pouch, but they only confirmed what had already been too obvious. We were expecting a new 'dynastic name' for the Nhu regime. At least, we in Hong Kong were just waiting for the formalization of the Ngô Đình Nhu takeover before resigning in good conscience. We did not know that many, and not least from Nhu's own Political Advisory Office, were preparing to take over from ***him***, even while he was informally overthrowing his brother.

Hot on the heels of Nhu's actions came U.S. Ambassador Henry Cabot Lodge, Jr., and together with a new set of American policy to be applied to Saigon, the Voice of America started a series of broadcasts denouncing the Ngô Đình Diệm regime. Refusing to be second to none, Trần Văn Chương added his two cents to the melee by announcing his resignation; whereupon his own daughter, Madame Nhu, no less dramatically denounced her father in no uncertain terms.

It is safe to say that at that period, the press of the world focused on Vietnam. The United Nations sent an investigation team to Vietnam led by Bửu Hội. With more fiery immolations, Madame Nhu unwittingly drew more hatred upon her and her husband by dismissing them as "monk barbecues." Indeed, as we had feared, President Diệm was no longer in control, whether in name or in fact. From then on, everything was exclusively Ngô Đình Nhu's show.

It was resentment of the Nhus that caused most Vietnamese to wish a rapid end to rule by the Ngô family. We naively thought that if Diệm could no longer control his brother, it was better for him to resign and let the mob (if not the Army) take care of the Nhus, especially the hated Madame Nhu. For instance, my daughter Marie exclaimed: "It's about time!" when she heard a VOA program listing the excesses of the Nhu regime and openly condemning it.

The surprising event for us in Hong Kong was the appearance of Dr. Trần Kim Tuyến. He arrived in late August and stayed until the coup was about to finish in Saigon before he hastily flew home to be jailed, contrary to what he imagined would happen to him. When he first appeared on the island, I was nonplussed. Was Nhu preparing the coup from Hong Kong? It soon came out that Dr. Tuyến was no longer 'in.' He had been exiled into the post of Consul General to Cairo but he resigned from there and fled to 'take refuge' in Hong Kong. Dr. Tuyến in exile and a refugee! Politics certainly has strange bedfellows.

In September a surprise arrival at the Consulate was Mr. Võ Văn Lang, brother of Võ Văn Hải. Lang told me he feared Ngô Đình Diệm could not emerge unscathed from recent events. What he had in mind frightened me, but I was far from believing that our 'Good Old Man' would be killed. It was true that over the years Diệm had changed so much that he was not the same man we knew and loved in New York. To be fair, who could be the same person after being President for eight years and in control of a government, undisputed and quasi-absolute for almost nine years before that?

We could no longer approach him and, toward the end, did not want to see him anymore, not because we hated him despite all the irritations we encountered trying to get in touch with him. It was because the whole work—and seeing him was part of the job—had become senseless, futile, and debilitating soon after we even started it. If Diệm's brothers Cẩn and Nhu and specifically their henchmen, gave us the strong impression that the Diệm government deserved to end if only to put an end to the entourage around the president, the man himself remained irreplaceable.

Realizing that it was impractical to try and separate the man from his brothers, rather than, for example, wishing to see Nhu take the place of his father-in-law in Washington, D.C., we hoped for an honorable exit where after having resigned, the President would live in exile once more with us in America. Indeed, that was what my wife and I had been telling each other for long months even before the Buddhist incidents started. As the crisis developed, we naively kept hoping that our dream would come true. For me and my wife also, badly needed a new life and it might as well continue where we had left off in 1953 but with a chastised and mellower Ngô Đình Diệm who this time, would remain our children's Maryknoll Grandpa for good.

Ten years of chaotic and heartbreaking politics (seeing it was his own brother who betrayed him) would make Diệm whole again and we could repay him for his kindness by keeping him with us for the rest of his life. Again, that was our naïve dream. It never entered our heads that anyone would deliberately kill him—not the Army, least of all the Americans—even if they were all Cabot Lodges!

IN THESE CONFUSING conditions, Vietnam's national day rolled around again, and we celebrated it half-heartedly at our Repulse Bay residence. Unknown to us of what was happening despite countless premonitions, we had simplified this last Independence Day to a minimum. We skipped the usual reception at the Repulse Bay Hotel. No invitation was sent to Hong Kong's Governor nor to the Consular Corps. In lieu of the reception we sent official announcement cards commemorating the day without any further formality.

On the evening of October 26, 1963, the Vietnamese community in Hong Kong gathered at the residence. Unlike preceding years, everyone was preoccupied and only distractedly went through the motions of celebration and rejoicing as **this** year felt markedly different. As a last omen, the dais-like enclosure of flowerpots and national flags surrounding the portrait of President Ngô Đình Diệm was inadvertently draped and decorated in such a way that it reminded me of Lenten decorations in a church. An unhappy combination of colors, perhaps, or a disposition of candles and flowers suggested an outer reflection of the workings of our inner subconsciousness. A collection subconsciousness, as it were, for it was not the work of any single individual but the common effort of many who helped prepare the feast and all who attended it.

The usual rounds of dining, drinking, speech-making and film-showing followed its tedious course. We were irritated to see Madame Nhu in the film showing off her Republican Women group, haughty and vain. The evening ended and we shook hands with the Vietnamese guests without suspecting that this evening was the last time we would see them.

Up in our bedroom, my wife and I glued our ears to the radio tuned to Saigon, trying to find out how the National Day celebrations were going on there. Was it being celebrated at all now that Nhu controlled everything? We heard a report of the Day's celebration with a military parade with President Diệm on the reviewing stand receiving the salutes presented to him by the passing regiments. Ears practically glued to the radio had been our periodic practice since the coup on November 11, 1960. We continued it every day after the Buddhist incident and its aftermath. We could not rely on official information from the Ministry which really was more coverup than fact besides coming too late to be of much use. Experience taught us that in the case of a coup d'etat, radio stations would be the first places to be controlled and the first news broadcast would be from whoever was in control.

It was 10 a.m. the following day when I decided to get away from it all. A delegation of Buddhist monks had sent word to the Consulate that they wished to meet me at my convenience for an 'explanation' of the 'antireligious' policy of my government. I silently withdrew via a private door I had made when the consulate moved to new premises. When I reached Repulse Bay, I called the office to let them know I was on my way to Manila, the Philippines, for a short rest. It took me just a few minutes to pack and off I went.

At Kai Tak Airport, the sunshine was glorious but there was a tempest in my heart. What was I running from, and where was I fleeing to? I no longer had any responsibility to discharge now that Vietnam was reduced to a single package: the Buddhist Affair. Even the Việt Cộng receded to the background. Was I instinctively guided to the Philippines because it was the only Catholic country in Southeast Asia where I would be left alone?

It happened that our ambassador to Manila, Trần Hữu Thế, was the protegé of Archbishop Ngô Đình Thục. Prior to assuming this post, he was replacing Father Cao Văn Luận as Rector of the University of Huế after the latter's resignation in protest of the government policy (read Nhu's) against the Buddhists. I had been incensed by the Archbishop's high-handedness and blaming the whole mess on him; I had been exasperated by Ngô Đình Nhu and his wife's handling of the Buddhist Problem, and especially their latest crackdown on Xá Lợi Pagoda. I had thought of running away from anything that reminded me of **them.** Instead, I ran smack into their Number One sycophant.

Mr. and Mrs. Bùi Công Văn in Hong Kong on National Day, October 1963

Repulse Bay residence decorated for National Day, October 1963

34. MURDER IN THE TANK

Manila, The Philippines, October 27, 1963

It was ironic that wanting to get away from it all, I hurried out of Hong Kong only to land in the center of the fiefdom of one of the basest flatterers of the reigning House of Ngô. There were legions of sycophants, but Thế stood head and shoulders above them all. A special protégé of Archbishop Ngô Đình Thục, Thế had been elevated to the rank of Minister of National Education through no merit of his own. He should have stayed put, seeing that most other people thought there was nowhere he could go except down. Thế was already at rock bottom both morally and intrinsically, but he believed—if we did not—that for him, anywhere he was told to go could only bring higher up!

In the thick of the Buddhist crisis, when Father Cao Văn Luận resigned as President of the University of Huế to protest the anti-Diệm policy of Ngô Đình Nhu, Trần Hữu Thế was ordered to fill the vacancy and he promptly obeyed. One had yet to see such an anomaly anywhere in the world: a Minister of Education-cum-University President hundreds of miles away from the country's capital.

And it was no sheer administrative monstrosity either. Huế being the Buddhist 'capital' where a bloody incident occurred that in all appearances, justified the seething indignation of the Buddhist clergy and layman alike. It took immense arrogance on the part of the Catholic Archbishop to replace an accommodating University President, himself a priest, with a newly converted and worthless Catholic. It took no less a first-rate cynicism on the part of a super-sycophant to jump onto this position.

After a few weeks trial in a sea of boiling outrage, however, Thế's intrepidity gave way, and he ran for his life. It would be amusing if we could witness the scene wherein, he faced the Archbishop! At any rate, a way out must be found not so much to save **his** face as that of the Archbishop. To send Thế back to the Education Ministry was no solution but lo! Trần Hữu Thế was given a third hat to add to the first two: With a snap of His Excellency's fingers, Thế became Ambassador Plenipotentiary to the Republic of the Philippines!

So, there we were. Thế was freshly launched on a new diplomatic career and doubly happy to be rescued from the lion's jaws. I was dejected and made more despondent at the sight of Thế at Manila Airport. As I could not reasonably start a row with him, I had to swallow my mounting wrath—with difficulty. This showed and Thế felt it. No doubt he understood it also, for he was not unintelligent, with tremendous patience, he went through the Immigration and Customs formalities with me, handling my papers himself and smiling all the time. Was all this deliberate? Could he not have sent an Embassy man instead? Was this part of the game? A redeeming ploy of sorts?

Whatever it was, I was not untouched. I knew that I was being unreasonable, and that self-righteousness always borders on excessive pride. I had no right to set myself up as judge of my fellowmen. If I thought Thế contemptible, I knew his apparent humility should have made me ashamed of myself, but I could not control myself very well. And I had the excuse of some pending denouement I felt about to befall me—and Thế served as a convenient scapegoat.

From the airport, the Ambassador drove me to the hotel he had reserved for me. I would be fetched later that evening for the Embassy's banquet that evening for National Day celebrations. Here, the festivities are observed one day afterwards for the convenience of Manila high society.

At 7 p.m., I was on the Embassy grounds nicely decorated with Japanese lanterns and multicolored lights around the front lawn on which tables were set waiting for invited guests. Waiters were busy moving to and fro. Ambassador Thế took me on a tour of the premises, and I made my greetings to Madame Trần Hữu Thế.

Soon guests arrived and together with them I stood on the receiving line. Dinner began and I noticed an almost total absence of Vietnamese people. It could have been a soiree for Filipinos and the Manila diplomatic Corps for all I knew. Neither was there a toast or formality of any sort: it could have been an ordinary dinner in the trade of a diplomatic representative. So much the better, I thought, for with a toast to the President of the Filippino Republic who was not present, a toast to the President of the Republic of Vietnam would be called for which would only heighten whatever tension may have been in many hearts.

During the later courses of the dinner, perhaps under the influence of one drink too many, I lost my composure and spoke rather loudly with the French Embassy guests I was seated with, tongue-lashing and otherwise denigrating my own government in Saigon. Embarrassed, Thế came to the table to mutter in my ear something like, "Just the same, it's **your** government as well as mine." Furious, I was about to give him more of the same when the Frenchmen dexterously complimented me on my French and the tense atmosphere lessened.

After the last guest had left, Thế and his wife detained me for a game of 'Four-color' cards which they knew I was very fond of. We sat down immediately for the game and played until dawn. Hoà, an embassy secretary, was the fourth hand at the game and he would be my guide for the duration of my stay in Manila. During the many hours of playing, doubtlessly many of my deliberate or unwitting remarks must have hurt them. It followed that the Ambassador avoided me for two days afterwards.

Manila, The Philippines, October 30, 1963

Today, while I was at the restaurant of the Shell Born Hotel where I had transferred to, after the telephone rang, an employee called out: "Telephone call for the Vietnamese Consul!" I stepped up to the counter and took the receiver, embarrassed because many GIs in the restaurant were eyeing me hostilely. Either "Consul" or "Vietnam" irked the soldiers or maybe both. I was deeply self-conscious and thought: "This is because Ngô Đình Diệm and I both live at the expense of the United States."

The Ambassador was on the line with an invitation to join him for a motor trip to Pak Snag Hang, a scenic resort in the highlands in north Manila on All Saints' Day, November 1st. I thanked him and accepted the invitation.

Over the last two days I had flirted with the idea of returning home to Saigon, thinking I might clear my mind if I could see happenings first-hand. I went to the Air France ticket office to inquire about flights, but I gave it up when I learned there were none to Saigon until the following week.

Hoà meanwhile, took up a bed in my hotel room and kept me company. When I went up to my room, Madam Cao Thái Bảo, wife of the Charge d'affaires in Bangkok, Thailand, had come to see me for a money matter. She had her son buried here in Manila and after All Souls' Day, when she visited his tomb, she would go to Hong Kong and needed a check cashed.

Manila, the Philippines, October 31, 1961

Hoà and I borrowed a car from the Embassy and drove to visit Los Banos in the north of the Philippines. We came to the Rockefeller Rice Research Institute where, by chance, I found working there Trương Đình Phú who had a Ph.D.

in Agriculture. Phú was the Illinois student who I shared a room with when I attended the First Vietnamese Catholic Students Association in America, back in 1952. We were so happy to be reunited after all those years—and in the Philippines of all places! Two Vietnamese students were also present. At the end of the day, the girls, Misses Diễm and Dung, joined Hoà and me for a holiday trip to Manila.

We deposited the girls at a boarding house for women and drove Phú back to the Shell Born Hotel to—as of old—share a room with me. Remembrances of things past cheered me up as Phú and I talked late into the night over a sound asleep Hoà curled up in his cot.

Manila, the Philippines, November 1, 1963

The Ambassador picked me up for our trip to the hill country with two other guests—Dr. Nguyễn Phước Đại whose wife was a congresswoman, and Dr. Tôn Thất Niệm, son of Tôn Thất Hội, our Ambassador to Laos who were in town for a medical conference. We left in the early morning and as it was a long drive, we only arrived at midday.

Thế had rented a treehouse built in the middle of a huge mango tree. Its rustic construction harmoniously matched the surrounding countryside of hills and lush green vegetation. The driver brought up the lavish picnic lunch Madame Thế had prepared for us, and we quickly changed into sport outfits for a 'boat ride' upstream.

Climbing down from our lofty lodgings, we walked to the shore of a nearby river, small and shallow, where we hired a canoe with its two oarsmen sitting at both ends.

All four of us settled in the middle and the ride began. The current was swift and strong at first and the oarsmen rowed with great vigor. Two high rock walls towered on both sides of the river and on them grew varieties of fern and moss cut through here and there by tiny springs gushing threads of silvery water that misted bony pine trees that seemed to lap up every drop they could.

The higher up we went, the shallower the river became so that the rowers had to carry us—canoe and all—over heaps of stone to the next stretch of water which flowed down thin and barely deep enough to keep the canoe with us in it afloat. The oarsmen had to pull and push the canoe slowly and painfully upstream.

The river just dried up at the end where it was supposed to begin—the source. After a long rest, the arduous descent began. We compared the scenery here to our own famous landscape of gorges and caverns, of seas and rocky islands leading to Chùa Hương in Hà Tây. Of course, Vietnam's scenery was judged the better by far.

Our conversation all the strenuous way up and down centered on the Buddhist crisis and the possible effects it could produce. We felt a vague anxiety but didn't really worry over much. The weather remained splendid with the sun radiant on an azure sky streaked with swift-moving satin hems of immaculate clouds. It was 1:30 p.m. when we climbed back up the treehouse and attacked with gusto the delicious lunch, eating in the native fashion by each of us carrying our portion in a large banana leaf.

The long drive back to Manila made us half-drowse in

the aggravating heat and as soon as we parted company, we went our separate ways to seek rest and refreshment. It was dark when I awoke later: streetlights were on and feeling listless I took a quick shower then dragged Phú out to the hotel nearby where the two doctors were staying. We went together for a Chinese dinner at The Peking Restaurant and whiled away a few hours at the Bay Side Night Club before returning around midnight to the Shell Born hotel.

A sudden anxiety overtook me when I seemed to be half-dreaming and undergoing, fully conscious now, the tail end of a vague but unpleasant nightmare. I saw by my watch read 2 a.m. I tiptoed out of my room, took the elevator down to the basement all-night bar, and sat by myself, hunched up at a corner in semi-darkness, a Manhattan cocktail at my elbow. I tried to review events of the last few days, the Saigon radio's reportage of President Diệm taking the military salutes, martial fanfares blaring, still resounded in my ears…the Buddhist delegation waylaying me at the Consulate from which I escaped through a secret door...the short intermittent rift between Ambassador Thế and me…the Pak Sang Hang oarsmen, their Hawaiian shirts dripping with sweat…and…at this hour…a probably seething Saigon, a cauldron boiling with hatred and steaming in its own juice. Feeling saturated by an unspeakable sadness, I shook off the ugly visions and unsteadily regained my bed.

Manila, The Philippines, All Souls' Day, November 2, 1963

I was still asleep the next day when the door banged

open and in rushed the two doctors Đại and Niệm, hands holding high above their heads two Manila Morning papers bearing in blood-red print the banner headlines: "COUP D'ÉTAT IN SAIGON!"

The room was instantly electrified. Phú, disheveled and aghast, shrieked out "My God! My God!" A terror-stricken Hoà stood upon his bedsheets as if petrified. The two doctors still holding the newspapers transfixed in a 'hands-up' posture read the scanty columns under the eight-column headlines: Manila had no details as yet and only repeated radio-monitored snippets and short summaries of preliminary news of a "Coup d'etat taking place in the South Vietnamese capital." We precipitately switched on our portable transistors which reproduced the same flimsy stories from Radio Manila.

We decided that a more powerful short-wave receiver was needed to get Radio Saigon transmissions. So, we rushed out to pile into the Embassy car and drove with Hoà's guidance to the home of a certain Captain Phi, our military liaison man in Manila. Not one of us thought to call the Vietnamese Embassy.

As our car approached Captain Phi's house, I heard incongruous but clear peals of note after note rising and falling in a crescendo gamut of piano notes. The music emanated from the captain's cottage and floated hesitatingly, as if from a learning hand in the morning air still fresh with night dew lingering in tiny droplets, shining and multicolored on green shrubs around. Ringing the gate bell did not stop the music, so while the gate was being opened for us, the scales continued up and down its detached and gay notes. Music in the house of a Vietnamese Army man this morning of all mornings!

A sharp image flashed into my mind of an Army rejoicing at its successful coup. Another image also returned to me of Syngman Rhee's coup d'etat in South Korea and how a when a young American diplomat celebrated that coup's success by happily pounding away at his Embassy's piano.

Captain Phi greeted us matter-of-factly. While we shook hands, his wife rose from the piano, her face radiant and half smiling, as if to herself, slowly closed the piano lid and withdrew behind a beaded curtain. A glance at the radio showed me that it was not on: perhaps it had been turned off while the lady of the house practiced her piano. Phi obligingly switched the radio on and fumbled with the knob trying to locate Saigon. Static cracked and martial music came through—here came Saigon radio.

WE LISTENED FOR about half an hour to repeated communiques by the Army of the Republic of Vietnam interspersed with martial music and patriotic songs at regular intervals, announcing again and again the success of the Coup. It began at 1:00 p.m. on November 1 and was about to reach its successful conclusion. Long lists of Army men's names were read of those who had come out for what was called the 'Revolution.' The name-reading seemed to go on endlessly when a voice announced "Attention! Attention! We have an important announcement." We all jumped up as if on springs. Captain Phi turned the volume up to full blast. It was 11:15 a.m. by my watch.

"WE HAVE LEARNED," the voice said, "THAT NGÔ ĐÌNH DIỆM AND NGÔ ĐÌNH NHU JUST COMMITTED SUICIDE." A short pause then: "WE REPEAT, NGÔ ĐÌNH DIỆM AND NGÔ ĐÌNH NHU HAVE JUST COMMITTED SUICIDE." We stood in frozen silence, each of us pursuing our own thoughts. We could hear each other's jerky breaths. My heart was pounding violently. Except for long static crackling and a volley of stray morse code that faded like a distant downpour, the house was plunged into a dead silence.

At length, a voice broke our group's quiet. Dr. Đại said: "With this piece of news, everything has changed." We all nodded in agreement. Even Captain Phi was moved, his previous indifference gone. I kept my silence because my mind was numb. I did not know what to say and if I did, I did not want to say anything. Then the beaded curtains moved and a woman's head timidly looked out: the lady of the house was not unmoved.

I walked back to my car seat in a daze and saw in my mind's eye the bloody corpses of President Ngô Đình Diệm and his brother, Nhu. Whatever the radio said and whatever the other men in the room said, I knew that the Ngô brothers **did not** commit suicide. I knew they were killed, assassinated, executed. In cold blood.

We soon parted company, each going his separate way never to see the other again, not in Manila, not in Saigon, not anywhere. Two hours later, I was on the plane taking me back to my family in Hong Kong.

Hong Kong, November 5, 1963

Professor Bửu Hội, who led the United Nations Investigation Team to Saigon, came alone to Hong Kong on his return to France, I met him at Kai Tak Airport, took him up to our Repulse Bay Road residence and over brandy and Mui Kwei Lo he gave me his confirmation of what I already knew. President Diệm and his brother, Nhu, had been shot and stabbed to death in an Armored Personnel Carrier—a tank. The junta's tale of suicide had deceived no one. The junta's revolution scared the professor out of his wits, and he begged for the first opportunity to flee Vietnam.

"The generals invited **you** home," Bửu Hội said, "and all the Heads of Mission, too. You'll have their telegram in a few days."

"How about you, Professor?" I asked. "You're an ambassador, too."

"Ah," he responded, "but I'm on a mission for **them**—that's why I'm out."

I refrained from telling him point blank that I knew his 'mission' was to try to convince as many diplomatic representatives as possible abroad to come home as soon as possible. He was likely to have suggested he undertake this 'mission' for the junta to allow for his urgent exodus. And although the generals did not trust him nor need his 'mission,' Bửu Hội's ailing old mother, a respected Bonze, and his own cowardice convinced them to let him go. So, he hurried to Hong Kong to 'discharge his duty' on the only victim he could think of—me! His next stop would be Paris, France, and safety.

Hong Kong, November 6, 1963

No Buddhist delegation called on me at the Consulate anymore. They had their revenge and could say, 'Justice was done.' And like a lion after a full repast, they lay down to digest the fruits of their victory. However, an entirely unexpected caller did come to my office: Professor Augustin Choy, a Korean who said he taught at the University in Tokyo, Japan. He was on his way back to Japan from Saigon where he was visiting close relations who were personnel at the Korean Embassy. He particularly stopped over in Hong Kong to look for me, a complete stranger to him, and stated his reasons:

"I saw with my own eyes the remains of President Ngô Đình Diệm and Mr. Nhu, blood-drenched and mangled—in the back of a tank parked at the headquarters of the Army General Staff. It's revolting! And my advice to you, Mr. Consul, is: Do not come back. I know they are calling all ambassadors home. Do not come home!"

As I did not know what to say, the meeting being both dramatic and unexpected, Professor Choy continued:

"Because I am a good friend of the Korean Ambassador, I was allowed to see the corpses. Very few people saw them. And believe me, the junta is doing what the Korean junta did a while back in my own poor country: they are tearing the country apart. Do not trust them with your life. I repeat: **Do not go home!**"

I took Choy to the Repulse Bay Hotel for a private luncheon during which I could prolong our *tête-a-tête* (face to face meeting) and learn more about what happened before, during, and after the onslaught that the junta called a 'revolution.' I thanked Choy then we parted company. Was it a last favor that the now dead Ngô Đình Diệm was granting me? It was God-sent nevertheless and a counterstroke that undid what Professor Bửu Hội was trying to do to me. "Man proposes" they say, "but God disposes."

Tokyo, Japan, November 15, 1963

My family and I left Hong Kong today and landed here in the afternoon. My family was detained at the Tokyo Airport because the Japanese found fault with my vaccination certificate. I called the Vietnamese Embassy, but no one came to our rescue, and I had to allow them to inoculate me again with a smallpox vaccine with the hope they would not require a quarantine. We exited customs soon after and found Mr. and Mrs. Nguyễn Văn Lộc, the 'orphaned' members of the Embassy who because they did not belong to the clique of then-Ambassador Nguyễn Huy Nghĩa, a protégé of Dr. Tuyến, were not given an Airport Pass despite their status as diplomatic personnel. We mourned President Diệm's death with the disconsolate Lộc, then quickly moved on to the Tokyo Hilton where a suite had been reserved for my family by Japan Airlines.

We gathered in the hotel room, the forlorn family composed of me, my wife, Auntie Cô Sáu, Marie (22), Dominic (15), Mỹ-Châu (13), and Muriel (11). Seven persons, morally shipwrecked, on their first leg to Paris,

France where we would be refugees for an indefinite time.

We saw Professor Augustin Choy that night, our benefactor who had warned us against coming home and into the lion's den. Mr. and Mrs. Nguyễn Văn Lộc stayed with us, the only Vietnamese friends left to us who were themselves precariously hanging on with a 'second-rate' status to an embassy whose new owners may or may not summarily dispose of him!

Haneda Airport, Japan, November 16, 1963

Professor Choy kindly drove all of us to the airport in his car and that of Miss Sato, his secretary. They and the Nguyễn Văn Lộcs waved goodbye to us from outside the no-admittance enclosure. We proceeded along the long walk to the gate to our plane when I realized that a confusing public address announcement had caused us to start too soon to our gate. We turned around to walk back, a long file of us, defeated and downhearted.

Leading the way, I carried a bulky briefcase; then came mom, her *áo dài* so conspicuously out of place and not matching with her worn out and sorrowful expression; Dominic came next lugging a heavy transistor shortwave radio; then Marie, Mỹ-Châu and Muriel trudged along each carrying her little possessions; and finally, my sister, Cô Sáu, brought up the rear, bewildered and at a loss.

We met in crossing on the interminable walk Mr. and Mrs. Ando, my former Japanese colleague in Hong Kong. They, too, were loaded down with baggage and 'democratically' plodding along like everyone else. We stopped and exchanged greetings. Ando's sympathy rather irked me, especially as he reminded me of the Japanese consul in Hong Kong who changed his mind at the last minute to grant us a visa to Japan. The American Consul General did the same. Only the French consul was helpful and granted gratis the equivalent of temporary residence visas for France for 'our Asian colleagues!'

On American territorial waters, about two hours to New York, on board the "Rotterdam" liner, November 2, 1964

Today is the first anniversary of the death of President Ngô Đình Diệm. We had asked the ship's chaplain, Father MacCarthy, to say a Requiem Mass for the late president and his brother. It was the first All Soul's Day after their death. We attended the mass and thanked the padre afterwards when he had this to say: "Nothing was good enough for the good president. I am glad I had the opportunity to pray for him."

The ship steadily worked its way towards New York and while Mom and even Marie had thoughts about returning to our old town, the kids did not remember anything about good old New York and were excitedly preparing to land on a brand-new big city to them. For Cô Sáu, who had traveled only to Hong Kong, she might have been getting ready to land on the moon!

The Rotterdam docked at New York's West Side Quay at 11:00 a.m. we had come full circle back to where the story of "Ngô Đình Diệm and I" began 12 years earlier. Riding along Broadway uptown to a rented apartment on West 86th Street, I recognized old landmarks like the Nemo

Theater, unchanged subway entrances in a more crowded city, and I thought that Ngô Đình Diệm had walked along these city streets when he came to our door, and we began a close relationship.

A few nights later, I revisited our old apartment on 111th Street and tried to find in the old walls, corridors, and marble steps leading to our front door ... an image, even an echo of my children's Grandpa Maryknoll's booming voice which, I felt sure, time and eventful tide could not totally efface from this world.

In the New York I long kept intact in my heart, this city and this neighborhood was full of Ngô Đình Diệm who walked with his duck's gait and carried under his bulging briefcase a bundle of toys for my children. He had never completely disappeared to me, dead though he might be to the world.

Kauai, Hawaii, February 7, 1965

Like Lawrence Durrell in his Alexandria Quartet, I must have been very sick to flee from the world and take refuge here on this island thousands of miles from civilization. Unlike Durrell or his hero, however, I did not come here a month ago to 'lick my wounds,' although I was w0unded indeed.

I came here immediately after spending five hours with Marshall Green, the 'young American diplomat' who while serving as Diplomatic Secretary at the U.S. Embassy in Seoul, pounded joyfully on a piano to celebrate the coup d'etat that deposed and later exiled old man Syngman Rhee. Green had advanced in age and career and by the time he became Consul General in Hong Kong, he could appreciate the harsh facts I told him about the underbelly of the U.S.-propped Ngô Đình Diệm government when he made his first courtesy call to me in 1961.

He was surprised and disbelieving at first, but when my Old Man Ngô Đình Diệm went down like Syngman Rhee, if more bloody and unnecessarily brutal, although no longer in Hong Kong but now promoted to Deputy Assistant Secretary for East Asian Affairs at the U.S. State Department, Green made it a point to invite me to his office for a frank review of things and men Vietnamese with my thorough and unrestricted prognostics for Vietnam's future.

The interview took place on New Year's Day, 1965. After five strenuous hours in Green's office in a building deserted for the holiday, I left confident that together with a 70-page paper I wrote on the subject, the United States would not walk in the erroneous steps of the French colonialists before the and commit an American Corps to 'fight Communism' in Vietnam.

I boarded a plane straight to Honolulu where I transferred to a smaller seaplane to reach this lost island of Kauai, the northernmost and least frequented island in search of quiet for some agonizing soul-searching of my own.

For a month during the empty hours of long days, I sat looking at the surf pounding its furious waves against the rocks. I was putting myself in Ngô Đình Diệm's place. What was the best I could have done for my country? How should I have conducted myself? Was it really his fault to have led Vietnam into such a mess? What could be the solution to, say, the last crisis of the Buddhist Affair?

Inexperienced in all things, I found a simplistic answer to my questions and wrote about it in my paper for Marshall Green. I had never before heard of the CIA, let alone of its wrongdoings like the Ngôs themselves, I had a blind trust in the U.S.A. My enemy was French colonialism and the same went for Ngô Đình Diệm. Both he and I, innocent and wishful thinking, we put our country's fate as well as our own, into the hands of the United States. With American help we could wrench back our independence from the French and defeat colonialism. But the very man who attained this goal, who was the first to symbolically occupy the Independence Palace and effectively recover our sovereignty—Ngô Đình Diệm—was, alas, the last man to see it intact.

For Contrary to what I had hoped, today the United States engaged in its first act of war in Vietnam and the first bombing of our land. Whether the U.S. realized it or not, it was stepping in the old shoes so recently discarded by the French. Echoes of the bombings the French rained on Vietnam's soil, over mountains and rivers, upon Cổ Am, Yên Bái, Rạch Gầm, resounded in my ears this morning. The ghost of Governor General Pierre Pasquier, the French Proconsul who pushed the button, seemed to wander about over the hills and valleys of this Hawaiian island, perhaps in search of his American counterpart who this morning did again what he used to do decades ago.

The death of Ngô Đình Diệm, murdered in a tank,

was not the end of Vietnam's difficulties. Rather, it was the beginning of a greater, more insurmountable obstacle. And both Vietnam and America will face a much darker future.

35. EPILOGUE

The pebble that bears the resemblance to a human face that I picked up from the tomb of Ngô Đình Diệm on a visit to Saigon in 1974 and brought back to America got lost the other day! My wife and I thought Mỹ-Nga unknowingly threw it away while cleaning the house. But lo! I found it lying snugly in the grass. We put it back under Ngô Đình Diệm's portrait, the same picture taken of him with us in New York and carried along wherever we went.

For us it represents the Old Man we knew, the one our children called Grandpa Maryknoll. Now, even our youngest Mỹ-Nga was already grown up when it was at her first month celebration that Diệm and I started a close relationship which he maintained until the end. Perhaps she still remembers something of Diệm. Certainly, her older sisters and brother do.

Ngô Đình Diệm has passed away. And so did the South Vietnam he wrenched back from the French. A South Vietnam belatedly mourning him and missing him—but to no avail.

Life goes on history may one day record the Ngô Đình

Diệm episode gracefully, with him being a "Patriot in his own way," as Hồ Chí Minh recognized it. And while history recognizes the latter as the winner of the northern half of Vietnam, it could also consider Diệm as conqueror of the southern half, with both patriots struggling all their lives for the same goal: a Vietnam free and independent.

As for my little tale, it's just a little story of NGÔ ĐÌNH DIỆM AND I.

www.ingramcontent.com/pod-product-compliance
Lightning Source LLC
LaVergne TN
LVHW101612210926
848480LV00008B/33
9798349470400